THE SOVEREIGN INDIVIDUAL

Mastering the Transition to the Information Age

JAMES DALE DAVIDSON *and*
LORD WILLIAM REES-MOGG

TOUCHSTONE
New York Toronto London Sydney New Delhi

Touchstone
An Imprint of Simon & Schuster, Inc.
1230 Avenue of the Americas
New York, NY 10020

This Touchstone trade paperback edition April 2020

TOUCHSTONE and colophon are registered trademarks of Simon &
Schuster, Inc.

For information about special discounts for bulk purchases, please
contact Simon & Schuster Special Sales at 1-866-506-1949 or
business@simonandschuster.com.

The Simon & Schuster Speakers Bureau can bring authors to your live event.
For more information or to book an event contact the Simon & Schuster
Speakers Bureau at 866-248-3049 or visit our website at
www.simonspeakers.com.

Interior design by Irving Perkins Associates, Inc.

40   39   38   37

The Library of Congress has cataloged the hardcover edition as follows:

Davidson, James Dale.
    The sovereign individual : how to survive and thrive during the collapse
of the welfare state / James Dale Davidson and Lord William Rees-Mogg.
        p.   cm.
    Includes index.
    1. Economic forecasting. 2. Twenty-first century—Forecasts.
3. Computers and civilization. 4. Information society. 5. World
politics—1989-   —Forecasting. I. Rees-Mogg, William, date.
II. Title.
HC59.15.D385   1997
338.9—dc21   96-48244
                                               CIP

ISBN 978-0-684-83272-2
ISBN 978-1-4391-4473-2 (ebook)

PREFACE

Medieval men despaired of the will. They thought of humans as wounded and weak. But they respected the intellect. They thought even humans, if we think carefully, have the power to answer the most profound questions of God and the Universe.

Modern men worship the will, but they despair of the intellect. The wisdom of crowds; the swerve of random particles; the influence of unconscious biases: all of these contemporary clichés are ways to talk about intellectual weakness—or ways to talk ourselves into it.

Lord William Rees-Mogg and James Dale Davidson do not promise answers about God and the Universe, nor do they supply any. But their investigation of "megapolitics"—an anatomy of the forces at work in history and a set of predictions for the near future—is unusual, or even countercultural, because it applies human reason to matters that we have been taught to leave to chance or fate.

Looking back almost a quarter century after the first publication of *The Sovereign Individual*, the easiest thing to do, and the thing most encouraged by the culture around us, is to look at what they got wrong—almost as if to reassure ourselves that there was no point all along in thinking carefully about the future.

And of course, there are some things they missed: above all, the rise of China. The twenty-first-century People's Republic of China under the Communist Party has created its very own version of the Information Age with decidedly nationalist, ethnically homogenous, profoundly statist characteristics. This is probably the single biggest "megapolitical" development since the book came out. To cite just one key illustration, Communist China has crushed the city-state of Hong Kong—whereas Rees-Mogg and Davidson had described Hong Kong as "a mental model of the kind of jurisdiction that we expect to see flourish in the Information Age."

On one account, this is a blind spot on the part of the authors. On another view, it can seem like China's Politburo must have been keen readers of *The Sovereign Individual*. It is only through a unique long-term awareness that looks back to Lenin and Stalin as well as forward to the Information Age that the Party's leaders prevailed amid the trends analyzed by this book.

Those trends—winner-take-all economics, jurisdictional competition, the shift away from mass production, and the arguable obsolescence of interstate warfare—are still at work today. The rise of China is less a refutation of Rees-Mogg and Davidson than a dramatic raising of the stakes they described.

In truth, the great conflict over our megapolitical future is only just beginning. On the dimension of technology, the conflict has two poles: AI and crypto. Artificial Intelligence holds out the prospect of finally solving what economists call the "calculation problem": AI could theoretically make it possible to centrally control an entire economy. It is no coincidence that AI is the favorite technology of the Communist Party of China. Strong cryptography, at the other pole, holds out the prospect of a decentralized and individualized world. If AI is communist, crypto is libertarian.

The future may lie somewhere between these two extreme poles. But we know the actions we take today will determine the overall outcome. Reading *The Sovereign Individual* in 2020 is a way to think carefully about the future that your own actions will help to create. It is an opportunity not to be wasted.

Peter Thiel
January 6, 2020
Los Angeles

To Annunziata and Brooke,
Sovereign Individuals in the new millennium

"The future is disorder. A door like this has cracked open five or six times since we got up on our hind legs. It is the best possible time to be alive, when almost everything you thought you knew is wrong."

—Tom Stoppard, Arcadia

CONTENTS

CONTENTS

CHAPTER 1
THE TRANSITION OF THE YEAR 2000

The Fourth Stage of Human Society

"It feels like something big is about to happen: graphs show us the yearly growth of populations, atmospheric concentrations of carbon dioxide, Net addresses, and Mbytes per dollar. They all soar up to an asymptote just beyond the turn of the century: The Singularity. The end of everything we know. The beginning of something we may never understand."[1]

—DANNY HILLIS

PREMONITIONS

The coming of the year 2000 has haunted the Western imagination for the past thousand years. Ever since the world failed to end at the turn of the first millennium after Christ, theologians, evangelists, poets, seers, and now, even computer programmers have looked to the end of this decade with an expectation that it would bring something momentous. No less an authority than Isaac Newton speculated that the world would end with the year 2000. Michel de Nostradamus, whose prophecies have been read by every generation since they were first published in 1568, forecast the coming of the Third Antichrist in July 1999.[2] Swiss psychologist Carl Jung, connoisseur of the "collective unconscious," envisioned the birth of a New Age in 1997. Such forecasts may easily be ridiculed. And so can the sober forecasts of economists, such as Dr. Edward Yardeni of Deutsche Bank Securities, who expects computer malfunctions on the millennial midnight to "disrupt the entire global economy."[3] But whether you view the Y2K computer problem as groundless hysteria ginned up by computer programmers and Information Technology consultants to stir up business, or as a mysterious instance of technology unfolding in concert with the prophetic imagination, there is no denying that circumstances at the eve of the millennium excite more than the usual morbid doubt about where the world is tending.

A sense of disquiet about the future has begun to color the optimism so characteristic of Western societies for the past 250 years. People everywhere are hesitant and worried. You see it in their faces. Hear it in their conversation. See it reflected in polls and registered in the ballot box. Just as an invisible, physical change of ions in the atmosphere signals that a thunderstorm is imminent even before the clouds darken and lightning strikes, so now, in the twilight of the millennium, premonitions of change are in the air. One person after another, each in his own way, senses that time is running out on a dying way of life. As the decade expires, a murderous century expires with it, and also a glorious millennium of human accomplishment. All draw to a close with the year 2000.

"For there is nothing covered that shall not be revealed, neither hid that shall not be known."

—MATTHEW 10:26

We believe that the modern phase of Western civilization will end with it. This book tells why. Like many earlier works, it is an attempt to see into a glass darkly, to sketch out the vague shapes and dimensions of a future that is still to be. In that sense, we mean our work to be apocalyptic—in the original meaning of the word. *Apokalypsis* means "unveiling" in Greek. We believe that a new stage in history—the Information Age—is about to be "unveiled."

"We are watching the beginnings of a new logical space, an instantaneous electronic everywhereness, which we may all access, enter into, and experience. We have, in short, the beginnings of a new kind of community. The virtual community becomes the model for a secular Kingdom of Heaven; as Jesus said there were many mansions in his Father's Kingdom, so there are many virtual communities, each reflecting their own needs and desires."

—MICHAEL GRASSO[4]

THE FOURTH STAGE OF HUMAN SOCIETY

The theme of this book is the new revolution of power which is liberating individuals at the expense of the twentieth-century nation-state. Innovations that alter the logic of violence in unprecedented ways are transforming the boundaries within which the future must lie. If our deductions are correct, you stand at the threshold of the most sweeping revolution in history. Faster than all but a few now imagine, microprocessing will subvert and destroy the nation-state, creating new forms of social organization in the process. This will be far from an easy transformation.

The challenge it will pose will be all the greater because it will happen with incredible speed compared with anything seen in the past. Through all of human history from its earliest beginnings until now, there have been only three basic stages of economic life: (1) hunting-and-gathering societies; (2) agricultural societies; and (3) industrial societies. Now, looming over the horizon, is something entirely new, the fourth stage of social organization: information societies.

Each of the previous stages of society has corresponded with distinctly different phases in the evolution and control of violence. As we explain in detail, information societies promise to dramatically reduce the returns to violence, in part because they transcend locality. The virtual reality of cyber-space, what novelist William Gibson characterized as a "consensual halluci-nation," will be as far beyond the reach of bullies as imagination can take it. In the new millennium, the advantage of controlling violence on a large scale will be far lower than it has been at any time since before the French Revolution. This will have profound consequences. One of these will be rising crime. When the payoff for organizing violence at a large scale tumbles, the payoff from violence at a smaller scale is likely to jump. Violence will become more random and localized. Organized crime will grow in scope. We explain why.

Another logical implication of falling returns to violence is the eclipse of politics, which is the stage for crime on the largest scale. There is much evidence that adherence to the civic myths of the twentieth-century nation-state is rapidly eroding. The death of Communism is merely the most strik-ing example. As we explore in detail, the collapse of morality and growing corruption among leaders of Western governments are not random develop-ments. They are evidence that the potential of the nation-state is exhausted. Even many of its leaders no longer believe the platitudes they mouth. Nor are they believed by others.

History Repeats Itself

This is a situation with striking parallels in the past. Whenever technological change has divorced the old forms from the new moving forces of the economy, moral standards shift, and people begin to treat those in command of the old institutions with growing disdain. This widespread revulsion often comes into evidence well before people develop a new coherent ideology of change. So it was in the late fifteenth century, when the medieval Church was the predominant institution of feudalism. Notwithstanding popular belief in "the sacredness of the sacerdotal office," both the higher and lower ranks of clergy were held in the utmost contempt—not unlike the popular attitude toward politicians and bureaucrats today.[5]

We believe that much can be learned by analogy between the situation at the end of the fifteenth century, when life had become thoroughly saturated by organized religion, and the situation today, when the world has become saturated with politics. The costs of supporting institutionalized religion at the end of the fifteenth century had reached a historic extreme, much as the costs of supporting government have reached a senile extreme today.

We know what happened to organized religion in the wake of the Gunpowder Revolution. Technological developments created strong incentives to downsize religious institutions and lower their costs. A similar technological revolution is destined to downsize radically the nation-state early in the new millennium.

"Today, after more than a century of electric technology, we have extended our central nervous system itself in a global embrace, abolishing both space and time as far as our planet is concerned."[6]

—MARSHALL MCLUHAN, 1964

The Information Revolution

As the breakdown of large systems accelerates, systematic compulsion will recede as a factor shaping economic life and the distribution of income. Efficiency will become more important than the dictates of power in the organization of social institutions. This means that provinces and even cities that can effectively uphold property rights and provide for the administration of justice, while consuming few resources, will be viable sovereignties in the Information Age, as they generally have not been during the last five centuries. An entirely new realm of economic activity that is not hostage to physical violence will emerge in cyberspace. The most obvious benefits will flow to the "cognitive elite," who will increasingly operate outside political boundaries. They are already equally at home in Frankfurt, London, New York, Buenos Aires, Los Angeles, Tokyo, and Hong Kong. Incomes will become more unequal within jurisdictions and more equal between them.

The Sovereign Individual explores the social and financial consequences of this revolutionary change. Our desire is to help you to take advantage of the opportunities of the new age and avoid being destroyed by its impact. If only half of what we expect to see happens, you face change of a magnitude with few precedents in history.

The transformation of the year 2000 will not only revolutionize the character of the world economy, it will do so more rapidly than any previous phase change. Unlike the Agricultural Revolution, the Information Revolution will not take millennia to do its work. Unlike the Industrial Revolution, its impact will not be spread over centuries. The Information Revolution will happen within a lifetime.

What is more, it will happen almost everywhere at once. Technical and economic innovations will no longer be confined to small portions of the globe. The transformation will be all but universal. And it will involve a break with the past so profound that it will almost bring to life the magical domain of the gods as imagined by the early agricultural peoples like the ancient Greeks. To a greater degree than most would now be willing to concede, it will prove difficult or impossible to preserve many contemporary institutions in the new millennium. When information societies take shape they will be as different from industrial societies as the Greece of Aeschylus was from the world of the cave dwellers.

PROMETHEUS UNBOUND: THE RISE OF THE SOVEREIGN INDIVIDUAL

"I know of no more encouraging fact than the unquestionable ability of man to elevate his life by conscious endeavor."

—HENRY DAVID THOREAU

The coming transformation is both good news and bad. The good news is that the Information Revolution will liberate individuals as never before. For the first time, those who can educate and motivate themselves will be almost entirely free to invent their own work and realize the full benefits of their own productivity. Genius will be unleashed, freed from both the oppression of government and the drags of racial and ethnic prejudice. In the Information Society, no one who is truly able will be detained by the ill-formed opinions of others. It will not matter what most of the people on earth might think of your race, your looks, your age, your sexual proclivities, or the way you wear your hair. In the cybereconomy, they will never see you. The ugly, the fat, the old, the disabled will vie with the young and beautiful on equal terms in utterly color-blind anonymity on the new frontiers of cyberspace.

Ideas Become Wealth

Merit, wherever it arises, will be rewarded as never before. In an environment where the greatest source of wealth will be the ideas you have in your head rather than physical capital alone, anyone who thinks clearly will potentially be rich. The Information Age will be the age of upward mobility. It will afford far more equal opportunity for the billions of humans in parts of the world that never shared fully in the prosperity of industrial society. The brightest, most successful and ambitious of these will emerge as truly Sovereign Individuals.

At first, only a handful will achieve full financial sovereignty. But this does not negate the advantages of financial independence. The fact that not everyone attains an equally vast fortune does not mean that it is futile or meaningless to become rich. There are 25,000 millionaires for every billionaire. If you are a millionaire and not a billionaire, that does not make you poor. Equally, in the future, one of the milestones by which you measure your financial success will be not just now many zeroes you can add to your net worth, but whether you can structure your affairs in a way that enables you to realize full individual autonomy and independence. The more clever you are, the less propulsion you will require to achieve financial escape velocity. Persons of even quite modest means will soar, as the gravitational pull of politics on the global economy weakens. Unprecedented financial independence will be a reachable goal in your lifetime or that of your children.

At the highest plateau of productivity, these Sovereign Individuals will compete and interact on terms that echo the relations among the gods in Greek myth. The elusive Mount Olympus of the next millennium will be in cyberspace—a realm without physical existence that will nonetheless develop what promises to be the world's largest economy by the second decade of the new millennium. By 2025, the cybereconomy will have many millions of participants. Some of them will be as rich as Bill Gates, worth tens of billions of dollars each. The cyberpoor may be those with an income of less than $200,000 a year. There will be no cyberwelfare. No cybertaxes and no cybergovernment. The cybereconomy, rather than China, could well be the greatest economic phenomenon of the next thirty years.

The good news is that politicians will no more be able to dominate, suppress, and regulate the greater part of commerce in this new realm than the legislators of the ancient Greek city-states could have trimmed the beard of Zeus. That is good news for the rich. And even better news for the not so rich. The obstacles and burdens that politics imposes are more obstacles to becoming rich than to being rich. The benefits of declining returns to violence and devolving jurisdictions will create scope for every energetic and ambitious person to benefit from the death of politics. Even the consumers of government services will benefit as entrepreneurs extend the benefits of competition. Heretofore, competition between jurisdictions has usually meant competition by means of violence to enforce the rule of a predominant group. Consequently, much of the ingenuity of interjurisdictional competition was channeled into military endeavor. But the advent of the cybereconomy will bring competition on new terms to provision of sovereignty services. A proliferation of jurisdictions will mean proliferating experimentation in new ways of enforcing contracts and otherwise securing the safety of persons and property. The liberation of a large part of the global economy from political control will oblige whatever remains of government as we have known it to operate on more nearly market terms. Governments will ultimately have little choice but to treat populations in territories they serve more like customers, and less in the way that organized criminals treat the victims of a shakedown racket.

Beyond Politics

What mythology described as the province of the gods will become a viable option for the individual—a life outside the reach of kings and councils. First in scores, then in hundreds, and ultimately in the millions, individuals will escape the shackles of politics. As they do, they will transform the character of governments, shrinking the realm of compulsion and widening the scope of private control over resources.

The emergence of the sovereign individual will demonstrate yet again the strange prophetic power of myth. Conceiving little of the laws of nature, the early agricultural peoples imagined that "powers we should call supernatural" were widely distributed. These powers were sometimes employed by men, sometimes by "incarnate human gods" who looked like men and interacted with them in what Sir James George Frazer described in *The Golden Bough* as "a great democracy." [7]

When the ancients imagined the children of Zeus living among them they were inspired by a deep belief in magic. They shared with other primitive agricultural peoples an awe of nature, and a superstitious conviction that nature's works were set in motion by individual volition, by magic. In that sense, there was nothing self-consciously prophetic about their view of nature and their gods. They were far from anticipating microtechnology. They could not have imagined its impact in altering the marginal productivity of individuals thousands of years later. They certainly could not have foreseen how it would shift the balance between power and efficiency and thus revolutionize the way that assets are created and protected. Yet what they imagined as they spun their myths has a strange resonance with the world you are likely to see.

Alt.Abracadabra

The "abracadabra" of the magic invocation, for example, bears a curious similarity to the password employed to access a computer. In some respects, high-speed computation has already made it possible to mimic the magic of the genie. Early generations of "digital servants" already obey the commands of those who control the computers in which they are sealed much as genies were sealed in magic lamps. The virtual reality of information technology will widen the realm of human wishes to make almost anything that can be imagined seem real. Telepresence will give living individuals the same capacity to span distance at supernatural speed and monitor events from afar that the Greeks supposed was enjoyed by Hermes and Apollo. The Sovereign Individuals of the Information Age, like the gods of ancient and primitive myths, will in due course enjoy a kind of "diplomatic immunity" from most of the political woes that have beset mortal human beings in most times and places.

The new Sovereign Individual will operate like the gods of myth in the same physical environment as the ordinary, subject citizen, but in a separate realm politically. Commanding vastly greater resources and beyond the reach of many forms of compulsion, the Sovereign Individual will redesign governments and reconfigure economies in the new millennium. The full implications of this change are all but unimaginable.

Genius and Nemesis

For anyone who loves human aspiration and success, the Information Age will provide a bounty. That is surely the best news in many generations. But it is bad news as well. The new organization of society implied by the triumph of individual autonomy and the true equalization of opportunity based upon merit will lead to very great rewards for merit and great individual autonomy. This will leave individuals far more responsible for themselves than they have been accustomed to being during the industrial period. It will also precipitate transition crises, including a possibly severe economic depression that will reduce the unearned advantage in living standards that has been enjoyed by residents of advanced industrial societies throughout the twentieth century. As we write, the top 15 percent of the world's population have an average per-capita income of $21,000 annually. The remaining 85 percent of the world have an average income of just $1,000. That huge, hoarded advantage from the past is bound to dissipate under the new conditions of the Information Age.

As it does, the capacity of nation-states to redistribute income on a large scale will collapse. Information technology facilitates dramatically increased competition between jurisdictions. When technology is mobile, and transactions occur in cyberspace, as they increasingly will do, governments will no longer be able to charge more for their services than they are worth to the people who pay for them. Anyone with a portable computer and a satellite link will be able to conduct almost any information business anywhere, and that includes almost the whole of the world's multitrillion-dollar financial transactions.

This means that you will no longer be obliged to live in a high-tax jurisdiction in order to earn high income. In the future, when most wealth can be earned anywhere, and even spent anywhere, governments that attempt to charge too much as the price of domicile will merely drive away their best customers. If our reasoning is correct, and we believe it is, the nation-state as we know it will not endure in anything like its present form.

THE END OF NATIONS

Changes that diminish the power of predominant institutions are both unsettling and dangerous. Just as monarchs, lords, popes, and potentates fought ruthlessly to preserve their accustomed privileges in the early stages of the modern period, so today's governments will employ violence, often of a covert and arbitrary kind, in the attempt to hold back the clock. Weakened by the challenge from technology, the state will treat increasingly autonomous individuals, its former citizens, with the same range of ruthlessness and diplomacy it has heretofore displayed in its dealing with other governments. The advent of this new stage in history was punctuated with a bang on August 20, 1998, when the United States fired about $200 million worth of Tomahawk BGM-109 sea-launched cruise missiles at targets allegedly associated with an exiled Saudi millionaire, Osama bin Laden. Bin Laden became the first person in history to have his satellite phone targeted for attack by cruise missiles. Simultaneously, the United States destroyed a pharmaceutical plant in Khartoum, Sudan, in Bin Laden's honor. The emergence of Bin Laden as the enemy-in-chief of the United States reflects a momentous change in the nature of warfare. A single individual, albeit one with hundreds of millions of dollars, can now be depicted as a plausible threat to the greatest military power of the Industrial era. In statements reminiscent of propaganda employed during the Cold War about the Soviet Union, the United States president and his national security aides portrayed Bin Laden, a private individual, as a transnational terrorist and leading enemy of the United States.

The same military logic that has seen Osama bin Laden elevated to a position as the chief enemy of the United States will assert itself in governments' internal relations with their subjects. Increasingly harsh techniques of exaction will be a logical corollary of the emergence of a new type of bargaining between governments and individuals. Technology will make individuals more nearly sovereign than ever before. And they will be treated that way. Sometimes violently, as enemies, sometimes as equal parties in negotiation, sometimes as allies. But however ruthlessly governments behave, particularly in the transition period, wedding the IRS with the CIA will avail them little. They will be increasingly required by the press of necessity to bargain with autonomous individuals whose resources will no longer be so easily controlled.

The changes implied by the Information Revolution will not only create a fiscal crisis for governments, they will tend to disintegrate all large structures. Fourteen empires have disappeared already in the twentieth century. The breakdown of empires is part of a process that will dissolve the nation-state itself. Government will have to adapt to the growing autonomy of the individual. Taxing capacity will plunge by 50–70 percent. This will tend to make smaller jurisdictions more successful. The challenge of setting competitive terms to attract able individuals and their capital will be more easily undertaken in enclaves than across continents.

We believe that as the modern nation-state decomposes, latter-day barbarians will increasingly come to exercise power behind the scenes. Groups like the Russian mafiya, which picks the bones of the former Soviet Union, other ethnic criminal gangs, nomenklaturas,* drug lords, and renegade covert agencies will be laws unto themselves. They already are. Far more than is widely understood, the modern barbarians have already infiltrated the forms of the nation-state without greatly changing its appearances. They are micro-parasites feeding on a dying system. As violent and unscrupulous as a state at war, these groups employ the techniques of the state on a smaller scale. Their growing influence and power are part of the downsizing of politics.

* Nomenklaturas are the entrenched elites that ruled the former Soviet Union and other state-run economies.

Microprocessing reduces the size that groups must attain in order to be effective in the use and control of violence. As this technological revolution unfolds, predatory violence will be organized more and more outside of central control. Efforts to contain violence will also devolve in ways that depend more upon efficiency than magnitude of power.

History in Reverse

The process by which the nation-state grew over the past five centuries will be put into reverse by the new logic of the Information Age. Local centers of power will reassert themselves as the state devolves into fragmented, overlapping sovereignties.[8] The growing power of organized crime is merely one reflection of this tendency. Multinational companies are already having to subcontract all but essential work. Some conglomerates, such as AT&T, Unisys, and ITT, have split themselves into several firms in order to function more profitably. The nation-state will devolve like an unwieldy conglomerate, but probably not before it is forced to do so by financial crises.

Not only is power in the world changing, but the work of the world is changing as well. This means that the way business operates will inevitably change. The "virtual corporation" is evidence of a sweeping transformation in the nature of the firm, facilitated by the drop in information and transaction costs. We explore the implications of the Information Revolution for dissolving corporations and doing away with the "good job." In the Information Age, a "job" will be a task to do, not a position you "have." Microprocessing has created entirely new horizons of economic activity that transcend territorial boundaries. This transcendence of frontiers and territories is perhaps the most revolutionary development since Adam and Eve straggled out of paradise under the sentence of their Maker: "In the sweat of thy face shalt thou eat bread." As technology revolutionizes the tools we use, it also antiquates our laws, reshapes our morals, and alters our perceptions. This book explains how.

Microprocessing and rapidly improving communications already make it possible for the individual to choose where to work. Transactions on the Internet or the World Wide Web can be encrypted and will soon be almost impossible for tax collectors to capture. Tax-free money already compounds far faster offshore than onshore funds still subject to the high tax burden imposed by the twentieth-century nation-state. After the turn of the millennium, much of the world's commerce will migrate into the new realm of cyberspace, a region where governments will have no more dominion than they exercise over the bottom of the sea or the outer planets. In cyberspace, the threats of physical violence that have been the alpha and omega of politics since time immemorial will vanish. In cyberspace, the meek and the mighty will meet on equal terms. Cyberspace is the ultimate off-shore jurisdiction. An economy with no taxes. Bermuda in the sky with diamonds.

When this greatest tax haven of them all is fully open for business, all funds will essentially be offshore funds at the discretion of their owner. This will have cascading consequences. The state has grown used to treating its taxpayers as a farmer treats his cows, keeping them in a field to be milked. Soon, the cows will have wings.

The Revenge of Nations

Like an angry farmer, the state will no doubt take desperate measures at first to tether and hobble its escaping herd. It will employ covert and even violent means to restrict access to liberating technologies. Such expedients will work only temporarily, if at all. The twentieth-century nation-state, with all its pretensions, will starve to death as its tax revenues decline.

When the state finds itself unable to meet its committed expenditure by raising tax revenues, it will resort to other, more desperate measures. Among them is printing money. Governments have grown used to enjoying a monopoly over currency that they could depreciate at will. This arbitrary inflation has been a prominent feature of the monetary policy of all twentieth-century states. Even the best national currency of the postwar period, the German mark, lost 71 percent of its value from January 1, 1949, through the end of June 1995. In the same period, the U.S. dollar lost 84 percent of its value.[9] This inflation had the same effect as a tax on all who hold the currency. As we explore later, inflation as revenue option will be largely foreclosed by the emergence of cybermoney. New technologies will allow the holders of wealth to bypass the national monopolies that have issued and regulated money in the modern period. Indeed, the credit crises that swept through Asia, Russia, and other emerging economies in 1997 and 1998 attest to the fact that national currencies and national credit ratings are anachronisms inimical to the smooth operation of the global economy. It is precisely the fact that the demands of sovereignty require all transactions within a jurisdiction to be denominated in a national currency that creates the vulnerability to mistakes by central bankers and attacks by speculators which precipitated deflationary crises in one jurisdiction after another. In the Information Age, individuals will be able to use cybercurrencies and thus declare their monetary independence. When individuals can conduct their own monetary policies over the World Wide Web it will matter less or not at all that the state continues to control the industrial-era printing presses. Their importance for controlling the world's wealth will be transcended by mathematical algorithms that have no physical existence. In the new millennium, cybermoney controlled by private markets will supersede fiat money issued by governments. Only the poor will be victims of inflation and ensuing collapses into deflation that are consequences of the artificial leverage which fiat money injects into the economy.

Lacking their accustomed scope to tax and inflate, governments, even in traditionally civil countries, will turn nasty. As income tax becomes uncollectible, older and more arbitrary methods of exaction will resurface. The ultimate form of withholding tax—*de facto* or even overt hostage-taking—will be introduced by governments desperate to prevent wealth from escaping beyond their reach. Unlucky individuals will find themselves singled out and held to ransom in an almost medieval fashion. Businesses that offer services that facilitate the realization of autonomy by individuals will be subject to infiltration, sabotage, and disruption. Arbitrary forfeiture of property, already commonplace in the United States, where it occurs five thousand times a week, will become even more pervasive. Governments will violate human rights, censor the free flow of information, sabotage useful technologies, and worse. For the same reasons that the late, departed Soviet Union tried in vain to suppress access to personal computers and Xerox machines, Western governments will seek to suppress the cybereconomy by totalitarian means.

RETURN OF THE LUDDITES

Such methods may prove popular among some population segments. The good news about individual liberation and autonomy will seem to be bad news to many who are frightened by the transition crisis and do not expect to be winners in the new configuration of society. The apparent popularity of the draconian capital controls imposed in 1998 by Malaysian prime minister Mahathir Mohamad in the wake of the Asian meltdown testifies to residual enthusiasm among many for the old-fashioned closed economy dominated by the nation-state. This nostalgia for the past will be fed by resentments inflamed by the inevitable transition crisis. The greatest resentment is likely to be centered among those of middle talent in currently rich countries. They particularly may come to feel that information technology poses a threat to their way of life. The beneficiaries of organized compulsion, including millions receiving income redistributed by governments, may resent the new freedom realized by Sovereign Individuals. Their upset will illustrate the truism that "where you stand is determined by where you sit."

> *"Sometimes I wondered how I could experience such deep misery over the fate of a handful of men I did not know, playing a game against another group of strangers in a ballpark hundreds of miles away. The answer is simple. I loved my teams. Although risky, caring was worth its price. Sports fired up my blood, excited me, made my heart pound. I liked having something at stake. Life was more vivid during a contest."*
>
> —CRAIG LAMBERT

It would be misleading, however, to attribute all the bad feelings that will be generated in the coming transition crisis to the bald desire to live at someone else's expense. More will be involved. The very character of human society suggests that there is bound to be a misguided moral dimension to the coming Luddite reaction. Think of it as a bald desire fitted with a moral toupee. We explore the moral and moralistic dimensions of the transition crisis. Self-interested grasping of a conscious kind has far less power to motivate actions than does self-righteous fury. While adherence to the civic myths of the twentieth century is rapidly falling away, they are not without their true believers. Many humans, as the passage quoted from Craig Lambert attests, are belongers, who place importance on being members of a group. The same need to identify that motivates fans of organized sports makes some partisans of nations. Everyone who came of age in the twentieth century has been inculcated in the duties and obligations of the twentieth-century citizen. The residual moral imperatives from industrial society will stimulate at least some neo-Luddite attacks on information technologies.

In this sense, this violence to come will be at least partially an expression of what we call "moral anachronism," the application of moral strictures drawn from one stage of economic life to the circumstances of another. Every stage of society requires its own moral rules to help individuals overcome incentive traps peculiar to the choices they face in that particular way of life. Just as a farming society could not live by the moral rules of a migratory Eskimo band, so the Information Society cannot satisfy moral imperatives that emerged to facilitate the success of a militant twentieth-century industrial state. We explain why.

In the next few years, moral anachronism will be in evidence at the core countries of the West in much the way that it has been witnessed at the periphery over the past five centuries. Western colonists and military expeditions stimulated such crises when they encountered indigenous hunting-and-gathering bands, as well as peoples whose societies were still organized for farming. The introduction of new technologies into anachronistic settings caused confusion and moral crises. The success of Christian missionaries in converting millions of indigenous peoples can be laid in large measure to the local crises caused by the sudden introduction of new power arrangements from the outside. Such encounters recurred over and over, from the sixteenth century through the early decades of the twentieth century. We expect similar clashes early in the new millennium as Information Societies supplant those organized along industrial lines.

The Nostalgia for Compulsion

The rise of the Information Society will not be wholly welcomed as a promising new phase of history, even among those who benefit from it most. Everyone will feel some misgivings. And many will despise innovations that undermine the territorial nation-state. It is a fact of human nature that radical change of any kind is almost always seen as a dramatic turn for the worse. Five hundred years ago, the courtiers gathered around the duke of Burgundy would have said that unfolding innovations that undermined feudalism were evil. They thought the world was rapidly spiraling downhill at the very time that later historians saw an explosion of human potential in the Renaissance. Likewise, what may someday be seen as a new Renaissance from the perspective of the next millennium will look frightening to tired twentieth-century eyes.

There is a high probability that some who are offended by the new ways, as well as many who are disadvantaged by them, will react unpleasantly. Their nostalgia for compulsion will probably turn violent. Encounters with these new "Luddites" will make the transition to radical new forms of social organization at least a measure of bad news for everyone. Get ready to duck. With the speed of change outracing the moral and economic capacity of many in living generations to adapt, you can expect to see a fierce and indignant resistance to the Information Revolution, notwithstanding its great promise to liberate the future.

You must understand and prepare for such unpleasantness. A series of transition crises lies ahead. Deflationary tribulations, such as the Asian contagion that swept through the Far East to Russia and other emerging economies in 1997 and 1998, will erupt sporadically as the dated national and international institutions left over from the Industrial Era prove inadequate to the challenges of the new, dispersed, transnational economy. The new information and communication technologies are more subversive of the modern state than any political threat to its predominance since Columbus sailed. This is important because those in power have seldom reacted peacefully to developments that undermined their authority. They are not likely to now.

The clash between the new and the old will shape the early years of the new millennium. We expect it to be a time of great danger and great reward, and a time of much diminished civility in some realms and unprecedented scope in others. Increasingly autonomous individuals and bankrupt, desperate governments will confront one another across a new divide. We expect to see a radical restructuring of the nature of sovereignty and the virtual death of politics before the transition is over. Instead of state domination and control of resources, you are destined to see the privatization of almost all services governments now provide. For inescapable reasons that we explore in this book, information technology will destroy the capacity of the state to charge more for its services than they are worth to you and other people who pay for them.

"Governments will have to deal with what sovereignty means."

—ROBERT MARTIN, CHIEF TECHNOLOGY OFFICER, LUCENT TECHNOLOGIES

Sovereignty Through Markets

To an extent that few would have imagined only a decade ago, individuals will achieve increasing autonomy over territorial nation-states through market mechanisms. All nation-states face bankruptcy and the rapid erosion of their authority. Mighty as they are, the power they retain is the power to obliterate, not to command. Their intercontinental missiles and aircraft carriers are already artifacts, as imposing and useless as the last warhorse of feudalism.

Information technology makes possible a dramatic extension of markets by altering the way that assets are created and protected. This is revolutionary. Indeed, it promises to be more revolutionary for industrial society than the advent of gunpowder proved to be for feudal agriculture. The transformation of the year 2000 implies the commercialization of sovereignty and the death of politics, no less than guns implied the demise of oath-based feudalism. Citizenship will go the way of chivalry.

We believe that the age of individual economic sovereignty is coming. Just as steel mills, telephone companies, mines, and railways that were once "nationalized" have been rapidly privatized throughout the world, you will soon see the ultimate form of privatization—the sweeping denationalization of the individual. The Sovereign Individual of the new millennium will no longer be an asset of the state, a *de facto* item on the treasury's balance sheet. After the transition of the year 2000, denationalized citizens will no longer be citizens as we know them, but customers.

BANDWIDTH TRUMPS BORDERS

The commercialization of sovereignty will make the terms and conditions of citizenship in the nation-state as dated as chivalric oaths seemed after the collapse of feudalism. Instead of relating to a powerful state as citizens to be taxed, the Sovereign Individuals of the twenty-first century will be customers of governments operating from a "new logical space." They will bargain for whatever minimal government they need and pay for it according to contract. The governments of the Information Age will be organized along different principles than those which the world has come to expect over the past several centuries. Some jurisdictions and sovereignty services will be formed through "assortive matching," a system by which affinities, including commercial affinities, are the basis upon which virtual jurisdictions earn allegiance. In rare cases, the new sovereignties may be holdovers of medieval organizations, like the 900-year-old Sovereign Military Hospitaller Order of St. John of Jerusalem, of Rhodes and of Malta. More commonly known as the Knights of Malta, the order is an affinity group for rich Catholics, with 10,000 current members and an annual income of several billions. The Knights of Malta issues its own passports, stamps, and money, and carries on full diplomatic relations with seventy countries. As we write it is negotiating with the Republic of Malta to reassume possession of Fort St. Angelo. Taking possession of the castle would give the Knights the missing ingredient of territoriality that will enable it to be recognized as a sovereignty. The Knights of Malta could once again become a sovereign microstate, instantly legitimized by a long history. It was from Fort St. Angelo that the Knights of Malta turned back the Turks in the Great Siege of 1565. Indeed, they ruled Malta for many years thereafter, until they were expelled by Napoleon in 1798. If the Knights of Malta were to return in the next few years, there could be no clearer evidence that the modern nation-state system, ushered in after the French Revolution, was merely an interlude in the longer sweep of history in which it has been the norm for many kinds of sovereignties to exist at the same time.

Still another and very different model for a postmodern sovereignty based on assortive matching is the Iridium satellite telephone network. At first glance, you may think it odd to treat a cellular telephone service as a kind of sovereignty. Yet Iridium has already received recognition as a virtual sovereignty by international authorities. As you may know, Iridium is a global cellular phone service that allows subscribers to receive calls on a single number, wherever they find themselves on the planet, from Featherston, New Zealand, to the Bolivian Chaco. To allow calls to be routed to Iridium subscribers anywhere on the globe, given the architecture of global telecoms, international telecom authorities had to agree to recognize Iridium as a virtual country, with its own country code: 8816. It is a short step logically from a virtual country comprising satellite telephone subscribers to sovereignty for more coherent virtual communities on the World Wide Web that span borders. Bandwidth, or the carrying capacity of a communications medium, has been expanding faster than computational capacity multiplied after the invention of transistors. If this trend to greater bandwidth continues, as we believe likely, it is only a matter of a few years, soon after the turn of the millennium, until bandwidth becomes sufficiently capacious to make technically possible the "metaverse," the alternative, cyberspace world imagined by the science fiction novelist Neal Stephenson. Stephenson's "metaverse" is a dense virtual community with its own laws. We believe it is inevitable that, as the cybereconomy becomes richer, its participants will seek and obtain exemption from the anachronistic laws of nation-states. The new cybercommunities will be at least as wealthy and competent at advancing their interests as the Sovereign Military Hospitaller Order of St. John of Jerusalem, of Rhodes and of Malta. Indeed, they will be more capable of asserting themselves because of far-reaching communications and information warfare capabilities. We explore still other models of fragmented sovereignty in which small groups can effectively lease the sovereignty of weak nation-states, and operate their own economic havens much as free ports and free trade zones are licensed to do today.

A new moral vocabulary will be required to describe the relations of Sovereign Individuals with one another and what remains of government. We suspect that as the terms of these new relations come into focus, they will offend many people who came of age as "citizens" of twentieth-century nation-states. The end of nations and the "denationalization of the individual" will deflate some warmly held notions, such as "equal protection under the law," that presuppose power relations that are soon to be obsolete. As virtual communities gain coherence, they will insist that their members be held accountable according to their own laws, rather than those of the former nation-states in which they happen to reside. Multiple systems of law will again coexist over the same geographic area, as they did in ancient and medieval times.

Just as attempts to preserve the power of knights in armor were doomed to fail in the face of gunpowder weapons, so the modern notions of nationalism and citizenship are destined to be short-circuited by microtechnology. Indeed, they will eventually become comic in much the way that the sacred principles of fifteenth-century feudalism fell to ridicule in the sixteenth century. The cherished civic notions of the twentieth century will be comic anachronisms to new generations after the transformation of the year 2000. The Don Quixote of the twenty-first century will not be a knight-errant struggling to revive the glories of feudalism but a bureaucrat in a brown suit, a tax collector yearning for a citizen to audit.

REVIVING LAWS OF THE MARCH

We seldom think of governments as competitive entities, except in the broadest sense, so the modern intuition about the range and possibilities of sovereignty has atrophied. In the past, when the power equation made it more difficult for groups to assert a stable monopoly of coercion, power was frequently fragmented, jurisdictions overlapped, and entities of many different kinds exercised one or more of the attributes of sovereignty. Not infrequently, the nominal overlord actually enjoyed scant power on the ground. Governments weaker than the nation-states are now faced with sustained competition in their ability to impose a monopoly of coercion over a local territory. This competition gave rise to adaptations in controlling violence and attracting allegiance that will soon be new again.

When the reach of lords and kings was weak, and the claims of one or more groups overlapped at a frontier, it frequently happened that neither could decisively dominate the other. In the Middle Ages, there were numerous frontier or "march" regions where sovereignties blended together. These violent frontiers persisted for decades or even centuries in the border areas of Europe. There were marches between areas of Celtic and English control in Ireland; between Wales and England, Scotland and England, Italy and France, France and Spain, Germany and the Slav frontiers of Central Europe, and between the Christian kingdoms of Spain and the Islamic kingdom of Granada. Such march regions developed distinct institutional and legal forms of a kind that we are likely to see again in the next millennium. Because of the competitive position of the two authorities, residents of march regions seldom paid tax. What is more, they usually had a choice in deciding whose laws they were to obey, a choice that was exercised through such legal concepts as "avowal" and "distraint" that have now all but vanished. We expect such concepts to become a prominent feature of the law of Information Societies.

Transcending Nationality

Before the nation-state, it was difficult to enumerate precisely the number of sovereignties that existed in the world because they overlapped in complex ways and many varied forms of organization exercised power. They will do so again. The dividing lines between territories tended to become clearly demarcated and fixed as borders in the nation-state system. They will become hazy again in the Information Age. In the new millennium, sovereignty will be fragmented once more. New entities will emerge exercising some but not all of the characteristics we have come to associate with governments.

Some of these new entities, like the Knights Templar and other religious military orders of the Middle Ages, may control considerable wealth and military power without controlling any fixed territory. They will be organized on principles that bear no relation to nationality at all. Members and leaders of religious corporations that exercised sovereign authority in parts of Europe in the Middle Ages in no sense derived their authority from national identity. They were of all ethnic backgrounds and professed to owe their allegiance to God, and not to any affinities that members of a nationality are supposed to share in common.

Merchant Republics of Cyberspace

You will also see the re-emergence of associations of merchants and wealthy individuals with semisovereign powers, like the Hanse (confederation of merchants) in the Middle Ages. The Hanse that operated in the French and Flemish fairs grew to encompass the merchants of sixty cities.[10] The "Hanseatic League," as it is redundantly known in English (the literal translation is "Leaguely League"), was an organization of Germanic merchant guilds that provided protection to members and negotiated trade treaties. It came to exercise semisovereign powers in a number of Northern European and Baltic cities. Such entities will re-emerge in place of the dying nation-state in the new millennium, providing protection and helping to enforce contracts in an unsafe world.

In short, the future is likely to confound the expectations of those who have absorbed the civic myths of twentieth-century industrial society. Among them are the illusions of social democracy that once thrilled and motivated the most gifted minds. They presuppose that societies evolve in whatever way governments wish them to—preferably in response to opinion polls and scrupulously counted votes. This was never as true as it seemed fifty years ago. Now it is an anachronism, as much an artifact of industrialism as a rusting smokestack. The civic myths reflect not only a mindset that sees society's problems as susceptible to engineering solutions; they also reflect a false confidence that resources and individuals will remain as vulnerable to political compulsion in the future as they have been in the twentieth century. We doubt it. Market forces, not political majorities, will compel societies to reconfigure themselves in ways that public opinion will neither comprehend nor welcome. As they do, the naïve view that history is what people wish it to be will prove wildly misleading.

It will therefore be crucial that you see the world anew. That means looking from the outside in to reanalyze much that you have probably taken for granted. This will enable you to come to a new understanding. If you fail to transcend conventional thinking at a time when conventional thinking is losing touch with reality, then you will be more likely to fall prey to an epidemic of disorientation that lies ahead. Disorientation breeds mistakes that could threaten your business, your investments, and your way of life.

"The universe rewards us for understanding it and punishes us for not understanding it. When we understand the universe, our plans work and we feel good. Conversely, if we try to fly by jumping off a cliff and flapping our arms the universe will kill us." [11]

—JACK COHEN AND IAN STEWART

Seeing Anew

To prepare yourself for the world that is coming you must understand why it will be different from what most experts tell you. That involves looking closely at the hidden causes of change. We have attempted to do this with an unorthodox analysis we call the study of megapolitics. In two previous volumes, *Blood in the Streets* and *The Great Reckoning,* we argued that the most important causes of change are not to be found in political manifestos or in the pronouncements of dead economists, but in the hidden factors that alter the boundaries where power is exercised. Often, subtle changes in climate, topography, microbes, and technology alter the logic of violence. They transform the way people organize their livelihoods and defend themselves.

Notice that our approach to understanding how the world changes is very different from that of most forecasters. We are not experts *in* anything, in the sense that we pretend to know a great deal more about certain "subjects" than those who have spent their entire careers cultivating highly specialized knowledge. To the contrary, we look from the outside in. We are knowledgeable *around* the subjects about which we make forecasts. Most of all, this involves seeing where the boundaries of necessity are drawn. When they change, society necessarily changes, no matter what people may wish to the contrary.

In our view, the key to understanding how societies evolve is to understand factors that determine the costs and rewards of employing violence. Every human society, from the hunting band to the empire, has been informed by the interactions of megapolitical factors that set the prevailing version of the "laws of nature." Life is always and everywhere complex. The lamb and the lion keep a delicate balance, interacting at the margin. If lions were suddenly more swift, they would catch prey that now escape. If lambs suddenly grew wings, lions would starve. The capacity to utilize and defend against violence is the crucial variable that alters life at the margin.

We put violence at the center of our theory of megapolitics for good reason. The control of violence is the most important dilemma every society faces. As we wrote in *The Great Reckoning:*

> The reason that people resort to violence is that it often pays. In some ways, the simplest thing a man can do if he wants money is to take it. That is no less true for an army of men seizing an oil field than it is for a single thug taking a wallet. Power, as William Playfair wrote, "has always sought the readiest road to wealth, by attacking those who were in possession of it."
>
> The challenge to prosperity is precisely that predatory violence does pay well in some circumstances. War does change things. It changes the rules. It changes the distribution of assets and income. It even determines who lives and who dies. It is precisely the fact that violence does pay that makes it hard to control.[12]

Thinking in these terms has helped us foresee a number of developments that better-informed experts insisted could never happen. For example, *Blood in the Streets,* published in early 1987, was our attempt to survey the first stages of the great megapolitical revolution now under way. We argued then that technological change was destabilizing the power equation in the world. Among our principal points:

- We said that American predominance was in decline, which would lead to economic imbalances and distress, including another 1929-style stock market crash. Experts were all but unanimous in denying that such a thing could happen. Yet within six months, in October 1987, world markets were convulsed by the most violent sell-off of the century.
- We told readers to expect the collapse of Communism. Again, experts laughed. Yet 1989 brought the events that "no one could have predicted." The Berlin Wall fell, as revolutions swept away Communist regimes from the Baltic to Bucharest.
- We explained why the multiethnic empire the Bolshevik nomenklatura inherited from the tsars would "inevitably crack apart." At the end of December 1991, the hammer-and-sickle banner was lowered over the Kremlin for the last time as the Soviet Union ceased to exist.
- During the height of the Reagan arms buildup, we argued that the world stood at the threshold of sweeping disarmament. This, too, was considered unlikely, if not preposterous. Yet the following seven years brought the most sweeping disarmament since the close of World War I.
- At a time when experts in North America and Europe were pointing to

Japan for support of the view that governments can successfully rig markets, we said otherwise. We forecast that the Japanese financial assets boom would end in a bust. Soon after the fall of the Berlin Wall, the Japanese stock market crashed, losing almost half its value. We continue to believe that its ultimate low could match or exceed the 89 percent loss that Wall Street suffered at the bottom after 1929.

- At a point when almost everyone, from the middle-class family to the world's largest real estate investors, appeared to believe that property markets could only rise and not fall, we warned that a real estate bust was in the offing. Within four years, real estate investors throughout the world lost more than $1 trillion as property values dropped.
- Long before it was obvious to the experts, we explained in *Blood in the Streets* that the income of blue-collar workers had decreased and was destined to continue falling on a long-term basis. As we write today, almost a decade later, it has at last begun to dawn on a sleepy world that this is true. Average hourly wages in the United States have fallen below those achieved in the second Eisenhower administration. In 1993, average annualized hourly wages in constant dollars were $18,808. In 1957, when Eisenhower was sworn in for his second term, U.S. annualized average hourly wages were $18,903.

While the main themes of *Blood in the Streets* have proven remarkably accurate with the benefit of hindsight, only a few years ago they were considered rank nonsense by the guardians of conventional thinking. A reviewer in *Newsweek* in 1987 reflected the closed mental climate of late industrial society when he dismissed our analysis as "an unthinking attack on reason."

You might imagine that *Newsweek* and similar publications would have recognized with the passage of time that our line of analysis had revealed something useful about the way the world was changing. Not a bit. The first edition of *The Great Reckoning* was greeted with the same sniggering hostility that welcomed *Blood in the Streets*. No less an authority than the *Wall Street Journal* categorically dismissed our analysis as the nattering of "your dopey aunt."

This chuckling aside, the themes of *The Great Reckoning* proved less ludicrous than the guardians of orthodoxy pretended.

- We extended our forecast of the death of the Soviet Union, exploring why Russia and the other former Soviet republics faced a future of growing civil disorder, hyperinflation, and falling living standards.
- We explained why the 1990s would be a decade of downsizing, including

for the first time a worldwide downsizing of governments as well as business entities.

- We also forecast that there would be a major redefinition of terms of income redistribution, with sharp cutbacks in the level of benefits. Hints of fiscal crisis appeared from Canada to Sweden, and American politicians began to talk of "ending welfare as we know it."

- We anticipated and explained why the "new world order" would prove to be a "new world disorder." Well before the atrocities in Bosnia engrossed the headlines, we warned that Yugoslavia would collapse into civil war.

- Before Somalia slid into anarchy, we explained why the pending collapse of governments in Africa would lead some countries there to be effectively placed into receivership.

- We forecast and explained why militant Islam would displace Marxism as the principal ideology of confrontation with the West.

- Years before the Oklahoma bombing and the attempt to blow up the World Trade Center, we explained why the United States faced an upsurge in terrorism.

- Before the headlines that told of the rioting that swept Los Angeles, Toronto, and other cities, we explained why the emergence of criminal subcultures among urban minorities was setting the stage for widespread criminal violence.

- We also anticipated "the final depression of the twentieth century," which began in Asia in 1989 and has been spreading back from the periphery toward the center of the global system. We said that the Japanese stock market would follow Wall Street's path after 1929, and that this would lead to credit collapse and depression. Although massive government intervention in Japan and elsewhere temporarily prevented markets from fully reflecting the deterioration of credit conditions, this only displaced and compounded economic distress, building pressures for competitive devaluations and a systemic credit collapse of the kind that imploded economies worldwide in the 1930s.

The Great Reckoning also spelled out a number of controversial theses that have not yet been confirmed, or have not reached the level of development that we forecast:

- We said that the Japanese stock market would follow Wall Street's path after 1929, and that this would lead to credit collapse and depression. Although unemployment rates in Spain, Finland, and a few other countries exceeded those of the 1930s, and a number of countries, including Japan, did experience local depressions, there has not yet been a systemic credit collapse of the kind that imploded economies worldwide in the 1930s.

- We argued that the breakdown of the command-and-control system in the former Soviet Union would lead to the spread of nuclear weapons into the hands of ministates, terrorists, and criminal gangs. To the world's good fortune, this has not come to pass, at least not to the degree that we feared. Press reports indicate that Iran purchased several tactical nuclear weapons on the black market; more worryingly, the *Times* of London reported on October 7, 1998, that "Osama bin Laden, the exiled millionaire Saudi terrorist leader, has acquired tactical nuclear weapons from the former Soviet Central Asian states, according to a leading Arab newspaper." That said, there has been no officially confirmed deployment or use of nuclear weapons from the arsenals of the former Soviet Union.
- We explained why the "War on Drugs" was a recipe for subverting the police and judicial systems of countries where drug use is widespread, particularly the United States. With tens of billions of dollars in hidden monopoly profits piling up each year, drug dealers have the means as well as the incentive to corrupt even apparently stable countries. While the world media have carried occasional stories hinting at high-level penetration of the U.S. political system by drug money, the full story has not yet been told.

Looking Where Others Don't

Notwithstanding the points where our forecasts were mistaken or seem mistaken in light of what is now known, the record stands to scrutiny. Much of what is likely to figure in future economic histories of the 1990s was forecast or anticipated and explained in *The Great Reckoning*. Many of our predictions were not simple extrapolations or extensions of trends, but forecasts of major departures from what has been considered normal since World War II. We warned that the 1990s would be dramatically different from the previous five decades. Reading the news of 1991 through 1998, we see that the themes of *The Great Reckoning* were borne out almost daily.

We see these developments not as examples of isolated difficulties, trouble here, trouble there, but as shocks and tremors that run along the same fault line. The old order is being toppled by a megapolitical earthquake that will revolutionize institutions and alter the way thinking people see the world.

In spite of the central role of violence in determining the way the world works, it attracts surprisingly little serious attention. Most political analysts and economists write as if violence were a minor irritant, like a fly buzzing around a cake, and not the chef who baked it.

Another Megapolitical Pioneer

In fact, there has been so little clear thinking about the role of violence in history that a bibliography of megapolitical analysis could be written on a single sheet of paper. In *The Great Reckoning,* we drew upon and elaborated arguments of an almost entirely forgotten classic of megapolitical analysis, William Playfair's *An Enquiry into the Permanent Causes of the Decline and Fall of Powerful and Wealthy Nations,* published in 1805. Here one of our departure points is the work of Frederic C. Lane. Lane was a medieval historian who wrote several penetrating essays on the role of violence in history during the 1940s and 1950s. Perhaps the most comprehensive of these was "Economic Consequences of Organized Violence," which appeared in the *Journal of Economic History* in 1958. Few people other than professional economists and historians have read it, and most of them seem not to have recognized its significance. Like Playfair, Lane wrote for an audience that did not yet exist.

Insights for the Information Age

Lane published his work on violence and the economic meaning of war well before the advent of the Information Age. He certainly was not writing in anticipation of microprocessing or the other technological revolutions now unfolding. Yet his insights into violence established a framework for understanding how society will be reconfigured in the Information Revolution.

The window Lane opened into the future was one through which he peered into the past. He was a medieval historian, and particularly a historian of a trading city, Venice, whose fortunes surged and sagged in a violent world. In thinking about how Venice rose and fell, his attention was attracted to issues that can help you understand the future. He saw the fact that how violence is organized and controlled plays a large role in determining "what uses are made of scarce resources." [13]

We believe that Lane's analyses of the competitive uses of violence has much to tell us about how life is likely to change in the Information Age. But don't expect most people to notice, much less follow, so unfashionably abstract an argument. While the attention of the world is riveted on dishonest debates and wayward personalities, the meanderings of megapolitics continue almost unnoted. The average North American has probably lavished one hundred times more attention on O. J. Simpson and Monica Lewinsky than he has on the new microtechnologies that are poised to antiquate his job and subvert the political system he depends on for unemployment compensation.

THE VANITY OF WISHES

The tendency to overlook what is fundamentally important is not confined solely to the couch dweller watching television. Conventional thinkers of all shapes and sizes observe one of the pretenses of the democratic nation-state —that the views people hold determine the way the world changes. Apparently sophisticated analysts lapse into explanations and forecasts that interpret major historical developments as if they were determined in a wishful way. A striking example of this type of reasoning appeared on the editorial page of the *New York Times* just as we were writing: "Goodbye, Nation-State, Hello . . . What?," by Nicholas Colchester.[14] Not only was the topic, the death of the nation-state, the very topic we are addressing, but its author presents himself as an excellent marker to illustrate how far removed our way of thinking is from the norm. Colchester is no simpleton. He wrote as editorial director of the *Economist* Intelligence Unit. If anyone should form a realistic view of the world it should be he. Yet his article clearly indicates in several places that "the coming of international government" is "now logically unstoppable."

Why? Because the nation-state is faltering and can no longer control economic forces.

In our view, this assumption verges on the absurd. To suppose that some specific new form of governance will emerge simply because another has failed is a fallacy. By that reasoning, Haiti and the Congo would long ago have had better government simply because what they had was so luminously inadequate.

Colchester's point of view, widely shared among the few who think about such things in North America and Europe, utterly fails to take into account the larger megapolitical forces that determine what types of political systems are actually viable. That is the focus of this book. When the technologies that are shaping the new millennium are considered, it is far more likely that we will see not one world government, but microgovernment, or even conditions approaching anarchy.

For every serious analysis of the role of violence in determining the rules by which everyone operates, dozens of books have been written about the intricacies of wheat subsidies, and hundreds more about arcane aspects of monetary policy. Much of this shortfall in thinking about the crucial issues that actually determine the course of history probably reflects the relative stability of the power configuration over the past several centuries. The bird that falls asleep on the back of a hippopotamus does not think about losing its perch until the hippo actually moves. Dreams, myths, and fantasies play a much larger role in informing the supposed social sciences than we commonly think.

This is particularly evident in the abundant literature of economic justice. Millions of words have been uttered and written about economic justice and injustice for each page devoted to careful analysis of how violence shapes society, and thus sets the boundaries within which economies must function. Yet formulations of economic justice in the modern context presuppose that society is dominated by an instrument of compulsion so powerful that it can take away and redistribute life's good things. Such power has existed for only a few generations of the modern period. Now it is fading away.

Big Brother on Social Security

Industrial technology gave governments greater instruments of control in the twentieth century than ever before. For a time, it seemed inevitable that governments would become so effective at monopolizing violence as to leave little room for individual autonomy. Nobody at mid-century was looking forward to the triumph of the Sovereign Individual.

Some of the shrewdest observers of the mid-twentieth century became convinced on the evidence of the day that the tendency of the nation-state to centralize power would lead to totalitarian domination over all aspects of life. In George Orwell's *1984* (1949), Big Brother was watching the individual vainly struggle to maintain a margin of autonomy and self-respect. It appeared to be a losing cause. Friedrich von Hayek's *The Road to Serfdom* (1944) took a more scholarly view in arguing that freedom was being lost to a new form of economic control that left the state as the master of everything. These works were written before the advent of microprocessing, which has incubated a whole range of technologies that enhance the capacity of small groups and even individuals to function independently of central authority.

As shrewd as observers like Hayek and Orwell were, they were unduly pessimistic. History has unfolded its surprises. Totalitarian Communism barely outlasted the year 1984. A new form of serfdom may yet emerge in the next millennium if governments succeed in suppressing the liberating aspects of microtechnology. But it is far more likely that we will see unprecedented opportunity and autonomy for the individual. What our parents worried about may prove to be no problem at all. What they took for granted as fixed and permanent features of social life now seem destined to disappear. Wherever necessity sets boundaries to human choice, we adjust, and reorganize our lives accordingly.

The Hazards of Forecasting

No doubt we put our small measure of dignity at risk in attempting to foresee and explain profound changes in the organization of life and the culture that binds it together. Most forecasts are doomed to make silly reading in the fullness of time. And the more dramatic the change they envision, the more embarrassingly wrong they tend to be. The world doesn't end. The ozone doesn't vanish. The coming Ice Age dissolves into global warming. Notwithstanding all the alarms to the contrary, there is still oil in the tank. Mr. Antrobus, the everyman of *The Skin of Our Teeth,* avoids freezing, survives wars and threatened economic calamities, and grows old ignoring the studied alarms of experts.

Most attempts to "unveil" the future soon turn out to be comic. Even where self-interest provides a strong incentive to clear thinking, forward vision is often myopic. In 1903, the Mercedes company said that "there would never be as many as 1 million automobiles worldwide. The reason was that it was implausible that as many as 1 million artisans worldwide would be trainable as chauffeurs." [15]

Recognizing this should stop our mouths. It doesn't. We are not afraid to stand in line for a due share of ridicule. If we mistake matters greatly, future generations may laugh as heartily as they please, presuming anyone remembers what we said. To dare a thought is to risk being wrong. We are hardly so stiff and useless that we are afraid to err. Far from it. We would rather venture thoughts that might prove useful to you than suppress them out of apprehension that they might prove overblown or embarrassing in retrospect.

As Arthur C. Clarke shrewdly noted, the two overriding reasons why attempts to anticipate the future usually fall flat are "Failure of Nerve and Failure of Imagination." [16] Of the two, he wrote, "Failure of Nerve seems to be the more common; it occurs when *even given all the relevant facts* the would-be prophet cannot see that they point to an inescapable conclusion. Some of these failures are so ludicrous as to be almost unbelievable." [17]

Where our exploration of the Information Revolution falls short, as it inevitably will, the cause will be due more to a lack of imagination than to a lack of nerve. Forecasting the future has always been a bold enterprise, one which properly excites skepticism. Perhaps time will prove that our deductions are wildly off the mark. Unlike Nostradamus, we do not pretend to be prophetic personalities. We do not foretell the future by stirring a wand in a bowl of water or by casting horoscopes. Nor do we write in cryptic verse. Our purpose is to provide you with a sober, detached analysis of issues that could prove to be of great importance to you.

We feel an obligation to set out our views, even where they seem heretical, precisely because they may not otherwise be heard. In the closed mental atmosphere of late industrial society, ideas do not traffic as freely as they should through the established media.

This book is written in a constructive spirit. It is the third we have written together, analyzing various stages of the great change now under way. Like *Blood in the Streets* and *The Great Reckoning,* it is a thought exercise. It explores the death of industrial society and its reconfiguration in new forms. We expect to see amazing paradoxes in the years to come. On the one hand, you will witness the realization of a new form of freedom, with the emergence of the Sovereign Individual. You can expect to see almost the complete liberation of productivity. At the same time, we expect to see the death of the modern nation-state. Many of the assurances of equality that Western people have grown to take for granted in the twentieth century are destined to die with it. We expect that representative democracy as it is now known will fade away, to be replaced by the new democracy of choice in the cybermarketplace. If our deductions are correct, the politics of the next century will be much more varied and less important than that to which we have become accustomed.

We are confident that our argument will be easy to follow, notwithstanding the fact that it leads through some territory that is the intellectual equivalent of the backwoods and bad neighborhoods. If our meaning is not entirely intelligible in places, that is not because we are being cute, or using the time-honored equivocation of those who pretend to foretell the future by making cryptic pronouncements. We are not equivocators. If our arguments are unclear, it is because we have failed the task of writing in a way that makes compelling ideas accessible. Unlike many forecasters, we want you to understand and even duplicate our line of thinking. It is based not upon psychic reveries or the gyrations of planets, but upon old-fashioned, ugly logic. For quite logical reasons, we believe that microprocessing will inevitably subvert and destroy the nation-state, creating new forms of social organization in the process. It is both necessary and possible for you to foresee at least some details of the new way of life that may be here sooner than you think.

Ironies of a Future Foretold

For centuries, the end of this millennium has been seen as a pregnant moment in history. More than 850 years ago, St. Malachy fixed 2000 as the date of the Last Judgment. American psychic Edgar Cayce said in 1934 that the earth would shift on its axis in the year 2000, causing California to split in two and inundating New York City and Japan. A Japanese rocket scientist, Hideo Itokawa, announced in 1980 that the alignment of the planets in a "Grand Cross" on August 18, 1999, would cause widespread environmental devastation, leading to the end of human life on earth.[18]

Such visions of apocalypse make a plump target for ridicule. After all, the year 2000, while an imposing round number, would appear to be only an arbitrary artifact of the Christian calendar as adopted in the West. Other calendars and dating systems calculate centuries and millennia from different starting points. By the reckoning of the Islamic calendar, for example, A.D. 2000 will be the year 1378. As ordinary-sounding as a year can be. According to the Chinese calendar, which repeats itself every sixty years, A.D. 2000 is just another year of the dragon. It is part of a continuous cycle that extends millennia into the past. Yet there is more than theological investment in the year 2000. Its importance is undergirded not only by Christian tradition, but by the limitations of mid-century information technology. The so-called Y2K or year 2000 computer problem, a potentially devastating logic flaw in billions of lines of computer code, could approximate apocalyptic conditions by closing down essential elements of industrial society on the millennial midnight. Many computers and microprocessors use software preserved and recycled from the earliest days of computers, when memory space, at $600,000 per megabyte, was more valuable than gold. To save expensive space, the early programmers tracked dates with only the last two numbers of the year. This convention of employing two-digit date fields was carried over into most software employed in mainframe computers, and even found wide use in personal computers and so-called embedded chips, microprocessors that are used to control almost everything, from VCRs to car ignition systems, security systems, telephones, the switching systems that control the telephone network, process and control systems in factories, power plants, oil refineries, chemical plants, pipelines and much more. Thus, abbreviated into a two-digit field, the year 1999 would be "99." The trouble is what happens when 00 comes up for the year 2000. Many computers will read this as 1900. This may make it impossible for many unremediated computers and other digital devices to recognize the year 2000 in date fields.

The result will be a massive problem of data corruption that will provide an accidental illustration of a new potential for information warfare. In the Information Age, potential adversaries will be able to wreak havoc by detonating "logic bombs" that sabotage the functions of essential systems by corrupting the data upon which their functioning depends. As a military exercise, for example, you would not need to shoot down an airplane, if you could corrupt data crucial to its safe operation. Data corruption can do almost as much as physical weapons can to thwart the function of a modern society. That this has potentially far-reaching consequences should be obvious on reflection. For example, the *Mail* of London reported on December 14, 1997, that airlines around the globe were planning to cancel hundreds of flights on January 1, 2000 out of fear that air traffic control systems could fail.[19] Potential problems include not only the air traffic systems, but also date-sensitive functions built into the airplanes themselves. According to

Boeing, many airplanes will require Y2K remediation. Many devices may have a problem if they try to log an event on an invalid date. The fly-by-wire computer-controlled systems that operate airplanes may malfunction if they are programmed to conclude that crucial maintenance was last performed in the year 1900. They many even go into an error loop and shut down.

The potentially lethal feedback effects of a logic time bomb that closes down noncompliant control systems could make the turn of the millennium a memorable date for unpleasant reasons. Remember, you can be affected by many devices that go into an error loop and shut down even if you are lucky enough not to find yourself in midair when the new millennium begins.

You would be well advised to avoid an accident arising from non-Y2K-compliant pacemakers, or simply inebriated millennial revelers, because if the pacemakers shut down, the phone system might also, so the ambulance might never come. Unless you live in Brazil or Ukraine, you are used to picking up the telephone or turning on the car phone and automatically getting a dial tone. Happily, you seldom have to concern yourself with the technical details of how the telephone system operates. But it turns out that phone network switches and routers are highly date dependent. All connections are logged to a date and time, which is crucial to calculating call duration for billing. If you happen to make a one-minute call at 11:59:30 on December 31, 1999, and at 12:00:00 the system reads your call as having had a negative duration of more than 99 years, error loops and shutdown are possible. While long-distance companies are spending great sums to upgrade their switches to make them year 2000 compliant, and local service providers presumably are too, if even a few smaller companies fail to comply and go down, the whole network could be affected. You will be lucky to get a dial tone on January 1, 2000.

In the words of the Y2K expert Peter de Jager, "If we lose the ability to make a phone call, then we lose everything. We lose electronic fund transfers, we lose trading, we lose branch banking." And the follow-on consequences of Y2K failures could come to more than that.

Today, no one knows how pervasively crucial systems will crash because of the year 2000 problem. Embedded systems that cannot be reprogrammed but must be replaced if nonfunctional on a date-sensitive basis are found in cars, trucks, and buses built after 1976. (Perhaps you won't be in an accident with vehicles driven by persons with noncompliant pacemakers, because their vehicles might not start.) Embedded systems are also widespread in all types of power plants, water and sewage systems, medical devices, military equipment, aircraft, offshore oil platforms, oil tankers, alarm systems, and elevators. While many assemblies of microprocessors perform no date-sensitive functions, they may nonetheless depend upon a clock, which may be Y2K sensitive, for their internal operations.

MAINFRAMES AND THE Y2K TIME BOMB

The large-scale command and control systems of government and major corporations that involve high transaction volumes on mainframe computers were the original focus of Y2K concern. Because they operate on big machines for which most software is decades old and mostly noncompliant, the original alarms about Y2K, first sounded by Peter de Jager early in the 1990s, have focused mainly on the need to upgrade operating systems for big, multiprocessing mainframes. Mr. de Jager voiced concern that there might not be enough programmers conversant with COBOL, the old mainframe language, to complete the necessary patches and repairs to date-sensitive code, even if every company and government agency with a vulnerable system had begun a crash program several years ago. Since this has not happened, and many operators of date-sensitive information systems have only just begun to assess their vulnerability, you can predict with a high degree of confidence that many mainframe systems will not be prepared to operate smoothly into the year 2000.

This is certainly a major concern because there is really no alternative to computer processing as the economy is now structured. Most businesses that are large enough to require a mainframe to handle their transactions are dependent upon transaction volumes that could not be managed with old-fashioned nineteenth-century paperwork systems. If such businesses were forced to revert to shuffling paper they could expect to complete only a fraction of their normal transaction volume. The revenue shock from such a drop-off in business would endanger the survival of all but the most highly capitalized companies.

Almost everything related to money—invoicing, purchasing, and payroll systems, plus inventory controls and regulatory compliance—would be fouled up. Huge quantities of data would be lost as computers crash or spew out false data in response to the Y2K problem. In some cases, it would actually prove a blessing if systems crash immediately rather than corrupting their data on a compounding basis until massive malfunction draws attention to the problem. What happens to files when a backup utility copies files originating on 07/04/99 to an update on 01/04/00? Who knows? Will the computer interpret a payment made on January 4, "1900," for an insurance policy as a signal that the policy has been in default for a century, resulting in a canceled policy that is stricken from the file? Will banks and finance company computers seek to assess a hundred years of interest on loans that span the shift to the new millennium? Will your banks and brokerage firms retain accurate records of your account balances and give you timely access to your funds? These are just some of the interesting quandaries that you will confront because of the Y2K problem.

"This is potentially the most destructive part of the year 2000 problem. This isn't the inconvenience part where your paycheck comes a few days late. This is the blood-in-the-streets part."

—DR. LEON KAPPELMAN, CO-CHAIR,
SOCIETY FOR INFORMATION MANAGEMENT'S YEAR 2000 WORKING GROUP

Also high on your list of concerns should be what happens if the electricity goes off because of Y2K-related malfunctions. Without electricity, even most systems that are not Y2K-impaired will not function: your refrigerator, your freezer, perhaps even your source of heat. Y2K compliance issues could effect safety-related access and control functions at nuclear power plants. For example, personnel at nuclear facilities wear dosimetry devices that measure the amount of radiation exposure they receive while in the plant. These devices are analyzed regularly, with the data on exposure amounts maintained on a computer system that controls personnel access to the facility. Obviously, if the controlling computers fail, they will make a hash of all the elaborate controls designed to insure safe operation and guarantee proper maintenance. But, more importantly, a Nuclear Regulatory Commission memo notes that many "non-safety-related, but important computer-based systems, primarily databases and data collection necessary for plant operations," are date sensitive.

The conventional generating plants are not less vulnerable to Y2K disruption. For one thing, coal-powered plants are susceptible to disruptions in the surface transportation system that brings the coal to the boilers. In the 1997–1998 winter heating season, operators of coal-fired electricity generation found themselves forced to reduce output in some instances because of a slowdown in rail deliveries of Western coal arising from the merger of the Southern Pacific and Union Pacific railway systems. The problem arose because of incompatibilities between the computer control and dispatch systems employed by the two railroads. According to a Union Pacific spokesman, integrating the two systems became a "nightmare," in spite of the fact that Union Pacific Technologies has been considered an industry leader in developing computerized transportation control systems. As a result of the programming difficulties, the railroad was unable to accurately track the movements of its freight cars. The failure of Union Pacific to master the assimilation of Southern Pacific is a bad omen about what could happen when Y2K logic time bombs disrupt transportation, power generation, and other aspects of the economy.

The biggest worry about the electric grid, however, arises from the fact that the whole system is subject to sensitive monitoring and computer control to transfer electricity from areas of surplus generation to those with a deficit. This process must be carefully monitored by computer to prevent power surges and system failures. All the transfers of electricity are logged to time and date for duration, much like a telephone connection. While heavy-duty mechanical relays are used to make the connections, they are controlled by computer systems. These computer controls, essential for load balancing, may fail for the same reasons as the phone networks. In fact, the power load distribution-control systems in North America are networked together through T-1 lines and telephone microwave links. So if the phone network fails, you can expect the electricity to go down as well. And remember, as the experience in Canada in January 1998 confirms, once the electricity shuts down over a wide area, getting the system running again is a challenge. A blackout may last for an inconveniently long time.

Y2K AND THE NUCLEAR ARSENAL

For modern economies to have the electricity turn off in the dead of winter would be disruptive and potentially health threatening, especially for those who depend upon electric heat and medical equipment. Yet the worst case scenario is even worse. According to John Koskinen, who heads President Clinton's Y2K Conversion Council, U.S. military arsenals may cease to function on the stroke of midnight, December 31, 1999. While indicating that he does not wish to touch off undue alarm, Koskinen adds, "It needs to be worried about." One concern about nuclear missiles "is if the data doesn't function and they actually go off."

Of course, this concern would apply with equal or greater force to Russian nuclear missiles. Russia's bankruptcy has made upgrades for Y2K compliance even more problematic than in the United States. And there is evidence that Russia is not yet taking Y2K conversion seriously. While one would pray that no accidental launches would occur, there should be little doubt that the turn of the year 2000 has a potential for aggravating global insecurity if for no other reason than that military communications systems in many countries may not function normally. As Koskinen puts it, "If you're sitting in a country and suddenly you can't quite figure out exactly what's happening, and your communications don't work as well, you get even more nervous." So put that on your list of Y2K worries. The logic time bomb could precipitate the launch of genuinely explosive bombs—a fact that highlights the danger from information warfare to centralized command and control systems.

If terrorists wish to strike any centralized system, they may pick December 31, 1999, as the date for action because it will be a time of maximum vulnerability of many systems. Not only will communications be strained at best, with the possibility that electricity may fail, vehicles may not start, police, fire, and ambulance 911 service may not work, and so on, but many other functions you probably take for granted, such as air traffic control, may cease to function. No power means no water from the tap. Sewage systems would fail. Traffic lights could turn off. Within a few hours of a genuine breakdown in the transportation system, food in grocery stores would be shopped out. (Or looted.) On the basis of recent experience in American cities, you could suppose that no power, no water, no heat for many, no light, and fragmented communications with emergency services, including police and fire, all add up to no civilization. While no one can be sure what the impact of the Y2K problem may be, it could extend to looting and rioting in the streets, especially if it becomes known that there could be widespread failures to issue payroll, welfare and pension checks.

"We shall not be what we have been, but we shall begin to be other."[20]

—JOACHIM DE FIORE

Premonitions of doom about the new millennium do not necessarily rest upon theology tied to the Christian faith, but they do fit within the millennial tradition of Joachim de Fiore whose mediations convinced him that Christ was only "the second hinge of history" and that another was destined to unfold."[21] So argues the philosopher Michael Grosso, who suggests that the Information Revolution is piloting human history toward the realization of the prophetic vision of the Western world. He calls this "technocalypse." Whether or not the development of technology is somehow informed by millennial visions, the Y2K phenomenon is an artifact of the predominant Western imagination of time. In a strange way, it could complement dreams, reveries and visions, or numerical interpretations of visions, like Newton's gloss on the prophecies of Daniel. These intuitive leaps begin with a perspective that takes the birth of Christ to be the central fact of history. They are compounded by the psychological power of large round numbers, which every trader will recognize as having an arresting quality. The two thousandth year of our epoch cannot help but become a focus for the imagination of intuitive people.

A critic could easily make these premonitions seem silly, without even addressing the ambiguous and debatable theological notions of the Apocalypse and the Last Judgment that give these visions so much of their power. Interestingly, however, the Y2K computer glitch trumps the errors of arithmetic that otherwise might seem to devalue the importance of the year 2000 even within the Christian framework. The year 2000 has the potential to become an inflection point for the next stage of history simply because it brings forward the arrival of the new millennium. In strict logic, the next millennium will not begin until 2001. The year 2000 will be only the last year of the twentieth century, the two thousandth year since Christ's birth. Or it would be had Christ been born in the first year of the Christian era. He was not. In 533, when Christ's birth replaced the founding date of Rome as the basis for calculating years according to the Western calendar, the monks who introduced the new convention miscalculated Christ's birth. It is now accepted that he was born in 4 B.C. On that basis, a full two thousand years since his birth were completed sometime in 1997. Hence Carl Jung's apparently odd launch date for the start of a New Age.

Giggle if you will, but we do not despise or dismiss intuitive understandings of history. Although our argument is grounded in logic, not in reveries, we are awed by the prophetic power of human consciousness. Time after time, it redeems the visions of madmen, psychics, and saints. So it may be with the transformation of the year 2000. The date that has long been fixed in the imagination of the West looks to be the inflection point that at least half confirms that history has a destiny. We cannot explain why this should be, but nonetheless we are convinced that it is so.

Our intuition is that history has a destiny, and that free will and determinism are two versions of the same phenomenon. The human interactions that form history behave as though they were informed by a kind of destiny. Just as an electron plasma, a dense gas of electrons, behaves as a complex system, so do human beings. The freedom of individual movement by the electrons turns out to be compatible with highly organized collective behavior. As David Bohm said of an electron plasma, human history is "a highly organized system which behaves as a whole."

Understanding the way the world works means developing a realistic intuition of the way that human society obeys the mathematics of natural processes. Reality is nonlinear. But most people's expectations are not. To understand the dynamics of change, you have to recognize that human society, like other complex systems in nature, is characterized by cycles and discontinuities. That means certain features of history have a tendency to repeat themselves, and the most important changes, when they occur, may be abrupt rather than gradual.

Among the cycles that permeate human life, a mysterious five-hundred-year cycle appears to mark major turning points in the history of Western civilization. As the year 2000 approaches, we are haunted by the strange fact that the final decade of each century divisible by five has marked a profound transition in Western civilization, a pattern of death and rebirth that marks new phases of social organization in much the way that death and birth delineate the cycle of human generations. This has been true since at least 500 B.C., when Greek democracy emerged with the constitutional reforms of Cleisthenes in 508 B.C. The following five centuries were a period of growth and intensification of the ancient economy, culminating in the birth of Christ in 4 B.C. This was also the time of the greatest prosperity of the ancient economy, when interest rates reached their lowest level prior to the modern period.

The next five centuries saw a gradual winding down of prosperity, leading to the collapse of the Roman Empire late in the fifth century A.D. William Playfair's summary is worth repeating: "When Rome was at its highest pitch of greatness . . . will be seen to be at the birth of Christ, that is, during the reign of Augustus, and by the same means it will be found declining gradually till the year 490."[22] It was then that the last legions dissolved, and the Western world sank into the Dark Ages.

During the following five centuries, the economy withered, long-distance trade ground to a halt, cities were depopulated, money vanished from circulation, and art and literacy almost disappeared. The disappearance of effective law with the collapse of the Roman Empire in the West led to the emergence of more primitive arrangements for settling disputes. The blood feud began to be significant at the end of the fifth century. The first recorded incident of trial by ordeal occurred precisely in the year 500.

Once again, a thousand years ago, the final decade of the tenth century witnessed another "tremendous upheaval in social and economic systems." Perhaps the least known of these transitions, the feudal revolution, began at a time of utter economic and political turmoil. In *The Transformation of the Year One Thousand*, Guy Bois, a professor of medieval history at the University of Paris, claims that this rupture at the end of the tenth century involved the complete collapse of the remnants of ancient institutions, and the emergence of something new out of the anarchy—feudalism.[23] In the words of Raoul Glaber, "It was said that the whole world, with one accord, shook off the tatters of antiquity."[24] The new system that suddenly emerged accommodated the slow revival of economic growth. The five centuries now known as the Middle Ages saw a rebirth of money and international trade, along with the rediscovery of arithmetic, literacy, and time awareness.

Then, in the final decade of the fifteenth century, there was yet another turning point. It was then that Europe emerged from the demographic deficit caused by the Black Death and almost immediately began to assert dominion over the rest of the globe. The "Gunpowder Revolution," the "Renaissance," and the "Reformation" are names given to different aspects of this transition that ushered in the Modern Age. It was announced with a bang when Charles VIII invaded Italy with new bronze cannon. It involved an opening to the world, epitomized by Columbus sailing to America in 1492. This opening to the New World launched a push toward the most dramatic economic growth in the experience of humanity. It involved a transformation of physics and astronomy that led to the creation of modern science. And its ideas were disseminated widely with the new technology of the printing press.

Now we sit at the threshold of another millennial transformation. The large command and control systems inherited from the Industrial Era may break down like the one-horse shay on the stroke of the millennial midnight. Yet whether or not the Y2K logic bomb precipitates an immediate collapse of industrial society, its days are numbered. We expect the advent of the Information Society to utterly transform the world, in ways that this book is meant to explain. You would be perfectly within your rights to doubt this, since no cycle that repeats itself only twice in a millennium has demonstrated enough iterations to be statistically significant. Indeed, even much shorter cycles have been viewed skeptically by economists demanding more statistically satisfying proof. "Professor Dennis Robertson once wrote that we had better wait a few centuries before being sure" about the existence of four-year and eight- to ten-year trade cycles.[25] By that standard, Professor Robertson would have to suspend judgment for about thirty thousand years to be sure that the five-hundred-year cycle is not a statistical fluke. We are less dogmatic, or more willing to take a hint. We recognize that the patterns of reality are more complex than the static- and linear-equilibrium models of most economists.

We believe that the coming of the year 2000 marks more than another convenient division along an endless continuum of time. We believe it will be an inflection point between the Old World and a New World to come. The Industrial Age is rapidly passing, and its demise may, ironically, be accelerated by the fact that early computer memory was so expensive that it encouraged the widespread adoption of two-digit date fields. When Hallerith punch cards could accommodate only eighty characters each, abbreviating dates seemed a prudent thing to do. Contrary to the expectations of the early programmers, however, their abbreviation of the date field endured four decades until the end of the millennium as an accidental logic bomb that could destroy a large part of Industrial society. The U.S. government's Office of Management and Budget described the problem in "Getting Federal Computers Ready for 2000," a report dated February 7, 1997. The OMB concludes of computers: "Unless they are fixed or replaced, they will fail at the turn of the century in one of three ways: they will reject legitimate entries, or they will compute erroneous results, or they simply will not run." These three outcomes in combination could cripple Industrial society. Its technology of mass production is destined to be eclipsed by a new technology of miniaturization in any event. A near-term crisis will merely accelerate the process. With the new information technology has come a new science of nonlinear dynamics, one whose startling conclusions are mere strands that have yet to be woven together into a comprehensive worldview. We live in the time of the computer, but our dreams are still spun on the loom. We continue to live by the metaphors and thoughts of industrialism. We don't yet imagine the world in terms of strange attractors. Our politics still straddles the industrial divide between right and left, as mapped by thinkers like Adam Smith and Karl Marx, who died before almost everyone now living was born.* The industrial worldview, incorporating the operating principles of industrial science, is still the "commonsense" intuition of educated opinion. It is our thesis that the "common sense" of the Industrial Age will no longer apply to many areas as the world is transformed.

More than eighty-five years after the day in 1911 when Oswald Spengler was seized with an intuition of a coming world war and "the decline of the West," we, too, see *a historical change of phase* occurring . . . at the point preordained for it hundreds of years ago."[26] Like Spengler, we see the impending death of Western civilization, and with it the collapse of the world order that has predominated these past five centuries, ever since Columbus sailed west to open contact with the New World. Yet unlike Spengler we see the birth of a new stage in Western civilization in the coming millennium.

---

* Adam Smith died in 1790, Karl Marx in 1883.

CHAPTER 2
MEGAPOLITICAL TRANSFORMATIONS IN HISTORIC PERSPECTIVE

"In history, as in nature, birth and death are equally balanced."[1]
—JOHAN HUIZINGA

THE WANING OF THE MODERN WORLD

In our view, you are witnessing nothing less than the waning of the Modern Age. It is a development driven by a ruthless but hidden logic. More than we commonly understand, more than CNN and the newspapers tell us, the next millennium will no longer be "modern." We say this not to imply that you face a savage or backward future, although that is possible, but to emphasize that the stage of history now opening will be qualitatively different from that into which you were born.

Something new is coming. Just as farming societies differed in kind from hunting-and-gathering bands, and industrial societies differed radically from feudal or yeoman agricultural systems, so the New World to come will mark a radical departure from anything seen before.

In the new millennium, economic and political life will no longer be organized on a gigantic scale under the domination of the nation-state as it was during the modern centuries. The civilization that brought you world war, the assembly line, social security, income tax, deodorant, and the toaster oven is dying. Deodorant and the toaster oven may survive. The others won't.

Like an ancient and once mighty man, the nation-state has a future numbered in years and days, and no longer in centuries and decades.

Governments have already lost much of their power to regulate and compel. The collapse of Communism marked the end of a long cycle of five centuries during which magnitude of power overwhelmed efficiency in the organization of government. It was a time when the returns to violence were high and rising. They no longer are. A phase transition of world-historic dimensions has already begun. Indeed, the future Gibbon who chronicles the decline and fall of the once–Modern Age in the next millennium may declare that it had already ended by the time you read this book. Looking back, he may say, as we do, that it ended with the fall of the Berlin Wall in 1989. Or with the death of the Soviet Union in 1991. Either date could come to stand as a defining event in the evolution of civilization, the end of what we now know as the Modern Age.

The fourth stage of human development is coming, and perhaps its least predictable feature is the new name under which it will be known. Call it "Post-Modern." Call it the "Cyber Society" or the "Information Age." Or make up your own name. No one knows what conceptual glue will stick a nickname to the next phase of history.

We do not even know that the five-hundred-year stretch of history just ending will continue to be thought of as "modern." If future historians know anything about word derivations, it will not be. A more descriptive title might be "The Age of the State" or "The Age of Violence." But such a name would fall outside the temporal spectrum that currently defines the epochs of history. "Modern," according to the *Oxford English Dictionary,* means "pertaining to the present and recent times, as distinguished from the remote past. . . . In historical use commonly applied (in contradiction to *ancient* and *medieval*) to the time subsequent to the MIDDLE AGES." [2]

Western people consciously thought of themselves as "modern" only when they came to understand that the medieval period was over. Before 1500, no one had ever thought of the feudal centuries as a "middle" period in Western civilization. The reason is obvious upon reflection: before an age can reasonably be seen as sandwiched in the "middle" of two other historic epochs, it must have already come to an end. Those living during the feudal centuries could not have imagined themselves as living in a halfway house between antiquity and modern civilization until it dawned on them not just that the medieval period was over, but also that medieval civilization differed dramatically from that of the Dark Ages or antiquity. [3]

Human cultures have blind spots. We have no vocabulary to describe paradigm changes in the largest boundaries of life, especially those happening around us. Notwithstanding the many dramatic changes that have unfolded since the time of Moses, only a few heretics have bothered to think about how the transitions from one phase of civilization to another actually unfold.

How are they triggered? What do they have in common? What patterns can help you tell when they begin and know when they are over? When will Great Britain or the United States come to an end? These are questions for which you would be hard-pressed to find conventional answers.

The Taboo on Foresight

To see "outside" an existing system is like being a stagehand trying to force a dialogue with a character in a play. It breaches a convention that helps keep the system functioning. Every social order incorporates among its key taboos the notion that people living in it should not think about how it will end and what rules may prevail in the new system that takes its place. Implicitly, whatever system exists is the last or the only system that will ever exist. Not that this is so baldly stated. Few who have ever read a history book would find such an assumption realistic if it was articulated. Nonetheless, that is the convention that rules the world. Every social system, however strongly or weakly it clings to power, pretends that its rules will never be superseded. They are the last word. Or perhaps the only word. Primitives assume that theirs is the only possible way of organizing life. More economically complicated systems that incorporate a sense of history usually place themselves at its apex. Whether they are Chinese mandarins in the court of the emperor, the Marxist nomenklatura in Stalin's Kremlin, or members of the House of Representatives in Washington, the powers-that-be either imagine no history at all or place themselves at the pinnacle of history, in a superior position compared to everyone who came before, and the vanguard of anything to come.

This is true for practical reasons. The more apparent it is that a system is nearing an end, the more reluctant people will be to adhere to its laws. Any social organization will therefore tend to discourage or play down analyses that anticipate its demise. This alone helps ensure that history's great transitions are seldom spotted as they happen. If you know nothing else about the future, you can rest assured that dramatic changes will be neither welcomed nor advertised by conventional thinkers.

You cannot depend upon conventional information sources to give you an objective and timely warning about how the world is changing and why. If you wish to understand the great transition now under way, you have little choice but to figure it out for yourself.

Beyond the Obvious

This means looking beyond the obvious. The record shows that even transitions that are undeniably real in retrospect may not be acknowledged for decades or even centuries after they happen. Consider the fall of Rome. It was probably the most important historic development in the first millennium of the Christian era. Yet long after Rome's demise, the fiction that it survived was held out to public view, like Lenin's embalmed corpse. No one who depended upon the pretenses of officials for his understanding of the "news" would have learned that Rome had fallen until long after that information ceased to matter.

The reason was not merely the inadequacy of communications in the ancient world. The outcome would have been much the same had CNN miraculously been in business, running its videotape in September 476. That is when the last Roman emperor in the West, Romulus Augustulus, was captured in Ravenna and forcibly retired to a villa in Campania on a pension. Even if Wolfe Blitzer had been there with minicams recording the news in 476, it is unlikely that he or anyone else would have dared to characterize those events as marking the end of the Roman Empire. That, of course, is exactly what latter historians said happened.

CNN editors probably would not have approved a headline story saying "Rome fell this evening." The powers-that-be denied that Rome had fallen. Peddlers of "news" seldom are partisans of controversy in ways that would undermine their own profits. They may be partisan. They may even be outrageously so. But they seldom report conclusions that would convince subscribers to cancel their subscriptions and head for the hills. Which is why few would have reported the fall of Rome even if it had been technologically possible. Experts would have come forth to say that it was ridiculous to speak of Rome falling. To have said otherwise would have been bad for business and, perhaps, bad for the health of those doing the reporting. The powers in late-fifth-century Rome were barbarians, and they denied that Rome had fallen.

But it was not merely a case of authorities' saying, "Don't report this or we will kill you." Part of the problem was that Rome was already so degenerate by the later decades of the fifth century that its "fall" genuinely eluded the notice of most people who lived through it. In fact, it was a generation later before Count Marcellinus first suggested that "The Western Roman Empire perished with this Augustulus."[4] Many more decades passed, perhaps centuries, before there was a common acknowledgment that the Roman Empire in the West no longer existed. Certainly Charlemagne believed that he was a legitimate Roman emperor in the year 800.

The point is not that Charlemagne and all who thought in conventional terms about the Roman Empire after 476 were fools. To the contrary. The characterization of social developments is frequently ambiguous. When the power of predominant institutions is brought into the bargain to reinforce a convenient conclusion, even one based largely on pretense, only someone of strong character and strong opinions would dare contradict it. If you try to put yourself in the position of a Roman of the late fifth century, it is easy to imagine how tempting it would have been to conclude that nothing had changed. That certainly was the optimistic conclusion. To have thought otherwise might have been frightening. And why come to a frightening conclusion when a reassuring one was at hand?

After all, a case could have been made that business would continue as usual. It had in the past. The Roman army, and particularly the frontier garrisons, had been barbarized for centuries.[5] By the third century, it had become regular practice for the army to proclaim a new emperor. By the fourth century, even officers were Germanized and frequently illiterate.[6] There had been many violent overthrows of emperors before Romulus Augustulus was removed from the throne. His departure might have seemed no different to his contemporaries than many other upheavals in a chaotic time. And he was sent packing with a pension. The very fact that he received a pension, even for a brief period before he was murdered, was a reassurance that the system survived. To an optimist, Odoacer, who deposed Romulus Augustulus, reunified rather than destroyed the empire. A son of Attila's sidekick Edecon, Odoacer was a clever man. He did not proclaim himself emperor. Instead, he convened the Senate and prevailed upon its too-suggestible members that they offer the emperorship and thus sovereignty over the whole empire to Zeno, the Eastern emperor in faraway Byzantium. Odoacer was merely to be Zeno's *patricius* to govern Italy.

As Will Durant wrote in *The Story of Civilization,* these changes did not appear to be the "fall of Rome" but merely "negligible shifts on the surface of the national scene."[7] When Rome fell, Odoacer said that Rome endured. He, along with almost everyone else, was keen to pretend that nothing had changed. They knew that "the glory that was Rome" was far better than the barbarism that was taking its place. Even the barbarians thought so. As C. W. Previte-Orton wrote in *The Shorter Cambridge Medieval History,* the end of the fifth century, when "the Emperors had been replaced by barbaric German kings," was a time of "persistent make-believe."[8]

"Persistent Make-Believe"

This "make-believe" involved the preservation of the façade of the old system, even as its essence was "deformed by barbarism."[9] The old forms of government remained the same when the last emperor was replaced by a barbarian "lieutenant." The Senate still met. "The praetorian prefecture and other high offices continued, and were held by eminent Romans." [10] Consuls were still nominated for a year. "The Roman civil administration survived intact." [11] Indeed, in some ways it remained intact until the birth of feudalism at the end of the tenth century. On public occasions, the old imperial insignia was still employed. Christianity was still the state religion. The barbarians still pretended to owe fealty to the Eastern emperor in Constantinople, and to the traditions of Roman law. In fact, in Durant's words, "in the West the great Empire was no more." [12]

So What?

The faraway example of the fall of Rome is relevant for a number of reasons as you contemplate conditions in the world today. Most books about the future are really books about the present. We have sought to remedy that defect by making this book about the future first of all a book about the past. We think that you are likely to draw a better perspective about what the future has in store if we illustrate important megapolitical points about the logic of violence with real examples from the past. History is an amazing teacher. The stories it has to tell are more interesting than any we could make up. And many of the more interesting relate to the fall of Rome. They document important lessons that could be relevant to your future in the Information Age.

First of all, the fall of Rome is one of history's more vivid examples of what happened in a major transition when the scale of government was collapsing. The transitions of the year 1000 also involved the collapse of central authority, and did so in a way that increased the complexity and scope of economic activity. The Gunpowder Revolution at the end of the fifteenth century involved major changes in institutions that tended to raise rather than shrink the scale of governance. Today, for the first time in a thousand years, megapolitical conditions in the West are undermining and destroying governments, corporate conglomerates, labor unions, and many other institutions that operate on a large scale.

Of course, the collapse in the scale of governance at the end of the Roman Empire had very different causes from those prevailing now, at the advent of the Information Age. Part of the reason that Rome fell is simply that it had expanded beyond the scale at which the economies of violence could be maintained. The cost of garrisoning the empire's far-flung borders exceeded the economic advantages that an ancient agricultural economy could support. The burden of taxation and regulation required to finance the military effort rose to exceed the carrying capacity of the economy. Corruption became endemic. A large part of the effort of military commanders, as historian Ramsay MacMullen has documented, was devoted to pursuit of "illicit profits of their command." [13] This they pursued by shaking down the population, what the fourth-century observer Synesius described as "the peace-time war, one almost worse than the barbarian war and arising from the military's indiscipline and the officers' greed." [14]

Another important contributing factor to Rome's collapse was a demographic deficit caused by the Antonine plagues. The collapse of the Roman population in many areas obviously contributed to economic and military weakness. Nothing of that kind has happened today, at least not yet. Taking a longer view, perhaps, the scourge of new "plagues" will compound the challenges of technological devolution in the new millennium. The unprecedented bulge in human population in the twentieth century creates a tempting target for rapidly mutating microparasites. Fears about the Ebola virus, or something like it, invading metropolitan populations may be well founded. But this is not the place to consider the coevolution of humans and diseases. As interesting a topic as that is, our argument at this juncture is not about why Rome fell, or even about whether the world today is vulnerable to some of the same influences that contributed to Roman decline. It is about something different—namely, the way that history's great transformations are perceived, or rather, misperceived as they happen.

People are always and everywhere to some degree conservative, with a small "c." That implies a reluctance to think in terms of dissolving venerable social conventions, overturning the accepted institutions, and defying the laws and values from which they drew their bearings. Few are inclined to imagine that apparently minor changes in climate or technology or some other variable can somehow be responsible for severing connections to the world of their fathers. The Romans were reluctant to acknowledge the changes unfolding around them. So are we.

Yet recognize it or not, we are living through a change of historical season, a transformation in the way people organize their livelihoods and defend themselves that is so far-reaching that it will inevitably transform the whole of society. The change will be so profound, in fact, that to understand it will require taking almost nothing for granted. You will be invited at almost every turn to believe that the coming Information Societies will be very like the industrial society you grew up in. We doubt it. Microprocessing will dissolve the mortar in the bricks. It will so profoundly alter the logic of violence that it will inevitably change the way people organize their livelihoods and defend themselves. Yet the tendency will be to downplay the inevitability of these changes, or to argue about their desirability as if it were within the fiat of industrial institutions to determine how history evolves.

The Grand Illusion

Authors who are in many ways better informed than we are will nevertheless lead you astray in thinking about the future because they are far too superficial in examining how societies work. For example, David Kline and Daniel Burstein have written a well-researched volume entitled *Road Warriors: Dreams and Nightmares Along the Information Highway*. It is full of admirable detail, but much of this detail is marshaled in arguing an illusion, the idea "that citizens can act together, consciously, to shape the spontaneous economic and natural processes going on around them." [15] Although it may not be obvious, this is equivalent to saying that feudalism might have survived if everyone had rededicated himself to chivalry. No one in a court of the late fifteenth century would have objected to such a sentiment. Indeed, it would have been heresy to do so. But it also would have been entirely misleading, an example of the snake trying to fit the future into its old skin.

The basic causes of change are precisely those that are not subject to conscious control. They are the factors that alter the conditions under which violence pays. Indeed, they are so remote from any obvious means of manipulation that they are not even subjects of political maneuvering in a world saturated with politics. No one ever marched in a demonstration shouting, "Increase scale economies in the production process." No banner has ever demanded, "Invent a weapons system that increases the importance of the infantry." No candidate ever promised to "alter the balance between efficiency and magnitude in protection against violence." Such slogans would be ridiculous, precisely because their goals are beyond the capacity of anyone to consciously affect. Yet as we will explore, these variables determine how the world works to a far greater degree than any political platform.

If you think about it carefully, it should be obvious that important transitions in history seldom are driven primarily by human wishes. They do not happen because people get fed up with one way of life and suddenly prefer another. A moment's reflection suggests why. If what people think and desire were the only determinants of what happens, then all the abrupt changes in history would have to be explained by wild mood swings unconnected to any change in the actual conditions of life. In fact, this never happens. Only in cases of medical problems affecting a few people do we see arbitrary fluctuations in mood that appear entirely divorced from any objective cause.

As a rule, large numbers of people do not suddenly and all at once decide to abandon their way of life simply because they find it amusing to do so. No forager ever said, "I am tired of living in prehistoric times, I would prefer the life of a peasant in a farming village." Any decisive swing in patterns of behavior and values is invariably a response to an actual change in the conditions of life. In this sense, at least, people are always realistic. If their views do change abruptly, it probably indicates that they have been confronted by some departure from familiar conditions: an invasion, a plague, a sudden climatic shift, or a technological revolution that alters their livelihoods or their ability to defend themselves.

Far from being the product of human desire, decisive historic changes more often than not confound the wish of most people for stability. When change occurs, it typically causes widespread disorientation, especially among those who lose income or social status. You will look in vain at public opinion polls or other measures of mood for an understanding of how the coming megapolitical transition is likely to unfold.

LIFE WITHOUT FORESIGHT

If we fail to perceive the great transition going on around us, it is partly because we do not desire to see. Our foraging forebears may have been just as obdurate, but they had a better excuse. No one ten thousand years ago could have foreseen the consequences of the Agricultural Revolution. Indeed, no one could have foreseen much of anything beyond where to find the next meal. When farming begàn, there was no record of past events from which to draw perspective on the future. There was not even a Western sense of time divided into orderly units, like seconds, minutes, hours, days, and so on, to measure out the years. Foragers lived in the "eternal present," without calendars, and indeed, without written records at all. They had no science, and no other intellectual apparatus for understanding cause and effect beyond their own intuitions. When it came to looking ahead, our primeval ancestors were blind. To cite the biblical metaphor, they had not yet eaten of the fruit of knowledge.

Learning from the Past

Luckily, we have a better vantage point. The past five hundred generations have given us analytic capabilities that our forebears lacked. Science and mathematics have helped unlock many of nature's secrets, giving us an understanding of cause and effect that approaches the magical when compared to that of the early foragers. Computational algorithms developed as a result of high-speed computers have shed new insights on the workings of complex, dynamic systems like the human economy. The painstaking development of political economy itself, although it falls well short of perfection, has honed understanding of the factors informing human action. Important among these is the recognition that people at all times and places tend to respond to incentives. Not always as mechanically as economists imagine, but they do respond. Costs and rewards matter. Changes in external conditions that raise the rewards or lower the costs of certain behavior will lead to more of that behavior, other things being equal.

Incentives Matter

The fact that people tend to respond to costs and rewards is an essential element of forecasting. You can say with a high degree of confidence that if you drop a hundred-dollar bill on the street, someone will soon pick it up, whether you are in New York, Mexico City, or Moscow. This is not as trivial as it seems. It shows why the clever people who say that forecasting is impossible are wrong. Any forecast that accurately anticipates the impact of incentives on behavior is likely to be broadly correct. And the greater the anticipated change in costs and rewards, the less trivial the implied forecast is likely to be.

The most far-reaching forecasts of all are likely to arise from recognizing the implications of shifting megapolitical variables. Violence is the ultimate boundary force on behavior; thus, if you can understand how the logic of violence will change, you can usefully predict where people will be dropping or picking up the equivalent of one-hundred-dollar bills in the future.

We do not mean by this that you can know the unknowable. We cannot tell you how to forecast winning lottery numbers or any truly random event. We have no way of knowing when or whether a terrorist will detonate an atomic blast in Manhattan. Or if an asteroid will strike Saudi Arabia. We cannot predict the coming of a new Ice Age, a sudden volcanic eruption, or the emergence of a new disease. The number of unknowable events that could alter the course of history is large. But knowing the unknowable is very different from drawing out the implications of what is already known. If you see a flash of lightning far away, you can forecast with a high degree of confidence that a thunderclap is due. Forecasting the consequences of megapolitical transitions involves much longer time frames, and less certain connections, but it is a similar kind of exercise.

Megapolitical catalysts for change usually appear well before their consequences manifest themselves. It took five thousand years for the full implications of the Agricultural Revolution to come to the surface. The transition from an agricultural society to an industrial society based on manufacturing and chemical power unfolded more quickly. It took centuries. The transition to the Information Society will happen more rapidly still, probably within a lifetime. Yet even allowing for the foreshortening of history, you can expect decades to pass before the full megapolitical impact of existing information technology is realized.

Major and Minor Megapolitical Transitions

This chapter analyzes some of the common features of megapolitical transitions. In following chapters we look more closely at the Agricultural Revolution, and the transition from farm to factory, the second of the previous great phase changes. Within the agricultural stage of civilization there were many minor megapolitical transitions such as the fall of Rome and the feudal revolution of the year 1000. These marked the waxing and waning of the power equation as governments rose and fell and the spoils of farming passed from one set of hands to another. The owners of sprawling estates under the Roman Empire, yeoman farmers in the European Dark Ages, and the lords and serfs of the feudal period all ate grain from the same fields. They lived under very different governments because of the cumulative impact of different technologies, fluctuations in climate, and the disruptive influences of disease.

Our purpose is not to thoroughly explain all of these changes. We do not pretend to do so, although we have sketched out some illustrations of the way that changing megapolitical variables have altered the way that power was exercised in the past. Governments have grown and shrunk as megapolitical fluctuations have lowered and raised the costs of projecting power.

Here are some summary points that you should keep in mind as you seek to understand the Information Revolution:

1. A shift in the megapolitical foundations of power normally unfolds far in advance of the actual revolutions in the use of power.
2. Incomes are usually falling when a major transition begins, often because a society has rendered itself crisis-prone by marginalizing resources due to population pressures.
3. Seeing "outside" of a system is usually taboo. People are frequently blind to the logic of violence in the existing society; therefore, they are almost always blind to changes in that logic, latent or overt. Megapolitical transitions are seldom recognized before they happen.
4. Major transitions always involve a cultural revolution, and usually entail clashes between adherents of the old and new values.
5. Megapolitical transitions are never popular, because they antiquate painstakingly acquired intellectual capital and confound established moral imperatives. They are not undertaken by popular demand, but in response to changes in the external conditions that alter the logic of violence in the local setting.

6. Transitions to new ways of organizing livelihoods or new types of government are initially confined to those areas where the megapolitical catalysts are at work.
7. With the possible exception of the early stages of farming, past transitions have always involved periods of social chaos and heightened violence due to disorientation and breakdown of the old system.
8. Corruption, moral decline, and inefficiency appear to be signal features of the final stages of a system.
9. The growing importance of technology in shaping the logic of violence has led to an acceleration of history, leaving each successive transition with less adaptive time than ever before.

History Speeds Up

With events unfolding many times faster than during previous transformations, early understanding of how the world will change could turn out to be far more useful to you than it would have been to your ancestors at an equivalent juncture in the past. Even if the first farmers had miraculously understood the full megapolitical implications of tilling the earth, this information would have been practically useless because thousands of years were to pass before the transition to the new phase of society was complete.

Not so today. History has sped up. Forecasts that correctly anticipate the megapolitical implications of new technology are likely to be far more useful today. If we can develop the implications of the current transition to the Information Society to the same extent that someone with current knowledge could have grasped the implications of past transitions to farm and factory, that information should be many times more valuable now. Put simply, the action horizon for megapolitical forecasts has shrunk to its most useful range, within the span of a single lifetime.

"Looking back over the centuries, or even if looking only at the present, we can clearly observe that many men have made their living, often a very good living, from their special skill in applying weapons of violence, and that their activities have had a very large part in determining what uses were made of scarce resources."[16]

—FREDERIC C. LANE

Our study of megapolitics is an attempt to do just that—to draw out the implications of the changing factors that alter the boundaries where violence is exercised. These megapolitical factors largely determine when and where violence pays. They also help inform the market distribution of income. As economic historian Frederic Lane so clearly put it, how violence is organized and controlled plays a large role in determining "what uses are made of scarce resources." [17]

A CRASH COURSE IN MEGAPOLITICS

The concept of megapolitics is a powerful one. It helps illuminate some of the major mysteries of history: how governments rise and fall and what types of institutions they become; the timing and outcome of wars; patterns of economic prosperity and decline. By raising or lowering the costs and rewards of projecting power, megapolitics governs the ability of people to impose their will on others. This has been true from the earliest human societies onward. It still is. We explored many of the important hidden megapolitical factors that determine the evolution of history in *Blood in the Streets* and *The Great Reckoning*. The key to unlocking the implications of megapolitical change is understanding the factors that precipitate revolutions in the use of violence. These variables can be somewhat arbitrarily grouped into four categories: topography, climate, microbes, and technology.

1. *Topography* is a crucial factor, as evidenced by the fact that control of violence on the open seas has never been monopolized as it has on land. No government's laws have ever exclusively applied there. This is a matter of the utmost importance in understanding how the organization of violence and protection will evolve as the economy migrates into cyberspace.

Topography, in conjunction with climate, had a major role to play in early history. The first states emerged on floodplains, surrounded by desert, such as in Mesopotamia and Egypt, where water for irrigation was plentiful but surrounding regions were too dry to support yeoman farming. Under such conditions, individual farmers faced a very high cost for failing to cooperate in maintaining the political structure. Without irrigation, which could be provided only on a large scale, crops would not grow. No crops meant starvation. The conditions that placed those who controlled the water in a desert in a position of strength made for despotic and rich government.

As we analyzed in *The Great Reckoning*, topographic conditions also played a major role in the prosperity of yeoman farmers in ancient Greece, enabling that region to become the cradle of Western democracy. Given the primitive transportation conditions prevailing in the Mediterranean region three thousand years ago, it was all but impossible for persons living more than a few miles from the sea to compete in the production of high-value crops of the ancient world, olives and grapes. If the oil and the wine had to be transported any distance overland, the portage costs were so great that they could not be sold at a profit. The elaborate shoreline of the Greek littoral meant that most areas of Greece were no more than twenty miles from the sea. This gave a decisive advantage to Greek farmers over their potential competitors in landlocked areas.

Because of this advantage in trading high-value products, Greek farmers earned high incomes from control of only small parcels of land. These high incomes enabled them to purchase costly armor. The famous hoplites of ancient Greece were farmers or landlords who armed themselves at their own expense. Both well armed and well motivated, the Greek hoplites were militarily formidable and could not be ignored. Topographic conditions were the foundation of Greek democracy, just as those of a different kind gave rise to the Oriental despotisms of Eygpt and elsewhere.

2. *Climate* also helps set the boundaries within which brute force can be exercised. A climatic change was the catalyst for the first major transition from foraging to farming. The end of the last Ice Age, about thirteen thousand years ago, led to a radical alteration in vegetation. Beginning in the Near East, where the Ice Age retreated first, a gradual rise in temperature and rainfall spread forests into areas that had previously been grasslands. In particular, the rapid spread of beech forests seriously curtailed the human diet. As Susan Alling Gregg put it in *Foragers and Farmers:*

> The establishment of beech forests must have had serious consequences for local human, plant and animal populations. The canopy of an oak forest is relatively open and allows large amounts of sunlight to reach the forest floor. An exuberant undergrowth of mixed shrubs, forbs, and grasses develops, and the diversity of plants supports a variety of wildlife. In contrast, the canopy of a beech forest is closed and the forest floor is heavily shaded. Other than a flush of spring annuals prior to the emergence of the leaves, only shade-tolerant sedges, ferns, and a few grasses are found." [18]

Over time, dense forests encroached on the open plains, spreading throughout Europe into the Eastern steppes. [19] The forests reduced the grazing area available to support large animals, making it increasingly difficult for the population of human foragers to support themselves.

The population of hunter-gatherers had swollen too greatly during the Ice Age prosperity to support itself on the dwindling herds of large mammals, many species of which were hunted to extinction. The transition to agriculture was not a choice of preference, but an improvisation adopted under duress to make up for shortfalls in the diet. Foraging continued to predominate in those areas farther north, where the warming trend had not adversely affected the habitats of large mammals, and in tropical rainforests, where the global warming trend did not have the perverse effect of reducing food supplies. Since the advent of farming, it has been far more common for changes to be precipitated by the cooling rather than the warming of the climate.

A modest understanding of the dynamics of climatic change in past societies could well prove useful in the event that climates continue to fluctuate. If you know that a drop of one degree Centigrade on average reduces the growing season by three to four weeks and shaves five hundred feet off the maximum elevation at which crops can be grown, then you know something about the boundary conditions that will confine people's action in the future.[20] You can use this knowledge to forecast changes in everything from grain prices to land values. You may even be able to draw informed conclusions about the likely impact of falling temperatures on real incomes and political stability. In the past, governments have been overthrown when crop failures extending over several years raised food prices and shrank disposable incomes.

For example, it is no coincidence that the seventeenth century, the coldest in the modern period, was also a period of revolution worldwide. A hidden megapolitical cause of this unhappiness was sharply colder weather. It was so cold, in fact, that wine froze on the "Sun King's" table at Versailles. Shortened growing seasons produced crop failures and undermined real income. Because of the colder weather, prosperity began to wind down into a long global depression that began around 1620. It proved drastically destabilizing. The economic crisis of the seventeenth century led to the world being overwhelmed by rebellions, many clustering in 1648, exactly two hundred years before another and more famous cycle of rebellions. Between 1640 and 1650, there were rebellions in Ireland, Scotland, England, Portugal, Catalonia, France, Moscow, Naples, Sicily, Brazil, Bohemia, Ukraine, Austria, Poland, Sweden, the Netherlands, and Turkey. Even China and Japan were swept with unrest.

It may also be no coincidence that mercantilism predominated in the seventeenth century during a period of shrinking trade. Economic closure was perhaps most pronounced at the end of the century, "when a terrible famine occurred." [21] By the eighteenth century, especially after 1750, warmer temperatures and higher crop yields had begun to raise real incomes in Western Europe sufficiently to expand demand for manufactured goods. More free-market policies were adopted. This led to a self-reinforcing burst of economic growth as industry expanded to a larger scale in what is commonly described as the Industrial Revolution. The growing importance of technology and manufactured output reduced the impact of the weather on economic cycles.

Even today, however, you should not underestimate the impact of suddenly colder weather in lowering real incomes—even in wealthy regions such as

North America. There is a strong tendency for societies to render themselves crisis-prone when the existing configuration of institutions has exhausted its potential. In the past, this tendency has often been manifested by population increases that stretched the carrying capacity of land to the limit. This happened both before the transition of the year 1000 and again at the end of the fifteenth century. The plunge in real income caused by crop failures and lower yields played a significant role in both instances in destroying the predominant institutions. Today the marginalization is manifested in the consumer credit markets. If sharply colder weather reduced crop yields and lowered disposable incomes, this would lead to debt default as well as tax rebellions. If the past is a guide, both economic closure and political instability could result.

3. *Microbes* convey power to harm or immunity from harm in ways that have often determined how power was exercised. This was certainly the case in the European conquest of the New World, as we explored in *The Great Reckoning*. European settlers, arriving from settled agricultural societies riddled with disease, brought with them relative immunity from childhood infections like measles. The Indians they encountered lived largely in thinly populated foraging bands. They possessed no such immunity and were decimated. Often, the greatest mortality occurred before white people even arrived, as Indians who first encountered Europeans on the coasts traveled inland with infections.

There are also microbiological barriers to the exercise of power. In *Blood in the Streets,* we discussed the role that potent strains of malaria served in making tropical Africa impervious to invasion by white men for many centuries. Before the discovery of quinine in the mid-nineteenth century, white armies could not survive in malarial regions, however superior their weapons might have been.

The interaction between humans and microbes has also produced important demographic effects that altered the costs and rewards of violence. When fluctuations in mortality are high due to epidemic disease, famine, or other causes, the relative risk of mortality in warfare falls. The declining frequency of eruptions in death rates from the sixteenth century onward helps explain smaller family size and, ultimately, the far lower tolerance of sudden death in war today as compared to the past. This has had the effect of lowering the tolerance for imperialism and raising the costs of projecting power in societies with low birthrates.

Contemporary societies, comprising small families, tend to find even small numbers of battle deaths intolerable. By contrast, early modern societies were much more tolerant of the mortality costs associated with imperialism. Before this century, most parents gave birth to many children, some of whom were expected to die randomly and suddenly from disease. In an era when early death was commonplace, would-be soldiers and their families faced the dangers of the battlefield with less resistance.

"Machinery is aggressive. The weaver becomes a web, the machinist a machine. If you do not use tools, they use you."

—EMERSON

---

4. *Technology* has played by far the largest role in determining the costs and rewards of projecting power during the modern centuries. The argument of this book presumes it will continue to do so. Technology has several crucial dimensions:

A. *Balance between offense and defense.* The balance between the offense and the defense implied by prevailing weapons technology helps determine the scale of political organization. When offensive capabilities are rising, the ability to project power at a distance predominates, jurisdictions tend to consolidate, and governments form on a larger scale. At other times, like now, defensive capabilities are rising. This makes it more costly to project power outside of core areas. Jurisdictions tend to devolve, and big governments break down into smaller ones.

B. *Equality and the predominance of the infantry.* A key feature determining the degree of equality among citizens is the nature of weapons technology. Weapons that are relatively cheap, can be employed by nonprofessionals, and enhance the military importance of infantry tend to equalize power. When Thomas Jefferson wrote that "all men are created equal," he was saying something that was much more true than a similar statement would have seemed centuries earlier. A farmer with his hunting rifle was not only as well armed as the typical British soldier with his Brown Bess, he was better armed. The farmer with the rifle could shoot at the soldier from a greater distance, and with greater accuracy than the soldier could return fire. This was a distinctly different circumstance from the Middle Ages, when a farmer with a pitchfork—he could not have afforded more—could scarcely have hoped to stand against a heavily armed knight on horseback. No one was writing in 1276 that "all men are created equal." At that time, in the most manifestly important sense, men were not equal. A single knight exercised far more brute force than dozens of peasants put together.

C. *Advantages and disadvantages of scale in violence.* Another variable that helps determine whether there are a few large governments or many small ones is the scale of organization required to deploy the prevailing weapons. When there are increasing returns to violence, it is more rewarding to operate governments at a large scale; therefore governments tend to get bigger. When a small group can command effective means of resisting an assault by a large group, which was the case during the Middle Ages, sovereignty tends to fragment. Small, independent authorities exercise many of the functions of government. As we explore in a latter chapter, we believe that the Information Age will bring the dawn of cybersoldiers, who will be heralds of devolution. Cybersoldiers could be deployed not merely by nation-states but by very small organizations, and even by individuals. Wars of the next millennium will include some almost bloodless battles fought with computers.

D. *Economies of scale in production.* Another important factor that weighs in the balance in determining whether ultimate power is exercised locally or from a distance is the scale of the predominant enterprises in which people gain their livelihoods. When crucial enterprises can function optimally only when they are organized on a large scale in an encompassing trading area, governments that expand to provide such a setting for enterprises under their protection may rake off enough additional wealth to pay the costs of maintaining a large political system. Under such conditions, the entire world economy usually functions more effectively where one supreme world power dominates all others, as the British Empire did in the nineteenth century.

But sometimes megapolitical variables combine to produce falling economies of scale. If the economic benefits of maintaining a large trading area dwindle, larger governments that previously prospered from exploiting the benefits of encompassing trading areas may begin to break apart—even if the balance of weaponry between offense and defense otherwise remains much as it had been.

E. *Dispersal of technology.* Still another factor that contributes to the power equation is the degree of dispersal of key technologies. When weapons or tools of production can be effectively hoarded or monopolized, they tend to centralize power. Even technologies that are essentially defensive in character, like the machine gun, proved to be potent offensive weapons, that contributed to a rising scale of governance during the period when they were not widely dispersed. When the European powers enjoyed a monopoly on machine guns late in the nineteenth century, they were able to use those weapons against peoples at the periphery to dramatically expand colonial empires. Later, in the twentieth century, when machine guns became widely available, especially in the wake of World War II, they were deployed to help destroy the power of empires. Other things being equal, the more widely dispersed key technologies are, the more widely dispersed power will tend to be, and the smaller the optimum scale of government.

THE SPEED OF MEGAPOLITICAL CHANGE

While technology is by far the most important factor today, and apparently growing more so, all four major megapolitical factors have played a role in determining the scale at which power could be exercised in the past.

Together, these factors determine whether the returns to violence continue to rise as violence is employed on a larger scale. This determines the importance of magnitude of firepower versus efficiency in employing resources. It also strongly influences the market distribution of income. The question is, What role will they command in the future? A key to estimating an answer lies in recognizing that these megapolitical variables mutate at dramatically different speeds.

Topography has been almost fixed through the whole of recorded history. Except for minor local effects involving the silting of harbors, landfills, or erosion, the topography of the earth is almost the same today as it was when Adam and Eve straggled out of Eden. And it is likely to remain so until another Ice Age recarves the landscapes of continents or some other drastic event disturbs the surface of the earth. At a more profound scale, geological ages seem to shift, perhaps in response to large meteorite strikes, over a period of 10 to 40 million years. Someday, there may again be geological upheavals that will alter significantly the topography of our planet. If that happens, you can safely assume that both the baseball and cricket seasons will be canceled.

Climate fluctuates much more actively than topography. In the last million years, climatic change has been responsible for most of the known variation in the features of the earth's surface. During Ice Ages, glaciers gouged new valleys, altered the course of rivers, severed islands from continents or joined them together by lowering the sea level. Fluctuations in climate have played a significant role in history, first in precipitating the Agricultural Revolution after the close of the last Ice Age, and later in destablizing regimes during periods of colder temperatures and drought.

Lately, there have been concerns over the possible impact of "global warming." These concerns cannot be dismissed out of hand. Yet, taking a longer perspective, the more likely risk appears to be a shift toward a colder, not a warmer climate. Study of temperature fluctuations based upon analysis of oxygen isotopes in core samples taken from the ocean floor show that the current period is the second warmest in more than 2 million years.[22] If temperatures were to turn colder, as they did in the seventeenth century, that might prove megapolitically destabilizing. Current alarms about global warming may in that sense be reassuring. To the extent that they are true, that assures that temperatures will continue to fluctuate within the abnormally warm and relatively benign range experienced for the past three centuries.

The rate of change in the influence of microbes on the exercise of power is more of a puzzle. Microbes can mutate very rapidly. This is especially true of viruses. The common cold, for example, mutates in an almost kaleidoscopic way. Yet although these mutations proceed apace, their impact in shifting the boundaries where power is exercised have been far less abrupt than technological change. Why? Part of the reason is that the normal balance of nature tends to make it beneficial for microbes to infect but not destroy host populations. Virulent infections that kill their hosts too readily tend to eradicate themselves in the process. The survival of microparasites depends upon their not being too rapidly or uniformly fatal to the hosts they invade.

That is not to say, of course, that there cannot be deadly eruptions of disease that alter the balance of power. Such episodes have figured prominently in history. The Black Death wiped out large fractions of the population of Eurasia and dealt a crushing blow to the fourteenth-century version of the international economy.

What Might Have Been

History can be understood in terms of what might have been as well as what was. We know of no reason that microparasites could not have continued to play havoc with human society during the modern period. For example, it is possible that microbiological barriers to the exercise of power, equivalent to malaria but more virulent, could have halted the Western invasion of the periphery in its tracks. The first intrepid Portuguese adventurers who sailed into African waters could have contracted a deadly retrovirus, a more communicable version of AIDS, that would have stopped the opening of the new trade route to Asia before it even began. Columbus, too, and the first waves of settlers in the New World might have encountered diseases that decimated them in the same way that indigenous local populations were affected by measles and other Western childhood diseases. Yet nothing of the kind happened, a coincidence that underlines the intuition that history has a destiny.

Microbes did far less to impede the consolidation of power in the modern period than to facilitate it. Western troops and colonists at the periphery often found that the technological advantages that allowed them to project power were underscored by microbiological ones. Westerners were armed with unseen biological weapons, their relative immunity to childhood diseases that frequently devastated native peoples. This gave voyagers from the West a distinct advantage that their antagonists from less densely settled regions lacked. As events unfolded, the disease transfer was almost entirely in one direction—from Europe outward. There was no equivalent transfer of disease in the other direction, from the periphery to the core.

As a possible counterexample, some have claimed that Western explorers imported syphilis from the New World to Europe. This is arguable. If true, however, it did not prove to be a significant barrier to the exercise of power. The major impact of syphilis was to shift sexual mores in the West.

From the end of the fifteenth century to the last quarter of the twentieth, the impact of microbes on industrial society was ever more benign. Notwithstanding the personal tragedies and unhappiness caused by outbreaks of tuberculosis, polio, and flu, no new diseases emerged in the modern period that even approached the megapolitical impact of the Antonine plagues or the Black Death. Improving public health, and the advent of vaccinations and antidotes, generally reduced the importance of infectious microbes during the modern period, thereby increasing the relative importance of technology in setting the boundaries where power was exercised.

The recent emergence of AIDS and alarms over the potential spread of exotic viruses are hints that the role of microbes may not be altogether as megapolitically benign in the future as it has been over the past five hundred years. But when or whether a new plague will infect the world is unknowable. An eruption of microparasites, such as a viral pandemic, rather than drastic changes in climate or topography, would more likely disrupt the megapolitical predominance of technology.

We have no way of monitoring or anticipating drastic departures from the nature of life on earth as we have known it. We cross our fingers and assume that the major megapolitical variables in the next millennium will be technological rather than microbiological. If luck continues to side with humanity, technology will continue to grow in prominence as the leading megapolitical variable.

It was not always such, however, as a review of the first great megapolitical transformation, the Agricultural Revolution, clearly shows.

CHAPTER 3
EAST OF EDEN

The Agricultural Revolution and the Sophistication of Violence

"And the Lord said unto Cain, Where is Abel, thy brother? And he said, I know not: Am I my brother's keeper? And he said, What hast thou done? the voice of thy brother's blood crieth unto me from the ground."

—GENESIS 4:9–10

Five hundred generations ago, the first phase change in the organization of human society began.[1] Our ancestors in several regions reluctantly picked up crude implements, sharpened stakes and makeshift hoes, and went to work. As they sowed the first crops, they also laid a new foundation for power in the world. The Agricultural Revolution was the first great economic and social revolution. It started with the expulsion from Eden and moved so slowly that farming had not completely displaced hunting and gathering in all suitable areas of the globe when the twentieth century opened. Experts believe that even in the Near East, where farming first emerged, it was introduced in "a long incremental process" that "may have taken five thousand years or more."[2]

It may seem an exaggeration to describe a process that stretched out over millennia as a "revolution." Yet that is precisely what the advent of farming was, a slow-motion revolution that transformed human life by altering the logic of violence. Wherever farming took root, violence emerged as a more important feature of social life. Hierarchies adept at manipulating or controlling violence came to dominate society.

Understanding the Agricultural Revolution is a first step toward understanding the Information Revolution. The introduction of tilling and harvesting provides a paradigm example of how an apparently simple shift in the character of work can radically alter the organization of society. Put this past revolution into perspective and you are in a far stronger position to forecast how history may unfold in response to the new logic of violence introduced with microprocessors.

To appreciate the revolutionary character of agriculture, you first need a picture of how the primeval society functioned before farming. We surveyed this in *The Great Reckoning* and offer a further sketch below. Hunting-and-gathering societies were the only forms of social organization through a long, prehistoric slumber when human life changed little or not at all from generation to generation. Anthropologists claim that humans have been hunters and gatherers for 99 percent of the time since we appeared on earth. Crucial to the long success and ultimate failure of hunting-and-gathering bands is the fact that they had to operate on a very small scale over a very wide area.

Foragers could survive only where population densities were light. To see why, think of the problems that larger groups would have posed. For one thing, a thousand hunters parading together across a landscape would have raised such a ruckus as to scare away the game they sought to trap. And even worse, had a small army of hunters occasionally managed to corner a huge herd of game, the food they harvested, including fruits and edible plants found in the wild, could not have remained plentiful for long. A large group of foragers would have laid waste to the countryside through overharvesting like a starving army in the Thirty Years War. Therefore, to minimize overkill, hunting bands had to be small. As Stephen Boyden writes in *Western Civilization in Biological Perspective,* "Most commonly, hunter-gatherer groups number between twenty-five and fifty individuals."[3]

To live on ten thousand acres in a temperate climate today is a luxury allowed only to the very rich. A family of hunter-gatherers could scarcely have survived on less. They generally required thousands of acres per person, even in areas that were most fertile for foraging. This suggests why the growth of human populations during periods particularly favorable to foraging may have created the basis for population crises. Because so much land was required to support a single person, the population densities of hunting-and-gathering societies had to be incredibly sparse. Before farming, humans were about as densely settled as bears.

With minor differences, the human diet resembled that of bears. Foraging societies depended upon food gathered from the open countryside or from nearby bodies of water. Although some gatherers were fishers, most were hunters who depended for a third to a fifth of their food upon protein from large mammals. Other than a few simple tools and objects carried around with them, hunter-gatherers had almost no technology at their disposal. They usually had no way to effectively store quantities of meat or other foods for later use. Most food had to be consumed soon after it was gathered or left to spoil. That is not say, of course, that some hunter-gatherers did not eat spoiled food. Eskimos, as Boyden reports, "are said to have a particular liking for decomposed food."[4] He repeats the observations of experts that Eskimos " 'bury fish heads and allow them to decay until the bones become of the same consistency as the flesh. They then knead the reeking mass into a paste and eat it'; they also enjoy the 'fat maggoty larvae of the caribou fly served raw . . . deer droppings, munched like berries . . . and marrow more than a year old, swarming with maggots.' "[5]

Other than such delicacies, foragers developed little surplus food. As anthropologist Gregg notes, "mobile populations generally do not store foodstuffs against seasonal or unexpected lows in resource availability." Consequently, foragers had little to steal. A division of labor that included specialization to employ violence was insupportable in settings where surplus food could not be stored. The logic of the hunt also dictated that violence among hunting-and-foraging bands could never rise above a small scale because the groups themselves had to remain tiny.

The small scale of foraging bands was advantageous in another way. Members of such small groups would have known one another intimately, a factor that made them more effective in working together. Decision-making becomes more difficult as numbers rise, because incentive traps proliferate. You need only think how hard it is to get a dozen people organized to go out to dinner. Imagine how hopeless would have been the task of organizing hundreds or thousands of persons to traipse around on a moveable feast. Lacking any sustained and separate political organization or bureaucracy required by specialization for war, hunting-and-gathering bands had to depend on persuasion and consensus—principles that work best among small groups with relatively easygoing attitudes.

Whether hunting-and-gathering bands were easygoing is open to debate. Sir Henry Maine refers to "the universal belligerency of primitive man." In his words, "It is not peace which is natural and primitive but war."[6] His view has been underlined by the work of evolutionary biologists. R. Paul Shaw and Yuwa Wong comment: "[T]here are strong indications that many of the injuries apparent in remains of Australopithecus, Homo erectus, and Homo sapiens of the European fourth and pre-fourth glacial periods resulted from combat."[7] But others doubt this. Experts like Stephen Boyden argue that primitive groups were usually not warlike or prone to violence. Social conventions developed to reduce internal tensions and facilitate the sharing of the hunt. Especially in areas where humans preyed on larger game, which was difficult for a single hunter to fell, religious and social doctrines emerged to facilitate the redistribution of any game that was taken with the whole group. The first priority of sharing of caloric resources was with other hunters. Necessity, rather than sentiment, was the spur. The first claim on the resources was exercised by the most economically competent and militarily strong, not by the sick and the weak. Undoubtedly, a major influence informing this priority was the fact that hunters in the prime of life were also militarily the most potent members of the small band. By assuring them a first claim on the hunt, the group minimized potentially lethal internal squabbling.

So long as population densities remained low, the foragers' gods were not militant gods but embodiments of natural forces or the animals they hunted. The scantiness of capital and open frontiers made war in most cases unnecessary. There were few neighbors outside one's own small family or clan to pose threats. Because foragers tended to roam in search of food, personal possessions beyond a bare minimum became an encumbrance. Those with few possessions necessarily experienced little property crime. When conflicts arose, the contending parties were often content to walk away because they had little invested in any given locale. Escape was an easy solution to personal feuds or exorbitant demands of other kinds. This does not mean that early humans were peaceful. They may have been violent and unpleasant to a degree we can scarcely imagine. But if they employed violence, it was mostly for personal reasons or, what may be worse, for sport.

The livelihoods of hunter-gatherers depended upon their functioning in small bands that allowed little or no scope for a division of labor other than along gender lines. They had no organized government, usually no permanent settlements, and no possibility for accumulating wealth. Even such basic building blocks of civilization as a written language were unknown in the primeval economy. Without a written language there could be no formal records and no history.

Overkill

The dynamic of foraging created very different incentives to work than those to which we have become accustomed since the advent of farming. The capital requirements for life as a forager were minimal. A few primitive tools and weapons sufficed. There was no outlet for investment, not even private property in land, except occasionally in quarries where flint or soapstone was mined.[8] As anthropologist Susan Alling Gregg wrote in *Foragers and Farmers*, "Ownership of and access to resources" was "held in common by the group."[9] With rare exceptions, such as fishers living on the shores of lakes, foragers usually had no fixed place of abode. Having no permanent homes, they had little need to work hard to acquire property or maintain it. They had no mortgage or taxes to pay, no furniture to buy. Their few consumer goods were animal skins, and personal adornments made by members of the group themselves. There was little incentive to acquire or accumulate anything that might have passed for money because there was little to buy. Under such conditions, savings for the foragers could have been no more than a rudimentary concept.

With no reason to earn and almost no division of labor, the concept of hard work as a virtue must have been foreign to hunting-and-gathering groups. Except during periods of unusual hardship, when protracted effort was required to find something to eat, little work was done because little was needed. There was literally nothing to be gained by working beyond the bare minimum required for survival. For the members of the typical hunting-and-gathering band, that meant working only about eight to fifteen hours a week.[10] Because a hunter's labor did not augment the food supply but could only reduce it, one who heroically labored overtime to kill more animals or pick more fruit than could be eaten before it spoiled contributed nothing to prosperity. To the contrary, overkill reduced the prospects of finding food in the future, and thus had a detrimental impact on the well-being of the group. That is why some foragers, such as Eskimos, punished or ostracized members of the band who engaged in overkill.

The example of the Eskimos punishing overkill is particularly telling, because they, far more than others, might well have been able to store meat by freezing it. Further, it would have been feasible to provide at least some storage for oils rendered from large marine animals. The fact that foragers generally chose not to do so reflects their far more passive interactions with nature. It may also indicate the degree to which cognition and mental processes are biased by culture. Constraints on learning and behavior in complex environments make adoption of some strategies far more difficult than would otherwise appear. As R. Paul Shaw and Yuwa Wong have written, "Because niches differ in many respects, so, too, do biases in learning."[11]

Seen in this perspective, the advent of agriculture entailed more than a change in diet; it also launched a great revolution in the organization of economic life and culture as well as a transformation of the logic of violence. Farming created large-scale capital assets in land and sometimes in irrigation systems. The crops and domesticated animals farmers raised were valuable assets. They could be stored, hoarded, and stolen. Because crops had to be tended over the entire growing season, from planting through harvest, migration away from threats became less attractive, especially in arid regions where opportunities to grow crops were confined to the small areas of the land with dependable water supplies. As escape became more difficult, opportunities for organized shakedowns and plunder increased. Farmers were subject to raids at harvesttime, which gradually raised the scale of warfare.

This tended to increase the size of societies because contests of violence more often than not were won by the larger group. As competition over land and control of its output became more intense, societies became more stationary. A division of labor became more apparent. Employment and slavery arose for the first time. Farmers and herders specialized in producing food. Potters produced containers in which food was stored. Priests prayed for rain and bountiful harvests. Specialists in violence, the forefathers of government, increasingly devoted themselves to plunder and protection from plunder. Along with the priests, they became the first wealthy persons in history.

In the early stages of agricultural societies, these warriors came to control a portion of the annual crop as a price of protection. In places where threats were minimal, yeoman farmers were sometimes able to retain a relatively large degree of autonomy. But as population densities rose, and competition over food intensified, especially in regions around deserts where productive land was at a premium, the warrior group could take a large fraction of total output. These warriors founded the first states with the proceeds of this rake-off, which reached as high as 25 percent of the grain crop and one-half the increase in herds of domesticated animals. Farming, therefore, dramatically increased the importance of coercion. The surge in resources capable of being plundered led to a large surge in plunder.

It took millennia for the full logic of the Agricultural Revolution to play itself out. For a long while, sparse populations of farmers in temperate regions may have lived much as their foraging forebears had done. Where land and rainfall were ample, farmers harvested crops on a small scale without much violent interference. But as populations rose over a period of several thousand years, farmers even in thinly settled regions became subject to erratic plunder that sometimes must have left them with insufficient seed to replant the next year's crop. Competitive plundering, or anarchy, was a possibility at one extreme, as well as unprotected communities living without any specialized organization to monopolize violence.

As time passed, the logic of violence inherent in agriculture imposed itself over an ever-wider terrain. The regions where farming and herding could continue without the predations of government receded to a few truly remote areas. The Kafir regions of Afghanistan, to cite an extreme example, resisted the imposition of government until the last decade of the nineteenth century. But in so doing, they were transformed centuries earlier into a quite militant society, organized along kinship lines. Such arrangements were not capable of mustering force on a large scale. Until the British brought modern weapons to the region, the Kafirs remained independent in their remote Bashgal and Waigal valleys because their redoubts were protected by features of topography, high mountains, and deserts that stood between them and conquerors from the outside.[12]

Over time, the basic logic of the Agricultural Revolution impressed itself on the societies where farming took hold. Farming sharply raised the scale at which human communities could form. Beginning about ten thousand years ago, cities began to emerge. Although tiny by today's standards, they were the centers of the first "civilizations," a word derived from *civitas,* which means "citizenship" or "inhabitants of a city" in Latin. Because farming created assets to plunder and to protect, it also created a requirement for inventory accounting. You cannot tax unless you can compile records and issue receipts. The symbols employed in the accountant's ledger became the rudiments of written language, an innovation that had never existed among hunters and gatherers.

Farming also extended the horizon over which humans had to solve problems. Hunting bands lived within an immediate time horizon. They seldom undertook projects that lasted more than a few days. But planting and harvesting a crop took months. Pursuing projects of a longer time frame led farmers to train their attentions on the stars. Detailed astronomical observations were a precondition for drawing up almanacs and calendars to serve as guides on when to best plant and reap. With the advent of farming, human horizons expanded.

PROPERTY

The move to a settled agricultural society resulted in the emergence of private property. Obviously, no one would be content to toil through the whole growing season to produce a crop just to see someone else wander along and harvest what he produced. The idea of property emerged as an inevitable consequence of farming. But the clarity of private property as a concept was attenuated by the logic of violence that also accompanied the introduction of farming. The emergence of property was confused by the fact that the megapolitical power of individuals was no longer as equal as it had been in foraging societies, where every healthy adult male was a hunter, as well armed as anyone else. Farming gave rise to specialization in violence. Precisely because it created something to steal, farming made investments in better weaponry profitable. The result was theft, much of it highly organized.

The powerful were now able to organize a new form of predation: a local monopoly of violence, or government. This sharply differentiated society, creating quite different circumstances for those who benefited from the plunder, and the mass of poor who tilled the fields. The few who controlled military power could now become rich, along with others who found favor with them. The god-kings and their allies, the various lesser, local potentates who ruled the first Near Eastern states, enjoyed much more nearly modern forms of property than the great mass who toiled beneath them.

Of course, it is anachronistic to think of a distinction between private and public wealth in the early agricultural societies. The ruling god-king had the full resources of the state at his disposal in a way that could hardly be distinguished from ownership of a sprawling estate. Much as in the feudal period of European history, all property was subject to the overlordship of higher potentates. Those down the chain of hierarchy found their property subject to attenuation at the whim of the ruler.

Yet to say that the potentate was not restrained by law does not mean that he could afford to seize anything he pleased. Costs and rewards impinged upon the freedom of the pharaoh as much as they do today upon the prime minister of Canada. And the pharaoh was much more constrained than contemporary leaders by the difficulties of transport and communication. Simply hauling loot from one spot to the next, especially when loot was measured mainly in the form of agricultural produce, involved a lot of loss from spoilage and theft. The proliferation of officials to check on one another reduced the loss due to pilfering but increased the total overhead costs the pharaoh had to bear. Decentralized authority, which optimized output under some circumstances, also gave rise to stronger local powers who sometimes blossomed into full-fledged challengers for dynastic control. Even Oriental despots were by no means free to do as they pleased. They had no choice but to recognize the balance of raw power as they found it.

Although everyone, including the rich, was subject to arbitrary expropriation, some were able to accumulate property of their own. Then as now, the state devoted much of its income to public works. Projects such as irrigation systems, religious monuments, and crypts for the kings provided opportunities for architects and artisans to earn income. Some well-situated individuals were able to accumulate considerable private property. In fact, a large portion of the surviving cuneiform tablets from Sumer, an early Mesopotamian civilization, record various acts of trade, most of which involve the transfer of property titles.

There was private property in the early agricultural societies, but seldom at the bottom of the social pyramid. The overwhelming majority of the population were peasants who were too poor to accumulate much wealth. In fact, with a few exceptions, most peasants, up until modern times, were so poor that they stood in constant danger of perishing from starvation any time that a drought or a flood or an infestation reduced crop yields. Hence the peasants were obliged to organize their affairs in a way that minimized the downside risks in bad years. Across the broad and impoverished stratum of society, a more primitive organization of property obtained. It increased the chance of survival at the expense of foreclosing the greater part of the opportunity to accumulate capital and rise in the economic system.

Peasant Insurance

The form that this bargain took was the adoption of what anthropologists and social historians describe as the "closed village." Almost every peasant society in premodern times had, as its main form of economic organization, the "closed village." Unlike more modern forms of economic organization, in which individuals tend to deal with many buyers and sellers in an open market, the households of the closed village joined together to operate like an informal corporation, or a large family, not in an open marketplace but in a closed system where all the economic transactions of the village tended to be struck with a single monopolist—the local landlord, or his agents among the village chiefs. The village as a whole would contract with the landlord, usually for payment in kind, for a high proportion of the crop, rather than a fixed rent. The proportional rent meant that the landlord absorbed part of the downside risk of a bad harvest. Of course, the landlord also took the greater part of the potential profit. Landlords also typically provided seed.

This convention also minimized the danger of starvation. It required that the landlord, rather than the peasant, save a disproportionate share of his part of the harvest. Because agricultural yields were appallingly low in many areas in the past, as many as two seeds had to be planted for every three harvested. Under such conditions, a bad harvest would mean mass starvation. The peasants rationally preferred an arrangement which would require the landlord to invest in their survival. At the cost of buying at monopolized prices, selling cheaply, and providing the landlord with in-kind labor, the peasants increased their chances of survival. A similar impulse led the typical peasant in a closed village economy to forgo the security of freehold property ownership. By putting themselves at the mercy of the village headman, a peasant family improved its chances of benefiting from the regular redistribution of fields. Not infrequently, the headman would take the best fields for himself and his favorites. But that was a risk that peasants had to tolerate in order to enjoy the survival insurance that confused village ownership of fields provided. At times when crop yields were miserably low, a difference in growing conditions of fields a hundred yards apart could make the difference between starvation and survival. Peasants frequently opted for the arrangement that lowered the downside risk, even at the cost of forgoing any hope of increased prosperity.

In general, risk-averse behavior has been common among all groups that operated along the margins of survival. The sheer challenge of survival in premodern societies always constrained the behavior of the poor. An interesting feature of this risk aversion, explored in *The Great Reckoning,* is that it reduced the range of peaceful economic behavior that individuals were socially permitted to adopt. Taboos and social constraints limited experimentation and innovative behavior, even at the obvious cost of forgoing potentially advantageous improvements in settled ways of doing things.[13] This was a rational reflection of the fact that experimentation increases the variability of results. Greater variability means not only potentially greater gains but— more ominously for those at the very margin of survival—potentially ruinous losses. A great part of the cultural energy of poor farming societies has always been devoted to suppressing experimentation. This repression, in effect, was their substitute for insurance policies. If they had insurance, or sufficient savings to self-insure their experiments, such strong social taboos would not be needed to help ensure survival.

Cultures are not matters of taste but systems of adaptation to specific circumstances that may prove irrelevant or even counterproductive in other settings. Humans live in a wide variety of habitats. The wide number of potential niches in which we live require variations in behavior that are too complex to be informed by instinct. Therefore, behavior is culturally programmed. For the vast majority in many agricultural societies, culture programmed them for survival, but little more than survival in an environment where the luxury of participating in open markets was reserved to others.

Personal ability and personal choice—individual "pursuit of happiness," in the modern sense—were suppressed by taboos and social restrictions that have always been most emphatic among the poor. Such restrictions were superseded only with great difficulty in societies with limited productivity. When and where agricultural productivity was higher, such as in ancient Greece, minor megapolitical revolutions occurred. Property took more modern forms. "Allod," or freehold property, emerged. Lands tended to rent for a fixed fee, and the tenant absorbed the economic risk as well as a higher portion of the profit if the crop was good. Higher savings allow self-insurance of riskier behavior. Under such conditions, yeoman farmers could rise above the rank of peasantry and sometimes even accumulate independent wealth.

The tendency for more market-like property rights and relationships to develop near the top of an economic hierarchy or, in rarer cases, across the whole economy, as societies emerged from poverty, is an important characteristic of social organization. It is equally important to note that the most common organization of agricultural society historically has been essentially feudal, with market relations at the top and the closed village system at the bottom. The great mass of peasants were tied to the land in almost all premodern agricultural societies. So long as agricultural productivity remained low, or higher productivity was dependent upon access to centralized hydraulic systems, the freedom and property rights of individual farmers at the bottom remained minimal. In such conditions, feudal forms of property prevailed. Land was held by tenure rather than through freehold title. Typically, rights of sale, gift, and inheritance were restricted.

Feudalism in its various forms was not only a response to ever-present risks of predatory violence. It also was a reaction to appallingly low rates of productivity. The two have tended to go hand in hand in farming societies. Each frequently contributed to the other. When public authority collapsed, property rights and prosperity tended to recede accordingly. Collapsing productivity also tended to undermine authority. While not every drought or adverse climatic change resulted in the breakdown of public authority, many did.

THE FEUDAL REVOLUTION OF THE YEAR 1000

Such was the case with the transformation of the year 1000, which launched the feudal revolution.[14] At that time, megapolitical and economic conditions differed in important ways from those we have come to think of as characterizing the Middle Ages. In the first few centuries after the fall of Rome, the economy of Western Europe withered. The Germanic kingdoms that took root in the territories of the former Roman Empire had assumed many functions of the Roman state, but at a much less ambitious level. Infrastructure more or less went untended. As the centuries passed, bridges and aqueducts fell into disrepair and became unusable. Roman coinage was still employed, but it practically disappeared from circulation. Land markets, which had thrived in Roman times, more or less dried up. Towns, which had been centers of Roman administration, virtually vanished along with the taxing power of the state. And so did almost every other accoutrement of civilization.

The "Dark Ages" were so named for a reason. Literacy became so rare that anyone who possessed the ability to read and write could expect immunity from prosecution for almost any crime, including murder. Artistic, scientific, and engineering skills that had been highly developed in Roman times disappeared. From road building to the grafting of vines and fruit trees, Western Europe ceased employing many techniques that had once been well known and practiced to a high standard. Even so ancient a device as the potter's wheel disappeared in many places. Mining operations contracted. Metallurgy receded. Irrigation works in the Mediterranean region disintegrated through neglect.[15] As historian Georges Duby observed, "At the end of the sixth century, Europe was a profoundly uncivilized place."[16] Although there was a brief renaissance of central authority under the rule of Charlemagne around the year 800, everything soon devolved again after his death.

A surprising corollary to this dreary landscape was the fact that the collapse of the Roman state probably raised the living standards of small farmers for several centuries. The Germanic kingdoms that dominated Western Europe during the Dark Ages incorporated some of the relatively easygoing social features common to their ancestral tribes, such as the legal equality of freeholders. As a consequence, small farmers in the Dark Ages were far freer than they were to be in the feudal centuries. By that we can also infer that they were more prosperous. As we analyzed above in exploring the logic of property forms under different conditions of productivity, freehold property has historically gone hand in hand with the relative prosperity of small farmers. The closed-village and feudal forms of property tended to emerge where the capacity of small farmers to make a living was more doubtful.

To be sure, the virtual collapse of commerce during the Dark Ages cost small farmers the benefits of trade and advantages of wider markets. The demise of the towns undermined the cash economy, but it also meant the rural population was no longer called upon to support the crushing burden of bureaucracy. As Guy Bois has written, the Roman town was a parasitic community, not a center of production: "In the Roman period, the dominant function of a city was of a political order. It lived primarily from the revenues draining into it from its surroundings by the agency of the land tax. . . . The town, in effect, produced little or nothing for the benefit of the surrounding countryside."[17] The collapse of Roman authority largely freed farmers in the countryside from taxes, which had sucked away "between one quarter to one third of the gross product of the land, without counting the various exactions suffered by small and middling landowners."[18] The taxes were so onerous, sometimes enforced by execution, that desertion of property by owners was widespread. The barbarians mercifully allowed these taxes to lapse.

Agri Deserti

The burdens of government were so greatly reduced by the barbarian conquests that an opening was created for the poor to obtain freehold property and keep it. Some of the *agri deserti,* or deserted farms abandoned by owners fleeing predatory taxation in the final years of the Roman Empire, were brought back into production. Notwithstanding the rude circumstances of the time and the fact that crop yields were ridiculously low by modern standards, the Dark Ages were a period of relative prosperity for Europe's smallholders. In fact, they were in a stronger position than they would be again until the modern era. For one thing, fewer hands were available to till the fertile land, large tracts of which had gone out of cultivation. Plagues, wars, and abandonment by owners escaping the collapsing Roman Empire had significantly depopulated areas previously under cultivation. Another advantage enjoyed by small farmers in the Dark Ages arose from the adoption in the sixth century of new farming technology: the heavy plow, often mounted on wheels. Used in tandem with an improved harness that allowed peasants to employ multiple oxen, the new technology made it much easier to clear forested land in Northern Europe.[19]

Under such conditions, the market for land contracted almost to the vanishing point. New land for farming could be had merely by clearing it and sharing part of each new parcel with the appropriate local authorities. This process, known as *assarting,* gave a comfortable outlet for population growth for centuries after Rome fell. Assarting became particularly attractive in thinly populated northern regions after warmer temperatures in the eighth century made farming more productive.

The leaders of the Germanic tribes who conquered former Roman territories had established themselves as large landholders. Most of the rest of the population farmed small plots—but under conditions very different from those that came later under feudalism. Wealthier landowners, or *masters,* represented about 7–10 percent of the population. It appears that before the year 1000, two-thirds of the villagers in a typical area of France were freehold landowners.[20] They owned about half of all the land in cultivation.[21] There were few serfs. *Coloni,* or tenant farmers, amounted to no more than 5 percent of the population. Slavery persisted, but on a much smaller scale than in Roman times.

The Germanic successor kingdoms to Rome were defended militarily by all free men who assembled to bear arms on the call of the king's local representative, the count. Even "small and middling proprietors" were expected to club together and send one of their number to fight with the infantry.[22] In the Edict of Pitres, Charles the Bald ordered all those who could afford to do so to muster for battle on horseback. Pope Gregory III had attempted to advance this military imperative a century earlier by banning the human consumption of horsemeat in 732.[23] But there was as yet little distinction in status or law between the infantry of freeholders and the cavalry. All free men participated in local judicial assemblies and could petition for dispute settlement to the count, an office that had existed since late Roman times. There was no nobility as such.

"A social phenomenon, new as a mass phenomenon, suddenly appeared on the horizons in the 980s: downward social mobility. Its first victims were the small allod-holders."[24]

—Guy Bois

As the Dark Ages wore on, however, several things happened to destabilize the relationships that had preserved the independence of the yeoman farmers and freeholders in the Germanic kingdoms that inherited power after Rome's fall:

1. Populations gradually recovered, placing greater pressures on the use of land. Over several centuries, much of the most fertile of the unclaimed land was brought into production, engendering growth in Northern Europe in particular. The increasing population of farmers relative to the supply of land made the labor of each farmer worth less. Most freehold titles were broken into ever smaller plots through inheritance. During the Dark Ages, children tended to share equally in the estates of their parents. The fragmentation of holdings at a time of rising population tended to place land at a premium once again and led to the re-emergence of active land markets by the mid-tenth century.

2. In the final decades of the tenth century, temperatures suddenly turned colder, with a devastating impact on farm output. Three successive crop failures led to severe famine from 982 to 984. Famine struck again after another crop failure in 994.[25] Then, in 997, the problem of falling crop yields was compounded by a plague, which struck small family holdings with particular force because the smallholders lacked the resources to replace labor supplied by lost family members. These clustered crop failures and disasters at first led the yeoman farmers to sink into debt. When yields failed to recover they could not pay their mortgages.

3. Power relations were progressively destabilized by the growing importance of heavy cavalry. Medieval historian Frances Gies describes the transformation of the armored cavalryman into the medieval knight:

Originally a personality of mediocre status raised above the peasant by his expensive horse and armor, the knight slowly improved his position in society until he became part of the nobility. Although knights remained the lowest rank of the upper class, knighthood acquired a unique cachet that made knighting an honor prized by the great nobility and even royalty. The cachet was primarily the product of the Church's policy of Christianizing knighthood by sanctifying the ceremony of knighting and by sponsoring a code of behavior known as chivalry, a code perhaps violated more often than honored, but exercising incontestable influence on the thought and conduct of posterity.[26]

As we recounted in *The Great Reckoning,* the invention of the stirrup gave the armed knight on horseback a formidable assault capability. He could now attack at full speed and not be thrown from the saddle by the impact of his lance striking a target. The military value of the heavy cavalry was further enhanced by an Asian invention that penetrated through Western Europe in the tenth century; the nailed iron horseshoe. This further improved the durability of the horse on the road.[27] Also adding to the improved effectiveness of the armed knight were the contoured saddle, which made it easier to wield heavy weapons, the spur, and the curb bit, which enabled a rider to control the horse with one hand while fighting.[28] Together, these apparently minor technological innovations dramatically devalued the military importance of the smallholders, who could not afford to maintain warhorses and arm themselves. The cheaper of the horses specially bred for war, the large chargers known as *destriers,* were worth four oxen or forty sheep. The more expensive warhorses cost ten oxen or one hundred sheep. Armor also cost a sum that no small holder could afford, equivalent to the price of sixty sheep.[29]

4. The fact that the colder weather, crop failures, famines, and plagues occurred during the run-up to the year 1000 also played a role in informing behavior. Many people were convinced that the end of the world or the Second Coming was at hand. Devout or frightened landowners, large and small, gave their land to the Church in preparation for apocalypse.

"Only a Poor Man Sells Land"

The unsettled conditions of the late tenth century paved the way for the feudal revolution. Clustered crop failures and disasters led the yeoman farmers to sink into debt. When crop yields failed to recover, the freeholders faced a desperate situation. Markets always place the greatest pressures on the weakest holders. Indeed, that is part of their virtue. They promote efficiency by removing assets from weak hands. But in late-tenth-century Europe, subsistence farming was practically the only occupation. Families who lost their land lost their only means of survival. Faced with this unpalatable prospect, many or most of the freehold farmers decided to give away their fields during the feudal revolution. In the words of Guy Bois, "The only sure way for a peasant to hold on to the land he tilled was to concede ownership of it to the Church, so he could retain its usufruct." [30] Others ceded some or all of their land to wealthier farmers in whom they had confidence, either friendly neighbors or relatives.

These property transfers were made on the condition that the farmer, his family, and his descendants were to remain to work the fields. The poor farmers were also to enjoy the reciprocal support of the more substantial holders, now the "nobles" who were able to afford horse and armor, and thus provide protection to the enlarged estates. Such a bargain can be seen from the new serf's point of view as a halfway station between continuing economic ownership and foreclosure. More often than not, it was a bargain he could not refuse.

Falling productivity not only placed poor farmers in a desperate economic dilemma; it also instigated an upsurge in predatory violence that undermined the security of property. Those without the resources to wrest a share of the available and inadequate supply of horses and fodder suddenly found that they and their property were no longer safe. To put their dilemma in contemporary terms, it was as if you were forced to arm yourself today with a new type of weapon, but the cost of doing so was $100,000. If you could not pay that price, you would be at the mercy of those who could.

Within a few years, the capacity of the king and the courts to enforce order collapsed.[31] Anyone with armor and a horse could now become a law unto himself. The result was a late-tenth-century version of *Blade Runner*, a melee of fighting and plunder that the constituted authorities were powerless to stop. Looting and attacks by armed knights disrupted the countryside. It is by no means obvious, however, that all the victims of this pillage were the poor. To the contrary, the elderly, physically weaker, or ill-prepared among the larger landholders made more attractive targets. They had more to steal.

It was not a coincidence that this happened at the very moment when colder weather, famine, and plague were placing a pinch on resources. The megapolitical conditions conducive to the breakdown of authority had been in place for some time. Their potential for altering the power relations in society was not realized, however, until a crisis was triggered. Crop failures and famines appear to have done just that. While the exact sequence of events is difficult to reconstruct, it appears that the looting was instigated, at least in part, by desperate conditions. Once the violence was unleashed, it became evident that no one could mobilize the force to stop it. The vast majority of poorly armed farmers certainly could do little. Even dozens of farmers on foot would have been outmatched by a single armed knight on horseback. The freehold farmers, like the constituted authorities, the kings with their counts, were powerless to prevent local land from being seized by armed warriors.

"The Peace of God"

In these desperate conditions, the Church helped to launch feudalism through its efforts to negotiate a truce in the violent countryside. Historian Guy Bois described the situation this way: "The impotence of the political authorities was such that the Church stood in for them in the attempt to restore order, in the movement known as 'The Peace of God.' 'Councils of Peace' proclaimed series of interdictions which were sanctioned by anathemas; vast 'assemblies of peace' received the oaths of the warriors. The movement originated in the French Midi (Council of Charroux in 989, Council of Narbonne in 990), then gradually spread. . . ." [32]

The bargain that the Church struck involved acknowledgment of the overlordship of armed knights in local communities in exchange for a cessation or tempering of the violence and looting. Land titles inscribed after the surge of violence in the late tenth century suddenly bore the title "nobilis" or "miles" as an indication of lordship. The nobility as a separate estate was created by the feudal revolution. Property transactions recorded to the same individuals only a few years earlier had listed no such distinction. [33]

Given falling productivity and the economic insecurity of the smallholders, the megapolitical power of the armed knights led inevitably to property holdings by feudal tenure. By the end of the first quarter of the eleventh century, yeoman farmers had largely disappeared. Their freeholdings had shrunk to a fraction of their previous extent and were now being worked just part-time. The small farmers or their descendants were serfs who spent most of their time laboring on the estates of feudal lords, lay and ecclesiastical.

The breakdown of order that accompanied the feudal revolution led to adjustments in behavior which reinforced feudalism. Among them was a surge in castle building. Castles had first appeared in northwest Europe as primitive wooden structures in the wake of Viking raids in the ninth century. Originally command centers for Carolingian officials, they became hereditary possessions after the feudal revolution. These early redoubts were far more primitive than they would later become, but they were nonetheless difficult to attack. Once erected, castles were razed only with the greatest effort. As they began to dot the countryside, the castles made it ever more implausible that the king or his counts could effectively challenge the local supremacy of the lords.

Contributions of the Church to Productivity

Feudalism was the response of agricultural society to the collapse of order at a time of low productivity. During the early stages of feudalism, the Church played an important and economically productive role. Among the Church's contributions:

1. In an environment where military power was decentralized, the Church was uniquely placed to maintain peace and develop rules of order that transcended fragmented, local sovereignties. This is a job that no secular power was positioned to do. The observations of the great religious authority A. R. Radcliffe-Brown are directly relevant here. He pointed out that "the

social function of a religion is independent of its truth or falsity." Even those that are "absurd and repulsive, such as those of some savage tribes, may be important and effective parts of the social machinery."[34] This was certainly the case with the Church in the early stages of feudalism. It helped create rules, as only a religion could, that enabled people to overcome incentive traps and behavioral dilemmas. Some of these were moral dilemmas common to all human life. But others were local dilemmas, unique to the prevailing megapolitical conditions. The medieval Church had a special role to play in restoring order in the countryside in the final years of the tenth century. By providing religious and ceremonial support to local authorities, the Church lowered the costs of establishing at least weak local monopolies of violence. By helping to establish order in this way, the Church contributed to the conditions that ultimately led to more stable configurations of power.

The Church continued to play a role for a long time thereafter in tempering the private wars and excesses of violence that otherwise could not be contained by civil authorities. The relative importance of the Church as opposed to secular authorities is reflected in the fact that by the eleventh century, the main administrative division of authority in most of Western Europe came to be the parish, rather than the old divisions of civil authority, the *ager* and *pagus* (town) that had persisted from Roman times through the Dark Ages.[35]

2. The Church was the main source for preserving and transmitting technical knowledge and information. The Church sponsored universities and provided the minimal education that medieval society enjoyed. The Church also provided a mechanism for reproducing books and manuscripts, including almost all contemporary information about farming and husbandry. The *scriptoria* of the Benedictine monasteries can be understood as an alternate technology to printing presses, which did not yet exist. Costly and inefficient as the scriptoria were, they were practically the only mechanism for reproducing and preserving written knowledge in the feudal period.

3. Partly because its farm managers were literate, the Church did a great deal to help improve the productivity of European farming, especially in the early stages of feudalism. Before the thirteenth century the farm managers of lay lords were almost all illiterates who kept records through an elaborate set of marks. Shrewd farmers though they may have been, they were in no position to benefit from any improvement in production methods that they could not invent themselves or see with their own eyes. The Church was therefore essential to improving the quality of grains, fruits, and breeding stock. Because of its extensive holdings spread over the entire European continent, the Church could send the most productive seed and breeding stock to areas where output lagged. The demand for sacramental wine in Northern Europe led monks to experiment with hardier varieties of grape

that could survive in colder climates. The Church also helped raise the productivity of medieval farming in other ways. Many of the uneconomically small plots donated to the Church during the feudal revolution were reconfigured to make them easier to farm. The Church also provided ancillary services required by small farming communities. In many areas, Church-owned mills ground grain into flour.

4. The Church undertook many functions that are today absorbed by government, including the provision of public infrastructure. This is part of the way that the Church helped overcome what economists call "public goods dilemmas" in an era of fragmented authority. Specific religious orders of the early-medieval Church devoted themselves to applied engineering tasks, like opening roads, rebuilding fallen bridges, and repairing dilapidated Roman aqueducts. They also cleared land, built dams, and drained swamps. A new monastic order, the Carthusians, dug the first "artesian" well in Artois, France. Using percussion drilling, they dug a small hole deep enough to create a well that needed no pump.[36] The Cistercian Order undertook to build and maintain precarious seawalls and dikes in the Low Countries of Europe. Farmers deeded land to Cistercian monasteries and then leased it back, while the monks undertook full responsibility for upkeep and repairs. Cistercians also took the lead in developing water-powered machines, which were adopted to such widespread uses as "pounding, lifting, grinding, and pressing."[37] The monastery of Clairvaux dug a two-mile-long canal from the River Aube.[38] The Church also intervened to build new roads and bridges where population centers had shifted outside the range of the old Roman garrison roads. Bishops granted indulgences to local lords who would build or repair river crossings and maintain hospices for travelers. An order of monks established by St. Bénezet, the Frères Pontifes, or "Brothers of the Bridge," built several of the longest bridges then existing, including the Pont d'Avignon, a massive twenty-arch structure over the Rhone with a combination chapel and tollbooth at one end. Even London Bridge, which stood until the nineteenth century, was constructed by a chaplain and financed in part by a contribution of 1,000 marks from the papal legate.[39]

5. The Church also helped incubate a more complex market. Cathedral construction, for example, differs in kind from public infrastructure, like bridges and aqueducts. In principle, at least, Church structures were used only for religious services and not as thoroughfares for commerce. Yet it should not be forgotten that construction of churches and cathedrals helped create and deepen markets for many artisanal and engineering skills. In the same way that military spending of the nation-state during the Cold War unintentionally helped incubate the Internet, so the building of medieval cathedrals led to spin-offs of other kinds, the incubation of commerce. The Church was a principal customer of the building trades and artisans. Church

purchases of silver for communion services, candelabra, and artworks to decorate churches helped to create a market for luxury goods that otherwise would not have existed.

In many ways, the Church helped to temper the ferocity of violence unleashed by armed knights during and after the "feudal revolution." Especially in the early centuries of feudalism, the Church contributed significantly to improving the productivity of the farming economy. It was an essential institution, well fitted to the needs of agrarian society at the close of the Dark Ages.

Vulnerability to Violence

In "[t]hirty or forty years of violent disturbances, the feudal revolution of the year 1000," [40] like the fall of Rome five centuries earlier, was a unique event, caused by a complex interplay of influences. Yet in one respect, the triumph of *mali homines* (wicked men) and the oppressions they wrought perfectly reflect the essential vulnerability of agricultural society to violence. In contrast to the foraging phase of human existence, farming introduced a quantum leap in organized violence and oppression.

From the very earliest, this was reflected in the more militant cultures of farming peoples. The gods of the early agricultural societies were gods of rainfall and flooding, whose functions reflected the preoccupations of those societies with factors that determined crop yields. The sender of rain or water was also often the god of war, invoked by the earliest kings, who were, above all else, warlords. [41]

The close connection between farming and warfare was reflected in the religious imagination of people whose lives were transformed by the innovations of the agricultural revolution. The expulsion from the Garden of Eden can be seen as a figurative account of the transformation of society from foraging to farming, from a free life with food picked from nature's bounty with little work to a life of hard labor.

PARADISE LOST

Farming set humanity on an entirely new course. The first farmers truly planted the seeds of civilization. From their toil came cities, armies, arithmetic, astronomy, dungeons, wine and whiskey, the written word, kings, slavery, and war. Yet notwithstanding all the drama that farming was to add to life, the shift away from the primeval economy appears to have been roundly unpopular from its earliest days. Witness the account preserved in the Book of Genesis, which tells the story of the expulsion from paradise. The biblical parable of the Garden of Eden is a fond recollection of the life of ease enjoyed by the forager in the wilderness. Scholars indicate that the word "Eden" appears to be derived from a Sumerian word for "wilderness."[42]

The transition from a free and sparsely settled life in the wild to a sedentary life in a farming village was a matter of deep regret, expressed not only in the Bible but also in humankind's continuing grudge against getting up in the morning and going to work. As Stephen Boyden wrote in *Western Civilization in Biological Perspective,* the new way of living that accompanied farming was "evodeviant."[43] Prior to the advent of farming, thousands of human generations lived as Adam did in Eden, at the invitation of his Maker: "Of every tree of the garden thou mayest freely eat." Hunters and gatherers had no crops to tend, no herd to watch, no taxes to pay. Like hoboes, foragers drifted where they pleased, worked little, and answered to no one.

With farming, a new way of life began, and on altogether more pressing terms. "Thorns also and thistles shall it bring forth to thee; and thou shalt eat the herb of the field; In the sweat of thy face shalt thou eat bread." Farming was hard work. The memory of life before farming was that of paradise lost.

More than they could have imagined, farmers created new conditions that drastically altered the logic of violence. It is not a coincidence that the Book of Genesis makes Cain, the first murderer, "a tiller of the ground." Indeed, it is part of the uncanny prophetic power of the Bible that its story was entrusted to shepherds who readily understood how farming gave leverage to violence. In a few verses the biblical account encapsulates logic that took thousands of years to play out. Farming was an incubator of disputes. Farming created stationary capital on an extensive scale, raising the payoff from violence and dramatically increasing the challenge of protecting assets. Farming made both crime and government paying propositions for the first time.

CHAPTER 4
THE LAST DAYS OF POLITICS

Parallels Between the Senile Decline of the Holy Mother Church and the Nanny State

"I also believe—and hope—that politics and economics will cease to be as important in the future as they have been in the past; the time will come when most of our present controversies on these matters will seem as trivial, or as meaningless, as the theological debates in which the keenest minds of the Middle Ages dissipated their energies."[1]

—ARTHUR C. CLARKE

To speak of the coming death of politics is bound to seem ridiculous or optimistic, depending on your disposition. Yet that is what the Information Revolution is likely to bring. For readers reared in a century saturated in politics, the idea that life could proceed without it may seem fanciful, the equivalent to claiming that one could live merely by absorbing nutrients from the air. Yet politics in the modern sense, as the preoccupation with controlling and rationalizing the power of the state, is mostly a modern invention. We believe it will end with the modern world just as the tangle of feudal duties and obligations that engrossed the attentions of people in the Middle Ages ended with the Middle Ages. During the feudal period, as historian Martin van Creveld points out, "politics did not exist (the very concept had yet to be invented, and dates back only to the sixteenth century)."[2]

The thought that politics, as we now know it, did not exist prior to the modern period may seem surprising, especially given that Aristotle had written an essay of that title in the days of Alexander the Great. But look closely. Words used in ancient texts are not necessarily contemporary concepts. Aristotle also wrote an essay entitled *Sophistical Refutations,* a term about as meaningless today as *Politics* was in the Middle Ages. The word simply was not in use. Its first known appearance in English dates to 1529.[3] Even then, "politics" appears to have been a pejorative, derived from an Old French word, *politique,* used to describe "opportunists and temporizers."[4]

It took almost two thousand years for Aristotle's latent concept to emerge with the meaning we now know. Why? Before the modern world could put Aristotle's word to a meaningful use, megapolitical conditions were required that dramatically raised the returns to violence. The Gunpowder Revolution, which we analyzed in *The Great Reckoning,* did just that. It raised the returns to violence far above what they had ever been. This made the question of who controlled the state more important than it had ever been. Logically and inevitably, politics emerged from the struggle to control the sharply increased spoils of power.

Politics began five centuries ago with the early stages of industrialism. Now it is dying. A widespread revulsion against politics and politicians is sweeping the world. You see it in news and speculation on the hidden details of Whitewater, and the poorly disguised murder of Vincent Foster. You see it in numerous other scandals touching President Bill Clinton. You see in it reports of embezzlement by leading congressmen from the House Post Office. You see it in scandals leading to resignations in John Major's circle, and similar scandals in France, reaching two recent prime ministers, Eduard Balladur and Alain Juppe. Even larger scandals have been revealed in Italy, where seven-time prime minister Giulio Andreotti was brought to the dock to stand trail on charges that included links to the Mafia and ordering the murder of Mino Pecorelli, an investigative journalist. Still other scandals have tarnished the reputation of Spanish prime minister Filipe Gonzales. Corruption allegations cost four Japanese prime ministers their jobs in the first five years of the 1990s. Canada's Justice Department alleged in a letter to Swiss authorities that former prime minister Brian Mulroney had received kickbacks on a C$1.8 billion sale of Airbus planes to Air Canada.[5] Willy Claes, the secretary-general of NATO, was forced to resign under a cloud of corruption allegations. Even in Sweden, Mona Sahlin, a deputy prime minister and presumptive prime minister, was forced to resign in the face of allegations that she used government credit cards to purchase diapers and other household goods. Almost everywhere you turn in countries with mature welfare states once thought of as well governed, people hate their political leaders.

Disdain as a Leading Indicator

Moral outrage against corrupt leaders is not an isolated historical phenomenon but a common precursor of change. It happens again and again whenever one era gives way to another. Whenever technological change has divorced the old forms from the new moving forces of the economy, moral standards shift, and people begin to treat those in command of the old institutions with growing disdain. This widespread revulsion comes into evidence well before people develop a new coherent ideology of change. As we write, there is as yet little evidence of an articulate rejection of politics. That will come later. It has not yet occurred to most of your contemporaries that a life without politics is possible. What we have in the final years of the twentieth century is inarticulate disdain.

Something similar happened in the late fifteenth century, but at that time it was religion rather than politics that was in the process of being downsized. Notwithstanding popular belief in "the sacredness of the sacerdotal office," [6] both the higher and lower ranks of clergy were held in the utmost contempt —not unlike the popular attitude toward politicians and bureaucrats today. It was widely believed that the upper clergy were corrupt, worldly, and venal. And not without reason. Several fifteenth-century popes openly sported bastards. The lower clergy were held in even lower esteem as they proliferated in country and town, begging for alms and frequently offering to sell God's grace and the forgiveness of sins to anyone who would put cash into the bargain.

Beneath the "crust of superficial piety" [7] was a corrupt and increasingly dysfunctional system. Many lost respect for those who ran it, long before anyone dared to say that it did not work. A life saturated with religion, making no distinction between the spiritual and the temporal, had exhausted its possibilities. Its end was inevitable long before Luther nailed his 95 theses on the church door at Wittenberg.

A SECULAR REFORMATION

We believe that the reaction against saturation politics is following a similar path. The death of the Soviet Union and the repudiation of socialism are part of a broad pattern of depoliticization sweeping the world. This is now most evident in a growing contempt for those who run the world's governments. It is driven only in part by the realization that they are corrupt, and prone to sell "indulgences" from political difficulty in exchange for campaign contributions or special help on commodity trades to subvene their personal finances.

The reaction against politicians is also motivated by the widening realization that much of what they do at great cost is futile, in the same way that organizing another pilgrimage of penitents to march barefoot in the snow, or the founding of yet another order of mendicant monks in the late fifteenth century, could have done little to improve productivity or relieve pressures on living standards.

The Last Days of the Holy Mother Church

At the end of the Middle Ages, the monolithic Church as an institution had grown senile and counterproductive, a marked change from its positive economic contribution five centuries earlier. As we explored in the last chapter, the Church played a leading role at the end of the tenth century in establishing order and facilitating economic recovery from the anarchy that marked the close of the Dark Ages. At that time, the Church was indispensable to the survival of large numbers of small freeholders and serfs who made up the bulk of the Western European population. By the end of the fifteenth century, the Church had become a major drag upon productivity. The burdens it imposed upon the population were pushing living standards down.

Much the same thing can be said of the nation-state today. It was a necessary adaptation to the new megapolitical conditions created by the Gunpowder Revolution five centuries ago. The nation-state widened the scope of markets and displaced fragmented local authorities at a time when more encompassing trading areas brought large returns. The fact that merchants almost everywhere in Europe spontaneously allied themselves to the monarch at the center as he maneuvered to consolidate authority is itself telling evidence that the nation-state in its early form was good for business. It helped lift the burdens on commerce imposed by feudal landlords and local magnates.

In a world where returns to violence were high and rising, the nation-state was a useful institution. But five centuries later, as this millennium draws to a close, megapolitical conditions have changed. Returns to violence are falling, and the nation-state, like the Church at the twilight of the Middle Ages, is an anachronism that has become a drag on growth and productivity.

Like the Church then, the nation-state today has exhausted its possibilities. It is bankrupt, an institution grown to a senile extreme. Like the Church then, it has served as the dominant form of social organization for five centuries. Having outlived the conditions that brought it into existence, it is ripe for a fall. And fall it will. Technology is precipitating a revolution in the exercise of power that will destroy the nation-state just as assuredly as gunpowder weapons and the printing press destroyed the monopoly of the medieval Church.

If our reasoning is correct, the nation-state will be replaced by new forms of sovereignty, some of them unique in history, some reminiscent of the city-states and medieval merchant republics of the premodern world. What was old will be new after the year 2000. And what was unimaginable will be commonplace. As the scale of technology plunges, governments will find that they must compete like corporations for income, charging no more for their services than they are worth to the people who pay for them. The full implications of this change are all but unimaginable.

THEN AND NOW

Something similar might have been said five hundred years ago, at the turn of the fifteenth century. Then as now, Western civilization stood at the threshold of a momentous transformation. Although almost no one knew it, medieval society was dying. Its death was neither widely anticipated nor understood. Nonetheless, the prevailing mood was one of deep gloom. This is common at the end of an era, as conventional thinkers sense that things are falling apart, that "the falcon cannot hear the falconer." Yet their mental inertia is often too great to comprehend the implications of the emerging configurations of power. Medieval historian Johan Huizinga wrote of the waning days of the Middle Ages, "The chroniclers of the fifteenth century have, nearly all, been the dupes of an absolute misappreciation of their times, of which the real moving forces escaped their attention." [8]

Myths Betrayed

Major changes in the underlying dynamics of power tend to confound conventional thinkers because they expose myths that rationalize the old order but lack any real explanatory power. At the end of the Middle Ages, as now, there was a particularly wide gap between the received myths and reality. As Huizinga said of the Europeans in the late fifteenth century, "Their whole system of ideas was permeated by the fiction that chivalry ruled the world." [9] This has a close second in the contemporary assumption that it is ruled by votes and popularity contests. Neither proposition stands up to close scrutiny. Indeed, the idea that the course of history is determined by democratic tallies of wishes is every bit as silly as the medieval notion that it is determined by an elaborated code of manners called chivalry.

The fact that saying so borders on heresy suggests how divorced conventional thinking is from a realistic grasp of the dynamics of power in late industrial society. It is an issue we examine closely in this book. In our view, voting was an effect rather than a cause of the megapolitical conditions that brought forth the modern nation-state. Mass democracy and the concept of citizenship flourished as the nation-state grew. They will falter as the nation-state falters, causing every bit as much dismay in Washington as the erosion of chivalry caused in the court of the duke of Burgundy five hundred years ago.

PARALLELS BETWEEN CHIVALRY AND CITIZENSHIP

If you can understand how and why the importance of chivalric oaths faded away with the transition to an industrial organization of society, you will be better positioned to see how citizenship as we now know it could fade away in the Information Age. Both served a similar function. They facilitated the exercise of power under two quite different sets of megapolitical conditions.

Feudal oaths prevailed at a time when defensive technology was paramount, sovereignties were fragmented, and private individuals and corporate bodies exercised military power in their own right. Before the Gunpowder Revolution, wars had normally been fought by small contingents of armed men. Even the most powerful monarchs did not have *militum perpetuum,* or standing armies. They drew their military support from their vassals, the greater lords, who in turn drew upon their vassals, the lesser lords, who in turn drew upon *their* vassals, the knights. The whole chain of allegiance carried down the hierarchy to the person of the meanest social standing who was considered worthy to bear arms.

Uniforms or Divergences?

Unlike a modern army, a medieval army before the rise of citizenship did not march on the field of battle outfitted in uniforms. To the contrary, each retainer or vassal, each knight, baronet, or lord of different degree had his own distinctive livery that reflected his place in the hierarchy. Instead of uniforms, there were divergences that emphasized the vertical structure of society in which each station was different. As Huizinga said, medieval warriors were distinguished by "outward signs of . . . divergences: liveries, colors, badges, party cries."[10]

Nor were wars fought only by governments or nations. As Martin van

Creveld has pointed out, modern notions of war, as stylized by strategists like Carl von Clausewitz, misrepresent the reality of premodern conflict. Van Creveld writes:

> For a thousand years after the fall of Rome, armed conflict was waged by different kinds of social entities. Among them were barbarian tribes, the Church, feudal barons of every rank, free cities, even private individuals. Nor were the "armies" of the period anything like those we know today; indeed, it is difficult to find a word that will do them justice. War was waged by shoals of retainers who donned military garb and followed their lord.[11]

Under such conditions, it was obviously crucial to the lord that his retainers actually "donned their military garb and followed." Hence the heavy emphasis placed upon the chivalric oath.

The honor of the medieval knight and the duty of the conscript soldier served parallel functions. The medieval man was bound by oaths to individuals and the Church in much the way that moderns are bound by citizenship to the nation-state. Violating an oath was the medieval equivalent of treason. People in late-medieval times went to extremes to avoid violating oaths, just as millions of modern citizens went to extremes in the World Wars, charging machine-gun nests to fulfill their duties as citizens.

Both chivalry and citizenship added an extra dimension to the simple calculus that would otherwise deter unindoctrinated human beings from going onto a battlefield and staying there when the going got rough. Chivalry and citizenship both led people to kill and to risk death. Only demanding and exaggerated values that are strongly reinforced by leading institutions can serve that function.

Circumventing Cost-Benefit Analysis

The success and survival of any system depends upon its capacity to marshal military effort in times of conflict and crisis. Obviously, the decision on the part of a medieval knight or a private in the trenches in World War I to risk his life in battle was not likely to be informed by a sober, cost-benefit calculation. Seldom are wars so easily fought, or do rewards for those who bear the brunt of the fighting so far overshadow the possible costs that an army of economic optimizers could be recruited to rush out to the battlefield. Almost every war and, indeed, most battles have moments in which the tide could turn on a heartbeat. As students of military history are well aware, the difference between defeat and victory is often told by the valor, bravery, and ferocity with which individual soldiers take up their task. If the men doing the fighting are not willing to die over a piece of ground that would not be worth a fig once the battle stops, then they probably will not prevail against an otherwise evenly matched foe.

This has important implications. The more effective sovereignties are in limiting defections and encouraging military effort, the more likely they are to prevail militarily. In warfare, the most useful value systems induce people to behave in ways that short-term rational calculation would rule out. No organization could mobilize military power effectively if the individuals it sent into battle felt free to calculate where their own best advantage lay, and join in the fight or run away accordingly. If so, they would almost never fight. Only under the most propitious circumstances, or the most desperate, would the rational person care to engage in a potentially lethal battle based upon short-term cost-benefit analysis. Perhaps *Homo economicus* might fight on a sunny day, when the forces on his side were overwhelming, the enemy weak, and the potential rewards of battle enticing. Perhaps. He might also fight if backed into a corner by marauding cannibals.

But those are extreme circumstances. What of the more common conditions of warfare, which are neither so attractive that they would pass the scrutiny of cost-benefit analysis nor so desperate that they afford no way out? It is here that concepts like chivalry and citizenship are important contributors to the successful use of military power. Long before a battle begins, predominant organizations must convince individuals that upholding certain duties to the lord, or the nation-state, are more important than life itself. The myths and rationalizations that societies employ to encourage risk-taking on the battlefield are a key part of their military prowess.

To be effective, these myths must be tailored to the prevailing megapolitical conditions. The fiction that chivalry rules the world means nothing today, especially in a city like New York. But it was the cherished myth of feudalism. It justified and rationalized the ties of obligation that bound everyone under the domination of the Church and a warlike nobility. At a time when private wars of covetousness were commonplace,[12] the exercise of power and the very survival of individuals depended upon the willingness of others to fulfill their promises of military service under conditions of duress. It was obviously crucial that those promises be dependable.

Before Nationality

Unlike today, the concept of nationality played little or no role in establishing sovereignty in the Middle Ages. Monarchs, as well as some princes of the Church and powerful lords, possessed territories by private right. In a way that has no modern analogy, these lords could sell or give away territories or acquire new ones by conveyance or marriage as well as by conquest. Today, you could hardly imagine the United States falling under the sovereignty of a non-English-speaking Portuguese president because he happened to marry the former American president's daughter. Yet something similar was commonplace in medieval Europe. Power passed by hereditary descent. Cities and countries changed sovereigns the way that antiques change owners. In many cases, sovereigns were not native to the regions in which their properties lay. Sometimes they did not speak the local language, or spoke it badly with heavy accents. But it made little difference to the ties of personal obligation whether a Spaniard was king of Athens, or an Austrian was king of Spain.

Corporate Sovereignty

Sovereignty was also exercised by religious corporations like the Knights Templar, the Knights of St. John, the Teutonic Knights, and the Knights of Malta. While the Knights of Malta still exist and as we write are poised to recover sovereignty over Fort St. Angelo in Malta, such hybrid institutions have had no modern counterparts. They combined religious, social, judicial, and financial activities with sovereignty over localities.[13] While they exercised territorial jurisdiction, they were almost the opposite of today's governments in that nationality played no role in the mobilization of their support or their scheme of governance. The members and officers of these religious orders were drawn from all parts of Christian Europe, or "Christendom," as it was known.

No one thought it appropriate or necessary that those who ruled be drawn from the local populations. The mobilization of support in the fragmented medieval scheme of governance did not depend upon a national identity or duty to the state, as in modern times, but upon personal loyalty and customary ties that had to be upheld as a matter of personal honor. Oaths to uphold these duties could be sworn by anyone from anywhere provided he was otherwise deemed worthy by his station in life.

The Vow

Chivalric vows bound individuals to one another and were sworn on the honor of those who were parties to them. As Huizinga wrote, "in making a vow, people imposed some privation upon themselves as a spur to accomplishment of the actions they were pledged to perform."[14] So much importance was placed upon honoring vows that people frequently risked death or suffered serious privations in order to avoid breaking their vows. Often, the oaths themselves bound individuals to perform as matters of honor acts that would probably seem ludicrous to you and most readers of this book.

For example, the Knights of the Star swore an oath never to retire "more than four acres from the battlefield, through which rule soon afterwards more than ninety of them lost their lives." [15] The prohibition on even tactical retreat is irrational as a military strategy. But it was a common imperative of the chivalric vows. Before the Battle of Agincourt, the king of England issued an order that knights on patrol should remove their armor, on grounds that it would have been incompatible with their honor to withdraw from enemy lines if they were wearing their coat armor. It so happened that the king himself got lost and passed by the village that had been night quarters for the vanguard of his army. Since he was wearing armor, his chivalric honor forbade him to simply turn around when he discovered his mistake and return to the village. He spent the night in an exposed position.

As silly as this example seems, King Henry probably did not miscalculate in thinking that he would have risked more in trespassing his honor by retreating, and thus setting a demoralizing example for his entire army, than he did by sleeping behind enemy lines.

The history of the Middle Ages is filled with examples of prominent people fulfilling pledges that would seem ridiculous to us. In many cases, the actions proposed involved no objective connection to any benefit other than a vivid demonstration of the importance those undertaking them placed upon the vow itself. Among the common vows: to keep one eye closed, to eat and drink only when standing, and to become a self-imposed cripple by entering a one-person chain gang. There was a widespread custom of wearing painful foot irons. If today you saw someone struggling along the street in a heavy leg iron, you would probably assume that he was insane, not that he was a man of great virtue. Yet in the context of chivalry, willingly donning such a device was a badge of honor. And there were many similar customs that would seem equally ludicrous today. As Huizinga describes it, many took a pledge "not to sleep in a bed on Saturday, not to take animal food on Friday, etc. One act of asceticism is heaped upon another: one nobleman promises to wear no armor, to drink no wine one day in every week, not to sleep in a bed, not to sit down to meals, to wear the hair shirt." [16]

Lent survives as a much moderated version of this self-imposed discomfort.

Many enthusiasts for vows formed orders that placed particularly difficult privations on their members as tests of honor. The Order of Galois and Galoises, for example, dressed during summers in "furs and fur-lined hoods and lighted a fire in the hearth, whereas in winter they were only allowed to wear a simple coat without fur; neither mantles, not hats, nor gloves, and had only very light bed clothes." As Huizinga reports, "It is not surprising that a great many members died of cold." [17]

> *"Medieval self-flagellation was a grim torture which people inflicted on themselves in the hope of inducing a judging and punishing God to put away his rod, to forgive their sins, to spare them the greater chastisements which would otherwise be theirs in this life and the next."* [18]
>
> —NORMAN COHN

Flagellation, Then and Now

It was a short step from the vow that imposed danger and privation to ordeals, pilgrimages, mortification, discomfort, and even purposefully self-inflicted injury. These could be seen as highly beneficial and praiseworthy in the medieval period. They were gestures of the seriousness with which vows were held, a logic that is not entirely foreign even today to fraternity or sorority initiations.

Stifling in summer, freezing in winter, or walking in barefoot pilgrimages in the snow was relatively tame compared to "the grim torture" of self-flagellation. This was a particularly medieval form of penance that came into being almost exactly at the same time feudalism began. It was first "adopted by hermits in the monastic communities of Camaldoli and Fonte Avellana early in the eleventh century." [19]

Rather than just walking barefoot in cold weather, flagellants organized processions in which they would march day and night, from one town to the next. "And each time they came to a town they would arrange themselves in groups before the church and flog themselves for hours on end." [20]

We believe that people in the future who look back at the era of the nation-state will find some of the undertakings done in the twentieth century in the name of citizenship as ludicrous as we consider self-flagellation. From the vantage point of the Information Society, the spectacle of soldiers in the modern period traveling halfway around the world to entertain death out of loyalty to the nation-state will come to be seen as grotesque and silly. It will seem not far different from some of the extraordinary and exaggerated rites of chivalry, like walking about in leg irons, which otherwise sensible people took pride in doing during the feudal period.

Chivalry Yields to Citizenship

Chivalry faded away, to be replaced by citizenship, when megapolitical conditions changed and the military purpose of the vow to one's lord was antiquated. The world of gunpowder weapons and industrial armies involved very different relations between the individuals who did the fighting and their commanders. Citizenship emerged when returns to violence were high and rising, and the state had vastly greater resources than the social entities that waged war in the medieval period. Because of its great power and wealth, the nation-state could strike a bargain directly with the mass of common soldiers who fought in its uniform.

Such bargains proved to be far cheaper to the state and much less trouble-some than attempts to assemble military forces by negotiating with powerful lords and local notables, each of whom was capable of resisting demands that ran counter to his interests as no individual citizen in the nation-state conceivably could.

For reasons we explore at greater depth later, citizenship crucially depended upon the fact that no individual or small group of individuals was megapolitically capable of exercising military power independently. As information technology alters the logic of battle, it will antiquate the myths of citizenship just as assuredly as gunpowder antiquated medieval chivalry.

Hell's Angels on Horseback

The aristocracy of mounted warriors that dominated Western Europe for centuries were hardly the gentlemen their descendants became. They were rough and violent. In today's terms they could be better understood as the medieval equivalent of motorcycle gangs. The rules of manners and pre-tenses of chivalry served more to temper their excesses than as a description of the way they really behaved. Even an encyclopedic account of the rules and obligations of chivalry would have revealed little or nothing about the foundations of the nobility's power.

Perfection as a Synonym for Exhaustion

The advent of effective gunpowder weapons at the end of the fifteenth century detonated a powerful blast under their feet—just as armed knights had perfected their art as never before. By then, careful breeding had finally produced a battle horse sixteen hands high, a steed with the stature to carry comfortably a mounted knight in full armor. Yet "perfection," as C. Northcote Parkinson shrewdly noted, "is achieved only by institutions on the point of collapse." [21] Just as the new warhorse was perfected, new weapons were deployed to blast horse and knight from the battlefield. These new gunpowder weapons could be fired by commoners. They required little skill to use but were expensive to procure in quantity. Their proliferation steadily increased the importance of commerce as compared to agriculture, which had been the foundation of the feudal economy.

War at a Higher Scale

How did gunpowder weapons precipitate such a transformation? For one thing, they raised the scale of fighting, which meant that waging war soon became far more costly than it had been during the medieval period. Before the Gunpowder Revolution, wars had normally been fought by groups so small that they could be levied over a small and poor territory. Gunpowder gave a new advantage to fighting on a larger scale. Only leaders with claims on rich subjects could afford to field effective forces under the new conditions. Those leaders who best accommodated the growth of commerce, usually monarchs who allied themselves with the urban merchants, found that they enjoyed a competitive advantage on the battlefield. In van Creveld's words, "thanks in part to the superior financial resources at their disposal, they could purchase more cannon than anybody else and blast the opposition to pieces." [22]

Even though it would be centuries before the full logic of gunpowder weapons would be unleashed in the citizen armies of the French Revolution, an early hint of the transformation of warfare by gunpowder was the adoption of military uniforms in the Renaissance. The uniforms aptly symbolize the new relations between the warrior and the nation-state that went hand in hand with the transition from chivalry to citizenship. In effect, the new nation-state would strike a "uniform" bargain with its citizens, unlike the special, divergent bargains struck by the monarch or the pope with a long chain of vassals under feudalism. In the old system, everyone had a different place in an architectonic hierarchy. Everyone had a bargain as unique as his coat of arms and the colorful pennants he flew.

Lowering the Opportunity Costs of Riches

Gunpowder weapons radically altered the nature of society in yet another way. They separated the exercise of power from physical strength, thereby lowering the opportunity costs of mercantile activity. Rich merchants no longer had to depend upon their own finesse and strength in hand-to-hand combat or on mercenaries of uncertain loyalty to defend themselves. They could hope to be defended by the new, larger armies of the great monarchs. As William Playfair said of the Middle Ages, "While human force was the power by which men were annoyed, in cases of hostility, . . . [t]o be wealthy and powerful long together was then impossible." [23] When gunpowder came along, it was impossible to be powerful without being rich.

Status and Static Understanding

For many of the same reasons that most people today are ill-prepared to anticipate the new dynamics of the Information Society, the leading thinkers of medieval society were unable to anticipate or understand the rise of commerce that played so important a part in shaping the modern period. Most people five centuries ago viewed their changing society in static terms. As Huizinga said, "Very little property is, in the modern sense, liquid, while power is not yet associated predominantly with money; it is still rather inherent in the person and depends on a sort of religious awe which he inspires; it makes itself felt by pomp and magnificence, or a numerous train of faithful followers. Feudal or hierarchic thought expresses the idea of grandeur by visible signs. . . ."[24] Because people in the late Middle Ages thought before all else of status, they were ill-prepared to comprehend that merchants could possibly contribute anything of importance to the life of. the realm. Almost without exception, merchants were commoners. They fit at the bottom of the three estates, below the nobility and the clergy.

Even the more perceptive thinkers of late-medieval society failed to appreciate the importance of commerce and other forms of enterprise outside of farming for accumulating wealth. To them, poverty was an apostolic virtue. They literally made no distinction between a wealthy banker and a beggar. In Huizinga's words, "No distinction in principle was made in the third estate, between rich and poor citizens, nor between townsmen and country-people."[25] Neither occupation nor wealth mattered in their scheme, merely chivalric status.

This blindness to the economic dimension of life was reinforced by churchmen, who were the ideological guardians of medieval life. They were so far from grasping the importance of commerce that one widely applauded fifteenth-century reform program proposed that all persons of nonnoble status be required to devote themselves exclusively to handicrafts or farm labor. No role was contemplated for commerce whatsoever.[26]

"The date 1492, conventionally used to separate medieval from modern history, serves as well as any other dividing point, for in the perspective of world history, Columbus's voyage symbolizes the beginning of a new relationship between Western Europe and the rest of the world."[27]

—FREDERIC C. LANE

THE BIRTH OF THE INDUSTRIAL AGE

Many of the keenest minds of the fifteenth century totally missed one of the more important developments in history, one that began under their eyes. The eclipse of feudalism marked the onset of the great modern phase of Western predominance. It was a period of rising returns to violence and rising scale in enterprise. For the past two and a half centuries, the modern economy has delivered an unparalleled rise in living standards for that fraction of the world that enjoyed its greatest benefits. The catalysts for these changes were new technologies, from gunpowder weapons to the printing press, which changed the boundaries of life in ways that few could grasp.

By the final decade of the fifteenth century, explorers like Columbus were just beginning to open an approach to vast, unknown continents. For the first time in the immemorial ages of human existence, the whole world was compassed. Galleons, new high-masted improvisations on Mediterranean galleys, circumnavigated the globe, charting the passages that were to become trade routes and thoroughfares for disease and conquest. Conquistadors wielding their new bronze cannon on sea and on shore blasted open new horizons. They found fortunes in gold and spices, planted the seeds of new cash crops, from tobacco to potatoes, and staked out new grazing lands for their cattle.

The First Industrial Technology

Just as the cannon was opening new economic horizons, the printing press opened new intellectual horizons. It was the first machine of mass production, a signature technology that marked the onset of industrialism. In saying this, we share the view advanced by Adam Smith in *The Wealth of Nations* that the Industrial Revolution had already happened well before he wrote. It had not reached maturity, to be sure, but the principles of mass production and the factory system were well established. His famous example of the pin manufacturers makes this case. Smith explains how eighteen separate operations are employed to produce pins. Because of specialized technology and the division of labor, each employee could make 4,800 times more pins in a day than an individual could fabricate on his own.[28]

Smith's example underscores the fact that the Industrial Revolution began centuries earlier than historians conventionally assume. Most textbooks would date its origins to the middle of the eighteenth century. That is not unreasonable as a date for the takeoff stage in the improvement of living standards. But the actual megapolitical transition between feudalism and industrialism began much earlier, at the end of the fifteenth century. Its impact was felt almost immediately in the transformation of dominant institutions, particularly in the eclipse of the medieval Church.

The historians who place the Industrial Revolution later are really measuring something else, the takeoff of living standards attributable to mass production powered by engines. This raised the value of unskilled labor and led to falling prices for a wide variety of consumer goods. Indeed, the fact that living standards began to rise sharply at different times in different countries is a tip-off that something other than the megapolitical transition is being measured. The *Cambridge Economic History of Europe* speaks of "Industrial Revolutions" in the plural, explicitly linking them to the sustained growth of national incomes.[29] In Japan and Russia, this income surge was delayed until the end of the nineteenth century. The rise in living standards and sustained growth of national income in other parts of Asia and some parts of Africa was a twentieth-century phenomenon. In some parts of Africa, sustained growth remains a dream to this day. But that does not mean that these regions are not living in the modern age.

Falling Income in Transition

The growth of income is not synonymous with the advent of industrialism. The shift to an industrial society was a megapolitical event, not measurable directly in income statistics. Indeed, real incomes for most Europeans fell for the first two centuries of the Industrial Age. They only began rising sometime after the beginning of the eighteenth century, and they did not recover to levels of 1250 until about 1750. We place the launch of the Industrial Age at the end of the fifteenth century. It was the industrial features of early-modern technology, including chemically powered weapons and printing presses, that precipitated the collapse of feudalism.

Lowering the Cost of Knowledge

The capacity to mass-produce books was incredibly subversive to medieval institutions, just as microtechnology will prove subversive to the modern nation-state. Printing rapidly undermined the Church's monopoly on the word of God, even as it created a new market for heresy. Ideas inimical to the closed feudal society spread rapidly, as 10 million books were published by the final decade of the fifteenth century. Because the Church attempted to suppress the printing press, most of the new volumes were published in those areas of Europe where the writ of established authority was the weakest. This may prove to be a close analogy with attempts by the U.S. government today to suppress encryption technology. The Church found that censorship did not suppress the spread of subversive technology; it merely assured that it was put to its most subversive use.

Depreciating the Monasteries

Many apparently innocent uses of the printing press were subversive because of their content. Merely the spread of knowledge of the fortunes to be earned by intrepid adventurers and merchants was itself a powerful solvent dissolving the bonds of feudal obligation. The temptation of new markets, along with the need and opportunity to fund armies and navies on a larger scale, gave money a value it had lacked in the feudal centuries. These new avenues for investment, reinforced by powerful weapons that raised the returns to violence, made it increasingly costly to the lord in the hinterlands or the merchant in the city to donate his capital to the Church. Thus the very creation of investment opportunities outside of landholdings destabilized the institutions of feudalism and undercut its ideology.

Another subversive consequence of the printing press was its effect in dramatically lowering the costs of reproducing information. A crucial reason why literacy and economic progress had been so minimal during the Middle Ages was the high cost of duplicating manuscripts by hand. As we have seen, one of the major productive functions assumed by the Church after the fall of Rome was reproducing books and manuscripts in Benedictine monasteries. This was an extremely costly undertaking. One of the more dramatic consequences of printing was to devalue the scriptoria, where monks labored day after day, month after month to produce manuscripts that could be duplicated in hours by printing presses. The new technology made the Benedictine scriptorium an obsolete and costly means of reproducing knowledge. This, in turn, made the religious orders and the Church that sustained the scribes less economically important.

Mass production of books ended the Church's monopoly on Scripture, as well as on other forms of information. The wider availability of books reduced the cost of literacy and thus multiplied the number of thinkers who were in a position to offer their own opinions on important subjects, particularly theological subjects. As theological historian Euan Cameron put it, "[a] series of publishing milestones" in the first two decades of the sixteenth century set the groundwork for the application of "modern text criticism to Scriptures."[30] This "threatened the monopoly" of the Church "by questioning corrupt readings of texts which had been used to support traditional dogmas."[31] This new knowledge encouraged the emergence of competitive Protestant sects who sought to formulate their own interpretations of the Bible. Mass production of books lowered the cost of heresy and gave the heretics large audiences of readers.

Publishing also helped destroy the medieval worldview. The greater availability and lower costs for information led to shifts away from a view of the world linked by symbolism rather than causal connections. "Symbolism's image of the world is distinguished by impeccable order, architectonic structure, hierarchic subordination. For each symbolic connexion implies a difference of rank or sanctity. . . . The walnut signifies Christ; the sweet kernel is His divine nature, the green and pulpy outer peel is His humanity, the wooden shell between is the cross. Thus all things raise the thoughts to the eternal. . . ."[32]

A symbolic mode of thinking not only complemented a hierarchic structure of society; it also suited illiteracy. Ideas conveyed by symbols in woodcuts were accessible to an illiterate population. By contrast, the advent of printing in the modern period led to the development of causal connections, employing the scientific method, for a literate population.

A PARALLEL FOR TODAY

Medieval society, seemingly so stable and secure in its beliefs in the middle of the fifteenth century, was rapidly transformed. Its predominant institution, the Church, saw its monopoly challenged and shattered. Authority that had been unquestioned for centuries was suddenly in dispute. Beliefs and loyalties more sacred than those that bind any citizen to a nation-state today were reconsidered and renounced within a few short years, all because of a technological revolution that came into its own in the last decade of the fifteenth century.

We believe that change as dramatic as that of five hundred years ago will happen again. The Information Revolution will destroy the monopoly of power of the nation-state as surely as the Gunpowder Revolution destroyed the Church's monopoly. There is a striking analogy between the situation at the end of the fifteenth century, when life had become thoroughly saturated by organized religion, and that of today, when the world has become saturated with politics. The Church then and the nation-state today are both examples of institutions grown to a senile extreme. Like the late-medieval Church, the nation-state at the end of the twentieth century is a deeply indebted institution that can no longer pay its way. Its operations are ever more irrelevant and even counterproductive to the prosperity of those who not long ago might have been its staunchest supporters.

"Impoverished, Grasping, and Extravagant"

Just as government today offers poor value for the money it collects, so did the Church at the end of the fifteenth century. As ecclesiastical historian

Euan Cameron put it, "[A]n impoverished local priesthood seemed to offer a poor service for the money it demanded; much of what was levied effectively 'disappeared' into enclosed monasteries or the arcane areas of higher education or administration. In spite of gifts prodigally given to some sectors of the Church, the institution as a whole managed to appear simultaneously impoverished, grasping, and extravagant."[33] It would be hard to deny the parallel with late-twentieth-century government.

Religious observances in the late fifteenth century grew like programs proliferating in welfare states today. Not only did special benedictions multiply endlessly, along with the supply of saints and saints' bones, but every year there were more churches, more convents, more monasteries, more friaries, more confessors (resident household priests), more preacherships, more cathedral chapters, more endowed chantries, more relic cults, more religious co-fraternities, more religious festivals, and new holy days. Services grew longer. Prayers and hymns grew more complicated. One after another, new mendicant orders appeared to beg for alms. The result was institutional overload similar to that characterizing heavily politicized societies today.

Religious festivals and feast days proliferated on all sides. Religious services grew more numerous, with special festivals in honor of the seven sorrows of Mary, of her sisters, and of all the saints of Jesus' genealogy.[34] For the faithful to meet their religious obligations became increasingly costly and burdensome, much as the costs of remaining within the law have proliferated today.

Innocents Pay

Then as now, the productive bore a growing burden of income redistribution. These costs were rising more sharply than anyone in authority recognized because of a shift in the use of capital. The relative advantage of holding land as compared to money capital was falling. Yet the medieval mind continued to think in terms of a status-bound society, where social position was determined by who you were, rather than by your skill in deploying capital effectively. Little or no consideration was given to the rising opportunity costs of staging exaggerated religious observances. These costs fell most heavily upon the more ambitious and hardworking peasants, burghers, and yeoman farmers, who depended more than the aristocracy upon deploying their capital usefully. They were obliged to shoulder a disproportionate cost of outfitting the tables at the endless feasts and holy days (holidays), as well as paying to support an extravagant Church bureaucracy.

Counterproductive Regulation

At the end of the fifteenth century, the Church largely controlled the regulatory powers that have since been assumed by governments. The Church dominated important areas of law, recording deeds, registering marriages, probating wills, licensing trades, titling land, and stipulating terms and conditions of commerce. The details of life were almost as thoroughly regulated by canon law as they are today by bureaucracy, and to much the same end. Just as political regulation today has become riddled with confusions and contradictions, so canon law was five hundred years ago. These regulations often suppressed and complicated commerce in ways that revealed that facilitating productivity was far from the minds of the regulators.

For example; it was forbidden to do business for an entire year on whatever day of the week the most recent twenty-eighth of December happened to fall. Thus if it was a Tuesday, no legal business could be conducted on Tuesdays as an obligatory expression of piety in honor of the Slaughter of the Innocents. On years when December 28 fell on any day other than Sunday, this injunction hampered the potential for many types of commerce, increasing costs by delaying transactions or forestalling them altogether.

Monopoly Pricing

Canon law was also imposed to reinforce monopoly prices. The Church earned significant revenues from the sale of alum mined from its properties in Tolfa, Italy. When some of its customers in the textile industry showed a preference for cheaper alum imported from Turkey, the Vatican attempted to sustain its monopoly pricing through canon law, declaring it sinful to use the less costly alum. Merchants who persisted in purchasing the cheaper Turkish product were excommunicated. The famous ban on eating meat on Friday originated in the same spirit. The Church was not only the largest feudal landholder; it also held major fisheries. Church Fathers discovered a theological necessity for the pious to eat fish, which not incidentally ensured a demand for their product at a time when transport and sanitary conditions discouraged fish consumption.

Like the nation-state today, the late-medieval Church not only regulated specific industries to directly underpin its own interests; it also made the most of its regulatory powers to gain revenue for itself in other ways. Clerics went to special pains to promulgate regulations and edicts that were difficult to abide by. For example, incest was very broadly defined, so that even remote cousins and persons related only by marriage required special dispensation from the Church to marry. As this included almost everyone in many small European villages before the era of modern travel, selling waivers for incestuous marriages became a thriving source of Church revenue. Even sex within marriage itself was tightly circumscribed by ecceliastic regulation. Sexual relations between spouses were illegal on Sundays, Wednesdays, and Fridays, as well as for forty days prior to Easter and Christmas. Further, couples were to abstain from sex for three days prior to receiving communion. In other words, married couples were forbidden to enjoy sex without an indulgence for a minimum of 55 percent of the days of the year. In *The Bishop's Brothels*, historian E. J. Burford suggests that these "idiotic" regulations of marriage helped stimulate the growth of medieval prostitution, from which the Church profited mightily.[35] Burford reports that the Bishop of Winchester was for many centuries the principal of London's Bankside brothels in Southwark. Further, ecclesiastical profiteering from prostitution was by no means merely a local English affair:

> Pope Sixtus IV (c. 1471) who allegedly caught syphilis from one of his many mistresses—became the first pope to issue licences to prostitutes and to levy a tax on their earnings, augmenting vastly the papal revenues in the process. Indeed the Roman Curia partly financed the building of St. Peter's by this tax and the sale of licences. His successor, Pope Leo X, is said to have made some twenty-two thousand gold ducats through the sale of licences, four times as much as he made by selling indulgences in Germany.[36]

Even the famous rule of celibacy imposed on priests was a lucrative source of revenue for the medieval Church. As Burford reports, the Church imposed "a racket known as *cullagium*," a fee imposed upon "concubinary priests."[37] This proved so lucrative that it was imposed uniformly upon all priests by bishops in France and Germany, in spite of the fact that the Lateran Council in 1215 had denounced "this disgraceful traffic by which such prelates regularly sell permission to sin."[38] It was merely one of many lucrative markets for the sale of licenses to infringe canon law and regulation, a trade motivated by the same logic that impels grasping politicians to seek arbitrary regulatory powers over commerce.

Indulgences

The power to regulate arbitrarily is also the power to sell an exemption from the harm such regulations can do. The Church sold permits, or "indulgences," authorizing everything from relief from petty burdens on commerce to permission to eat dairy products in Lent. These "indulgences" were not only sold at high prices to the aristocracy and the rich burghers. They were also packaged as lottery prizes much like the government-run lotteries of today to attract the pennies of the poor.[39] The trade in indulgences increased as the Church's expenditures outran its income. This led many to infer the obvious, that the institutional Church was using its powers primarily to raise revenues. As a contemporary critic put it, "[C]anon law was instituted solely for the purpose of making a great deal of money; whoever would be a Christian has to buy his way out of its provisions." [40]

Bureaucratic Overload

The costs of supporting institutionalized religion at the end of the fifteenth century had reached a historic extreme, much as the costs of supporting government have reached a senile extreme today. The more life was saturated with religion, the more expensive and bureaucratic the Church became. In Cameron's words, "It was far easier to find people to fill the vastly increased number of Church posts at the end of the Middle Ages, than to find money to pay for them." [41] Just as bankrupt governments today scrounge for revenues in counterproductive ways, so did the Church five hundred years ago. Indeed, the churchmen used some of the same predatory tricks mastered by the politicians today.

The medieval Church five hundred years ago, like the nation-state today, consumed more of society's resources than it ever had before, or ever would again. The Church then, like the state today, seemed incapable of functioning and sustaining itself on even record amounts of revenue. Just as the state has come to dominate late-industrial economies, spending more than half of all revenue in some Western European countries, so the Church dominated the late-feudal economy, draining resources and retarding growth.

Deficit Spending in the Fifteenth Century

The Church resorted to every conceivable expedient to squeeze more money out of its charges to feed its overgrown bureaucracy. Regions directly under the lordship of the Church were required to pay higher and higher taxes. In provinces and kingdoms where the Church lacked direct taxing power, the Vatican imposed "annates," a payment to be made by the local sovereign in lieu of direct ecclesiastic taxes.

The Church, like the state today, also raided its own coffers, diverting funds from benefactions earmarked for specific uses to pay for general overhead expenses. Benefices and venal religious offices were openly sold, as were the income streams from tithes. In effect, the interests in tithes became the ecclesiastic equivalent of bonds issued by modern governments to finance their chronic deficits.

While the Church was the ideological defender of feudalism and critic of commerce and capitalism, like the nation-state today, it utilized every available marketing technique to optimize its own revenues. The Church operated a thriving business in the sale of sacramentals, including consecrated candles, palms blessed on Palm Sunday, "herbs blessed on the Feast of the Assumption, and especially the varieties of Holy Water." [42]

Like today's politicians who threaten constituents with curtailed garbage pickup and other indignities if they decline to pay higher taxes, religious authorities in the fifteenth century were also prone to cutting off religious services to blackmail congregations into paying arbitrary fines. Often the fines were imposed for some petty offense done by a few persons who need not even have been members of the congregation in question. For example, in 1436, Bishop Jacques Du Chatelier, "a very ostentatious, grasping man," closed the Church of the Innocents in Paris for twenty-two days, halting all religious services while waiting for an impossibly large fine to be paid by two beggars. The men had quarreled in the church and shed a few drops of blood, which the bishop claimed had deconsecrated the church. He would not allow anyone to use the church for weddings, burials, or the normal sacraments of the calendar until his fine was paid. [43]

> *The Italian Stewes (to make the Pope good cheer)*
> *payd twentie thousand Duckets in a yeere.*
> *Besides they give a Priest (t'amend his fee)*
> *the profit of a whore, or two or three. . . .*
> *Methinkes it must be a bad Divintie*
> *that with the Stewes hath such affinitie.* [44]

—Fifteenth-century English ballad

Hatred of Church Leaders

Little wonder that the common opinion of the late fifteenth century despised the higher and lower clergy, much as common opinion in highly politicized societies today despises the bureaucracy and politicians. As Johan Huizinga put it, "Hatred is the right word to use in this context, for hatred it was, latent, but general and persistent. The people never wearied of hearing the vices of the clergy arraigned." [45] Part of the reason that people were commonly convinced that the Church was "grasping and extravagant" is that it was true. "The worldliness of the higher ranks of the clergy and the deterioration of the lower grades" [46] were too obvious to miss. From the parish priest to the pope himself, the clergy appeared to be corrupt as only the personnel of a predominant institution can be.

Five hundred years ago, the pope, Alexander VI, made even Giulio Andreotti and Bill Clinton seem like exemplars of integrity. Alexander VI was known for his wild parties. As a cardinal in Siena, he staged a famous orgy to which only "Siena's most beautiful young women had been invited, but their 'husbands, fathers, and brothers' had been excluded."[47] The Siena orgy was famous, but it later proved to be tame compared to those Alexander threw after becoming pope. Perhaps the most lurid of those was the so-called Ballet of the Chestnuts, which involved Rome's "fifty most beautiful whores" in a copulation contest with the Church Fathers and other important Romans. As William Manchester describes it, "Servants kept score of each man's orgasms, for the pope greatly admired virility. . . . After everyone was exhausted, His Holiness distributed prizes—cloaks, boots, caps, and fine silken tunics. The winners, the diarist wrote, were those who made love with those courtesans the greatest number of times."[48]

Alexander fathered at least seven and perhaps eight illegitimate children. One of his apparent sons, Giovanni, was the so-called Infans Romanus, born to Alexander's illegitimate daughter, Lucrezia Borgia, when she was eighteen. In a secret papal bull, Alexander admitted fathering Giovanni. If he was not the father, he was certainly the grandfather on both sides. The pope was involved in a three-way incestuous affair with Lucrezia, who was also the mistress of Juan, duke of Gandia, Alexander's oldest illegitimate son, as well as the mistress of another illegitimate son, Cardinal Cesare Borgia. Cesare was the prince of the Church who served as Niccolò Machiavelli's inspiration for *The Prince.* Cesare was a killer, as was the pope, who was known to have plotted several murders. One or the other of them apparently became jealous of Juan, whose lifeless body was fished out of the Tiber River on June 15, 1497.[49]

The leadership of the late-medieval Church was as corrupt as the leadership of the nation-state today.

"Today I have twice become a father. God's blessing on it."[50]

—RODOLPH AGRICOLA, on hearing that his concubine
had given birth to a son on the day he was elected abbot

HYPOCRISY

Beneath a "superficial crust of piety," late-medieval society was remarkably blasphemous, irreverent, and debauched. Churches were the favorite trysting places of young men and women, and frequent gathering spots of prostitutes and vendors of obscene pictures. Historians report that "the irreverence of daily religious practice was almost unbounded."[51] Choristers hired to chant for the souls of the dead commonly substituted profane words in the mass. Vigils and processions, which played a far bigger role in medieval religious practice than they do today, were nonetheless "disgraced by ribaldry, mockery and drinking." So said late-medieval Europe's leading theological authority, Denis the Carthusian.[52]

While such a report could be challenged as the griping of a stiff-lipped moralist, it is merely one of many accounts that paint the same picture. There is ample reason to believe that the bawdy and the sacred were frequently close companions in medieval life. Pilgrimages, for example, so often degenerated into riot and debauchery that high-minded reformers argued without success that they be suppressed. Local religious processions also provided regular occasions for mobs to vandalize, loot, and generally indulge in whatever drunken antics caught their fancy. Even when people sat still to hear mass, it was frequently not a sober experience. Prodigious quantities of wine were consumed in church, especially on festival nights. Accounts from the Council of Strasbourg show that those who "watched in prayer" on St. Adolphus Night drank 1,100 liters of wine provided by the council in honor of the saint.

Jean Gerson, a leading fifteenth-century theologian, reports that "the most sacred festivals, even Christmas night," were spent "in debauchery, playing at cards, swearing and blaspheming." When admonished for these lapses, the common people "plead the example of the nobility and the clergy, who behave in like manner with impunity."[53]

Piety and Compassion

The piety that rationalized the saturation of society by organized religion in the late Middle Ages served the same purpose as the "compassion" that is meant to justify the political domination of life today. The sale of indulgences to satisfy a desire for piety without morals parallels lavish welfare spending to slake the pretense of compassion without charity. It was largely immaterial whether the actual effect of received practices was to improve moral character or save souls, just as it is largely immaterial whether a welfare program actually improves the lives of the people to whom it is directed. "Piety," like "compassion," was an almost superstitious invocation.

In a time when causal relationships were scarcely understood, rituals and sacraments of the Church permeated every phase of life. ". . . A journey, a task, a visit, were equally attended by a thousand formalities: benedictions, ceremonies, formulas."[54] Prayers inscribed on pieces of parchment were strung like necklaces on those suffering from fevers. Malnourished girls draped locks of their hair in front of the image of St. Urban to prevent further hair loss. Peasants in Navarre marched in processions behind an image of St. Peter to solicit rain during droughts.[55] People eagerly adopted these and other "ineffective techniques to allay anxiety when effective ones were not available." [56]

Two Wrongs to Make a Rite

People were so firmly convinced of the miraculous qualities attaching to the relics of saints that the death of any notably pious person frequently occasioned a mad rush to divide up the body. After Thomas Aquinas died in the monastery of Fossanuova, the monks there decapitated and boiled his body in order to secure control of his bones. When St. Elizabeth of Hungary was lying in state, "a crowd of worshippers came and cut or tore strips of the linen enveloping her face; they cut off the hair, the nails, even the nipples." [57]

Piety Without Virtue

The medieval mind saw the saints and their relics as part of the arsenal of faith in a world that was colder in winter, darker at night, and more desperate in the face of disease than any reader of this book will have been likely to know. More emphatically than in the modern period, people in the Middle Ages believed that demons were real, that God actively intervened in the world, and that prayer, penance, and pilgrimages earned divine favor.

To say simply that people believed in God could convey neither the intensity of their adherence nor the apparent ease with which medieval piety seemed to bed down with sin. Belief in the efficacy of rites, rituals, and sacraments was so pervasive that it perhaps inevitably undercut the urgency of behaving in a virtuous way. For any sin or spiritual defect there was a remedy, a penance that would clear the slate, in what came to be a "mathematics of salvation." [58] Religion became so all-pervasive that its sincerity necessarily began to flag. As Huizinga put it, "Religion penetrating all relations in life means a constant blending of the spheres of holy and of profane thought. Holy things will become too common to be deeply felt." [59] And so it was.

DOWNSIZING THE CHURCH

By the end of the fifteenth century, the Church was not only as corrupt as the nation-state today; it was also a major drag on economic growth. The Church engrossed large amounts of capital in unproductive ways, imposing burdens that limited the output of society and suppressed commerce. These burdens, like those imposed by the nation-state today, were numerous. We know what happened to organized religion in the wake of the Gunpowder Revolution: it created strong incentives to downsize religious institutions and lower their costs. When the traditional Church declined to do this, Protestant sects seized the opportunity to compete. In so doing they employed almost every device imaginable to reduce the cost of living a pious life:

- They built spare new churches and sometimes stripped the altars of older ones to free capital for other uses.
- They revised Christian doctrine in ways that lowered costs, emphasizing faith over good deeds as a key to salvation.
- They developed a new, terse liturgy, pared or eliminated feast days, and abolished numerous sacraments.
- They closed monasteries and nunneries, and stopped giving alms to mendicant orders. Poverty went from being an apostolic virtue to an unwelcome and often blameworthy social problem.[60]

To understand how downsizing the Church liberated productivity, you have to review the many ways that the Church stood in the way of growth before its monopoly was broken. Much as the nation-state does today, the Church at the end of the fifteenth century imposed an incredible burden of excess costs.

1. Direct costs such as tithes, taxes, and fees fed the overgrown ecclesiastical bureaucracy. Tithes were common to Protestant churches that replaced the medieval "Holy Mother Church" also, but they tended not to be collectible in urban areas. In effect, the end of the Church's monopoly led to declining marginal tax rates in regions with the most highly developed commerce.

2. Religious doctrines made saving difficult. The arch-villain of the medieval Church was the "miser," the person who saved his gold at the risk of his soul. The requirement for the faithful to fund "good deeds" entailed costly contributions to the Church. The doctrine of "satisfactions" obliged those concerned about salvation to endow masses or "chantries" in order to avoid purgatory. Luther attacked this directly in the eighth and thirteenth of his ninety-five theses. He wrote that "the dying will pay all their debts by their death."[61] In other words, the capital of the Protestant believer was available to pass on to his heirs. Under Protestant doctrine, there was no need to endow chantries to repeat masses, usually for thirty years, and sometimes, for the very wealthy, in perpetuity.

3. The ideology of the medieval Church also encouraged diversion of capital into acquisition of relics. Numerous relic cults were endowed with

large sums to acquire physical objects associated with Christ or various saints. The very wealthy even assembled personal collections of relics. For example, the Elector Frederick of Saxony amassed a collection of nineteen thousand relics, some acquired on a pilgrimage to Jerusalem in 1493. His collection included what he believed to be "the body of a holy innocent, Mary's milk, and straw from the stable of the Nativity." [62] Presumably, the return on capital invested in these relics was low. The shift to an emphasis on faith and the notion of the elect downgraded the importance of acquisition of the trappings of Christian life for use as charms and encouraged money to find more productive channels that paid a return that the monarch could tap.

4. The advent of Protestant denominations broke the medieval Church's economic monopolies, and led to a significant weakening of regulation. As we have seen, canon law was frequently bent to support Church monopolies and commercial interests. Because the new denominations had fewer economic interests to protect and promote, their version of religious doctrine tended to result in a freer system, with fewer inhibitions of commerce.

5. The Protestant revolution abolished many of the rites and rituals of the medieval Church that burdened the time of the faithful. Rites, sacraments, and holy days had been elaborated to absorb almost the entire calendar by the late fifteenth century. This ceremonial overload was a logical outgrowth of the Church's insistence "that one could multiply acts of prayer or worship as often as one liked and gain benefits from them." [63] Multiply they did. Productivity was taxed by longer and more elaborate services, obligations to recite repetitious prayers in penance, and the proliferation of feast days of saints during which no work could be done. Numerous regulations and ceremonies punctuated the day and the seasons, considerably shrinking the time available for productive tasks. This may have done little to interrupt the rhythms of medieval farming, in which 90 percent or more of the population was engaged. There were many periods during the seasons when field labor was not required on a daily basis. The yield of crops under medieval conditions probably varied more with the weather and uncontrollable rhythms of infestation than from any marginal addition of labor beyond the minimum that the Church calendar accommodated.

The larger problem of lost productivity did not fall so much in farming as in other areas. The Church's demands on time were far less compatible with craft work, manufacturing, transport, commerce, or any other undertaking where productivity and profitability were likely to be crucially determined by the amount of time devoted to the task.

It may not be a coincidence that the great transition at the end of the fifteenth century occurred at a time when land rents were rising and real wages for the peasantry were in decline. Increased population pressures had reduced the yield from the common lands, often found surrounding rivers and streams, upon which peasants depended to graze their livestock, and in some cases, for fish and firewood. The whittling down of living standards placed increasingly urgent pressures on peasants to find alternative sources of income. As a result, "more and more of the rural population turned to small-scale manufacturing for the market, above all in textiles, in the process known as 'putting-out' or 'proto-industrialization.' "[64] The ceremonial burdens on time imposed by the Church stood in the way of efforts by the more ambitious peasants to supplement their farming income by craft work, as indeed they inhibited any redeployment of effort in new economic directions.

One of the more pronounced contributions that Protestant sects made to productivity was the scrapping of forty feast days. This not only saved the considerable costs of staging the festivals, including outfitting the village tables with food and drink; it also freed a great deal of valuable time. Implicitly, everyone who stopped honoring the forty banished feast days could add three hundred man-hours or more to his annual productivity. In short, the scrapping of ceremonial overload in the medieval Church opened the way for an appreciable increase in output simply by freeing time that would otherwise have been lost to commerce.

6. The break in the Church's monopoly disgorged vast amounts of assets that were yielding low returns under Church management—a situation with obvious parallels to state holdings late in the twentieth century. The Church was the largest feudal landholder by far. Its grip on the land matched that of the state in highly politicized societies today—exceeding 50 percent of the total in some European countries such as Bohemia. According to canon law, once a property came under the control of the Church, it could not be alienated. Thus the holdings of Church land tended steadily to rise, as the Church received more and more testamentary gifts from the faithful for financing various social welfare services, chantries, and other activities.

While it is difficult to measure precisely the relative productivity of Church holdings, it must have been far lower at the end of the Middle Ages than it was in the early part of that epoch. By the fourteenth century, increased emphasis upon production for the market rather than subsistence farming had led most lay lords to turn from illiterate headmen to professional managers to optimize the output of their holdings. Their incentives probably led them to quickly outstrip the output of Church properties, which in theory usually did not accrue to anyone's private profit. No doubt some of the more worldly prince-bishops husbanded their estates in ways indistinguishable from those of the lay lords. Yet the productivity of other Church properties would surely have suffered from failures of indifferent management by a huge, far-flung institution, whose drawbacks would have been similar to the drawbacks of state and communal ownership today. It is obvious, as well, that the seizure of the monasteries rearrayed resources that were no longer needed for the reproduction of books and manuscripts after the advent of the printing press.

7. As we detailed in *The Great Reckoning,* some of the Protestant sects immediately responded to the Gunpowder Revolution by altering their doctrines in ways that encouraged commerce, such as by lifting the injunction against usury, or lending at interest. The ideological opposition of the medieval Church to capitalism was a drag on growth. The main ideological thrust of Church teachings was to reinforce feudalism, in which the Church had a large stake, as the largest feudal landholder. Consciously, or not, the Church tended to make religious virtues of its own economic interests, while militating against the development of manufacturing and independent commercial wealth that were destined to destabilize the feudal system. Injunctions against "avarice," for example, applied mainly to commercial transactions rather than feudal levies, and never to the sale of indulgences. The infamous attempts by the Church to fix a "just price" for items in commerce tended to suppress economic returns on those products and services where the Church itself was not a producer.

The ban on "usury" was a signal example of the Church's resistance to commercial innovation. Banking and credit were crucial to the development of larger-scale commercial enterprises. By restricting the availability of credit, the Church retarded growth.

8. More subtly, the new denominations' focus upon the Bible as a text helped demolish the medieval Church's mode of thought as well as its ideology. Both placed obstacles in the way of growth. The cultural programming of the late Middle Ages encouraged people to see the world in terms of symbolic similitude rather than cause and effect. This short-circuited reasoning. It also pointed away from a mercantile conception of life. Thinking in terms of symbolic equivalences does not easily translate into thinking in terms of market values. "The three estates represent the qualities of the Virgin. The seven electors of the Empire signify the virtues; the five towns of Artois and Hainault, which in 1477 remained faithful to the house of Burgundy, are the five wise virgins. . . . In the same way shoes mean care and diligence, stockings perseverance, the garter resolution, etc." [65] As this example quoted from the distinguished medieval historian Johan Huizinga suggests, thinking was dominated by dogma, rigid symbols, and allegory that tied together every aspect of life in terms of hierarchic subordination. Every occupation, every part, every color, every number, even every element of grammar was tied into a grand system of religious conceptions.

Thus the mundane bits and pieces of life were interpreted not in terms of their causal connections, but in terms of static symbols and allegories. Sometimes personifying virtues and vices, each thing stood for something, which stood for something else again, in ways that often blocked rather than clarified cause and effect. To confuse matters further, relationships were often arbitrarily bound together in systems of numbers. Sevens played a particularly important role. There were the seven virtues, the seven deadly sins, the seven supplications of the Lord's Prayer, the seven Gifts of the Holy Spirit, the seven moments of the passion, the seven beatitudes, and the seven sacraments, "represented by the seven animals and followed by the seven diseases." [66]

Fifteenth-Century Journalism

A fifteenth-century news story, if it had been written, would not have answered any of the classic questions of reporting facts, except indirectly through allegoric personification. Consider this report, in a private diary, of the Burgundian murders in fifteenth-century Paris:

> Then arose the goddess of Discord, who lived in the tower of Evil Counsel, and awoke Wrath, the mad woman, and Covetousness and Rage and Vengeance, and they took up arms of all sorts and cast out Reason, Justice, Remembrance of God, and Moderation most shamefully. Then Madness them enraged, and Murder and Slaughter killed, cut down, put to death, massacred all they found in the prisons. . . . and Covetousness tucked up her skirts into her belt with Rapine, her daughter, and Larceny, her son. . . . Afterward, the aforesaid people went by guidance of their goddesses, that is to say, Wrath, Covetousness, and Vengeance, who led them through all the public prisons of Paris, etc.[67]

The shift away from the medieval paradigm helped prepare people to think in "modern" terms about cause and effect, rather than in terms of symbolic linkages and allegoric personification.

It is not necessary to argue that the doctrine and mode of thinking of the late-medieval Church were insincere to see that they tended to fit closely with the needs of agrarian feudalism, while allowing very little place for commerce, much less industrial development. It was rather a case of the Church as a predominant institution shaping moral, cultural, and legal constraints in ways that were closely fitted to the imperatives of feudalism. For this very reason, they were ill-suited to the needs of industrial society, just as the moral, cultural, and legal constraints of the modern nation-state are ill-suited to facilitating commerce in the Information Age. We believe that the state will be revolutionized, just as the Church was, to facilitate the realization of the new potential.

The Protestant doctrine that heaven could be attained by faith alone and without the benefit of endowed prayers for the dead was cast as a theological issue. Yet it was theology to fit the economic realities of a new age. It met the obvious need for a more cost-effective path to salvation at a time when the opportunity costs of sinking additional capital into the bloated ecclesiastical bureaucracy had suddenly risen. People had minded less giving their money to the Church when there was no other outlet for it. But when they suddenly saw the chance to make one hundred times their capital financing a spice voyage to the East, or get a lesser, but still promising sum of 40 percent per annum financing a battalion for the king, they understandably sought the grace of God where their own interests lay.

Many merchants and other commoners soon became far richer than their forebears had been under feudalism. The sharp acceleration of living standards among the merchants and small manufacturers of the early-modern period was widely unpopular among those whose incomes and way of life were collapsing with feudalism. The weakening of the Church's monopoly and the increased megapolitical power of the rich led to a sharp reduction in income redistribution. The peasants and urban poor who were not immediate beneficiaries of the new system were bitterly envious of those who were. Huizinga described the prevailing attitude, in what could well be an important parallel with the Information Revolution: "Hatred of rich people, especially of the new rich, who were then very numerous, is general." [68]

An equally striking parallel arose from a tremendous surge in crime. The breakdown of the old order almost always unleashes a surge in crime, if not the outright anarchy of the feudal revolution we explored in the last chapter. At the end of the Middle Ages, crime also skyrocketed as the old systems of social control broke down. In Huizinga's words, "[C]rime came to be regarded as a menace to order and society." [69] It could be equally menacing in the future.

The modern world was born in the confusion of new technologies, new ideas, and the stench of black powder. Gunpowder weapons and improved shipping destabilized the military foundation of feudalism, even as new communications technology undermined its ideology. Among the elements that the new technology of printing helped reveal was the corruption of the Church, whose hierarchy as well as rank and file were already held in low regard by a society that paradoxically placed religion at the center of everything. It is a paradox with an obvious contemporary parallel in the disillusionment with politicians and bureaucrats, in a society that places politics at the center of everything.

The end of the fifteenth century was a time of disillusion, confusion, pessimism, and despair. A time much like now.

CHAPTER 5

THE LIFE AND DEATH OF THE NATION-STATE

Democracy and Nationalism as Resource Strategies in the Age of Violence

"Most important of all, success in war depends on having enough money to provide whatever the enterprise needs."[1]

—ROBERT DE BALSAC, 1502

THE RUBBLE OF HISTORY

On November 9 and 10, 1989, television broadcast to the world scenes of exuberant East Berliners dismantling the Berlin Wall with sledgehammers. Fledgling entrepreneurs among the crowd picked up pieces of the wall that were later marketed to capitalists far and wide as souvenir paperweights. A brisk business in these relics was done for years thereafter. Even as we write, one can still encounter occasional ads in small magazines offering bits of old East German concrete for sale at prices ordinarily commanded by high-grade silver ore. We believe that those who bought the Berlin Wall paperweights should be in no rush to sell. They hold mementos of something bigger than the collapse of Communism. We believe that the Berlin Wall became the most important pile of historical rubble since the walls of San Giovanni were blasted to smithereens almost five centuries earlier in February 1495.[2]

The leveling of San Giovanni by the French king Charles VIII was the first blast of the Gunpowder Revolution. It marked the end of the feudal phase of history and the advent of industrialism, as we outlined earlier. The destruction of the Berlin Wall marks another historical watershed, the passage between the Industrial Age and the new Information Age. Never has there been so great a symbolic triumph of efficiency over power. When the walls of San Giovanni fell, it was a stark demonstration that the economic returns to violence in the world had risen sharply. The fall of the Berlin Wall says something different, namely that returns to violence are now falling. This is something that few have even begun to recognize, but it will have dramatic consequences.

For reasons we explore in this chapter, the Berlin Wall may prove to be far more symbolic of the whole era of the industrial nation-state than those in the crowd that night in Berlin or the millions watching from a distance understood. The Berlin Wall was built to a very different purpose than the walls of San Giovanni—to prevent people on the inside from escaping rather than to prevent predators on the outside from entering. That fact alone is a telling indicator of the rise in the power of the state from the fifteenth to the twentieth centuries. And in more ways than one.

For centuries, the nation-state made all outward-facing walls redundant and unnecessary. The level of monopoly that the state exercised over coercion in those areas where it first took hold made them both more peaceful internally and more formidable militarily than any sovereignties the world had seen before. The state used the resources extracted from a largely disarmed population to crush small-scale predators. The nation-state became history's most successful instrument for seizing resources. Its success was based upon its superior ability to extract the wealth of its citizens.

"MTV is more than a purveyor of music videos—and a promotional tool of the recording industry. It's the first truly global network, the first network to deliver a single stream of programming in virtually every country in the world. In the process, MTV is creating a single sense of shared global reality for its viewers, children and young adults. Recent research has found that young people around the planet more and more share not just common pop icons and common tastes, but common expectations for their careers, common sets of values about what is meaningful in life and what there is to be afraid of, a

common sense that politics is less important than their own abilities in shaping their futures."[3]

—JIM TAYLOR AND WATTS WACKER, *The 500-Year Delta:*
What Happens After What Comes Next

"Love It or Leave It" (Unless You Are Rich)

Before the transition from the nation-state to the new sovereignties of the Information Age is complete, many residents of the largest and most powerful Western nation-states, like their counterparts in East Berlin in 1989, will be plotting to find their way out. For the generations that came of age before World War II, or early in the Cold War, moving across borders is traumatic. But for new generations, who draw their bearings from a more global perspective, abandoning the country of their birth is not the unthinkable decision it would be for older persons who are more deeply inculcated with the ideology of the nation-state. Jim Taylor and Watts Wacker report the intriguing results of a mass survey of 25,000 middle-class high school students on five continents. In a sampling conducted during the 1995–96 school year by Brainwaves Group, a New York consumer-research firm, nine of ten students agreed that "it's up to me to get what I want of life." More strikingly, "almost half the teens said they expected to leave the country of their birth in pursuit of their goals."[4] Perhaps because he is tuned in to the attitudes of the MTV generation, as the first presidential candidate to campaign on MTV, Bill Clinton has sought to make it more difficult for Americans to "leave the country of their birth in pursuit of their goals." In 1995, at about the same time that the high school students were declaring their intentions to seek independence, the President of the United States proposed the enactment of an exit tax, a "Berlin Wall for Capital," that would require wealthy Americans to pay a substantial ransom to escape with even part of their money.

Clinton's ransom is not only reminiscent of the late East German state's policy of treating its citizens as assets; it also calls to mind the increasingly draconian measures taken to shore up the fiscal position of the Roman Empire in decline. This passage from *The Cambridge Ancient History* tells the story.

> Thus began the fierce endeavor of the State to squeeze the population to the last drop. Since economic resources fell short of what was needed, the strong fought to secure the chief share for themselves with a violence and unscrupulousness well in keeping with the origin of those in power and with a soldiery accustomed to plunder. The full rigour of the law was let loose on the popula-

tion. Soldiers acted as bailiffs or wandered as secret police through the land. Those who suffered most were, of course, the propertied class. It was relatively easy to lay hands on their property, and in an emergency, they were the class from whom something could be extorted most frequently and quickly.[5]

When failing systems have the power to do so, they often impose penal burdens upon those seeking to escape. Again, we quote *The Cambridge Ancient History:* "If the propertied class buried their money, or sacrificed two-thirds of their estate to escape from a magistracy, or went so far as to give up their whole property in order to get free of the domains rent, and the non-propertied class ran away, the State replied by increasing the pressure."

This is worth remembering as you plan ahead. The twilight of state systems in the past has seldom been a polite, orderly process. We mentioned the nasty habits of Roman tax collectors in Chapter 2. The large numbers of *agri deserti,* or abandoned farms, in Western Europe after the collapse of the Roman Empire reflected only a small part of a wider problem. In fact, exactions tended to be relatively mild in Gaul, and in the frontier areas that comprise current-day Luxembourg and Germany. In Rome's most fertile region, Egypt, where farming was more productive because of irrigation, desertion by owners was an even bigger problem. The question of whether to attempt escape, the *ultimum refugium,* as it was known in Latin, became the overriding quandary of almost everyone with property. Records show that "among the common questions which used to be put to an oracle in Egypt three standard types were: 'Am I to become a beggar?' 'Shall I take to flight?' and 'Is my flight to be stopped?' "[6]

Clinton's proposal says yes. It is an early version of an obstacle to escape that is likely to grow more onerous as the fiscal resources of the nation-state slip away. Of course, the first U.S. version of an exit barrier is more benign than Erich Honecker's concrete and barbed wire. It also involves greater price sensitivity, with the burden falling only on "billionaires" with taxable estates above $600,000. Nonetheless, it was justified with similar arguments to those once propounded by Honecker in defense of the late German Democratic Republic's most famous public works project. Honecker claimed that the East German state had a substantial investment in would-be refugees. He pointed out that allowing them to leave freely would create an economic disadvantage for the state, which required their efforts in East Germany.

If you accept the premise that people are or ought to be assets of the state, Honecker's wall made sense. Berlin without a wall was a loophole to the Communists, just as escape from U.S. tax jurisdiction was a loophole to Clinton's IRS. Clinton's arguments about escaping billionaires, aside from showing a politician's usual disregard for the integrity of numbers, were similar in kind to Honecker's, but somewhat less logical because the U.S. government, in fact, does not have a large economic investment in wealthy citizens who might seek to flee. It is not a question of their having been educated at state expense and wanting to slip away and practice law somewhere else. The overwhelming majority of those to whom the exit tax would apply have created their wealth by their own efforts and in spite of, not because of, the U.S. government.

With the top 1 percent of taxpayers paying 30.2 percent of the total income tax in the United States (1995), it is not a question of the rich failing to repay any genuine investment the state may have made in their education or economic prosperity. To the contrary. Those who pay most of the bills pay vastly more than the value of any benefits they receive. With an average annual tax payment exceeding $125,000, taxes cost the top 1 percent of American taxpayers far more than they now realize. Assuming they could earn even a 10 percent return on the excess tax paid by each over a forty-year period, each $5,000 of annual excess tax payment reduced their net worth by $2.2 million. At a 20 percent rate of return, each $5,000 of excess tax reduces net worth by $44 million.

As the millennium approaches, the new megapolitical conditions of the Information Age will make it increasingly obvious that the nation-state inherited from the industrial era is a predatory institution. With each year that passes, it will seem less a boon to prosperity and more an obstacle, one from which the individual will want an escape. It is an escape that desperate governments will be loath to allow. The stability and even the survival of Western welfare states depends upon their ability to continue extracting a huge fraction of the world's total output for redistribution to a subset of voters in the OECD countries. This requires that the taxes imposed upon the most productive citizens of the currently rich countries be priced at supermonopoly rates, hundreds or even thousands of times higher than the actual cost of the services that governments provide in return.

THE LIFE AND DEATH OF THE NATION-STATE

The fall of the Berlin Wall was more than just a visible symbol of the death of Communism. It was a defeat for the entire world system of nation-states and a triumph of efficiency and markets. The fulcrum of power underlying history has shifted. We believe that the fall of the Berlin Wall in 1989 culminates the era of the nation-state, a peculiar two-hundred-year phase in history that began with the French Revolution. States have existed for six thousand years. But before the nineteenth century, they accounted for only a small fraction of the world's sovereignties. Their ascendancy began and ended in revolution. The great events of 1789 launched Europe on a course toward truly national governments. The great events of 1989 marked the death of Communism and an assertion of control by market forces over massed power. Those two revolutions, exactly two hundred years apart, define the era in which the nation-state predominated in the Great Power system. The Great Powers, in turn, dominated the world, spreading or imposing state systems on even the most remote tribal enclave.

The triumph of the state as the principal vehicle for organizing violence in the world was not a matter of ideology. It was necessitated by the hidden logic of violence. It was, as we like to say, a megapolitical event, determined not so much by the wishes of theorists and statesmen, or even by the maneuvering of generals, as by the hidden leverage of violence, which moved history in the way that Archimedes once dreamt of moving the world.

States have been the norm for the past two hundred years of the modern period. But in the longer sweep of history, states have been rare. They have always depended upon extraordinary megapolitical conditions for their viability. Prior to the modern period, most states were "Oriental despotisms," agricultural societies in deserts dependent upon control of irrigation systems for their survival. Even the Roman Empire, through its control of Egypt and North Africa, was indirectly a hydraulic society. But not enough of one to survive. Rome, like most premodern states, ultimately lacked the capacity to compel adherence to the monopoly of violence that the ability to starve people provides. The Roman state outside of Africa could not cut off water for growing crops by denying unsubmissive people access to the irrigation system. Such hydraulic systems supplied more leverage to violence than any other megapolitical configuration in the ancient economy. Whoever controlled the water in these societies could extract spoils at a level almost comparable to the percentage of total output absorbed by modern nation-states.[7]

Magnitude over Efficiency

Gunpowder enabled states to expand more easily outside the confines of rice paddies and arid river valleys. The nature of gunpowder weapons and the character of the industrial economy created great advantages of scale in warfare. This led to high and rising returns to violence. As historian Charles Tilly put it, "[S]tates having the largest coercive means tended to win wars; efficiency (the ratio of output to input) came second to effectiveness (total output)."[8] With governments mostly organized on a large scale, even the few small sovereignties that survived, like Monaco or Andorra, needed the recognition of the larger states to ensure their independence. Only big governments with ever-greater command of resources could compete on the battlefield.

The Great Unanswered Question

This brings us to one of the great unanswered puzzles of modern history: why the Cold War that came at the conclusion of the Great Power system pitted as its final contenders Communist dictatorships against democratic welfare states. This issue has been so little examined that it actually seemed plausible to many when a State Department analyst, Francis Fukuyama, proclaimed "the end of history" after the Berlin Wall fell. The enthusiastic audience his work elicited took too much for granted. Apparently neither the author nor many others had bothered to ask a fundamental question: What common characteristics of state socialism and welfare-state democracies led them to be the final contenders for world domination?

This is an important issue. After all, dozens of contending systems of sovereignty have come and gone in the past five centuries, including absolute monarchies, tribal enclaves, prince-bishoprics, direct rule by the pope, sultanates, city-states, and Anabaptist colonies. Today, most people would be surprised to learn that a hospital management company, with its own armed forces, could rule a country for centuries. Yet something very like that happened. For three hundred years after 1228, the Teutonic Knights of St. Mary's Hospital at Jerusalem, later united with the Knights of the Sword of Livonia, ruled East Prussia and various territories in Eastern Europe, including parts of Lithuania and Poland. Then came the Gunpowder Revolution. Within decades, the Teutonic Knights were expelled as sovereigns of all their territories and their Grand Master was of no more military importance than a chess champion. Why? Why did so many other systems of sovereignty dwindle to insignificance while the great struggle for world power at the end of the Industrial Age saw mass democracies lined up against state socialist systems?

Unimpeded Control

Our theory of megapolitics points to the answer. It is rather like asking why sumo wrestlers tend to be fat. The answer is that a lean sumo wrestler, however impressive his ratio of strength to weight, cannot compete with another wrestler who is gigantic. As Tilly suggests, the important issue was "effectiveness (total output)," not "efficiency (the ratio of output to input)." In an increasingly violent world, the systems that predominated through five centuries of competition were necessarily those that facilitated the greatest access to resources needed to make war on a large scale.

How did this work?

In the case of Communism, the answer is obvious. Under Communism, those who controlled the state controlled almost everything. If you had been a citizen of the Soviet Union during the Cold War, the KGB could have taken your toothbrush if they had thought it useful for their purposes to do so. They could have taken your teeth. According to credible estimates that have become more credible since the opening of former Soviet archives in 1992, secret police and other agents of the late Soviet state took the lives of 50 million persons in seventy-four years of rule. The state socialist system was in a position to mobilize anything that existed within its boundaries for its military, with little likelihood that anyone living there would argue.

In the case of Western democracies, the story is less obvious, partly because we are accustomed to think of democracy in stark contrast to Communism. In terms of the Industrial Age, the two systems were indeed great opposites. But seen from the perspective of the Information Age, the two systems had more in common than you might suspect. Both facilitated unimpeded control of resources by government. The difference was that the democratic welfare state placed even greater resources in the hands of the state than the state socialist systems.

This is a clear-cut example of a rare phenomenon, less being more. The state socialist system was predicated upon the doctrine that the state owned everything. The democratic welfare state, by contrast, made more modest claims, and thereby employed superior incentives to mobilize greater output. Instead of laying claim to everything in the beginning, governments in the West allowed individuals to own property and accumulate wealth. Then, after the wealth had been accumulated, the Western nation-states taxed a large fraction of it away. Property taxes, income taxes, and estate taxes at high levels furnished the democratic welfare state with prodigious quantities of resources compared to those available through the state socialist systems.

Inefficiency, Where It Counted

Compared to Communism, the welfare state was indeed a far more efficient system. But compared to other systems for accumulating wealth, such as a genuine laissez-faire enclave like colonial Hong Kong, the welfare state was inefficient. Again, less was more. It was precisely this inefficiency that made the welfare state supreme during the megapolitical conditions of the Industrial Age.

When you come to understand why, you are much closer to recognizing what the fall of the Berlin Wall and the death of Communism really mean. Far from assuring that the democratic welfare state will be a triumphant system, as has been widely assumed, it was more like seeing that a fraternal twin has died of old age. The same megapolitical revolution that killed Communism is also likely to undermine and destroy democratic welfare states as we have known them in the twentieth century.

WHO CONTROLS GOVERNMENT?

The key to this unorthodox conclusion lies in recognizing where the control of democratic government is lodged. It is an issue that is not as simple as it may seem. In the modern era, the question of who controls the government has almost always been asked as a political question. It has had many answers, but almost uniformly these involved identifying the political party, group, or faction that dominated the control of a particular state at a particular moment. You have heard of governments controlled by capitalists. Governments controlled by labor. Governments controlled by Catholics, and by Islamic fundamentalists. Governments controlled by tribal and racial groups; governments controlled by Hutus and governments by whites. You have also heard of governments controlled by occupational groups, such as lawyers or bankers. You have heard of governments controlled by rural interests, by big-city machines and by people living in the suburbs. And you have certainly heard of governments controlled by political parties, by Democrats, Conservatives, Christian Democrats, Liberals, Radicals, Republicans, and Socialists.

But you probably have not heard much about a government controlled by its customers. Economic historian Frederic Lane laid the basis for a new way of understanding where the control of government lies in some of his lucid essays on the economic consequences of violence discussed earlier. Thinking about government as an economic unit that sells protection led Lane to analyze the control of government in economic rather than political terms. In this view, there are three basic alternatives in the control of government, each of which entails a fundamentally different set of incentives: proprietors, employees, and customers.

Proprietors

In rare cases, even today, governments are sometimes controlled by a proprietor, usually a hereditary leader who for all intents and purposes owns the country. For example, the Sultan of Brunei treats the government of Brunei somewhat like a proprietorship. This was more common among lords of the Middle Ages, who treated their fiefs as proprietorships to optimize their incomes.

Lane described the incentives of "the owners of the production-producing enterprise" as follows:

> An interest in maximizing profits would lead him, while maintaining prices, to try to reduce his costs. He would, like Henry VII of England or Louis XI of France, use inexpensive wiles, at least as inexpensive devices as possible, to affirm his legitimacy, to maintain domestic order, and to distract neighboring princes so that his own military expenses would be low. From lowered costs, or from the increased exactions made possible by the firmness of his monopoly, or from a combination, he accumulated a surplus. . . . "[9]

Governments controlled by proprietors have strong incentives to reduce the costs of providing protection or monopolizing violence in a given area. But so long as their rule is secure, they have little incentive to reduce the price (tax) they charge their customers below the rate that optimizes revenues. The higher the price a monopolist can charge, and the lower his actual costs, the greater the profit he will make. The ideal fiscal policy for a government controlled by its proprietors would be a huge surplus. When governments can keep their revenues high but cut their costs, this has a large impact on the use of resources. Labor and other valuable inputs that would otherwise be wasted providing unnecessarily expensive protection become available instead for investment and other purposes. The higher the monarch can raise his profit by lowering costs, the more resources are freed. When these resources are used for investment, they provide a stimulus for growth. But even if they are used for conspicuous consumption, they help create and feed new markets that otherwise would not exist if the resources had been wasted to produce inefficient "protection."

Employees

It is easy to characterize the incentives that prevail for governments controlled by their employees. They would be similar incentives in other employee-controlled organizations. First and foremost, employee-run organizations tend to favor any policy that increases employment and oppose measures which reduce jobs. As Lane put it, "When employees as a whole controlled, they had little interest in minimizing the amounts exacted for protection and none in minimizing that large part of costs represented by labor costs, by their own salaries. Maximizing size was more to their taste also."[10] A government controlled by its employees would seldom have incentives to either reduce the costs of government or the price charged to their customers. However, where conditions impose strong price resistance, in the form of opposition to higher taxes, governments controlled by employees would be more likely to let their revenues fall below their outlays than to cut their outlays. In other words, their incentives imply that they may be inclined toward chronic deficits, as governments controlled by proprietors would not be.

Customers

Are there examples of governments controlled by their customers? Yes. Lane was inspired to analyze the control of government in economic terms by the example of the medieval merchant republics, like Venice. There a group of wholesale merchants who required protection effectively controlled the government for centuries. They were genuinely customers for the protection service government provided, not proprietors. They paid for the service. They did not seek to profit from their control of government's monopoly of violence. If some did, they were prevented from doing so by the other customers for long periods of time. Other examples of governments controlled by their customers include democracies and republics with limited franchise, such as the ancient democracies, or the American republic in its founding period. At that time, only those who paid for the government, about 10 percent of the population, were allowed to vote.

Governments controlled by their customers, like those of proprietors, have incentives to reduce their operating costs as far as possible. But unlike governments controlled by either proprietors or employees, governments actually controlled by their customers have incentives to hold down the prices they charge. Where customers rule, governments are lean and generally unobtrusive, with low operating costs, minimal employment, and low taxes. A government controlled by its customers sets tax rates not to optimize the amount the government can collect but rather to optimize the amount that the customers can retain. Like typical enterprises in competitive markets, even a monopoly controlled by its customers would be compelled to move toward efficiency. It would not be able to charge a price, in the form of taxes, that exceeded costs by more than a bare margin.

THE ROLE OF DEMOCRACY: VOTERS AS EMPLOYEES AND CUSTOMERS

Lane treats democracy in the conventional way in assuming that it brings violence-using and violence-producing enterprises "increasingly under the control of their customers."[11] This is certainly the politically correct conclusion. But is it true? We think not. Look closely at how modern democracies function.

First of all, they have few characteristics of those competitive industries where the terms of trade are clearly controlled by their customers. For one thing, democratic governments typically spend only a bare fraction of their total outlays on the service of protection, which is their core activity. In the United States, for example, state and local governments spend just 3.5 percent of their total outlays on the provision of police, as well as courts and prisons. Add military spending, and the fraction of revenues devoted to protection is still only about 10 percent. Another revealing hint that mass democracy is not controlled by its customers is the fact that contemporary political culture, inherited from the Industrial Age, would consider it outrageous if policies on crucial issues were actually informed by the interests of the people who pay the bills. Imagine the uproar if a U.S. president or a British prime minister proposed to allow the group of citizens who pay the majority of the taxes to determine which programs of government should continue and which groups of employees should be fired. This would deeply offend expectations of how government should operate, in a way that allowing government employees to determine whose taxes should be raised would not.

Yet when you think about it, when customers really are in the driver's seat it would be considered outrageous that they should not get what they want. If you went into a store to buy furniture, and the salespeople took your money but then proceeded to ignore your requests and consult others about how to spend your money, you would quite rightly be upset. You would not think it normal or justifiable if the employees of the store argued that you really did not deserve the furniture, and that it should be shipped instead to someone whom they found more worthy. The fact that something very like this happens in dealings with government shows how little control its "customers" actually have.

By any measure, the costs of democratic government have surged out of control, unlike the typical situation where customer preferences force vendors to be efficient. Most democracies run chronic deficits. This is a fiscal policy characteristic of control by employees. Governments seem notably resistant to reducing the costs of their operations. An almost universal complaint about contemporary government worldwide is that political programs, once established, can be curtailed only with great difficulty. To fire a government employee is all but impossible. In fact, one of the principal advantages arising from privatization of formerly state-owned functions is that private control usually makes it far easier to weed out unnecessary employment. From Britain to Argentina, it has not been uncommon for the new private managers to shed 50–95 percent of former state employees.

Think, as well, of the basis upon which the fiscal terms of government's protection service is priced. For the most part, you would look in vain for hints of competitive influences on tax rates according to which government services are priced. Even the occasional debates about lowering taxes that have interrupted normal political discourse in recent years betray how far removed democratic government has normally been from control by its customers. Advocates of lower taxes sometimes have argued that government revenues would actually increase because rates previously had been set so high that they discouraged economic activity.

The trade-off they normally intended to highlight was not competition between jurisdictions but something much more amazing. They did not argue that because tax rates in Hong Kong were only 15 percent, rates in the United States or Germany must be no higher than 15 percent. To the contrary. Tax debates have normally assumed that the trade-off facing the taxpayer was not between doing business in one jurisdiction or doing it in another, but between doing business at penal rates or taking a holiday. You were told that productive individuals subject to predatory taxation would walk away from their in-boxes and go golfing if their tax burdens were not eased.

The fact that such an argument could even arise shows how far removed from a competitive footing the protection costs imposed by democratic welfare states have been. The terms of progressive income taxation, which emerged in every democratic welfare state during the course of the twentieth century, are dramatically unlike pricing provisions that would be preferred by customers. This can easily be seen by comparing taxation imposed to support a monopolistic provision of protection with tariffs for telephone service, which until recently was a monopoly in most places. Customers would scream bloody murder if a telephone company attempted to charge for calls on the same basis that income taxes are imposed. Suppose the phone company sent a bill for $50,000 for a call to London, just because you happened to conclude a deal worth $125,000 during a conversation. Neither you nor any other customer in his right mind would pay it. But that is exactly the basis upon which income taxes are assessed in every democratic welfare state.

When you think closely about the terms under which industrial democracies have operated, it is more logical to treat them as a form of government controlled by their employees. Thinking of mass democracy as government controlled by its employees helps explain the difficulty of changing government policy. Government in many respects appears to be run for the benefit of employees. For example, government schools in most democratic countries seem to malfunction chronically and without remedy. If customers truly were in the driver's seat, they would find it easier to set new policy directions. Those who pay for democratic government seldom set the terms of government spending. Instead, government functions as a co-op that is both outside of proprietary control and operating as a natural monopoly. Prices bear little relation to costs. The quality of service is generally low compared to that in private enterprise. Customer grievances are hard to remedy. In short, mass democracy leads to control of government by its "employees."

But wait. You may be saying that in most jurisdictions there are many more voters than there are persons on the government payroll. How could it be possible for employees to dominate under such conditions? The welfare state emerged to answer exactly this quandary. Since there were not otherwise enough employees to create a working majority, increasing numbers of voters were effectively put on the payroll to receive transfer payments of all kinds. In effect, the recipients of transfer payments and subsidies became pseudo employees of government who were able to dispense with the bother of reporting every day to work. It was a result dictated by the megapolitical logic of the industrial age.

When the magnitude of coercive force is more important than the efficient deployment of resources, as was the case prior to 1989, it is all but impossible for most governments to be controlled by their customers. As the example of the late Soviet Union illustrated so well, until a few years ago it was possible for states to exercise great power in the world even while wasting resources on a massive scale. When returns to violence are high and rising, magnitude means more than efficiency. Larger entities tend to prevail over smaller ones. Those governments that are more effective in mobilizing military resources, even at the cost of wasting many of them, tend to prevail over those that utilize resources more efficiently.

Think what this means. It inescapably implies that when magnitude means more than efficiency, governments controlled by their customers cannot prevail, and often, cannot survive. Under such conditions, the entities that will be most effectively militarily are those that commandeer the most resources for war. But governments that are truly controlled by their customers who pay their bills are unlikely to have carte blanche to reach into the pockets of everyone to extract resources.

Customers normally wish to see the prices they pay for any product or service, including protection, lowered and kept under control. If the Western democracies had been under customer control during the Cold War, that fact alone would have made them weaker competitors militarily, because it would almost certainly have curtailed the flow of resources into the government. Remember, where customers rule, both prices and costs should be expected to be under tight control. But this is hardly what happened. The welfare states were manifestly the winners of the spending contest during the Cold War. Commentators of all stripes cited as a factor in their triumph their ability to spend the Soviet Union into bankruptcy.

It is precisely this fact that highlights the way in which the inefficiencies of democracy made it megapolitically predominant during a period of rising returns to violence. Massive military spending, with all its waste, represents a distinctly suboptimal deployment of capital for private gain. We suggested earlier that while welfare states were economically efficient as compared to state socialist systems, they are far less efficient for the creation of wealth than *laissez-faire* enclaves, like Hong Kong. Ironically, it was this very inefficiency of the democratic welfare state as compared to a more unencumbered free-market system that made it successful—in the megapolitical conditions of industrialism.

How did inefficiency fostered by democracy become a factor in its success during the Age of Violence? The key to unraveling this apparent paradox lies in recognizing two points:

1. Success for a sovereignty in the modern period lay not in creating wealth but in creating a military force capable of deploying overpowering violence against any other state. Money was needed to do that, but money itself could not win a battle. The challenge was not to create a system with the most efficient economy or the most rapid rate of growth, but to create a system that could extract more resources and channel them into the military. By its nature, military spending is an area where the financial returns *per se* are low or nonexistent.

2. The easiest way to obtain permission to invest funds in activities with little or no direct financial return, like tax payments, is to ask for permission from someone other than the person whose money is coveted. One of the ways that the Dutch were able to purchase Manhattan for twenty-three dollars' worth of beads is that the particular Indians to whom they made the offer were not the ones who properly owned it. "Getting to yes," as the marketing people say, is much easier under those terms. Suppose, for example, that as authors of this book we wanted you to pay not its cover price but 40 percent of your annual income for a copy. We would be far likelier to get permission to do so if we asked someone else, and did not have to ask you. In fact, we would be far more persuasive if we could rely instead upon the consent of several people you do not even know. We could hold an *ad hoc* election, what H. L. Mencken described, with less exaggeration than he might have thought, as "an advanced auction of stolen goods." And to make the example more realistic, we would agree to share some of the money we collected from you with these anonymous bystanders in exchange for their support.

That is the role the modern democratic welfare state evolved to fulfill. It was an unsurpassed system in the Industrial Age because it was both efficient and inefficient where it counted. It combined the efficiency of private ownership and incentives for the creation of wealth with a mechanism to facilitate essentially unchecked access to that wealth. Democracy kept the pockets of wealth producers open. It succeeded militarily during the high-water period of rising returns to violence in the world precisely because it made it difficult for customers to effectively restrict the taxes the government collected or other ways of funding the outlay of resources for the military, such as inflation.

Why Customers Could Not Dominate

Those who paid for "protection" during the modern period were not in a position to successfully deny resources to the sovereign, even acting collectively, when doing so would simply have exposed them to being overpowered by other, possibly more hostile states. This was an obvious consideration during the Cold War. The customers, or taxpayers, who bore a disproportionate share of the cost of government in the leading Western industrial states were in no position to refuse to pay hefty taxes. The result would have been to expose themselves to total confiscation by the Soviet Union or another aggressive group capable of organizing violence.

Industrialism and Democracy

Taking a longer view, mass democracy may prove to be an anachronism that will not long survive the end of the Industrial Age. Certainly, mass democracy and the nation-state emerged together with the French Revolution at the end of the eighteenth century, probably as a response to a surge in real income. Incomes had begun to rise significantly in Western Europe about 1750, partly as a result of warmer weather. This coincided with a period of technological innovation that displaced skilled jobs of artisans with equipment that could be operated by unskilled workers, even women and children. This new industrial equipment raised earnings for unskilled workers, making the income distribution more equal.

The crucial trigger point of revolution may not have been, as is often thought, the perverse idea that people tend to revolt when conditions improve. More important may be the fact that when incomes had risen to a certain level, it at last became practical for the early-modern state to circumvent the private intermediaries and powerful magnates with whom they had previously bargained for resources, and move to a system of "direct rule" in which a national government dealt directly with individual citizens, taxing them at ever higher rates and demanding poorly compensated military service in exchange for provision of various benefits.[12]

Because the emerging middle class soon had enough money to tax, it was no longer essential, as it previously had been, for rulers to negotiate with powerful landlords or great merchants who were, as historian Charles Tilly wrote, "in a position to prevent the creation of a powerful state" that would "seize their assets and cramp their transactions." [13] It is easy to see why governments were more successful in extracting resources when they dealt with millions of citizens individually rather than with a relative handful of lords, dukes, earls, bishops, contract mercenaries, free cities, and other semisovereign entities with whom the rulers of European states were obliged to negotiate prior to the mid-eighteenth century.

Rising real incomes allowed governments to adopt a strategy that placed more resources under their control. Small sums taken in taxes from millions could produce more revenue than larger amounts paid by a few powerful people. What is more, the many were far easier to deal with than the few, who were generally unwilling to give their money away and were far better placed to resist.

After all, the typical farmer, small merchant, or worker possessed vanishingly small resources as compared to the state itself. It was not even remotely possible that the typical private individual in Western Europe on the eve of the French Revolution could have effectively bargained with the state to reduce his tax rate, or mounted an effective resistance to government plans and policies that threatened his interests. But this is precisely what powerful private magnates had done for centuries and would continue to do. They effectively resisted and bargained with rulers, restraining their ability to commandeer resources.

"Going to war accelerated the move from indirect to direct rule. Almost any state that makes war finds that it cannot pay for the effort from its accumulated reserves and current revenues. Almost all warmaking states borrow extensively, raise taxes, and seize the means of combat—including men—from reluctant citizens who have other uses for their resources." [14]

—CHARLES TILLY

The example of Poland in the mid-eighteenth century illustrates this perfectly. In 1760, the Polish national army comprised eighteen thousand soldiers. This was a meager force compared to the armies commanded by rulers of neighboring Austria, Prussia, and Russia, the least of whom could control a standing army of 100,000 soldiers. In fact, the Polish national army in 1760 was small even in comparison with other units under arms within Poland. The combined forces of the Polish nobility were thirty thousand men. [15]

If the Polish king had been able to interact directly with millions of individual Poles and tax them directly, rather than being limited to extracting resources indirectly through the contributions of the powerful Polish magnates, there is little doubt that the Polish central government would have been in a position to raise far more revenues, and thus pay for a larger army.

Against ordinary individuals, who were not in a position to act in concert with millions of other ordinary individuals, the central authorities were to prove irresistibly powerful everywhere. But the king of Poland lacked the option of directly taxing his citizens in 1760. He had to deal through the lords, wealthy merchants, and other notables, who were a small, cohesive group. They could and did act in concert to keep the king from commandeering their resources without their consent. Given that the Polish nobility had far more troops than he did, the king was in no position to insist.

As it turned out, the military disadvantage of failing to circumvent the wealthy and powerful in gathering resources was decisive in the Age of Violence. Within a few years, Poland ceased to exist as an independent country. It was conquered by invasions from Austria, Prussia, and Russia, three countries with armies each of which was many times bigger than Poland's small force. In each of those countries, the rulers had found paths to circumvent the capacity of the wealthy merchants and the nobility to limit the commandeering of their resources.

After the French Revolution

The French Revolution resulted in an even greater surge in the size of armies, a fact that demonstrated the strength of the democratic strategy when returns to violence were rising. The bargain governments struck from the French Revolution onward was to provide an unprecedented degree of involvement in the lives of average people, in exchange for their participation in wars in place of mercenaries, and paying a growing burden of taxes from their rising incomes.

As Tilly said,

> The state's sphere expanded far beyond its military core, and its citizens began to make claims on it for a very wide range of protection, adjudication, production, and distribution. As national legislatures extended their own ranges well beyond the approval of taxation, they became the targets of claims from all well-organized groups whose interests the state did or could affect. Direct rule and mass national politics grew up together, and reinforced each other mightily.[16]

The same logic that was true in the eighteenth century remained true until 1989, when the Berlin Wall fell. As the Industrial Age advanced, incomes for unskilled work continued to rise, making mass democracy an even more effective method of optimizing the extraction of resources. As a result, government grew and grew, adding about 0.5 percent to its total claims on annual income in the average industrial country over the twentieth century.

During the Industrial Age prior to 1989, democracy emerged as the most militarily effective form of government precisely because democracy made it difficult or impossible to impose effective limits on the commandeering of resources by the state. Generous provision of welfare benefits to one and all invited a majority of voters to become, in effect, employees of the government. This became the predominant political feature of all leading industrial countries because voters were in a weak position to effectively control the government in their role as customers for the service of protection. Not only did they face the aggressive menace of Communist systems, which could produce large resources for military purposes since the state controlled the entire economy, but true taxpayer control of government was also impractical for another reason.

Millions of average citizens cannot work together effectively to protect their interests. Because the obstacles to their cooperation are high, and the return to any individual for successfully defending the group's common interests is minimal, millions of ordinary citizens will not be as successful in withholding their assets from the government as will smaller groups with more favorable incentives.

Other things being equal, therefore, you would expect a higher proportion of total resources to be commandeered by government in a mass democracy than in an oligarchy, or in a system of fragmented sovereignty where magnates wielded military power and fielded their own armies, as they did everywhere in early-modern Europe prior to the eighteenth century.

Thus a crucial though seldom examined reason for the growth of democracy in the Western world is the relative importance of negotiation costs at a time when returns to violence were rising. It was always costlier to draw resources from the few than from the many.

A relatively small, elite group of rich represent a more coherent and effective body than a large mass of citizens. The small group has stronger incentives to work together. It will almost inevitably be more effective at protecting its interests than will a mass group.[17] And even if most members of the group choose not to cooperate with any common action, a few who are rich may be capable of deploying enough resources to get the job done.

With democratic decision-making, the nation-state could exercise power much more completely over millions of persons, who could not easily cooperate to act collectively in their own behalf, than it could in dealings with a much smaller number who could more easily overcome the organizational difficulties of defending their concentrated interests. Democracy had the still more compelling advantage of creating a legitimizing decision rule that allowed the state to tap the resources of the well-to-do without having to bargain directly for their permission. In short, democracy as a decision mechanism was well fitted to the megapolitical conditions of the Industrial Age. It complemented the nation-state because it facilitated the concentration of military power in the hands of those running it at a time when the magnitude of force brought to bear was more important than the efficiency with which it was mobilized.

This was demonstrated decisively with the French Revolution, which raised the magnitude of military force on the battlefield. Thereafter, other competitive nation-states had little choice but to converge on a similar organization, with legitimacy ultimately tied to democratic decision-making.

To summarize, the democratic nation-state succeeded during the past two centuries for these hidden reasons:

1. There were rising returns to violence that made magnitude of force more important than efficiency as a governing principle.
2. Incomes rose sufficiently above subsistence that it became possible for the state to collect large amounts of total resources without having to negotiate with powerful magnates who were capable of resisting.
3. Democracy proved sufficiently compatible with the operation of free markets to be conducive to the generation of increasing amounts of wealth.
4. Democracy facilitated domination of government by its "employees," thereby assuring that it would be difficult to curtail expenditures, including military expenditures.
5. Democracy as a decision-rule proved to be an effective antidote to the ability of the wealthy to act in concert to restrict the nation-state's ability to tax or otherwise protect their assets from invasion.

Democracy became the militarily winning strategy because it facilitated the gathering of more resources into the hands of the state. Compared to other styles of sovereignty that depended for their legitimacy on other principles, such as the feudal levy, the divine right of kings, corporate religious duty, or the voluntary contributions of the rich, mass democracy became militarily the most potent because it was the surest way to gather resources in an industrial economy.

"The nation, as a culturally defined community, is the highest symbolic value of modernity; it has been endowed with a quasi-sacred character equalled only by religion. In fact, this quasi-sacred character derives from religion. In

practice, the nation has become either the modern, secular substitute of religion or its most powerful ally. In modern times the communal sentiments generated by the nation are highly regarded and sought after as the basis for group loyalty. . . . That the modern state is often the beneficiary should hardly be surprising given its paramount power." [18]

—JOSEP R. LLOBERA

Nationalism

Much the same can be said of nationalism, which became a corollary to mass democracy. States that could employ nationalism found that they could mobilize larger armies at a smaller cost. Nationalism was an invention that enabled a state to increase the scale at which it was militarily effective. Like politics itself, nationalism is mostly a modern invention. As sociologist Josep Llobera has shown in his richly documented book on the rise of nationalism, the nation is an imagined community that in large measure came into being as a way of mobilizing state power during the French Revolution. As he puts it, "In the modern sense of the term, national consciousness has only existed since the French Revolution, since the time when in 1789 the Constituent Assembly equated the people of France with the French nation." [19]

Nationalism made it easier to mobilize power and control large numbers of people. Nation-states formed by underlining and emphasizing characteristics that people held in common, particularly spoken language. This facilitated rule without the intervention of intermediaries. It simplified the tasks of bureaucracy. Edicts that need only be promulgated in one language can be dispatched more quickly and with less confusion than those that must be translated into a Babel of tongues. Nationalism, therefore, tended to lower the cost of controlling larger areas. Before nationalism, the early-modern state required the aid of lords, dukes, earls, bishops, free cities, and other corporate and ethnic intermediaries, from tax "farmers" to military contract merchants and mercenaries to collect revenues, raise troops and conduct other government functions.

Nationalism also decisively lowered the costs of mobilizing military personnel by encouraging group identification with the interests of the state. There was such a substantial advantage in harnessing group feeling to the interests of the state that most states, even the allegedly internationalist Soviet Union, converged on nationalism as a complementary ideology.

Seen in a longer perspective, nationalism is as much an anomaly as the state itself. As historian William McNeill has documented, polyethnic sovereignties were the norm in the past. [20] In McNeill's words, "The idea that a government rightfully should rule only over citizens of a single ethnos started to develop in Western Europe towards the end of the Middle Ages." [21] An early nationalist entity was the Prussian League (Preussicher Bund), which formed in 1440 in opposition to rule by the Teutonic Order. Some of the characteristics of the order were highlighted earlier as a polar example of a sovereignty unlike the nation-state. The Teutonic Order was a kind of chartered company almost none of whose members were native to Prussia. Its headquarters shifted at various times from Bremen and Lübeck to Jerusalem to Acre to Venice and on to Marienberg on the Vistula. At one time it ruled the district of Burzenland in Transylvania. It is not surprising that a sovereignty so unlike a state would became the object of one of the early attempts to mobilize national feeling as a factor in organizing power. However, as an indication of how different early nationalism was from later varieties, the German-speaking nobles of the Prussian League petitioned the king of Poland to place Prussia under Polish rule, largely because even then the Polish king was a relatively weak monarch who was not expected to rule with the same rigor as the Teutonic Order.

Nationalism, in its early incarnations, came into play just prior to the Gunpowder Revolution. It continued to develop as the early-modern state developed, taking a quantum leap in importance at the time of the French Revolution. We believe that nationalism as an idea of force has already begun to recede. It probably reached its heyday with Woodrow Wilson's attempt to endow every ethnic group in Europe with its own state at the close of World War I. It is now a reactionary force, inflamed in places with falling incomes and declining prospects like Serbia.

As we explore later, we expect nationalism to be a major rallying theme of persons with low skills nostalgic for compulsion as the welfare state collapses in the Western democracies. You haven't seen anything yet. For most persons in the West the fallout from the death of Communism has seemed relatively benign. You have seen a drop in military spending, a plunge in aluminum prices, and a new source of hockey players for the NHL. That is the good news. It is news that most people who came of age in the twentieth century could applaud, especially if they are hockey fans. Most of the news that is destined to prove less popular is still to come.

With the passage of the Industrial Age, the megapolitical conditions that democracy satisfied are rapidly ceasing to exist. Therefore, it is doubtful that mass democracy and the welfare state will survive long in the new megapolitical conditions of the Information Age.

"Congress was not a temple of democracy, it was a market for bartering laws."

—ALBERTO FUJIMORI, president of Peru

Indeed, future historians may report that we have already seen the first postmodern coup—the remarkable padlocking of the congress in Peru in 1993. This was hardly an event that attracted much favorable notice in the leading industrial democracies. But it may turn out to mean more in the fullness of time than conventional analysts would suggest. The few who have thought about it tend to see it as just another power grab of the kind that has become depressingly familiar in the history of Latin America. But we see it as perhaps the first step toward delegitimizing a form of governance whose immediate megapolitical reason for being has begun to disappear with the transition to the Information Age. Fujimori's closure of the congress is a symptom of the ultimate devaluation of political promises. A similar fate could await other legislatures when their credit is exhausted.

The shift in technology that is eroding industrialism has trapped many countries with governments that no longer work. Or work badly. Legislatures, in particular, appear to be increasingly dysfunctional. They grind out laws that might have been merely stupid fifty years ago but are dangerous today. This was spectacularly obvious in Peru, where the internal sovereignty of the state had almost collapsed by 1993.

"Attacks, kidnappings, rapes and murders have coincided with increasingly aggressive driving habits and unsafe streets. The police have gradually lost control of the situation and some of their members have been involved in scandals and become seasoned criminals. . . . People have gradually grown used to living outside the law. Theft, illegal seizure and factory takeovers have become everyday occurrences. . . . "[22]

—HERNANDO DE SOTO

Peru in Ruins

In a sense, Peru was no longer a modern nation-state in 1993. It still had a flag and an army, but most of its institutions lay in ruins. Even the prisons had been taken over by the inmates. This disintegration could be traced to a number of causes, but most expert attempts to explain it miss the real point. Peru was an early casualty of the technological change that is making closed economies dysfunctional and undermining central authority everywhere. These megapolitical stresses are compounded because decision-making institutions like the Peruvian congress are trapped by perverse incentives into aggravating the very problems that they most need to solve.

Representative democracy in Peru was like a pair of loaded dice. As a decision mechanism for aggrandizing the state, it was unsurpassed. But when new circumstances called for devolving power, the inherent biases that made democracy so useful under the old megapolitical conditions made it increasingly dysfunctional. The very laws passed by the congress were rapidly destroying any foundation of value or respect for the law. As de Soto put it in *The Other Path,* "Small interest groups fight among themselves, cause bankruptcies, implicate public officials. Governments hand out privileges. The law is used to give and take away far more than morality permits." [23] A congress like that in Peru, entirely in thrall to special-interest groups, has all the moral stature of a gang of fences auctioning off stolen goods. It made the free market illegal, and consequently made the law ridiculous. As de Soto writes of the pre-Fujimori period:

> A complete subversion of ends and means has turned the life of Peruvian society upside down, to the point that there are acts which, although officially criminal, are no longer condemned by the collective consciousness. Smuggling is a case in point. Everyone, from the aristocratic lady to the humblest man, acquires smuggled goods. No one has scruples about it; on the contrary, it is viewed as a kind of challenge to individual ingenuity or as revenge against the state.
>
> This infiltration of violence and criminality into everyday life has been accompanied by increasing poverty and deprivation. In general terms, Peruvians' real average income had declined steadily over the last ten years and is now at the level of twenty years ago. Mountains of garbage pile up on all sides. Night and day, legions of beggars, car washers, and scavengers besiege passersby, asking for money. The mentally ill swarm naked in the streets, stinking of urine. Children, single mothers, and cripples beg for alms on every corner.
>
> ... The traditional centralism of our society has proved clearly incapable of satisfying the manifold needs of a country in transition. [24]

De Soto described the abandonment of the grotesque legal economy for the black market that was under way before Fujimori padlocked the congress as "an invisible revolution."

We are positive about the benefits of the free market, but much less positive about the promise of a society in which the law is as degraded as the money. The world that de Soto described in Peru prior to 1993 was a "Clockwork Orange" world, where overly centralized and dysfunctional government institutions were literally destroying the civil society.

This is what Fujimori set out to change. He had slashed inflation by turning off the printing presses. He had also managed to fire fifty thousand government employees, and to trim some subsidies. He had made a start toward balancing the budget. His program of reform included comprehensive plans to create free markets and privatize industry. But as in the former Soviet Union, most of the important elements of Fujimori's reform were yet to be adopted in 1993, including the first round of large-scale privatization of state banks, mining companies, and utilities. Instead of enacting these necessary proposals, Peru's congress, like the Russian congress that challenged Yeltsin's reforms in Moscow, sought to move backwards. Their plan: restore subsidies from an empty treasury, pad the payroll, and protect any and all vested interests, especially the bureaucracy—exactly what you would expect of a government controlled by its employees.

Fujimori claimed that the congress of Peru was dithering and corrupt, a fact with which almost everyone agreed. He further claimed that congressional dithering and corruption made it impossible to reform Peru's collapsing economy or combat a violent assault by narco-terrorists and nihilistic Sendero Luminoso (Shining Path) guerrillas.

The 70 Percent Solution

So Fujimori closed the Congress, an act that might have indicated that he was as authoritarian as many earlier Latin American leaders. But we thought, and said so at the time, that Fujimori had correctly identified a fundamental impediment to reform. The extravagant official elegies for the Peruvian congress by American editorial writers and officials of the State Department were not shared by the people of Peru. While North Americans carried on as if Peru's congress were the incarnation of freedom and civilization, the Peruvian people cheered. President Fujimori's popularity shot up above 70 percent when he sent the congress home. And he was later reelected to a second term in a landslide. Most citizens apparently saw their legislature more as an obstacle to their well-being than as an expression of their rights. In 1994, real economic growth in Peru reached 12.9 percent, the highest on the planet.

Deflation of Political Promises

We saw Peru's turmoil less as a throwback to the dictatorships of the past than as an early installment of a broader transition crisis. You can expect to see crises of misgovernment in many countries as political promises are deflated and governments run out of credit. Ultimately, new institutional forms will have to emerge that are capable of preserving freedom in the new technological conditions, while at the same time giving expression and life to the common interests that all citizens share.

Few have begun to think about the incompatibility between some of the institutions of industrial government and the megapolitics of postindustrial society. Whether these contradictions are explicitly acknowledged or not, however, their consequences will become increasingly obvious as examples of political failure compound around the world. Institutions of government that emerged in the modern period reflect the megapolitical conditions of one or more centuries ago. The Information Age will require new mechanisms of representation to avoid chronic dysfunction and even social collapse.

When the Berlin Wall fell in 1989, it not only signaled the end of the Cold War; it was also the outer sign of a silent earthquake in the foundations of power in the world. It was the end of the long period of rising returns to violence. The fall of Communism, which we forecast in 1987 in *Blood in the Streets* and even earlier in our monthly newsletter, *Strategic Investment,* was not merely the repudiation of an ideology. It was the outward marker of the most important development in the history of violence over the past five centuries. If our analysis is correct, the organization of society is bound to change to reflect growing diseconomies of scale in the employment of violence. The boundaries within which the future must lie have been redrawn.

CHAPTER 6
THE MEGAPOLITICS OF THE INFORMATION AGE

The Triumph of Efficiency over Power

"... it is computerized information, not manpower or mass production. that increasingly drives the U.S. economy and that will win wars in a world wired for 500 TV channels. The computerized information exists in cyberspace—the new dimension created by endless reproduction of computer networks, satellites, modems, databases and the public Internet."[1]

—NEIL MUNRO

On December 30, 1936, auto workers angling for higher pay forcibly seized two of General Motors' main plants at Flint, Michigan. They idled machines, turned off the assembly lines, and made themselves at home. Workers who had been employed to operate the factories sat down in an industrial confrontation that was to last for many weeks. It was a drama punctuated by violent riots and the fluctuating allegiances of the police, the Michigan militia, and political figures at all levels of government. Seeing little progress in forcing their demands, the union struck again on February 1, 1937. Union activists forcibly took over GM's Chevrolet factory in Flint. By occupying and closing

General Motors' key factories, the workers effectively paralyzed the company's productive capacity. In the ten days following the seizure of the third plant, GM produced only 153 automobiles in the United States.

We revisit this news flash from sixty years ago to place the revolution in megapolitical conditions now under way into clearer perspective. The GM sitdown strike happened within the lifetimes of some readers of this book. Yet we believe that sit-down strikes will prove as anachronistic in the Information Age as slaves slogging across the desert with giant stones in tow to erect funeral pyramids for the pharaohs. While labor unions and their tactics of intimidation became so familiar in the industrial period as to be an unquestioned part of the social landscape, they depended upon special megapolitical conditions that are rapidly fading away. There will be no Chevrolets and no UAW to strike on the Information Superhighway.

The fortunes of governments will follow those of their counterparts, the unions, into decline. Institutionalized coercion of the kind that played a crucial role in twentieth-century society will no longer be possible. Technology is precipitating a profound change in the logic of extortion and protection.

". . . there be no Propriety, no Dominion, no Mine and Thine distinct; but only that to be every man's that he can get; and for so long, as he can keep it." [2]

—THOMAS HOBBES

Extortion and Protection

Throughout history, violence has been a dagger pointed at the heart of the economy. As Thomas Schelling shrewdly put it, "The power to hurt—to destroy things that somebody treasures, to inflict pain and grief—is a kind of bargaining power, not easy to use but used often. In the underworld it is the basis for blackmail, extortion, and kidnapping, in the commercial world, for boycotts, strikes, and lockouts. . . . It is often the basis for discipline, civilian and military; and gods use it to exact discipline." [3] A government's capacity to tax ultimately depends upon the same vulnerabilities as do private shakedowns and extortion. Although we tend not to perceive it in these terms, the proportion of assets that are controlled and spent coercively, through crime and government, provides a rough measure of the megapolitical balance between extortion and protection. If technology made the protection of assets difficult, crime would tend to be widespread, and so would union activity. Under such circumstances, protection by government would therefore command a premium. Taxes would be high. Where taxes are lower and wage rates in the workplace are determined by market forces rather than through political intervention or coercion, technology has tipped the balance toward protection.

The technological imbalance between extortion and protection reached an extreme at the end of the third quarter of the twentieth century. In some advanced Western societies more than a majority of resources were commandeered by governments. The incomes of a large fraction of the population were either set by fiat or determined under the influence of coercion, such as by strikes and threats of violence in other forms. The welfare state and the trade union were both artifacts of technology, sharing the spoils of the triumph of power over efficiency in the twentieth century. They could not have existed if not for the technologies, military and civilian, that raised the returns to violence during the Industrial Age.

The capacity to create assets has always entailed some vulnerability to extortion. The greater the assets created or possessed, the higher the price to be paid, in one way or another. Either you paid off everyone who gained the leverage to employ violence for extortion, or you paid for military power capable of defeating any shakedown attempt by brute force.

"Violence shall no more be heard in thy land, wasting nor destruction within thy borders . . ."

—Isaiah 60:18

The Mathematics of Protection

Now the dagger of violence could soon be blunted. Information technology promises to alter dramatically the balance between protection and extortion, making protection of assets in many cases much easier, and extortion more difficult. The technology of the Information Age makes it possible to create assets that are outside the reach of many forms of coercion. This new asymmetry between protection and extortion rests upon a fundamental truth of mathematics. It is easier to multiply than to divide. As basic as this truth is, however, its far-reaching consequences were disguised prior to the advent of microprocessors. High-speed computers have facilitated many billions of times more computations in the past decade than were undertaken in all the previous history of the world. This leap in computation has allowed us for the first time to fathom some of the universal characteristics of complexity. What the computers show is that complex systems can be built and understood only from the bottom up. Multiplying prime numbers is simple. But disaggregating complexity by trying to decompose the product of large prime numbers is all but impossible. Kevin Kelly, editor of *Wired,* puts it this way: "To multiply several prime numbers into a larger product is easy; any elementary school kid can do it. But the world's supercomputers choke while trying to unravel a product into its simple primes."[4]

The Logic of Complex Systems

The cybereconomy will inevitably be shaped by this profound mathematical truth. It already has an obvious expression in powerful encryption algorithms. As we explore later in this chapter, these algorithms will allow the creation of a new, protected realm of cybercommerce in which the leverage of violence will be greatly reduced. The balance between extortion and protection will tip dramatically in the direction of protection. This will facilitate the emergence of an economy that depends more upon spontaneous adaptive mechanisms and less upon conscious decision-making and resource allocation through bureaucracy. The new system in which protection will be at the forefront will be very different from that which arose from the predominance of compulsion in the industrial period.

Command-and-Control Systems Are Primitive

We wrote in *The Great Reckoning* that the computer is enabling us to "see" the formerly invisible complexity inherent in a whole range of systems.* Not only does advanced computational capability enable us to better understand the dynamics of complex systems; it also enables us to harness those complexities in productive ways. In a sense, this is not even a choice but an inevitability if the economy is to advance beyond the inflexible central-control stage of development. Such a system, which depends upon linear relationships, is fundamentally primitive. Government appropriation inevitably dragoons resources from high-value complex uses to low-value primitive uses. It is a process that is limited by the same mathematical asymmetry that prevents the unraveling of the product of large prime numbers. Dividing the spoils can never be anything but primitive.

Everything Gets More Complex

Everywhere you look in the universe, you see systems attaining greater complexity as they evolve. This is true in astrophysics. It is true in a puddle. Leave rainwater alone in a low spot and it will grow more complex. Ad-

* See Chapter 8 of *The Great Reckoning,* "Linear Expectations in a Nonlinear World: How the Telescope Led Us to Compute; How the Computer Can Help Us to See."

vanced systems of every variety are complex adaptive systems without an authority in charge. Every complex system in nature, of which the market economy is the most evident social manifestation, depends upon dispersed capabilities. Systems that work most effectively under the widest range of conditions depend for their resilience upon spontaneous order that accommodates novel possibilities. Life itself is such a complex system. Billions of potential combinations of genes produce a single human individual. Sorting among them would confound any bureaucracy.

Twenty-five years ago, that could only have been an intuition. Today it is demonstrable. The closer computers bring us to understanding the mathematics of artificial life, the better we understand the mathematics of real life, which are those of biological complexity. These secrets of complexity, harnessed through information technology, are allowing economies to be reconfigured into more complex forms. The Internet and the World Wide Web have already taken on characteristics of an organic system, as Kevin Kelly suggests in *Out of Control: The New Biology of Machines, Social Systems, and the Economic World.*[5] In his words, nature is "an idea factory. Vital, postindustrial paradigms are hidden in every jungly ant hill. . . . The wholesale transfer of bio-logic into machines should fill us with awe. When the union of the born and the made is complete, our fabrications will learn, adapt, heal themselves, and evolve. This is a power we have hardly dreamt of yet."[6]

Indeed, the consequences of the "wholesale transfer of bio-logic into machines" are bound to be far-reaching. There has always been a strong tendency for social systems to mimic the characteristics of prevailing technology. This is something that Marx got right. Gigantic factories coincided with the age of big government. Microprocessing is miniaturizing institutions. If our analysis is correct, the technology of the Information Age will ultimately create an economy better suited to exploit the advantages of complexity.

Yet the megapolitical dimensions of such a change are so little understood that even most of those who have recognized its mathematical importance have done so in an anachronistic way. It is simply difficult to grasp and internalize fully the likelihood that technological change in the next few years will antiquate most of the political forms and concepts of the modern world. For example, the late physicist Heinz Pagels wrote in his farseeing book, *The Dreams of Reason,* "I am convinced that the nations and people who master the new science of Complexity will become the economic, cultural, and political superpowers of the next century."[7] It is an impressive forecast. But we believe it is bound to be wrong, not because it is misperceived, but precisely because it will prove more right than Dr. Pagels dared to express. Societies that reconfigure themselves to become more complex adaptive systems will indeed prosper. But when they do, they are unlikely to be nations, much less "political superpowers." The more likely immediate beneficiaries of increased complexity of social systems will be the Sovereign Individuals of the new millennium.

As Pagels's forecast stands, it is the equivalent to a shaman of a hunting band of five hundred generations ago telling his men as they crouched around the campfire, "I am convinced that the first hunting band to master the new science of irrigated planting will have more free time for storytelling than even those guys over at the lake who catch the big fish." As right as he was about the importance of complexity, Pagels overlooked the most basic fact of all. When the logic of violence changes, society changes.

THE LOGIC OF VIOLENCE

To see how and why, it is necessary to focus on several facets of megapolitics that are seldom brought to your attention. These are issues that were explored by historian Frederic C. Lane, whose work on violence and the economic meaning of war is discussed elsewhere in this volume. When Lane wrote in the middle of this century, the Information Society was nowhere in sight. Under the circumstances, he may well have supposed that the competition to employ violence in the world had reached its final stage with the appearance of the nation-state. There is no hint in his works that he anticipated microprocessing or believed that it was technologically feasible to create assets in cyberspace, a realm without physical existence. Lane had nothing to say about the implications of the possibility that large amounts of commerce could be made all but immune from the leverage of violence.

While Lane did not foresee the technological revolutions now unfolding, his insights into the various stages of the monopolization of violence in the past were so lucid that they have obvious application to the emerging Information Revolution. Lane's study of the violent medieval world attracted his attention to issues that conventional economists and historians have tended to neglect. He saw that how violence is organized and controlled plays a large role in determining "what uses are made of scarce resources." [8] Lane also recognized that while production of violence is not usually considered part of economic output, the control of violence is crucial to the economy. The primary role of government is to provide protection against violence. As he put it,

> Every economic enterprise needs and pays for protection, protection against the destruction or armed seizure of its capital and the forceful disruption of its labor. In highly organized societies the production of this utility, protection, is

one of the functions of a special association or enterprise called government. Indeed, one of the most distinctive characteristics of governments is their attempt to create law and order by using force themselves and by controlling through various means the use of force by others."[9]

That is a point that is apparently too basic to appear in textbooks, or to form a part of the civic discussion that presumably determines the course of politics. But it is also too basic to ignore if you wish to understand the unfolding Information Revolution. Protection of life and property is indeed a crucial need that has bedeviled every society that ever existed. How to fend off violent aggression is history's central dilemma. It cannot easily be solved, notwithstanding the fact that protection can be provided in more than one way.

The Close of an Age

As we write, the megapolitical consequences of the Information Age are only beginning to be felt. The economic change of recent decades has been from the primacy of manufactures to that of information and computation, from machine power to microprocessing, from factory to workstation, from mass production to small teams, or even to persons working alone. As the scale of enterprise falls, so does the potential for sabotage and blackmail in the workplace. Smaller-scale operations are much more difficult to organize by unions.

Microtechnology allows firms to be smaller, more footloose targets. Many deal in services or products with negligible natural-resource content. In principle, these businesses could be conducted almost anywhere on the planet. They are not trapped at a specific location, like a mine or a port. Therefore, in the fullness of time, they will be far less susceptible to being taxed, either by unions or by politicians. An old Chinese folk wisdom holds, "Of all the thirty-six ways to get out of trouble, the best way is—leave."[10]

In the Information Age, that Oriental wisdom will be easily applied. If operations become uncomfortable due to excessive demands in one location, it will be far easier to move. Indeed, as we explore below, it will be possible in the Information Age to create virtual corporations whose domicile in any jurisdiction will be entirely contingent on the spot market. An overnight increase in the degree of attempted extortion, either by governments or others, could lead to the activities and assets of the virtual corporation fleeing the jurisdiction at the speed of light.

The growing integration of microtechnology into industrial processes means that even those firms that still deal in manufactured products with great economies of scale are no longer as vulnerable to the leverage of violence as they once were. An example illustrating this point is the collapse of the United Auto Workers union's lengthy strike against Caterpillar, which was called off in the waning days of 1995 after almost two years. Unlike the assembly lines of the 1930s, today's Caterpillar plant employs far more skilled workers. Pressed by foreign competition, Caterpillar farmed out much of its low-skill work, closed inefficient plants, and spent almost $2 billion computerizing machine tools and installing assembly robots. Even the strike itself helped spur labor-saving efficiencies. The company now claims to need two thousand fewer employees than when the walkout began.[11]

The megapolitics of the production process has altered more drastically than most people realize. This change is not yet clearly visible, partly because there is always a lag between a revolution in megapolitical conditions and the institutional changes it inevitably precipitates. Further, the rapid evolution of microprocessing technology means that products are now on the horizon whose megapolitical consequences can be anticipated even before they exist. They will make for a far different world.

EXPLOITATION OF THE CAPITALISTS BY THE WORKERS

The character of technology through most of the twentieth century made the forcible seizure of a factory, or a sit-down strike, a hard tactic for owners or managers to counter. As historian Robert S. McElvaine put it, a sit-down strike "made it difficult for employers to break the strike without doing the same to their own equipment."[12] In effect, the workers physically held the owners' capital to ransom. For reasons we explore below, larger industrial companies proved easier targets for unions to exploit than smaller firms. In 1937, General Motors was perhaps the leading industrial corporation in the world. Its factories were among the largest and most costly aggregations of machinery ever assembled, employing many thousands of workers. Every hour, every day that the GM plants were forced to sit idle cost the company a small fortune. A strike that remained unsettled for weeks, like that in the winter of 1936–37, meant rapidly ballooning losses.

Defying Supply and Demand

Unable to produce automobiles after the seizure of its third plant, GM soon capitulated to the union. This was hardly an economic decision based upon the supply and demand for labor. Far from it. When General Motors acceded to the union demands there were nine million persons unemployed in the United States, 14 percent of the workforce. Most of those without work would gladly have taken jobs at GM. They certainly had the skills to fill assembly-line jobs, although you might not know this from most contemporary accounts. A delicate etiquette shrouded straightforward analysis of labor relations during the industrial period. One of its pretenses was the idea that factory jobs, particularly in the middle of the twentieth century, were skilled work. This was untrue. Most factory jobs could have been performed by almost anyone capable of showing up on time. They required little or no training, not even the ability to read or write. As recently as the 1980s, large fractions of the General Motors workforce were either illiterate, innumerate, or both. Until the 1990s, the typical assembly-line worker at GM received only one day of orientation before taking his place on the assembly line. A job you can learn in a single day is not skilled work.

Yet in 1937, with unskilled and skilled workers alike lined up begging for jobs, GM factory workers were able to coerce their employers into a pay hike. Their success had much more to do with the dynamics of violence than with the supply and demand for labor. In March 1937, the month following the settlement of the GM confrontation, there were 170 more sit-down strikes in the United States. Most were successful. Similar episodes occurred in every industrialized country. The workers simply seized the factories and ransomed them back to the owners. It was a tactic of great simplicity, and one that in most cases was profitable and fun for those participating. One sit-down striker wrote, "I am having a great time, something new, something different, lots of grub and music." [13]

The GM sit-down strike of 1936–37 and the other forcible plant seizures of the time were examples of a phenomenon we described in *Blood in the Streets* as "the exploitation of the capitalists by the workers." This was not the view that Pete Seeger set to music in his sad songs. But unless you are planning a career as a folk singer in a blue-collar neighborhood the important thing to focus on is not the popular interpretation but the underlying reality. Wherever you look in history there is generally a layer of rationalization and make-believe that disguises the true megapolitical foundations of any systematic extortion. If you take the rationalizations at face value, you are unlikely to grasp what is really going on.

DECIPHERING THE LOGIC OF EXTORTION

To recognize the megapolitical implications of the current shift to the Information Age, you have to strip away the cant and focus on the real logic of violence in society. This is like stripping away the layers of an overripe onion. It may bring tears to your eyes, but don't look away. We first examine the logic of extortion in the workplace, then extend the analysis to broader issues involving the creation and protection of assets, and the nature of modern government. To a greater degree than most people imagine, the prosperity of government, like that of unions, was directly correlated to the leverage available for extortion. That leverage was much lower in the nineteenth century than in the twentieth. In the next millennium, it will fall almost to the vanishing point.

The whole logic of government and the character of power have been transformed by microprocessing. This may seem exaggerated when you first think about it. But look closely. The prosperity of governments has gone hand in hand with the prosperity of labor unions in the twentieth century. Before this century, most governments commandeered far fewer resources than the militant welfare states to which we have become accustomed. Likewise, unions were small or insignificant factors in economic life prior to this century. The ability of workers to coerce their employers into paying above-market wages depended upon the same megapolitical conditions that allowed governments to extract 40 percent or more of the economy's output in taxes.

Workplace Extortion Before the Twentieth Century

The rise and fall of union extortion of the capitalists can be readily explained by the changing megapolitics of the production process. In 1776, when Adam Smith published *The Wealth of Nations,* conditions for extortion in the workplace were sufficiently unfavorable that "combinations" by workmen "to raise the price of their labour" were seldom tenable. Most manufacturing firms were tiny and family-run. Larger-scale industrial activities were just beginning to emerge. This did not rule out opportunities for violence, but it gave them little leverage. Indeed, during Smith's time and well into the nineteenth century, unions were generally considered illegal combinations in the Great Britain, the United States, and other common-law countries. Adam Smith described attempted strikes in these terms: "Their usual pretences are sometimes the high price of provisions; sometimes the great profit which their master make by their work. . . . [T]hey have always recourse to the loudest clamour, and sometimes to the most shocking violence and outrage."[14] Nonetheless, the workmen "very seldom derive any advantage of those tumultuous combinations," except "the punishment or ruin of the ringleaders."[15]

Scale economies in industry and firm size grew during the nineteenth century. Yet most individuals continued to work for themselves as farmers or small proprietors, and union organizing efforts, like those described by Adam Smith, continued to "generally end in nothing."[16] The legal and political standing of unions changed only as the scale of enterprise rose. The first unions that succeeded in organizing were craft unions of highly skilled workers, who normally organized without extensive violence. They tended to settle for wage increases that matched the marginal costs of replacing them. Unions for unskilled workers were another story. They tended to exploit the shift to firms of larger scale by singling out for organizing efforts precisely those industries that were especially vulnerable to coercion, either because they operated at a larger scale or the character of the operations exposed their owners to physical sabotage. This pattern was borne out from Newcastle to Argentina.[17]

An early example of violent labor movements in the United States was an attack on the Chesapeake and Ohio Canal in 1834. Unlike most early-nineteenth-century businesses, the C&O Canal was not a contained and easily protected operation. As originally planned, it was to have stretched 342 miles, with a 3,000-foot rise from the lower Potomac to the upper Ohio.[18] Digging such a ditch was a big job that never quite got completed. Nonetheless, a large number of workers were employed trying to do it, some of whom were not long in recognizing that the canal could be easily incapacitated. Indeed, without regular maintenance, it could be sabotaged by muskrats burrowing under the towpath. In operation, the canal's locks and channels could be ruined simply by careless use, floods from heavy rains, or battering by untowed boats. It was a simple matter for strikers to blockade the waterway with sunken boats or other debris. In early 1834, rioting among rival gangs of Irish workers on the C&O led to an attempt to make good this potential and seize the canal. The effort failed, however, leaving five persons dead, after President Andrew Jackson sent federal troops from Ft. McHenry to disperse the workers.

Mines and railroads also offered early targets of choice for union activism in America. Like the C&O Canal, they, too, were highly vulnerable to sabotage. Mines, for example, could be flooded, or blockaded at the entrance. Simply killing the mules that towed the ore cars out of underground mines created a difficult and unpleasant situation for the owners. Likewise, railroad trackbeds stretched over many miles, and could be guarded only with difficulty. It was relatively easy for union thugs to attack mines and railroads and do substantial economic damage. Such attacks became commonplace during attempts to organize effective unions. These efforts were generally most intense during periods when real wages were rising due to deflation. When owners attempted to adjust nominal wages, this often triggered protests leading to violence. Such incidents were widespread in the depression that followed the Panic of 1873.

In December 1874, open warfare erupted in the anthracite coalfields of eastern Pennsylvania. The unions organized a violent strike force in the guise of a secret society named the Ancient Order of Hibernians. Also known as the "Molly Maguires," after an Irish revolutionary, this group was known for "terrorizing the coal fields and preventing those miners who wished to work from doing so. Sabotage and destruction of property, outright murder and assassination, were all charged against its members." [19]

There was also recurring violence among railroad employees. For example, there were serious outbreaks in July 1877 aimed at destroying the property of both the Pennsylvania and Baltimore & Ohio railroads. Workers took over switches, tore up tracks, sealed off caryards, disabled locomotives, sabotaged, then looted trains, and worse. In Pittsburgh, roundhouses of the Pennsylvania Railroad were set ablaze with hundreds of people inside. Dozens were killed, two thousand railcars were burned and looted and the machine shop was destroyed, along with a grain elevator and 125 locomotives. Federal troops intervened to restore order. [20]

Although these early strikes were interpreted sympathetically by socialist and union activists, they inspired little public support. Notwithstanding the inherent vulnerability of industries such as mines and railroads, overall megapolitical conditions were not yet favorable to the exploitation of the capitalists by the workers. The scale of enterprise was too small to facilitate systematic extortion. While there were vulnerable industries, they employed too small a fraction of the population to allow the benefits of the coercion against employers to be broadly shared. Without such support, they were unsustainable because owners could depend upon the government for protection. While unions sometimes attempted through intimidation to prevent local officials from enforcing injunctions, these efforts, too, were seldom successful. Even the most violent strikes were usually suppressed within days or weeks by military means.

Blackmail Made Easy

There is a lesson to be learned for the Information Age in the fact that union attempts to achieve wages above market-clearing levels were seldom successful when firm size was small. Not even those lines of business that were clearly vulnerable to sabotage, such as canals, railways, streetcars, and mines, were easily brought under control. This is not because the unions shrank from using violence. To the contrary. Violence was lavishly employed, sometimes against high-profile individuals. For example, in a case celebrated in the American labor movement as a case of "miners' vengeance," Governor Frank Steunenberg of Idaho, who had opposed an attempt by miners to blockade properties at Coeur d'Alene, was assassinated by a bomb tossed by a contract killer hired by the union. [21] But even murder and threats of murder were usually insufficient to obtain union recognition prior to the emergence of large-scale factories and mass-production enterprises in the twentieth century.

To understand why the circumstances of unions underwent such a change in the twentieth century, you must look at the characteristics of production technology. Something definitely changed with the rapid rise of blue-collar factory employment in the early decades of the twentieth century. This change made businesses at the forefront of the economy especially vulnerable to extortion. In fact, the physical characteristics of industrial technology almost invited workers to employ coercion to shake down the capitalists. Consider:

1. *There was a high natural-resource content in most industrial products.* This tended to anchor production to a limited number of locations, almost in the way that mines must be located where the ore bodies are. Factories placed near transportation centers with convenient access to parts suppliers and raw materials had significant operating advantages. This made it easier for coercive organizations, like governments and unions, to extract some of those advantages for themselves.

2. *Rising economies of scale led to very large enterprises.* Early-nineteenth-century factories had been relatively small. But as scale economies increased with the assembly line during the twentieth century, the size and cost of facilities at the forefront of the production process rose rapidly. This made them easier targets in several ways. For example, significant scale economies tend to go hand in hand with long product cycles. Long product cycles make for more stable markets. This, in turn, invites predatory targeting of firms because it implies that there are longer-term benefits to capture.

3. *The number of competitors in leading industries fell sharply.* It was not uncommon during the industrial period to find only a handful of firms competing for billion-dollar markets. This contributed to making these firms targets for union extortion. It is far simpler to attack five firms than five thousand. The very concentration of industry was itself a factor that facilitated extortion. This advantage was self-reinforcing because the firms coerced into paying monopoly wages were unlikely to face stiff competition from others who were not also burdened by above-market labor costs. Unions could therefore drain a considerable portion of the profits of such firms without exposing them to immediate bankruptcy. Obviously, if employers had routinely gone broke whenever they were forced to pay above-market wages, workers would have gained little by coercing them to do so.

4. *The capital requirements for fixed investment rose to match the scale of enterprise.* This not only increased the vulnerability of capital and magnified the costs of plant closures; it also made it increasingly unlikely that a modern factory could be owned by a single individual or family, except through inheritance from someone who had launched the business at a smaller scale. In order to fund the massive costs of tooling and operating a large factory, the wealth of hundreds or thousands of people had to be pooled

together in capital markets. This tended to make it more difficult for the splintered and almost anonymous owners to defend their property. They had little choice but to rely upon professional managers who seldom held more than a bare chemical trace of the outstanding shares of the company. Reliance on subordinate managers weakened the resistance of firms to extortion. The managers lacked strong incentives to risk life and limb protecting the property of the firm. Their efforts seldom matched the kind of militancy commonly seen among owners of liquor stores and other small businesses when their property comes under threat.

5. *Greater firm size also meant that more of the total workforce was employed in fewer firms than at any time in the past.* In some cases, tens of thousands of workers found employment in a single company. In military terms, the owners and managers were starkly outnumbered by persons employed in subordinate positions. Ratios of thirty to one or worse were common. This disadvantage rose with firm size because massive numbers of workers assembled together could more easily employ violence in an anonymous way. Under such conditions, the workers were unlikely to have had any meaningful contact or relationships with the owners of the factory. The anonymous character of these relationships no doubt made it easier for workers to dismiss the importance of the owners' property rights.

6. *Massed employment in a small number of firms was a broad social phenomenon.* This further enhanced the megapolitical advantages enjoyed by unions as compared to the nineteenth century in America, when most people were self-employed or working in small firms. In 1940, 60 percent of the American workforce had blue-collar jobs.[22] As a consequence, support for the use of extortion to raise wages spread among a large number who imagined they might benefit by it. This was illustrated by a 1938–39 study of the views of 1,700 people in Akron, Ohio, toward corporate property. The survey found that 68 percent of the CIO Rubber Workers had very little or no sympathy with the concept of corporate property, "while only one percent were found in the classification of strong support of corporate property rights."[23] On the other hand, not a single businessman, even a small proprietor, fell into the same category of "strong opposition to corporate property; 94 percent received ratings in the range of extremely high support for the rights of property."[24]

7. *Assembly-line technology was inherently sequential.* The fact that the whole production process depended upon the movement and assembly of parts in a fixed sequence created additional vulnerabilities to disruption. In effect, the assembly line was like a railroad within factory walls. If the track could be blocked, or the availability of a single part could be cut off, the whole production process was brought to a halt.

8. *Assembly-line technology standardized work.* This reduced the vari-

ability of output for persons of different skills working with the same tools. In fact, a crucial objective of factory design was to create a system in which a genius and a moron on successive shifts of the assembly line would produce the same product. What might be called "stupid" machines were designed to be capable of only one kind of output. This made it unnecessary for even the buyer of a Cadillac to inquire about the identity of the line workers who produced his vehicle. All the products were meant to be alike, whatever the differences in skills and intelligence between the workers who produced them.

The fact that unskilled workers on the assembly line could produce the same product as more able individuals contributed to the egalitarian agenda by making it appear that everyone's economic contributions were equal. Entrepreneurial skills and mental effort seemed less important. The magic of modern production appeared to lie in the machines themselves. If they could not actually have been designed by everyone, they nevertheless appeared to be intellectually accessible to almost everyone. This gave more plausibility to the fiction that unskilled labor was being "exploited" by factory owners who could be cut out of the equation with no loss to anyone but themselves. "We learned we can take the plant," as one GM striker put it. "We already knew how to run them. If General Motors isn't careful we'll put two and two together." [25]

These characteristics of industrial technology led uniformly to the creation of labor unions to exploit the vulnerability to shakedowns, and to larger governments that fattened on the high taxes that could be imposed upon large-scale industrial facilities. This did not happen once or twice, it happened everywhere large-scale industry took root. Time after time, unions emerged to employ violence to achieve wages considerably above market levels. They were able to do this because industrial factories tended to be expensive, conspicuous, immobile, and costly. They could scarcely be hidden. They could not be moved. Every moment they were out of service meant that their staggering costs were not being amortized.

All this made them sitting ducks for coercive shakedowns, a fact that is far more obvious in the history of labor unions than the prevailing ideology of the twentieth century would have you believe. The noted economist Henry Simons framed the issue in 1944:

> Labor organization without large powers of coercion and intimidation is an unreal abstraction. Unions now have such powers; they always have had and always will have, so long as they persist in the present form. Where the power is small or insecurely possessed, it must be exercised overtly and extensively; large and unchallenged, it becomes like the power of government, confidently held, respectfully regarded, and rarely displayed conspicuously." [26]

As precise as Simons's analysis is, however, he was wrong about a crucial point. He presumed that unions "always will have" what he described as "large powers of coercion and intimidation." In fact, unions are fading away, not merely in the United States and Great Britain, but in other mature industrial societies. The reason they are fading, what Simons missed and what even many union organizers fail to understand, is that the shift to an Information Society has altered megapolitical conditions in crucial ways that sharply increase the security of property. Microtechnology has already begun to prove subversive of the extortion that supports the welfare state because even in the commercial realm it creates very different incentives from those of the industrial period.

1. *Information technology has negligible natural-resource content.* It confers few if any inherent advantages of location. Most information technology is highly portable. Because it can function independent of place, information technology increases the mobility of ideas, persons, and capital. General Motors could not pack up its three assembly lines in Flint, Michigan, and fly away. A software company can. The owners can download their algorithms into portable computers and take the next plane out. Such firms also have an added inducement to escape high taxes or union demands for monopoly wages. Smaller firms tend to have more competitors. If you have dozens or even hundreds of competitors tempting your customers, you cannot afford to pay politicians or your employees much more than they are actually worth. If you alone tried to do so, your costs would be higher than your competitors and you would go broke. The absence of significant operating advantages in a given locale means that coercive organizations, like governments and unions, will inevitably have less leverage to exploit in trying to extract some of those advantages for themselves.

2. *Information technology lowers the scale of enterprise.* This makes for smaller firm size, which implies a larger number of competitors. Increased competition reduces the potential for extortion by raising the number of targets that must be physically controlled in order to raise wages or tax rates above competitive levels. The sharp fall in the average size of firms facilitated by information technology has already reduced the number of persons employed in subordinate positions. In the United States, for example, widely reported estimates suggest that as many as 30 million persons worked alone in their own firms in 1996. Obviously, these 30 million are unlikely to go on strike against themselves. It is only slightly less plausible that the additional millions who work in small firms with a handful of employees would attempt to coerce their employers into paying above-market wages.

In the Information Age, workers who wish to raise their wages through extortion will lack the military advantage of overwhelming numbers that made them more formidable within the factory. The fewer persons employed in any firm, the fewer the opportunities for anonymous violence. For this reason alone, ten thousand workers divided among five hundred firms would pose a lesser threat to the property of those firms than ten thousand workers in a single firm, even if the ratio of workers to owners/managers were exactly the same.

3. *Falling scale in enterprise also implies that efforts to secure above-market wages are less likely to command broad social support, as they did in the industrial period.* Unions seeking to shake down employers are much more likely to find themselves in the situation of the canal workers, railroad employees, and miners of the nineteenth century. Even where a few firms with large-scale economies remain as holdovers from the Industrial Age, they will do so in a context of widely dispersed employment in small firms. The preponderance of small firms and smallholders suggests greater social support for property rights even if the desire to redistribute income remains unaltered.

4. *Information technology lowers capital costs,* which also tends to increase competition by facilitating entrepreneurship and allowing more people to work independently. Lower capital requirements not only reduce barriers to entry; they also reduce "barriers to exit." In other words, they imply that firms are likely to have fewer assets relative to income, and therefore less ability to sustain losses. Not only will they tend to have less recourse to banks for borrowing; firms in the Information Age are also likely to have fewer physical assets to capture.

5. *Information technology shortens the product cycle.* This makes for more rapid product obsolescence. This, too, tends to make any gains that might be achieved by extorting above-market wages short-lived. In highly competitive markets, wages that are too high may lead directly to a rapid loss of jobs and even bankruptcy for the firm. Grasping for temporarily higher wages at the expense of placing your job in jeopardy is like burning your furniture to make the house a few degrees warmer.

6. *Information technology is not sequential but simultaneous and dispersed.* Unlike the assembly line, information technology can accommodate multiple processes at the same time. It disperses activities on networks, allowing for redundancy and substitution between workstations that could number in the thousands or even the millions and be anywhere on earth. In increasing numbers of activities, it is possible for people to cooperate without ever coming into physical contact with one another. As virtual reality and video conferencing become more advanced, the trend toward dispersal of functions and telecommuting will accelerate. This is the Information Age equivalent of "putting out," which broke the power of the medieval guilds.

The fact that fewer and fewer people will be working together in smoky factories not only takes away an important advantage that workers formerly enjoyed in engineering shakedowns of capitalists; it also makes it increasingly difficult even to distinguish from racketeering the type of extortion that has been acceptable in the workplace. Heretofore, only persons who have worked together and been employed by a firm in a common setting have been permitted to use violence in the attempt to raise their incomes. But if the "workplace" does not exist as a central location, and most of the functions are dispersed to subcontractors and telecommuters, there is very little to distinguish from a shakedown racket their efforts to extort money from their clients or "employers."

For example, is a telecommuter who demands extra cash under threat of infecting the company's computers with a virus a worker on strike? Or an Internet racketeer?

Whether he is one or the other will prove to be a distinction without a difference. The reaction of the targeted firms is likely to be much the same in any event. Technical solutions to information sabotage, like improved encryption and network security, that would answer the danger of an outside hacker should also render moot the capacity of the disgruntled employee or subcontractor to impose damage on parties with whom he regularly or sporadically deals.

Of course, it might be suggested that the worker or telecommuter could always report to the office and carry on a more traditional strike there. But even this may not be as simple as it would seem in the Information Age. The capacity of information technology to transcend locality and disperse economic functions means that for the first time employees and employers need not even reside in the same jurisdictions. Here, we are not talking about the difference between being in the boroughs of Mayfair and Peckham, but of employers in Bermuda and telecommuters in New Delhi.

Furthermore, if the Indians became infatuated by accounts of the great GM strikes of 1936–37 and determined to journey to Bermuda to picket, they might find no physical office at all when they arrived. Chiat/Day, a large advertising company, has already set about dismantling its headquarters. Its employees, or subcontractors, stay in touch through call-forwarding and the Internet. When it becomes necessary to assemble talent teams to coordinate work on account projects, they rent hotel meeting rooms. When the project is over they check out.

The fact that microprocessing helps to liberate and disperse the production process from the fixed sequence of the assembly line greatly reduces the leverage formerly enjoyed by coercive institutions like unions and governments. If the assembly line were like a railroad within factory walls that could easily be captured by a sit-down strike, cyberspace is an unbounded realm without physical existence. It cannot be occupied by force or held to ransom. The position of employees wishing to use violence as leverage to extract higher incomes will be far weaker in the Information Age than it was for the sit-down strikers at General Motors in 1936–37.

7. *Microprocessing individualizes work.* Industrial technology standardized work. Anyone using the same tools would produce the same output. Microtechnology has started replacing "stupid" machines with more intelligent technology capable of highly variable output. The increased variability of output for persons using the same tools has profound implications, many of which we explore in coming chapters. Among the more important is the fact that where output varies, incomes vary as well. Most of the value in fields where skill varies will tend to be created by a small number of persons. This is a common characteristic of the most highly competitive markets. It is quite evident, for example, in sports. Many millions of young people worldwide play various versions of football. But 99 percent of the money that is spent to watch football games is paid to see the performances of a tiny fraction of the total number of players. Likewise, the world is full of aspiring actors and actresses. Yet only a relatively small number become stars. Equally, tens of thousands of books are published annually. But most of the royalty money is paid to a small number of best-selling authors who can really entertain their readers. Unhappily, we are not among them.

The vast variability of output among persons employing the same equipment poses yet another obstacle to extortion. It creates a major bargaining problem about how to share the payoff. Where a relatively small proportion of those participating in a given activity create most of the value, it is all but mathematically impossible for them to be left better off by a coerced outcome that averages incomes. One software programmer may devise an algorithm for controlling a robot that proves to be worth millions. Another, working with identical equipment, may write a program worth nothing. The more productive programmer is no more likely to wish to have his income tied to that of his compatriot than Tom Clancy is to agree to average his book royalties with ours.

Even the early stages of the Information Revolution have made it far more obvious than it was in 1975 that skills and mental ability are crucial variables in economic output. This has already vaporized the once-proud rationalization for extortion of the capitalists by the workers that prevailed during the industrial period. The fantasy that unskilled labor actually created the value that seemed to be pocketed in a disproportionate share by the capitalists and entrepreneurs is already an anachronism. It is not even a plausible fiction in the case of information technology. When the programmer sits down to write code, there is too direct a line of attribution between his skill and his product to allow for much mistake about who is responsible. It is obvious beyond dispute that an illiterate or semi-literate could not program a computer. It is therefore equally obvious that any value in programs compiled by others could not have been stolen from him. This is why cries of "exploitation" by workers are now heard mainly among janitors.

Information technology is making it plain that the problem faced by persons of low skill is not that their productive capacities are being unfairly taken advantage of, but rather the fear that they may lack the ability to make a real economic contribution. As Kevin Kelly suggests in *Out of Control,* the "Upstart" car company of the Information Age may be the brainchild of "a dozen people," who will outsource most of their parts, and still produce cars more carefully customized and tailored to their buyer's wishes than anything yet seen from Detroit or Tokyo: "Cars, each one customer-tailored, are ordered by a network of customers and shipped the minute they are done. Molds for the car's body are rapidly shaped by computer-guided lasers, and fed designs generated by customer response and target marketing. A flexible line of robots assembles the cars. Robot repair and improvement is outsourced to a robot company." [27]

"Tools with a Voice"

To an increasing extent, unskilled work can be done by automated machines, robots, and computational systems, like digital assistants. When Aristotle described slaves as "tools with a voice," he was talking about human beings. In the not-distant future, "tools with a voice," like the genies of fable, will be able to speak and follow instructions, and even handle complex assignments. Rapidly increasing computational power has already brought forth a number of primitive applications of voice recognition, such as hands-free telephones and computers that perform mathematical computations following verbal instructions. Computers that convert speech to text were already being marketed in late 1996 as we write. As pattern-recognition capabilities improve, computers linked to voice synthesizers will operate through networks to perform numerous functions formerly undertaken by humans employed as telephone operators, secretaries, travel agents, administrative assistants, chess champions, claims processors, composers, bond traders, cyberwar specialists, weapons analysts, or even street-smart flirts who answer the telephones on 900 calls.

Michael Mauldin of Carnegie-Mellon University has programmed a "bot," an artificial personality named Julia, who is capable of fooling almost anyone with whom she converses on the Internet. According to press reports, Julia is a "wise-cracking dame who lives out her life in a role-playing game on the Internet. She is smart, funny and loves to flirt. She is also a bit of a hockey whiz and able to come up with the perfect sarcastic comment on a moment's notice. Julia, however, is no lady. She is a bot, an artificial intelligence that exists only in the ether of the Internet." [28] The startling progress that has already been made in programming artificial intelligence and digital servants leaves little doubt that many practical applications are still to come. This has significant megapolitical consequences.

The Individual as an Ensemble

Development of "tools with a voice" for multiple applications creates the possibility for dispersal of the individual into multiple simultaneous activities. The individual will no longer be singular, but potentially an ensemble of dozens or perhaps even thousands of activities undertaken through intelligent agents. This will not only greatly enhance the productive capability of the most talented individuals; it will also make the Sovereign Individual potentially far more formidable militarily than the individual has ever been before.

Not only will one individual be able to manifestly multiply his activities by employing an essentially unlimited number of intelligent agents. He or she will even be able to act after death. For the first time, an individual will be capable of carrying on elaborate tasks even if he is biologically dead. It will no longer be possible for either an enemy at war or a criminal to completely extinguish the capability of an individual to retaliate by killing him. This is one of the more revolutionary innovations in the logic of violence in the whole of history.

Insights for the Information Age

The biggest changes in life occur to variables that no one watches. Or to put it another way, we take for granted variables that have fluctuated very little for centuries or even hundreds of generations. For most of history, if not for most of human existence, the balance between protection and extortion has fluctuated within a narrow margin, with extortion always holding the upper hand. Now that is about to change. Information technology is laying the groundwork for a fundamental shift in the factors that determine the costs and rewards of resorting to violence. The fact that intelligent agents will be available to investigate and perhaps retaliate in one fashion or another against those who initiate violence is merely a hint of this new vista in protection. Twenty-five years ago, the following statement would have been no more than the ranting of a crank: "If you kill me, I will sweep the money out of your bank accounts and give it to charities in Nepal." After the turn of the millennium, it may not be. Whether it would prove to be a practical threat would be determined by factors of time and place. Yet even if the would-be miscreant's accounts proved to be impermeable, there would surely be other costly mischief that an army of intelligent agents could impose in retaliation for a crime. Think about it.

New Alternatives in Protection

This is only one of many ways to enhance protection that are being opened by the technology of the Information Age, most of which tend to undermine the near-monopoly on protection and extortion that has been enjoyed by governments in the past two centuries. Even without the new technological razzle-dazzle, there have always been alternatives for protection, not all of which have tended to be monopolized by government.

A person who feels threatened may simply run away. When the world was young and horizons were open, the option to flee was commonly employed. When people worry about losses due to theft or vandalism, they may elect to purchase insurance policies to indemnify such risks. Curses and spells, although weak forms of protection, have also saved lives and warded off acts of theft. They sometimes work in societies where predators are superstitious. Valuables may also be protected by being hidden. This is sometimes an effective method when it can be employed. Assets can be buried. Secured with locks. Placed behind high walls. And rigged with sirens and electronic monitoring devices. But hiding person and property have not always been practical.

For all the variety of means of protection that have been employed historically, one method has dominated all others—the capacity to trump violence with violence, to call on greater force to overwhelm anyone who would assault you or steal your property. The question is where you can turn for such a service, and how you can motivate anyone to risk life and limb to help you battle thugs who might initiate force against you. Sometimes close relatives have answered the call. Sometimes tribal and clan-based groups have served as an unofficial police, responding to violence against any of their members with blood vendettas. Sometimes mercenaries or private guards have been employed to fend off attack, but not always as usefully as you might wish. The new intelligent agents of the Information Age, although their activities will be largely confined to cyberspace, add a new alternative. Their loyalties, unlike those of the mercenaries, private guards, and even remote cousins, will be beyond dispute.

The Paradoxes of Power

The use of violence to protect against violence is fraught with paradoxes. Under conditions that have heretofore existed, any group or agency that you could employ to successfully protect your life and wealth from attack would also necessarily have had the capacity to take either. That is a drawback for which there is no easy answer. Normally, you could look to competition to keep providers of an economic service from ignoring the wishes of their customers. But where violence is concerned, direct competition often has perverse results. In the past, it has usually led to increased violence. When two would-be protective agencies send their forces to arrest one another, the result is more akin to civil war than protection. When you are seeking protection from violence you normally do not wish to increase the output of violence but to suppress it. And to suppress it on terms that do not allow the plundering of the customers who pay for the protection service in the first place.

". . . during the time men live without a common power to keep them all in awe, they are in that condition which is called war: and such a war, as is of every man, against every man . . . wherein men live without other security than what their own strength and their own inventions shall furnish them withal."

—THOMAS HOBBES

Monopoly and Anarchy

This is why anarchy, or "the war of all against all," as Hobbes described it, has seldom been a satisfactory state of affairs. Local competition in the use of violence has usually meant paying higher costs for protection and enjoying less of it. Occasionally, freethinking enthusiasts for the market have suggested that market mechanisms alone would be sufficient to provide for policing of property rights and protection of life, without any need for a sovereignty whatsoever.[29] Some of the analytics have been elegant, but the fact remains that free-market provision of police and justice services has not proven viable under the megapolitical conditions of industrialism. Only primitive societies where behavior is highly stereotyped and populations are tiny and homogeneous have been able to survive without governments to provide the service of locally monopolizing protection through violence.

Examples of anarchic societies above the level of the hunting-and-gathering tribe are few and ancient. They are all among the simplest economies of isolated rainwater farmers. The Kafirs in pre-Muslim Afghanistan. Some Irish tribes in the Dark Ages. Some Indian bands in Brazil, Venezuela, and Paraguay. Other aboriginals in scattered parts of the world. Their methods of organizing protection without government are known only to connoisseurs of extreme cases. If you would like to learn more about them, we cite several books in our Notes that contain more details.[30] Primitive groups were able to function without a distinct organization specializing in violence only because they were small, closed societies. And they were isolated. They could draw on tight kinship relations to defend against most violent threats on a limited scale, which were the only sort they were likely to encounter. When they encountered larger threats, organized by states, they were over-powered and subjected to rule monopolized by outside groups. This happened over and over. Wherever societies have formed at a scale above bands and tribes, especially where trade routes brought different peoples into contact, specialists in violence have always emerged to plunder any surplus more peaceful people could produce. When technological conditions raised the returns to violence, they doomed societies that were not organized to channel large resources into making war.

"Which princes were rendering the service of police? Which were racketeers or even plunderers? A plunderer could become in effect the chief of police as soon as he regularized his 'take,' adapted it to the capacity to pay, defended his preserve against other plunderers, and maintained his territorial monopoly long enough for custom to make it legitimate."[31]

—FREDERIC C. LANE

Government as a Seller of Protection

As we have said at several points, government's principal economic function from the perspective of those who pay the taxes is to provide protection of life and property. Yet the government often operates like organized crime, extracting resources from people within its sphere of operations as tribute or plunder. Government is not only a protection service; it is also a protection racket. While government provides protection against violence originating with others, like the protection racket it also charges customers for protection against harm that it would otherwise impose itself. The first action is an economic service. The second is a racket. In practice, the distinction between the two forms of "protection" may be difficult to make. Governments, as Charles Tilly has pointed out, may perhaps be best understood as "our largest examples of organized crime."[32]

The activities of even the best government usually involved some mixture of the economic service of protection combined with extortion. Historically, both pursuits could be optimized if the government could impose a near-monopoly on coercion within the territories where it operates. In cases where a single armed group could establish predominance in the use of violence, the quality of the protection service it could provide was normally far superior to what could be had from one of several competing protection agencies thrown into battle over the same territory.

A Natural Monopoly on Land

Achievement of a local monopoly of coercion not only allowed a government to more effectively protect its potential customers from violence initiated by others; it also greatly reduced the government's operating costs. As Lane put it, "The violence-using, violence-controlling industry was a natural monopoly, at least on land. Within territorial limits, the service it rendered could be produced much more cheaply by a monopoly." [33] Thus a "monopoly of the use of force within a contiguous territory enabled a protection-producing enterprise to improve its product and reduce its costs." [34] Such a governing organization could offer more protection with less expense if it did not have to engage in incessant military actions to fend off competitive groups seeking to extract protection payments from its customers.

The prospect that information technology will help "relax" the assumption that sovereignty must be based upon a territorial monopoly has already attracted the attention of political theorists. It is the theme of *Beyond Sovereignty: Territory and Political Economy in the Twenty-first Century*, by David J. Elkins. Elkins echoes our thesis that monopoly governments are destined to be disintermediated much as religious monopolies were in the years following 1500. He writes: "We used to assume that religions should have their own territory or 'turf.' As nations replaced universal religions as the sovereign arbiters of life and death, the 'compactness' and 'boundedness' of religion gave way to our now familiar intermingling of believers in the same area. Instead, we refuse to countenance the intermingling of nations, or provinces for that matter, although I believe this assumption is in the process of breaking down." [35] He goes on to argue, in keeping with our view, that territorial monopolies on sovereignty can be broken down without anarchy, as evidenced by the split in sovereignty between national and provincial governments in a federal system like Canada's, and by the condominium government involving joint French and British sovereignty that characterized some Pacific Islands for much of this century. Thus, while territorial monopolies on sovereignty have rarely been unbundled by force, they can be unbundled by agreement. According to Elkins, and we agree, "The territorial nation has been a bundle or basket into which other facets of our lives are fit. It is similar to the economic concept of a 'basket' of goods—you cannot easily get items individually but must take them collectively. In a restaurant, one can order *'a la carte'*; but as far as our identities are concerned, we must take what nations have bundled together, which amounts to *'table d'hote.'* . . . Government *a la carte* will seem natural to citizens in the twenty-first century." [36] There is no development that will contribute more dramatically to the disaggregation of sovereignty and the rise of government à la carte than the emergence of a cybereconomy that altogether transcends physical borders.

"As frequencies rise and wavelengths drop, digital performance improves exponentially. Bandwidth rises, power usage shrinks, antenna size shrinks, interference collapses, error rates plummet."

—GEORGE GILDER

THE LAW OF THE TELECOSM REPEALS THE LAWS OF NATIONS

We are not alone in seeing that bandwidth (or the carrying capacity of communications media) is destined to trump the territorial state. Jim Taylor and Watts Wacker, authors of *The 500-Year Delta: What Happens After What Comes Next,* do not define their argument as we do, but they see clearly that "access creates globalism, and globalism disrupts political systems by making the concept of borders obsolete. As borders disappear, the concept of taxation, which supports governments, becomes increasingly fragile. . . . As borders disappear, the concept of entitlement—the belief that because you were born in a particular place, you are entitled to the economic advantages associated with that place—falls apart, and as it falls apart, the perks of nationhood fall apart with it. And as all that happens, the ideals that underlie nationhood—patriotism, democracy, the state, the melting pot, unification, responsible participation, whatever they happen to be in whatever nation one is living in—get relegated to the junk heap of history." [37] Without saying so explicitly, they, too, apparently sense that history is moving toward the liberation of the Sovereign Individual. As they say, "On the horizon waits a much purer form of individualism than democracy as we now understand it allows." [38] How will this happen? Taylor and Wacker see a powerful dynamic at work:

> The simple fact is that the larger sense of patriotism—a love of nation, a sense of filial duty to it—is not a particularly useful predisposition to have any longer. . . . Citizens who thrive in the global society will identify themselves globally. They will make political, social, and economic choices based not on national identity, but on how those choices relate to themselves directly and to people like them around the world. . . . Nations and corporations who thrive will organize themselves accordingly. They will maximize the freedom to

know, to go, to do, and to be. Nations and corporations that don't, that continue to fight rear-guard actions based on nostalgia, will atrophy.[39]

The devaluation of physical borders implied by the tripling of bandwidth each year and the geometric growth of the Internet and World Wide Web will accelerate the process of disintermediating governments. Indeed, a continuation of the annual tripling of bandwidth until the year 2012 would imply a billionfold growth in bandwidth since 1993, when George Gilder first suggested that bandwidth was destined to compound even faster than the capacity of microprocessors. If this comes to pass—as we believe it will, to judge by recent breakthroughs in integrated optics—the abundance of communications capability that would be created would result in a fantastic increase in cybercommerce. With wave division multiplexing, a single fiber strand, as thin as a human hair, has the capacity to carry one trillion bits per second.[40] In other words, a single fiber optic cable could accommodate twenty-five times more bits than the total load of all of the world's communications networks combined. The capacity for expansion is stupefying. With this much communications capacity unleashed, vastly more money will be spent on communication because it will be so cheap. And such established media as dedicated telephony and television will become anachronisms. The World Wide Web will deliver a richer mix of signals to every computer than consumers experience with network television today. As the bandwidth revolution unfolds, it will draw people more and more into the borderless virtual world of online communities and cybercommerce, a world with enough graphic density to become the "metaverse," the kind of alternative, cyberspace reality imagined by the science fiction novelist Neal Stephenson. Stephenson's "metaverse" is a virtual community with its own laws, princes, and villains.[41] As ever more economic activity is drawn into cyberspace, the value of the state's monopoly power within borders will shrink, giving states a growing incentive to franchise and fragment their sovereignty.

Just as nation-states today have incentives to host free ports, free-trade zones, and zona francas, so they will have incentives to lease their sovereignty. We have already discussed the well-advanced negotiations between the nine-hundred-year-old Sovereign Military Hospitaller Order of St. John of Jerusalem, of Rhodes and of Malta, more commonly known as the Knights of Malta, and the Republic of Malta to return sovereignty over Fort St. Angelo to the order. We expect these negotiations to be successfully concluded. Others will follow. Some nation-states will cede sovereignty over small enclaves and remote areas to entirely new affinity groups and virtual communities. Indeed, it is not unlikely that commercial entities, such as security firms and hotel chains, will bid for sovereignty over small patches of territory. Wackenhut, Pinkerton, and Argenbright may, in the future, offer hybrid gated retirement communities and tax-free zones in attractive climates around the world. Religious entities, like the Knights of Malta, but representing every conceivable denomination, will try in their own ways to make heaven incarnate in certain out-of-the-way corners of the earth. Even wealthy individuals and families will possess their own plots where they will exercise limited sovereignty, issue their own stamps and passports, and maintain a Web site.

MONOPOLY AND PLUNDER

Note that the incentives to share or lease sovereignty for a fee are quite different from those that have historically faced rulers exposed to military competition with their local monopoly of coercion. Leased sovereignty is no more destabilizing than hosting a free-trade zone. By contrast, military competition for power, of the kind pursued by battling warlords and guerrilla bands, directly affects whether the would-be government has stronger incentives to protect people within its grasp or to plunder them. Where contending groups wrestle and maneuver in uneasy balance, the incentives to use predatory violence increase. Plunder becomes more attractive. Because power is less stable, and the local monopoly of coercion less secure, the time horizons of those with the capacity to employ violence shrinks. The "king of the mountain" may stand on such a slippery slope that he could not expect to survive long enough to realize a share of the substantial gains that ultimately result from containing violence. When that is the case, there is little to prevent those who command what passes for government from employing their power to terrorize and pillage society.

The logic of force, therefore, tells you that the more competing armed groups there are operating in any territory, the higher the likelihood that they will resort to predatory violence. Without a single overwhelming power to suppress freelance violence, it tends to proliferate, and many of the gains of economic and social cooperation go up in smoke.

The damage that can occur when violence is given full reign in a condition of anarchy is demonstrated by the fate of China under the warlords in the 1920s. It is a story we recounted in *The Great Reckoning*. The competing warlords imposed great damage in areas where there was no single, overwhelming power to keep them in check. Similar stories illustrating a similar point have been broadcast to the world in living color by CNN news crews braving the streets of Mogadishu, Somalia. The armed forces of Somalia's warlords, nicknamed the "technicals," brought anarchy to that sad country before the United States led a massive military intervention to contain them. When the commanding might of U.S. forces was withdrawn, the technicals brought out their weapons again, and anarchy resumed. A report in the *Washington Post* observed:

> [P]ickup trucks mounted with antiaircraft guns are once again plowing the dusty, rubble-strewn streets. Back too are the swaggering young men in T-shirts and Kalashnikov rifles slung over their shoulders, extorting money from passing cars and buses at makeshift roadblocks. One militia-controlled neighborhood here is so heavily armed that locals refer to it as "Bosnia-Herzegovina."
>
> Travelling around this city's mean streets today is strikingly reminiscent of the days in 1992, when chaotic warfare among rival militias plunged Somalia into anarchy and a famine that prompted a U.S.-led military intervention. Once again, to traverse Mogadishu, travelers must hire a carload of armed thugs, hoping they will deliver protection for a hundred bucks a day, plus time off for lunch.[42]

The examples of Somalia, Rwanda, and others you will soon see on television offer a Technicolor proof that violent competition for control of territory does not yield the same immediate economic gains as other forms of competition. To the contrary. The roving bandits and looters who compete under anarchy lack even the weak incentives to protect productive activity that sometimes lighten even the heavy hand of dictators when their rule is secure.

"The society of what we call the modern age is characterized, above all in the West, by a certain level of monopolization. Free use of military weapons is denied the individual and reserved to a central authority of whatever kind, and likewise the taxation of the property or income of individuals is concentrated in the hands of a central social authority. The financial means thus flowing into this central authority maintain its monopoly of military force, while this in turn maintains the monopoly of taxation. Neither has in any sense precedence over the other; they are two sides of the same monopoly. If one disappears the other automatically follows; the monopoly rule may sometimes be shaken more strongly on one side than on the other."[43]

—NORBERT ELIAS

THE EVOLUTION OF PROTECTION

Lane developed an argument that we have misappropriated for our purposes in imagining how the Information Age may unfold. He argued that the history of Western economies since the Dark Ages can be interpreted in terms of four stages of competition and monopoly in the organization of violence. While Lane is largely silent about the megapolitical factors that we identify as influencing the scale at which governments operate, his exploration of the economics of violence coincides closely with the argument we spelled out in *Blood in the Streets* and *The Great Reckoning,* and elsewhere in this volume.

We have already analyzed some of the megapolitical factors that played a role in the evolution of Western society following the fall of Rome. Lane also examined this period, focusing on the economic consequences of that competition to monopolize violence. He discerned four important stages in the functioning of economies over the past thousand years, each involving a different phase in the organization of violence.*

Out of the Dark Ages

The first stage is one of "anarchy and plunder" that marked the feudal revolution of a thousand years ago. While Lane does not specify the dates for any of his summary periods, arithmetic sets the boundary of his first period quite clearly, and his description of the stage of "anarchy and plunder" seems to match conditions during the transition from the Dark Ages when the use of violence was "highly competitive, even on land." [44] He does not say why, but when violence is "highly competitive," this usually means that there are significant obstacles to the projection of power at any distance. In military terms, defense is predominant over the offense.

For reasons we explained in Chapter 3, this stage of "anarchy and plunder" coincided with falling productivity of agriculture due to adverse climatic changes. Since technology offered few effective economies of scale to help in securing a monopoly of violence at the time, competition between would-be rulers was widespread. Economic activity was smothered.

The weakness of the economy made the problem of establishing a stable order worse. To create a local monopoly of violence involved too high a cost in military activity in proportion to the meager value of economic turnover. Without the capacity to enforce an effective monopoly over an economically viable territory, the armed knights on horseback terrorized and plundered while providing little in the way of "protection" for their customers.

Feudalism

"The second stage begins when small regional or provincial monopolies are established. Agricultural production then rises, and most of the surplus is

---

* Note that Lane's four stages of competition and monopoly in the use of violence are different from the four stages in the organization of economic life that we identify—namely, foraging, farming, industrialism, and the Information Age.

collected by recently established monopolists of violence."[45] Still, the surplus is relatively meager during this second stage, which we identify with the early Middle Ages. Economic growth is held down by the absence of advantages of scale in the organization of violence, which keeps the military costs of enforcing local monopolies high. But while the costs remain high, the price that minisovereignties can charge for protection rises, since economic activity expands when anarchy is curtailed.

"During a late phase of the second stage many tribute takers attract customers by special offers to agricultural and commercial enterprise. They offer protection at low prices for those who will bring new lands into cultivation, and special policing services to encourage trade such as that organized by the Counts of Champagne for merchants coming to their fairs."[46] In other words, when they were able to establish a sufficient control over territory to negotiate credibly, local warlords did what local merchants do when they need to increase market share: they discounted their services to attract customers. The warlords later used the added resources from additional economic activity to consolidate their control over larger territories. Once that control was firmly established, they began to enjoy more of the advantages of monopoly. Their military costs for policing tended to fall, and they could also increase the price they charged without worrying that this made their service less attractive to customers.

In this complicated stage in Western history, those who employ violence, the medieval lords and monarchs, take most of the surplus above subsistence. There are few merchants. The most successful are those who are best able to evade or minimize the taxes, fees, and other costs imposed by those demanding money for "protection services."

The Early-Modern Period

A third stage is reached when the merchants and landowners who are not also specialists in violence "are getting more of the economy's surplus than are fief holders and monarchs. . . . In this third stage, the enterprises specializing in the use of violence receive less of the surplus than do enterprises that buy protection from the governments."[47] Since successful merchants are more likely to reinvest their profits than consume them, the higher profits of merchants in that stage in history led to self-reinforcing growth.

The Factory Age

Lane identifies the passage from the third to the fourth stage with the emergence of technological and industrial innovations as more important factors in earning profits than lowering the costs of protection. By this, Lane seems to refer to the period since 1750. From that time on, the character of technology began to play a clearly dominating role in the prosperity of regions. To take an extreme case, even areas where no government existed at all, as was the case in some parts of New Zealand, for example, prior to 1840, were not likely to become highly prosperous simply because they paid no taxes. At that point in history, innovations in industrial technology were more important to achieving profits than any savings that could be had by lowering the costs for protection, even to zero. As the scale of government rose, the credit and financing mechanisms originally pioneered by governments to raise resources for military operations became available to finance business enterprises of larger scale.

Although Lane does not say so, the concentration of technological advantages in a given locale reduced the competition between jurisdictions and allowed "enterprises specializing in the use of violence," or governments, to charge higher prices. When there are large technological gaps between the competitors in one jurisdiction and another, as there were during the Industrial Age, entrepreneurs in the jurisdictions with the best technology tend to make more money, even though they may have to pay higher taxes and other costs to their governments.

Plunder with a Smile

Governments in the Industrial Age enjoyed a delightful monopoly to exploit. Their actual costs for providing protection of life and limb were vanishingly small relative to the prices (taxes) they charged. Yet they really were in a realm where competition was so perverse that they could engage far more in the business of plunder than in that of protection and still have that fact go all but unnoticed. It was a rare moment in history.

The drawbacks of anarchy under the megapolitical conditions of industrialism made competition in protection services within the same territory technologically infeasible. The only way to achieve effective protection under those conditions was to command a greater capability to employ violence. Therefore there was little to be gained by attempting to better distinguish that portion of one's taxes that went, in Lane's words, "as payment for the service rendered" from "another part that one is tempted to call plunder."[48] The distinction was surely real enough. But since one was stuck paying the taxes in any event, developing it fully had little to commend it other than satisfying morbid curiosity. As Lane said, no matter what portion of the taxes was plunder they were a price one had to pay "to avoid more severe losses."[49]

The Rise of Incomes Under Industrialism

Part of the reason this dilemma was tolerable during the past two centuries of domination by the nation-state was the fact that incomes were rising dramatically, particularly in the jurisdictions where most industrial development was confined. Those running the OECD governments took a higher percentage of incomes almost every year. But the increase in plunder was nonetheless accompanied by far greater prosperity, and a greater inequality of wealth with the rest of the world. Under such conditions, objections to the surge of taxation were inevitably marginal and insufficient to deflect events from their logical progression. Indeed, for reasons spelled out in previous chapters, the military survival of an industrial nation-state largely depended upon the fact that no effective limits could be placed upon its claims on the resources of its citizens.

In every industrial state, policies meandered in more or less the same direction. At the high-water mark of industrialism after World War II, the rate of marginal income taxes reached 90 percent or higher. This was a far more aggressive assertion of the right of the state to extract resources than even the Oriental despots of the early hydraulic civilizations were prone to make. Yet the industrial version of plunder followed its own logic. Much of it was determined by the character of industrial technology in the first half of the twentieth century that we described earlier.

This technology made it all but inevitable that the state would seize and redistribute a large fraction of income, with much of the burden of the plunder falling upon a small segment of capitalists. Most industrial processes were heavily dependent on natural resources, and therefore tied to the sites where the resources were located. A steel mill, a mine, or a port could be moved only at staggering expense, or not at all. Such facilities were therefore stationary targets that could easily be taxed. Property, corporate, and severance taxes grew sharply over this century. So did income taxes, first on the capitalists, but eventually on the workers themselves. The advent of large-scale industrial employment made a broadly based income tax practical. Wages could be garnished at the source, with the tax authorities coordinating collections with the accounting departments of industrial firms. We take this for granted today, but collecting an income tax at the factory gate was a far simpler task than fanning out over the countryside to squeeze a portion of the profits from millions of independent craftsmen and farmers.

In short, industrial technology tended to make taxation more routinized, more predictable, and less personally dangerous than taxation in many earlier periods. Nonetheless, it extracted a higher percentage of society's resources than any form of sovereignty had done before.

Protecting What?

The fact that societies could become richer while the total percentage of income absorbed in taxes rose significantly invites a question about the character of the protection that governments provided to industrial economies. What were they protecting? Our answer: primarily industrial installations with high capital costs and significant vulnerability to attack. The presence of large-scale industrial firms would not have been possible in a disordered environment with more competitive violence, even if the result of the competition had been to shrink the overall share of output taken by government.

This is why capital-intensive operations are uneconomic in the American slums, as well as in Third World societies where ad hoc violence is endemic. Industrial society as a whole was able to proceed because a certain kind of order was established and maintained. Enterprises were subject to regular, predictable shakedowns, rather than erratic violence.

Even during the height of industrialism, it was always an exaggeration to speak of a government employing a "monopoly of force." All governments try to maintain such a monopoly, but as we have seen, employees of industrial corporations usually found that they were able to employ violence against their employers. As long as the general public has access to any arms at all, or a disorderly crowd retains the physical capacity to overturn a bus or throw rocks at police, those who control the government do not totally monopolize force. They merely control predominant force, dominant to a degree that it becomes uneconomic for most people to compete with them under existing conditions.

"A Net-based government can operate only by consent of the governed. Any Net government must therefore provide its citizens with real benefits if it wants them to stick around. Those benefits may not be just personal goods or services, but rather the broader benefits of a regulatory regime: a clean, transparent marketplace with defined rules and consequences, or a supervised community where children can trust the people they encounter of individual's privacy is protected."[50]

—ESTHER DYSON

The Information Age

The Information Age is bringing into being a fifth stage in the evolution of competition in the use of violence in the West. This stage was not anticipated by Lane. This fifth phase involves competition in cyberspace, an arena not subject to monopolization by any "violence-using enterprise." It is not subject to monopolization because it is not a territory.

Although Lane's argument incorporates conventional postwar assumptions about the inevitability of the nation-state, he recognized a point that will be more crucial to understanding the future than it may have seemed forty or fifty years ago. That is the fact that governments have never established stable monopolies of coercion over the open sea. Think about it. No government's laws have ever exclusively applied there. This is a matter of the utmost importance in understanding how the organization of violence and protection will evolve as the economy migrates into cyberspace, which has no physical existence at all. For the same reasons that Lane noted in observing that no government has ever been able to monopolize violence on the sea, it is even less likely that a government could successfully monopolize an infinite realm without physical boundaries.

COMPETITION WITHOUT ANARCHY

In the past, when conditions made it difficult for any single violence-wielding entity to establish a monopoly, the results were anarchy and plunder. The Information Age, however, has changed the technological terms under which violence is organized and done so in a profound way. Unlike the past, when the inability to monopolize protection in a region meant higher military costs and lower economic returns, the fact that governments cannot monopolize cyberspace actually implies lower military costs and higher economic returns. This is because information technology creates a new dimension in protection. For the first time in history, information technology allows for the creation and protection of assets that lie entirely outside the realm of any individual government's territorial monopoly on violence.

"Countries in which the units of political power and governance are multiple and which lack a central, stable, unchallenged supervisory source of jurisdiction and power have to devise their own working solutions for dealing with the problems raised by such frontiers."[51]

—REES DAVIES

The Analogy with the Frontier

Cyberspace is in one sense the equivalent of a technologically protected march region of the kind that existed in border areas during the Middle Ages. In the past, when the reach of lords and kings was weak, and the claims of one or more overlapped at a frontier, something akin to competitive government existed. A look at how the march regions functioned could give insights into how laws of the march or something like them may migrate into cyberspace.

Andorra survives as a kind of fossilized march region between France and Spain, an artifact of megapolitical conditions that made it difficult for either kingdom to dominate the other in that cold and almost inaccessible area of 190 square miles in the Pyrenees. In 1278, an agreement was struck dividing suzerainty over Andorra between local French and Spanish feudal lords, the French count of Foix and the Spanish bishop of Urgel. Each appointed one of two "viquiers" who sparingly exercised the minimal authority of government in Andorra, mostly by commanding the tiny Andorran militia, now a police force. The count's role was long ago superseded by history. The French government now stands in for him from Paris. Among its duties is to accept half of the annual tribute that Andorra pays, an amount less than a single month's rent in a fleabag apartment. The bishop of Urgel continues to receive his share of the tribute, just as his predecessors did in the Middle Ages.

As the split tribute implies, there have been two sources of "supervisory jurisdiction and power" rather than one in Andorra. Appeals from Andorran civil suits were traditionally lodged either with the Episcopal College of Urgel or the Court of Cassation in Paris.

A consequence of Andorra's ambiguous position was that almost no laws were enacted. Andorra has enjoyed vanishingly small government and no taxes for more than seven hundred years. Today, that gives it a growing appeal as a tax haven. But until a generation ago, Andorra was famously poor. Once thickly wooded, it was deforested over the centuries by residents trying to stay warm in the bitter winters. The whole place is snowed shut from November through April each year. Even in summer, Andorra is so cold that crops grow only on the southern slopes. If our description makes it seem unappealing, you have just learned the secret of its success. Andorra survived as a feudal enclave in the age of the nation-state because it was remote and dirt-poor.

At one time, there were numerous medieval frontier or "march" regions where sovereignties blended together. These violent frontiers persisted for decades or sometimes for centuries in the border areas of Europe. Most were poor. As we mentioned earlier, there were marches between areas of Celtic and English control in Ireland; between Wales and England, Scotland and

England, Italy and France, France and Spain, Germany and the Slav frontiers of Central Europe, and between the Christian kingdoms of Spain and the Islamic kingdom of Granada. Like Andorra, these march regions developed distinct institutional and legal forms of a kind that we are likely to see again in the next millennium.

Because of the competitive position of the two authorities, each of which was weak, rulers would sometimes even solicit volunteers among their subjects to settle in march regions in order to increase the reach of their authority. Almost as a matter of course, the subjects were lured into settling in the march by freedom from taxes. Given the delicate margins upon which they competed, if either authority in a march attempted to impose taxes, he would make it more difficult for his followers to make ends meet, as well as give everyone a reason to affiliate with his competitor. Therefore, residents of a march usually had a choice in deciding whose laws they were to obey. This choice was based upon the weakness of the competing authorities; it was not an ideological gesture.

Nonetheless, practical difficulties arose that had to be resolved. Under feudalism, landlords who owned property on both sides of a nominal frontier faced a serious conflict of duties. For example, a lord on the frontier of Scotland and England who held properties in both kingdoms could theoretically owe military service to both in the event of war. To resolve this contradictory obligation, almost everyone up and down the feudal hierarchy could choose whose laws to obey through a legal process called avowal.

Information technology will create equivalent opportunities for competitive choice in domiciling economic activities, but with important differences. One is that unlike the medieval frontier societies, cyberspace is likely to be in due course the richest of economic realms. It will therefore tend to be a growing rather than a receding frontier. Few persons at the core regions of medieval society would have wished to move to frontiers without strong inducements, often including religious imperatives, because these regions tended to be violent and poor. Therefore, they did not act as magnets drawing resources out of the control of the authorities. Cyberspace will.

Secondly, the new frontier will not be a duopoly, which invites collusion between the two authorities to compromise over their frontier claims. Such compromises tended not to be effective during the medieval period for two reasons: there were frequently sharp cultural gaps between the rival authorities; and more important, they lacked the physical capacity to impose a negotiated settlement, having insufficient military power on the ground. During the era of the nation-state, when national authorities did come to exercise sufficient military power to impose solutions, most march regions and vague frontiers disappeared. Border fixing became the norm. That is a stable solution if duopolists of violence face the prospect of dividing their authority over contiguous regions. But the competition in domiciling trans-actions in the cybereconomy will not be between two authorities, but between hundreds of authorities throughout the globe. For the territorial states to create an effective cartel to keep tax rates high will be all but impossible. This will be true for the same reason that collusion to enjoy monopoly prices in markets with hundreds of competitors does not work.

For evidence, consider the move by the Seychelles, a tiny country in the Indian Ocean, to enact a new investment law that U.S. government officials describe as a "Welcome Criminals" act. Under the law, anyone who invests $10 million in the Seychelles will not only be guaranteed protection against extradition, but will be issued a diplomatic passport. Contrary to the assertions of the U.S. government, however, the intended beneficiaries are not drug dealers, who are generally under the protection of more important governments in any event, but independent entrepreneurs who have become politically incorrect. The first potential beneficiary of the Seychelles law is a white South African who became wealthy by circumventing the economic sanctions against the former apartheid regime. Now he faces the danger of economic retribution by the new South African government and is willing to pay the Seychelles for protection.[52]

Whatever the merits of any individual case, the example shows why attempts by governments to maintain a cartel for protection on the ground are doomed to failure. Unlike the medieval frontier, in which the competition was between two authorities only, the frontier in cybercommerce will be between hundreds of jurisdictions, with the number probably rising rapidly to thousands.

In the age of the virtual corporation, individuals will choose to domicile their income-earning activities in a jurisdiction that provides the best service at the lowest cost. In other words, sovereignty will be commercialized. Unlike medieval frontier societies, which were in most cases impoverished and violent, cyberspace will be neither. The competition that information technology is driving governments to engage in is not competition of a military kind, but competition in quality and price of an economic service —genuine protection. In short, governments will be obliged to give customers what they want.

The Diminished Utility of Violence

This is not to say, of course, that governments will resign from employing violence. Far from it. Rather, what we are saying is that violence is losing a good deal of its leverage. One possible reaction on the part of governments would be to intensify their use of violence in local settings in an attempt to compensate for its declining global significance. Whatever governments do, however, they will be unable to saturate cyberspace with violence in the way that they saturated the territories they monopolized with violence in the modern world. No matter how many governments try to enter cyberspace, they will be no more capable or powerful in that realm than anyone else.

Ironically, attempts by nation-states to wage "information wars" to dominate or thwart access to cyberspace would probably only accelerate their own demise. The tendency toward the devolution of large systems is already powerful because of the fallaway of scale economies and the rising costs of holding fragmenting social groups together. The irony of information wars is that they could well impose more of a shock to the brittle systems left over from the Industrial Age than to the emerging information economy itself.

As long as essential information technology continues to function, cyber-commerce could proceed in tandem with the struggles of information war in a way that could never happen in a territorial war. You could not imagine millions of commercial transactions taking place at the front in one of the twentieth century's wars. But virtual wars may not exhaust any capacity of cyberspace to host multiple activities. And because virtual reality does not exist, there will be little danger of proximity, and almost none of being hit by exploding virtual shrapnel.

Vulnerability of Large-Scale Systems

The dangers of information war will mostly be dangers to large-scale industrial systems that operate with central command and control. Military authorities in the United States and other leading nation-states are both planning for and fearing acts of information sabotage that could have severe consequences for disabling large systems. An act of cyberwarfare could close down a telephone switching station, disrupt air traffic control, or sabotage a pumping system that regulates the flow of water to a city. A programmed virus could even close down conventional or nuclear generators, turning off segments of the electric grid. So-called logic bombs could scramble a great deal of information, the most sensitive of which is in central control systems operating vulnerable, large-scale systems inherited from the Industrial Age. Short of a massive and comprehensive destruction of all information technology, which would bring the world economy literally to a halt, cybercommerce and virtual reality will remain beyond the capacity of any government to stifle, much less monopolize.

Even one of the signal drawbacks of information technology, the apparent vulnerability of information-storage systems to decay and destruction, has been largely resolved by new archival technology. A new system called "High-Density Read-Only Memory," or "HD-ROM," employs an ion mill similar to those used in computer-aided manufacturing systems to create archives in a vacuum. Storage capacity is now as high as 25,000 megabytes per square inch. Unlike earlier systems that were vulnerable to early decay and disruption by shock, data stored in HD-ROM promises to be around for the duration. One of HD-ROM's developers, Bruce Lamartine, says, "It's virtually impervious to the ravages of time, thermal and mechanical shock, or the electromagnetic fields that are so destructive to other storage mediums." [53] Even the detonation of a blast by nuclear terrorists would not necessarily scramble or destroy vital information, such as the codes to digital money, upon which the smooth functioning of a cybereconomy will depend.

"Modern armies are so dependent on information that it is possible to blind and deafen them in order to achieve victory without fighting in the conventional sense." [54]

—COL. ALAN CAMPEN, U.S.A.F. (Ret.)

SUPERPOWERS OF VIRTUAL WARFARE

The assumptions of the nation-state at war will make less and less megapolitical sense as the importance of information in warfare increases. Because it has no physical existence, cyberspace is not a realm in which magnitudes as we know them in the physical world carry any commanding importance. It does not matter how many programmers were involved in stipulating a sequence of commands. All that matters is whether the program functions. The Sovereign Individual may truly count for as much in cyberspace as does a nation-state, with its seat in the UN, its own flag, and an army deployed on the ground. In purely economic terms, some Sovereign Individuals already command investible incomes in the hundreds of millions annually, sums that exceed the discretionary spending power of some of the bankrupt nation-states. But that is not all. In terms of virtual warfare waged through the manipulation of information, some individuals may loom as large or larger than many of the world's states. One bizarre genius, working with digital servants, could theoretically achieve the same impact in a cyberwar as a nation-state. Bill Gates certainly could.

In this sense, the age of the Sovereign Individual is not merely a slogan. A hacker, or a small group of mathematicians, not to mention a company like Microsoft, or almost any computer software company, could in principle do any or all of the things that the Pentagon's Cyber War Task Force has up its sleeves. There are hundreds of firms in the Silicon Valley and elsewhere that already have a greater capacity to wage a cyberwar than 90 percent of the existing nation-states.

Events of 1998 brought testimony from the U.S. President and his top aides that the leading enemy of the United States was not another nation-state, but Osama bin Laden, an exiled Saudi millionaire. The claim that Bin Laden, an individual, was a significant threat to the greatest military power of the Industrial Age was backed up by a barrage of cruise missiles. We are not altogether convinced that Bin Laden was not merely picked out to play the part of the "Richard Jewell of the Nairobi bombing." But be that as it may, if an individual like Bin Laden could be convincing as a dire threat to the United States as a terrorist, he or another multimillionaire could be even more convincing as a cyberterrorist, for cybertechnology puts individuals at a lesser disadvantage in confronting large groups than they face in the realm of explosives and missiles.

The presumption that governments will continue to monopolize life on the ground as alternative avenues for protection open on all sides is an anachronism. A far more likely outcome is that nation-states will have to be reconfigured to reduce their vulnerability to computer viruses, logic bombs, infected wires, and trapdoor programs that could be monitored by the U.S. National Security Agency, or some teenage hacker.

The megapolitical logic of cyberspace suggests that central command-and-control systems that currently dominate the world's large-scale infrastructure will have to be replaced by multicentric models of security with distributed capabilities so they cannot be easily captured or blocked by a computer virus. New types of software, known as agoric open systems, will replace command-and-control software inherited from the Industrial Age. That older software allocated computational capacity according to rigid priorities in much the same way that the central planners at Gosplan in the former Soviet Union used to allocate goods to boxcars by rigid rules. The new systems are controlled by algorithms that mock market mechanisms to allocate resources more efficiently by an internal bidding process that mimics the competitive processes in the brain. Instead of giant computer monopolies conducting important command-and-control functions, they will be decentralized in the new millennium.

There is no better example of the resilience of distributed networks compared to command-and-control systems than that given by Digital Equipment at its Palo Alto research lab. An engineer opened the door to a closet that housed the company's own computer network. As recounted by Kevin Kelly, the engineer dramatically "yanked a cable out of its guts. The network routed around the breach and didn't falter a bit." [55]

The Information Age will not only facilitate competition without anarchy in cyberspace; it will inevitably lead to the redesign of important systems left over from industrialism. Such a reconfiguration is essential to make them less vulnerable to mischief that could come from anyone or anywhere. Just as the Industrial Age inevitably led to the reconfiguration of institutions that were left over from the medieval period, such as schools and universities, so the leftover institutions of the Industrial Age are likely to devolve in miniature form, in ways that reflect the logic of microtechnology.

The need for protection against bandits on the Information Superhighway will require widespread adopting of public key–private key encryption algorithms. These already allow any individual user of a personal computer to encode any message more securely than the Pentagon could have sealed its launch codes only a generation ago. These powerful, unbreakable forms of encryption will be necessary to secure financial transactions from hackers and thieves.

They will also be necessary for another reason. Private financial institutions and central banks will adopt unbreakable encryption algorithms when they realize that the U.S. government—and it may not be alone—has the capacity to penetrate current bank software and computer systems to literally bankrupt a country or sweep the bank account of anyone living almost anywhere. There is no technological reason why any individual or any country should leave his financial deposits or transactions at the mercy of the U.S. National Security Agency or the successors to the KGB, or any similar organization, licit or illicit.

Encryption algorithms impenetrable by governments are not daydreams. They are available already as shareware over the Internet. When low-orbit satellite systems are fully operable, individuals using advanced personal computers with antennae no larger than those on portable phones will be able to communicate anywhere on the globe without even interfacing with the telephone system. It will no more be possible for a government to monopolize cyberspace, a realm with no physical existence at all, than it would have been for medieval knights to control transactions in the industrial period astride a heavy charger.

Protection by Stealth

Information societies will place vast resources outside the realm of predation. When cyberspace comes increasingly to host financial transactions and other forms of commerce, the resources employed there will be more or less immune to ordinary shakedowns and theft. Therefore, predators will be unable to harness as large a share of resources as they do today and have done through much of the twentieth century.

Inevitably, therefore, government protection of a large part of the world's wealth will be redundant. Government will be no better situated to protect a bank balance in cyberspace than you are. As government will be less necessary, its relative price is likely to fall for that reason alone. There are others.

With a large and growing share of financial transactions occurring in cyberspace in the new millennium, individuals will have a choice of jurisdictions in which to lodge them. This will create intense competition to price government's services (the taxes it charges) on a nonmonopolistic basis. This is revolutionary. As George Melloan argued in *The Wall Street Journal*, the one institution that has most successfully resisted the forces of global competition has been the welfare state. "A study by researchers at the Wharton School and the Australian National University discussed the forces coming to bear on income transfers. Geoffrey Garrett and Deborah Mitchell concluded that 'there is virtually no evidence that increased market integration has put downward pressures on their most fundamental welfare programs.' To the contrary, they write, 'governments have invariably responded to increased integration into international markets by increasing income transfers.' "[56] The advent of the cybereconomy will at long last finally expose the welfare state to genuine competition. It will change the nature of sovereignties and transform economies, as the balance between protection and extortion swings more completely on the side of protection than it has ever done before.

Chapter 7
TRANSCENDING LOCALITY

The Emergence of the Cybereconomy

"The real issue is control. The Internet is too widespread to be easily dominated by any single government. By creating a seamless global-economic zone, anti-sovereign and unregulatable, the Internet calls into question the very idea of a nation-state."[1]

—JOHN PERRY BARLOW

The Information Superhighway has become one of the more familiar metaphors of the early days of the digital age. It is remarkable not only for its pervasiveness, but also for the common misunderstanding it betrays about the cybereconomy. A highway, after all, is an industrial version of a footpath, a network for the physical transit of people and goods. The information economy is not like a highway, a railroad, or a pipeline. It does not haul or transport information from point to point the way the Trans-Canada Highway carries heavy trucks from Alberta to New Brunswick. What the world calls the "Information Superhighway" is not merely a transit link. It is the destination.

Cyberspace transcends locality. It involves nothing less than the instantaneous sharing of data everywhere and nowhere at once. The emerging information economy is based in the interconnections linking and relinking millions of users of millions of computers. Its essence lies in the new possibilities that arise from these connections. As John Perry Barlow put it, "What the Net offers is the promise of a new social space, global and anti-sovereign, within which anybody, anywhere can express to the rest of humanity whatever he or she believes without fear. There is in these new media a foreshadowing of the intellectual and economic liberty that might undo all the authoritarian powers on earth." [2]

Cyberspace, like the imaginary realm of Homer's gods, is a realm apart from the familiar terrestrial world of farm and factory. Yet its consequences will not be imaginary, but real. To a far greater extent than many now understand, the instantaneous sharing of information will be like a solvent dissolving large institutions. It will not only alter the logic of violence, as we have already explored; it will radically alter information and transaction costs that determine how businesses organize and the way the economy functions. We expect microprocessing to change the economic organization of the world.

"It is today possible, to a greater extent than at any time in the world's history, for a company to locate anywhere, to use resources from anywhere to produce a product that can be sold anywhere."

—MILTON FRIEDMAN

THE TYRANNY OF PLACE

The fact that the fading industrial era's first stab at conceiving the information economy is to think of it in terms of a gigantic public works project tells you how grounded our thinking is in the paradigms of the past. It is rather like hearing farmers at the end of the eighteenth century describe a factory as "a farm with a roof." Yet the "superhighway" metaphor is more revealing than that. It also betrays the extent to which we are hostage to the tyranny of place. Even when technology enables us to transcend locality, the instrument of our deliverance is given a nickname describing it as a route from place to place. Like salmon marked by their homing instinct, our consciousness is still deeply etched by notions of locality.

For the whole of history until now, economies have been tethered to a local geographic area. Most people who lived before the twentieth century passed their days like *de facto* prisoners under house arrest, seldom venturing more than a few days' walk from where they were born. A journey of any distance was the work of generations. Only occasionally did some crisis

—war, pestilence, an adverse shift in climate—stimulate a broad migration. To move human beings out of a wretched village required something spectacular and pressing. Nothing less could stimulate people to bundle up their belongings and wander off in search of a better life.

Until recently, the few who looked outside their own locale for opportunity often became famous. Consider that Marco Polo is still renowned for having traipsed the Eurasian continent to visit the court of the Great Khan. He was the exception in his time. Few other travelogues survive from the premodern period. Among the more widely read, *Mandeville's Travels*, written in French in 1357, is notable for having been composed by someone who probably never left Europe. Mandeville conveys delightful and often fanciful details about life around the globe, including the suggestion that many Ethiopians have only one foot: "[T]he foot is so large that it shadoweth all the body against the sun when they will lie and rest them."[3] Clearly, few of Mandeville's contemporaries who read his popular story were likely to have known that his Ethiopian "Bigfoot" did not exist.

Not until the modern age began with the journeys of exploration at the very end of the fifteenth century were there sustained contacts between the continents. Intrepid captains like Christopher Columbus and Vasco da Gama who set out to capture the spice trade were extraordinary enough to be remembered in every literate household for the better part of five centuries.

From the advent of farming until recent generations, life was characterized by its immobility. This is all but forgotten today, particularly in the European settlement colonies of the "New World," where movement is more fluid and everyone tends to draw his perspective from the vantage point of an immigrant. A theme of elementary education in North America is that the colonists came from Europe seeking freedom and opportunity, which is true. What is seldom told, however, is how reluctant most people were to take the trip, even when faced with destitution at home. The few who did migrate suffered what are in today's terms unimaginable ordeals to establish themselves. Only the most enterprising or the most desperate of the poor came. In the middle of the seventeenth century, inmates locked up in Bridewell, London's notorious house of correction, revolted to show "their unwillingness to go to Virginia."[4] In 1720, there were riots in the streets of Paris to free vagabonds, thieves, and murderers scheduled for deportation to Louisiana.

Narrow Horizons

Physical difficulties of communication and transport, compounded at most times and places by limited language skills, kept the focus of human action narrow and local. As recently as the early twentieth century, it was common

to find Chinese villages lying only five miles apart speaking mutually unintelligible dialects, even along the coast. The local organization of almost all
economies imposed a penalty of narrow markets and lost opportunity. Factor
costs were kept high due to limited competition. Access to specialized skills
was minimal. With incomes so low they scraped the margins of destitution,
and no access to outside capital or efficient insurance markets, small farmers
in much of the world were trapped in poverty. We have explored some of the
difficulties imposed upon peasants by the confines of closed village life.
Even now, as we write, at least a billion people, mostly in Asia and Africa,
struggle to survive on less than a dollar a day.

"ALL POLITICS IS LOCAL"

To a greater extent than is commonly realized, the immobility of people
and their assets has informed the way we see the world. Even those who
seem most ready to agree that the earth is a small place as the twentieth
century ends continue to think in terms constrained by antiquated concepts
of industrial politics. This is underscored by a slogan that became popular
among environmentalists in the 1980s: "Think globally but act locally." It is
an injunction that mirrors the logic of politics, a logic that has always turned
on local power advantages.

The local habit of mind has been dictated by the megapolitics of all past
societies. All topographical features that serve as barriers or facilitators to
the exercise of power are local. Every river, every mountain, every island is
local. Climate is local. Temperature, rainfall, and growing conditions vary as
you climb up and over a mountain. Every microbe that circulates, circulates
somewhere, and not in some other place.

Little wonder that the tyranny of place permeates our concepts of how
society must organize and function. The power advantages that have given
one group or another a local monopoly on violence have heretofore always
originated someplace and faded along the megapolitical margins where borders are drawn. That is why there has never been a world government.

While the importance of place to the exercise of power has rarely been
made explicit, some advocates of compulsion to redistribute the rewards of
human action began to sense the declining leverage of place as long ago as
the 1930s. They saw in modern transportation a division of social space
between the highly paid and the poor. This fear was captured by John Dos
Passos in *The Big Money:* "The 'vag' sits on the edge of the highway,
broken, hungry. Overhead, flies a transcontinental plane filled with highly
paid executives. The upper class has taken to the air, the lower class to the
road: there is no longer any bond between them, they are two nations." [5]

This is another way of saying that improved transportation reduced the leverage of extortion simply by increasing the choice of places where successful persons might choose to be. Certainly, the vagabond on the road below was in no position to press for a handout from those flying overhead. The tendencies that Dos Passos observed sixty years ago have only become more pronounced.

Mass Transit

In 1995, a million persons crossed borders somewhere in the world each day. This represents a startling change from the past. Before the twentieth century, travel was so infrequent that most borders were simply frontiers, not barriers to transit. Passports were unknown. The development of ocean liners, trains, and other improved forms of transportation dramatically increased movement. But this movement became more heavily regulated by states whose powers were increased by the same improvements in transportation and communications that made civilian travel cheaper and easier. The advent of movies and, especially, television also did a great deal to open horizons and stimulate travel and immigration. Yet until now, the bedrock assumptions of social and economic organization have remained anchored in locality.

"... to avoid that Failure of Nerve for which history exacts so merciless a penalty—we must have the courage to follow all technical extrapolations to their logical conclusion."[6]

—ARTHUR C. CLARKE

THE ERROR OF MINIMAL EXPECTATIONS

The geographic tether on imagination is still so tight that some experts examining the Internet in 1995 concluded that it has little commercial potential and almost no significance other than as an electronic medium for chat and an outlet for pornography. The many doubters of the economic importance of cyberspace are the Colonel Blimps of the Information Age. Their complacency rivals that of the British establishment facing the decline of the empire in the 1930s. Whenever elites find themselves threatened, their first reaction is denial. This is evidenced by the fond hope that the Internet will never amount to much, sometimes endorsed by authorities who should know better. We referred earlier to David Kline and Daniel Burstein's work, *Road Warriors: Dreams and Nightmares Along the Information Highway.* Their dismissal of the economic potential of the Net is another proof that being technically well-informed is not synonymous with understanding the consequences of technology.[7]

Even the most technically expert observers in the past have frequently failed to grasp the implications of new technologies. A British parliamentary committee, convened in 1878 to consider the prospects for Thomas Edison's incandescent lamp, reported Edison's ideas to be "good enough for our transatlantic friends, . . . but unworthy of the attention of practical or scientific men."[8] Thomas Edison himself was a man of great vision, but he thought that the phonograph he invented would be employed mainly by businessmen for dictation. Only a short time before the Wright brothers proved that airplanes would fly, the distinguished American astronomer Simon Newcomb authoritatively demonstrated why heavier-than-air flight was impossible. He concluded: "The demonstration that no possible combination of known substances, known forms of machinery and known forms of force, can be united in a practical machine by which men shall fly long distances through the air, seems to the writer as complete as it is possible for the demonstration of any physical fact to be."[9] Soon after airplanes began to fly, another renowned astronomer, William H. Pickering, explained to the public why commercial travel would never get off the ground: "The popular mind often pictures gigantic flying machines speeding across the Atlantic and carrying innumerable passengers in a way analogous to our modern steamships. . . . [I]t is clear that with our present devices there is no hope of competing for racing speed with either our locomotives or our automobiles."[10] We have previously recalled another wildly inaccurate prophecy about the potential of a new technology—the forecast from the beginning of the twentieth century by the makers of Mercedes that there would never be more than a million automobiles worldwide. Again, they knew more about automobiles than almost anyone but they could not have been more wrong in estimating the impact of autos on society.

Given this tradition of clueless misunderstandings, it is hardly surprising that many observers are slow to grasp the most important implications of the new information technology—the fact that it transcends the tyranny of place. The new technology creates for the first time an infinite, nonterrestrial realm for economic activity. It opens an option to explore the new frontiers of the cybereconomy, to "think globally and act globally." This chapter explains why.

BEYOND LOCALITY

The processing and use of information is rapidly replacing and modifying physical products as the most important source of profit. This has major consequences. Information technology divorces income-earning potential from residence in any specific geographic location. Since a greater and greater portion of the value of products and services will be created by adding ideas and knowledge to the product, an ever-smaller component of value-added will be subject to capture within local jurisdictions. Ideas can be formulated anywhere and transmitted globally at the speed of light. This inevitably means that the information economy will be dramatically different from the economy of the Factory Age.

We would concede to the critics that a recital of the tasks you could have undertaken through the Internet in 1998 might seem mundane. There is, after all, nothing terribly revolutionary about reading an article about gardening on the Net, or buying a case of wine long-distance. However, the potential of the cybereconomy cannot be judged solely on its early beginnings, any more than the potential of the automobile to transform society could have been judged by what you could have seen around you in 1900. We expect the cybereconomy to evolve through several stages.

1. The most primitive manifestations of the Information Age involve the Net simply as an information medium to facilitate what are otherwise ordinary industrial-era transactions. At this point, the Net is no more than an exotic delivery system for catalogues. Virtual Vineyards, for example, one of the first cybermerchants, simply sells wine from a page on the World Wide Web. Such transactions are not yet directly subversive of the old institutions. They employ industrial currency, and take place within identifiable jurisdictions. These uses of the Internet have little such megapolitical impact.

2. An intermediate stage of Internet commerce will employ information technology in ways that would have been impossible in the industrial era, such as in long-distance accounting or medical diagnosis. More examples of these new applications of advanced computational power are spelled out below. The second stage of Net commerce will still function within the old institutional framework, employing national currencies and submitting to the jurisdiction of nation-states. The merchants who employ the Net for sales will not yet employ it to bank their profits, only to earn revenues. These profits made on Internet transactions will still be subject to taxation.

3. A more advanced stage will mark the transition to true cybercommerce. Not only will transactions occur over the Net, but they will migrate outside the jurisdiction of nation-states. Payment will be rendered in cybercurrency. Profits will be booked in cyberbanks. Investments will be made in cyberbrokerages. Many transactions will not be subject to taxation. At this stage, cybercommerce will begin to have significant megapolitical consequences of the kind we have already outlined. The powers of governments over traditional areas of the economy will be transformed by the new logic

of the Net. Extraterritorial regulatory power will collapse. Jurisdictions will devolve. The structure of firms will change, and so will the nature of work and employment.

This outline of the stages of the Information Revolution is only the barest sketch of what could be the most far-reaching economic transformation ever.

THE GLOBALIZATION OF COMMERCE

In the Information Age, most current jurisdictional advantages will be eroded rapidly by technology. New types of advantages will emerge. Falling communications costs have already reduced the need for proximity as a necessary condition of doing business. In 1946, it was technically possible for an investor in London to place an order with a broker in New York. But only the largest and most compelling transaction would have justified doing so: a three-minute phone call between New York and London cost $650. Today, it costs $0.91. The price of an intercontinental phone call has plunged by more than 99 percent in half a century.

Convergent Communication

Soon, the difference between intercontinental chat and a local call may be minimal. So, too, may be the differences among your telephone, your computer, and your television. All will be interactive communications devices, more easily distinguished on ergonomic than functional grounds. You will be able to hold a voice conversation over the Internet using microphones and speakers on your personal computer. Or watch a movie. You will be able to talk back to your television, and communicate vast amounts of data through the network provided by the television entertainment media. As the industrial-era distinction between various forms of communication breaks down and costs plunge, more and more services will bill you by time of use rather than according to the destination of your messages. Conversation or data transmission anywhere in the world will cost little more than a local call did in most jurisdictions in 1985.

Internet Unwired

Low-orbit satellites and other approaches to wireless technology will transmit feeds back and forth directly to a beeper in your pocket, a portable computer, or a workstation, without interfacing with a local telephone operating or TV cable system at all. In short, the Internet will be unwired. The first steps in that direction are bound to be halting because of the relatively slow speed of data transmission in the early wireless media and the difficulties of "hearing" weak signals broadcast from subscriber devices, some of which will be mobile and battery-powered. Nonetheless, these technical problems will be tackled and solved as bandwidth increases.

Business Without Borders

Continued expansion of computational power will lead to better compression technology, speeding data flow. Widespread adoption of existing public key/private key encryption algorithms will allow providers, such as satellite systems, to incorporate the billing function into the service, lowering costs. Simultaneous with the service, vendors will be able to debit accounts loaded on personal computers in much the way that France Telecom debits the "smart cards" employed in Paris phone boxes.

Your Phone Becomes a Bank

The difference is that in the near future, you will be able to earn credits to your account with all manner of transactions and carry your phone box with you. Your PC will be the branch office of your bank and global money brokerage, as well as the equivalent of the Paris kiosk where you buy your anonymous phone card. And like the smart-card pay phones that are useless to thieves if broken open with a crowbar, your computer could only be raided by someone capable of breaking or manipulating sophisticated computer code. That would leave out a lot of ruffians capable of manipulating a crowbar. With proper encryption, nothing in your computer could be deciphered or misused.

By the turn of the millennium, you will be able to transact business almost anywhere north of Antarctica. Anywhere wired or digital cellular telephone is available. Anywhere interactive cable television systems are in use. Anywhere a satellite is overhead or other wireless transmission systems are in place. You will be able to speak, transmit data, and journey via virtual reality over borders and boundaries at will. Telephone numbers that identify the locale of the speaker by area codes are likely to be superseded by universal access numbers, which will reach the party with whom you wish to communicate anywhere on the planet. Witness Iridium.

Understanding Chinese

You will not only be able to talk and send a fax. In time, you will be able to shorten a multiyear learning process and converse in Chinese with a factory foreman in Shanghai. It will no longer matter as much that you do not speak his language or dialect. His words may be in Chinese but you will hear them roughly translated into English. He will hear your conversation in Chinese. In time, the capacity to employ instantaneous translation will significantly increase competition in regions where obstacles of language and idiom have heretofore been significant. When that happens, it will matter little or not at all that the Chinese government may not wish the call to be placed.

Customized Media

As the world grows closer together, you will have a greater opportunity than at any time in history to customize your particular place in it. Even the information you receive on a regular basis from the media will be information of your choosing. The mass media will become the individualized media. If you are interested in chess above all else, or are a keen cat fancier, you will be able to program your evening news broadcast to feature information important to you about cats or chess. No longer will you be at the mercy of Dan Rather or the BBC for the news that reaches you. You will be able to select news compiled and edited according to your instructions.

From Mass to Customized Production

If the news is slow, you can access a virtual catalogue on the World Wide Web. If you see a pair of trousers that you almost like, you can adjust the width of the cuff when you place your order. It will be custom-cut and tailored to fit your body by robots in Malaysia from photographs scanned into your computer and transmitted through the Net.

Cyberbroking

You will be able to use cybermoney to make investments as well as pay for services and products. If you live in a jurisdiction like the United States that heavily regulates your investment options, you can choose to domicile your activities in a jurisdiction that permits the freedom to pursue a full range of investment options. Whether you live in Cleveland or Belo Horizonte, you can do your investment business in Bermuda, the Cayman Islands, Rio de Janeiro, or Buenos Aires. Wherever you find yourself, the use of digital resources will widen as the cybereconomy evolves. You will be able to employ expert systems to help select your investments, and cyberaccountants and -bookkeepers to monitor the progress of your holdings on a real-time basis.

Virtual Culture

When you are not reviewing profit-and-loss data, you may take a virtual visit to the Louvre. Your trip may require you to pay a royalty payment equivalent to one-third of a penny to Bill Gates, or someone of equal foresight who has purchased the virtual-reality rights to tour the museum. While you are wondering whether the Mona Lisa had trouble with her teeth, your computer could be downloading S. I. Hsiung's translation of *The Romance of the Western Chamber.* At times of your choosing, your personal communications system will read the text aloud like a bard of old. Multitasking programs will allow you to perform many functions simultaneously.

Shopping for Jurisdictions on the Net

If you are inspired by your dose of the classics, you can organize a virtual corporation to market dramatic productions of famous literature for viewing through three-dimensional retinal display. Instead of being projected into the air, the images will be projected directly onto the retinas of viewers with low-energy lasers fluctuating fifty thousand times a second. This technology, already under development by MicroVision of Seattle, Washington, will allow many persons who are legally blind to see. Before undertaking the project, you could instruct your digital assistant to canvass the current contract offers of protection for manufacturing facilities in Malaysia, China, Peru, Brazil, and the Czech Republic. When you pick a location, you will be able to have your company incorporated in one hour in the Bahamas, courtesy of the St. George's Trust Company. Your instructions will place all the company's liquid assets in a cyberaccount in a cyberbank that is domiciled simultaneously in Newfoundland, the Cayman Islands, Uruguay, Argentina, and Liechtenstein. If any of the jurisdictions attempt to withdraw operating authority or seize the assets of depositors, the assets will automatically be transferred to another jurisdiction at the speed of light.

QUALITATIVE ADVANCES

Many of the transactions you soon will be able to perform in cyberspace would have been impossible in the Industrial Age, and not simply because they cross a language barrier. Sending your digital assistants to locate untranslated articles published in Hungarian scientific journals is qualitatively different from talking to a librarian. Sitting in on an Oxford tutorial from a distance of five thousand miles is not the same as taking the tutorial when you are sleeping within six miles of Carfax. And playing the roulette wheel at the Hôtel de Paris, Monte Carlo, is a novel experience when you can do it via virtual reality from a party at Punte del Este, Uruguay.

A Cybervisit to the Cyberdoctor

In short order, faster than many experts now think possible, activities will migrate into the cybereconomy that combine technologies in novel ways to transcend the tyranny of place and the antiquated institutions of the industrial economy. One day soon, if you have a stomachache, you will be able to consult a digital doctor, an expert system with an encyclopedic knowledge of symptoms, maladies, and antidotes. It will access your medical history in encrypted form, ask whether your pain happens after eating or before meals. Whether it is sharp or dull, persistent or episodic. Whatever questions doctors ask, the digital doctor will ask. It may determine that you drink too much wine, or not enough. You may be referred to a cyberspecialist. If you need an operation, a cybersurgeon in Bermuda may perform the operation long-distance with the aid of specialized equipment that performs micro-incisions.

Life-and-Death Information Processing

This may sound like science fiction. But many of the components of cyber-surgery are already in place. Others will be functional by the time you read this book. General Electric has introduced a new magnetic resonance treatment machine (MRT) into fifteen hospitals around the world. The machine is expected to have a three-year research-and-development phase, but after that it is likely to spread rapidly and become a norm for many types of surgery. It is one example, but a good one, of the way in which technology is changing society.

Most of us are familiar with magnetic resonance imaging (MRI) machines, in which magnetic resonance techniques are used to provide doctors with soft-tissue images for diagnostic purposes. They provide better images of soft tissues than X-rays or ultrasound, and have become an essential part of modern diagnostic techniques, particularly in cancers. They have, however, two significant limitations at present. The tube does not allow free access to the patient; the machines are of limited power.

Cybersurgery

General Electric has redesigned magnetic resonance machines so that they can be used for treatment as well as diagnosis. The power has been upped five times. The tube has, in effect, been cut in two, so the patient will lie between two doughnut-shaped units, rather than being fully enclosed. Instead of taking an image and then performing surgery in the light of that image, the surgeon will be able to see what he is doing as he does it. MRT will be combined with noninvasive, or less invasive, surgery using microtechniques. Instead of having to make large incisions with scalpels, the surgeon will make micro incisions with probes, and will be able to see what the probes reveal as he operates. He will perform the surgery from the image rather than by looking directly into the body. In principle, the probes will be operable from a distance. They will be able to destroy tumors with laser or cryogenic—heating or freezing—devices of great precision.

This will permit operations that are now impossible, particularly in neurosurgery, where tumors often lie very close to essential parts of the brain. It will also permit repeated operations, when the trauma of the traditional surgical operation cannot be repeated without unacceptable damage.

Some researchers believe that the knife for soft-tissue surgery may be looked back on as an obsolete relic by 2010. A lot of fear, and much of the aftershock, will be taken out of surgery if that is true. Obviously, this is very good news for the patient. Operations which now take hours to perform, and have to be followed by days or weeks in the hospital, will take only half an hour, and may not require hospitalization at all. Indeed, the surgeon and the patient may never even be in the same room. But what will this do to hospitals and surgeons?

Fewer Microsurgeons Doing More

There will be a revolution in surgery. In training, a third of young surgeons have failed to acquire the skills needed for microsurgery. A third are just able to do it, and a third become excellent. Similar proportions are found in conversion courses for senior surgeons. Fewer surgeons will be able to carry out more operations in a shorter time. It is likely that health care insurers and individuals seeking surgery will insist on outcome statistics for each surgeon, which will vary rather widely. Patients will want to go to surgeons who produce the best results, particularly if their conditions are life-threatening. In some cases, the best surgeons may operate long-distance. They may perform the whole operation from another jurisdiction where taxes are lower and courts do not honor exorbitant malpractice claims.

Digital Lawyers

Before agreeing to perform an operation, the skilled surgeon will probably call upon a digital lawyer to draft an instant contract that specifies and limits liability based upon the size and characteristics of the tumor revealed in images displayed by the magnetic resonance machine. Digital lawyers will be information-retrieval systems that automate selection of contract provisions, employing artificial intelligence processes such as neural networks to customize private contracts to meet transnational legal conditions. Participants in most high-value or important transactions will not only shop for suitable partners with whom to conduct a business; they will also shop for a suitable domicile for their transactions.

Emergency Consultation

To continue the example of cybersurgery, the technology of the Information Age will place a premium on the highest skills in surgery, as it will in almost every endeavor. Patients have been willing to pay such a premium for as long as there have been knives. But limits on information and the difficulty of shopping for surgeons in an emergency in any given locale made the market for surgery a very imperfect one. It will be less imperfect in the Information Age. A patient facing the need for an operation in twenty-four hours, or perhaps even forty-five minutes, could deputize digital assistants to locate the top ten surgeons worldwide available to perform such a task remotely, review their success rates in similar cases, and solicit offers for their particular case from corresponding digital servants. All of this could be canvassed in a matter of moments. As a consequence, the most-favored 10 percent of surgeons will have a far larger share in the global market for surgery. The MRT machine, plus microsurgery techniques, will raise the premium for their work. Surgeons with less skill will focus on residual local markets.

This life-and-death example helps suggest some of the revolutionary consequences of the liberation of economies from the tyranny of place. Someone may object that General Electric's MRT machine was not meant to be employed long-distance. Perhaps, but this misses the point. It or some equipment like it soon will be. When operations are better performed by surgeons watching a screen than looking at the patient directly, it will matter less than we now suppose where the surgeon and his screen are located. Increasing numbers of services are destined to be reconfigured to reflect the fact that information technology allows persons anywhere on the globe to interact in even so delicate a matter as surgery.

In activities that require less precise equipment, and involve lower risks of failure, the cybereconomy will flourish even more rapidly.

"The financial policy of the welfare state requires that there be no way for the owners of wealth to protect themselves."

—ALAN GREENSPAN

THE DEVALUATION OF COMPULSION

In almost every competitive area, including most of the world's multitrillion-dollar investment activity, the migration of transactions into cyberspace will be driven by an almost hydraulic pressure—the impetus to avoid predatory taxation, including the tax that inflation places upon everyone who holds his wealth in a national currency.

Escaping the Protection Racket

You do not need to think long about the megapolitics of the Information Age to realize that predatory taxes and inflation of the kind imposed as a matter of right by the wealthiest industrial countries upon their citizens will be preposterously uncompetitive on the new frontier of cyberspace. Soon after the turn of the millennium, anyone who pays income taxes at rates currently imposed will be doing so out of choice. As Frederic C. Lane pointed out, history shows that on "the frontiers and on the high seas, where no one had an enduring monopoly in the use of violence, merchants avoided payment of exactions which were so high that protection could be obtained more cheaply by other means." [11]

The cybereconomy provides just such an alternative. No government will be able to monopolize it. And the information technologies comprised by it will provide cheaper and more effective protection for financial assets than most governments ever had reason to provide.

The Black Magic of Compound Interest

Remember, each $5,000 of annual tax payments paid over forty years slashes your net worth by $2.2 million, assuming you could realize just a 10 percent return on your capital. At a 20 percent return, the compound loss balloons to about $44 million. For high-income earners in a high-tax country, the cumulative losses from predatory taxation over a lifetime are staggering. Most will lose more than they ever had.

This sounds impossible, but the mathematics are clear. It is something that you can confirm for yourself with a pocket calculator. The top 1 percent of taxpayers in the United States pay an average of more than $125,000 in federal income taxes annually. For a fraction of that amount, $45,000 a year, one would be welcome to live under a private tax treaty in Switzerland, and enjoy law and order provided by what is arguably the most honest police and judicial system in the world. From this perspective, the additional $80,000 a year of income tax paid above that generous level might well be classified as tribute or plunder. Forty-five thousand dollars is certainly a substantial payment toward the maintenance of law and order, considering that police protection is meant to be a public good. In theory, public goods can be extended to additional users at a marginal cost of zero. The Swiss are glad to have you pay a negotiated fixed tax of $45,000 (50,000 Swiss francs) per year because they make an annual profit of $45,000 on every millionaire who signs up.

Compared to the Swiss alternative, the lifetime losses from paying federal income tax at U.S. rates would be $705 million for an investor who could average a 20 percent rate of return. But remember, that assumes an annual tax payment of $45,000. Compared to a tax haven like Bermuda, where the income tax is zero, the lifetime loss for paying taxes at American rates would be about $1.1 billion.

You may object that an annual return of 20 percent is a high rate of return. No doubt you would be right. But given the startling growth in Asia in recent decades, many investors in the world have achieved that and better. The compound rate of return in Hong Kong real estate since 1950 has been more than 20 percent per annum. Even some economies that are less widely known for growth have afforded easy opportunities for high profits. You could have pocketed an average real return of more than 30 percent annually in U.S. dollar deposits in Paraguayan banks over the last three decades. High investment returns are easier to realize in some places than others, but skilled investors can certainly achieve profits of 20 percent or more in good years, even if they do not consistently match the performances of George Soros or Warren Buffet.

Obviously, the higher the rate of return that you could earn on your capital, the greater the opportunity costs that predatory income and capital gains taxes impose. But the conclusion that the loss is huge, indeed greater than the total amount of wealth that you may ever accumulate, does not depend upon your being able to achieve outlandish rates of return. Some mutual funds operating in the United States have averaged annual gains of more than 10 percent for more than half a century. If you could do no better than that and you are among the top 1 percent of American earners, then your net worth is reduced by more than $33 million just by the income tax you pay in excess of $45,000 annually. Compared to a jurisdiction without income tax, the loss is $55 million.

$55 Rather Than $55 Million

If the profit-maximizing assumptions of economists are correct, as we believe they generally are, one of the more certain predictions you could make is that most people would act to salvage $55 million if they could. That is our prediction. When the black magic of compound interest becomes more clear in the minds of successful people in high-tax countries, they will begin to shop in earnest among jurisdictions, just as they now shop for automobiles or compare rates on insurance policies. If you doubt it, merely stop people at random on the streets of New York or Toronto and ask whether they would move to Bermuda for $55 million. The question answers itself. The quandary it poses is reminiscent of that Mark Twain imagined in deciding whether he would prefer to spend the night with Lillian Russell stark naked or General Grant in full dress uniform. He did not deliberate long. Residents of mature welfare states, particularly the United States, may be slower on the uptake, but only because they are not yet aware of the choice they face. In the fullness of time, they will be. You or anyone motivated by the desire to live a better life will see the attraction of reducing the losses you suffer from predatory taxation. You need merely lodge your transactions in cyberspace. This will, of course, be illegal in many jurisdictions. But old laws seldom can resist new technology. In the 1980s, it was illegal in the United States to send a fax message. The U.S. Post Office considered faxes to be first-class mail, over which the U.S. Post Office claimed an ancient monopoly. An edict to that effect was issued reiterating the requirement that all fax transmissions be routed to the nearest post office for delivery with regular mail. Billions of fax messages later, it is unclear whether anyone ever complied with that law. If so, compliance was fleeting. The advantages of operating in the emerging cybereconomy are even more compelling than sidestepping the post office in sending a fax.

Widespread adoption of public-key/private-key encryption technologies will soon allow many economic activities to be completed anywhere you please. As James Bennet, technology editor of *Strategic Investment,* has written:

> Enforcement of laws and particularly tax codes has become heavily dependent on surveillance of communications and transactions. Once the next logical steps have been taken, and offshore banking locations offer the services of communication in hard RSA-encrypted electronic mail using account numbers derived from public-key systems, financial transactions will be almost impossible to monitor at the bank or in communications. Even if the tax authorities were to plant a mole in the offshore bank, or burglarize the bank records, they would not be able to identify depositors.[12]

To a degree that has never before been possible, individuals will be able to determine where to domicile their economic activities and how much income tax they prefer to pay. Many transactions in the Information Age will not need to be domiciled in any territorial sovereignty at all. Those that do will increasingly find their way to places like Bermuda, the Cayman Islands,

Uruguay, or similar jurisdictions that do not impose income taxes or other costly transaction burdens on commerce.

From Monopoly to Competition

Governments have become accustomed to imposing "protection services" that are, in Frederic C. Lane's words, "of poor quality and outrageously overpriced." [13] This habit of charging far more than government's services are actually worth developed through centuries of monopoly. Taxes were ruthlessly raised on anyone who seemed capable of paying—precisely because governments had a monopoly or near-monopoly on coercion. This tradition of monopoly will clash in a profound way with the new megapolitical possibilities of cybercommerce.

Encryption will make it easy to protect transactions in cyberspace. The cost of an effective encryption software program, like PGP, is less than the commission charged by a full-service broker on a trade of one hundred shares. Yet it will render almost any transaction invisible and impervious to governments and thieves for many years to come. The new technology of the Information Age will effectively protect cyberassets at a vanishingly small cost. For $55 rather than $55 million, participants in the cybereconomy will enjoy better actual protection of their assets than they enjoyed during the industrial era or at any previous time in history. Easily used encryption algorithms and the capacity to shop between terrestrial domiciles for transactions will provide effective protection against the largest source of predation, nation-states themselves.

That is not to say that territorial governments will be entirely outmaneuvered. They will still be able to exploit vulnerabilities to personal harm in order to extract head taxes, or perhaps even hold wealthy individuals to outright ransom. They will also be able to enforce collection of consumption taxes. Yet protection, the most important service governments provide, will be put on a more nearly competitive basis. Less of the cost that productive people pay for protection will be available to be seized and reallocated by political authorities. Technological innovations will place a large and growing portion of the world's wealth outside the reach of governments. This will reduce the risks of trade, sharply lowering, in historian Janet Abu-Lughod's words, "the proportion of all costs" that otherwise would have had to be "allocated to transit duties, tribute, or simple extortion." [14]

It has been rare in history to find governments truly constrained by competition. In the few times when something remotely like this has happened, governments were weak and technologies were similar between jurisdictions. As Lane suggested, the principal factor affecting profitability under such conditions tends to be the difference in protection costs paid by different entrepreneurs. The medieval merchant who had to pay twenty tolls to bring his goods to market could not compete with a merchant who had to pay only four tolls to deliver the same goods to the customer. Similar conditions are destined to return with the Information Age. Profitability will once again be determined not so much by technological advantage as by your success in minimizing the costs you are forced to pay for protection.

This new economic dynamic directly contradicts the desire of government left over from the industrial era to impose monopoly pricing for its protection services. But, like it or not, the old system will be nonviable in the new competitive environment of the Information Age. Any government that insists upon lumbering its citizens with heavy taxes that competitors do not pay will merely assure that profits and wealth gravitate someplace else. Therefore, the failure of the mature welfare states to curtail taxes over the long term will be self-correcting. Governments that tax too much will simply make residence anywhere within their power a bankrupting liability.

". . . as the king by his prerogative may make money of what matter and form he pleaseth, and establish the standard of it, so may he change his money in substance and impression, and enhance or debase the value of it, or entirely decry and annul it. . . ."[15]

—FROM AN ENGLISH COURT DECISION, 1604

THE DEATH OF SEIGNIORAGE

Governments will not only lose their power to tax many forms of income and capital; they are also destined to lose their power of compulsion over money. In the past, megapolitical transitions have been associated with changes in the character of money.

- The introduction of coinage helped launch the five-hundred-year cycle of expansion in the ancient economy that culminated with the birth of Christ and the lowest interest rates before the modern period.
- The advent of the Dark Ages coincided with virtual closure of the mints. While Roman coinage continued to circulate, quantities of money dwindled along with trade in a self-reinforcing downward spiral.
- The feudal revolution coincided with a reintroduction of money, coinage, bills of exchange, and other devices for settling commercial transactions. In particular, a surge in European silver production from new mines at Rammelsberg, Germany, facilitated an increase in the circulation of coin that helped lubricate commerce.

- The greatest revolution in money prior to the Information Age came with the advent of industrialism. The early-modern state consolidated its power in the Gunpowder Revolution. As its control increased, the state asserted its power over money, and came to rely heavily upon the signature technology of industrialism, the printing press. The first implement of mass production, the printing press, has been widely used by governments in the modern period to mass-produce paper money.

Paper money is a distinctly industrial product. It would have been impractical before the printing press to duplicate receipts or certificates that became paper currency. Certainly, monks in the scriptoria would not have spent their time well drawing fifty-pound notes. Paper money also contributed significantly to the power of the state, not only by generating profits from depreciating the currency, but by giving the state leverage over who could accumulate wealth. As Abu-Lughod put it, "when paper money backed by the state become the approved currency, the chances for amassing capital in opposition to or independent of the state machinery became difficult." [16]

CYBERCASH

Now the advent of the Information Age implies another revolution in the character of money. As cybercommerce begins, it will lead inevitably to cybermoney. This new form of money will reset the odds, reducing the capacity of the world's nation-states to determine who becomes a Sovereign Individual. A crucial part of this change will come about because of the effect of information technology in liberating the holders of wealth from expropriation through inflation. Soon, you will pay for almost any transaction over the Net or World Wide Web at the same time you place it, using cybercash.

This new digital form of money is destined to play a pivotal role in cybercommerce. It will consist of encrypted sequences of multihundred-digit prime numbers. Unique, anonymous, and verifiable, this money will accommodate the largest transactions. It will also be divisible into the tiniest fraction of value. It will be tradable at a keystroke in a multitrillion-dollar wholesale market without borders.

Dialing Without Dollars

Inevitably, this new cybermoney will be denationalized. When Sovereign Individuals can deal across borders in a realm with no physical reality, they will no longer need to tolerate the long-rehearsed practice of governments degrading the value of their money through inflation. Why should they?

Control over money will migrate from the halls of power to the global marketplace. Any individual or firm with access to cyberspace will be able to easily shift out of any currency that appears in danger of depreciation. Unlike today, there will be no necessity to deal in legal tender. Indeed, in transactions spanning the globe it will be likely that at least one party to every transaction will find himself dealing in a currency that is not legal tender to him.

Disadvantages of Barter Reduced

You will be able to trade in any medium you wish in the cybereconomy. As the late Nobel Prize–winning economist F. A. Hayek argued, there is "no clear distinction between money and non-money." He wrote, " although we usually assume there is a sharp line of distinction between what is money and what is not—and the law generally tries to make such a distinction—so far as the causal effects of monetary events are concerned, there is no such clear difference. What we find is rather a continuum in which objects of various degrees of liquidity, or with values which can fluctuate independently of each other, shade into each other in the degree to which they function as money."[17] Digital money on global computer networks will make every object on Hayek's continuum of liquidity more liquid—except government paper. One consequence will be that barter will become far more practical. Increasing numbers of objects and services will be offered in specific bids for other objects and services. These potential transactions will be widely advertised throughout the world on the Net, which will increase their liquidity by magnitudes.

One of the principal drawbacks of barter has always been the difficulty of matching a person with one specific demand with another who had exactly that on offer and was seeking to acquire for himself exactly what the first proposed to trade. Primitive barter stumbled over the daunting improbability of exactly matching two parties wishing to exchange in a local market. Cash transcended the limitations of barter, and its advantages will continue to be compelling in most transactions. But vast increases in computational power and the globalization of commerce in cyberspace also reduce the drawbacks of barter. The odds of finding someone with exactly reciprocal desires to yours increase dramatically when you can sort instantly across the entire world rather than drawing on only those whom you might meet locally.

Not Subject to Counterfeiting

While paper money will no doubt remain in circulation as a residual medium of exchange for the poor and computer-illiterate, money for high-value transactions will be privatized. Cybermoney will no longer be denominated only in national units like the paper money of the industrial period. It probably will be defined in terms of grams or ounces of gold, as finely divisible as gold itself. Or it may be defined in terms of other real stores of value. Even where different pricing measures are used, or certain transactions continue to be denominated in national currencies, cybermoney will serve the consumers far better than nationalized money ever did. Rapidly advancing computational capacity will diminish the difficulties of adjusting prices to various media of exchange to the vanishing point. Each transaction will involve the transfer of encrypted multihundred-digit prime-number sequences. Unlike the paper-money receipts issued by governments during the gold-standard era, which could be duplicated at will, the new digital gold standard or its barter equivalents will be almost impossible to counterfeit for the fundamental mathematical reason that it is all but impossible to unravel the product of multihundred-digit prime numbers. All receipts will be verifiably unique.

The names of traditional currencies like the "pound" and the "peso" reflect the fact that they originated as measures of weight of specific quantities of precious metals. The pound sterling was once upon a time a pound of sterling silver. Paper money in the West began as warehouse or safe-deposit receipts for quantities of precious metals. Governments issuing these receipts soon found that they could print far more of them than they could actually redeem from their supply of bullion. This was easy. No individual holding a gold or silver certificate could distinguish any information about the actual supply of precious metals from his receipt. Other than the serial numbers, all the receipts looked alike, a fact that appealed to counterfeiters as well as politicians and bankers seeking to profit from inflating the supply of money.

Cybermoney will be all but impossible to counterfeit in this way, officially or unofficially. The verifiability of the digital receipts rules out this classic expedient for expropriating wealth through inflation. The new digital money of the Information Age will return control over the medium of exchange to the owners of wealth, who wish to preserve it, rather than to nation-states that wish to spirit it away.

The Transaction Cost of "Free" Currency

Use of this new cybermoney will substantially free you from the power of the state. Earlier, we cited the dreary record of the world's nation-states in maintaining the value of their currencies over the past half century. No currency has suffered a smaller loss from inflation since World War II than the German mark. Yet even so, 71 percent of its value vanished between January 1, 1949, and the end of June 1995. The world reserve currency during this period, the U.S. dollar, lost 84 percent of its value.[18] This is a measure of the wealth that governments expropriated by exploiting their territorial monopolies on legal tender.

Note that there is no intrinsic necessity that currency depreciate or that the nominal cost of living rise every year. To the contrary. The technical challenge of maintaining the purchasing power of savings is trivial. You can see this merely by looking at the long-term purchasing power of gold. Between January 1, 1949, and the end of June 1995, while the best of nationalized currencies lost almost three-quarters of its value, the purchasing power of gold actually rose. As documented by Professor Roy W. Jastrom in his book *The Golden Constant,* gold has maintained its purchasing power, with minor fluctuations, for as far back as reliable price records are available, to 1560 in the case of England.

National currencies linked to gold have also maintained their purchasing power when military exigencies were not pressing. The value of the British pound sterling rose, rather than fell, during the relatively peaceful nineteenth century even though it was only weakly linked to gold. The new megapolitical conditions of the Information Age make feasible not a weak link, like the gold standard, but a strong link, reinforced for the first time by vastly improved information and computational resources in the hands of consumers.

The threat of the speedy loss of their whole business if they failed to meet expectations (and how any government organization would be certain to abuse the opportunity to play with raw material prices!) would provide a much stronger safeguard than any that could be devised against a government monopoly.[19]

—FRIEDRICH A. VON HAYEK

Privatizing Money

Friedrich von Hayek argued in 1976 that the use of competitive, private currencies would eradicate inflation.[20] Without legal-tender requirements forcing acceptance of an inflating currency within a jurisdiction, Hayek argued, market competition would force the private issuers of currency to preserve the value of their exchange media. Any issuer of a private currency failing to maintain its value would soon lose its customers. The evolution of encrypted cybercash will bring Hayek's logic vividly to life.

The theory of "free banking," as it is called, is not merely a hypothetical academic speculation. Private competing currencies circulated in Scotland from early in the eighteenth century until 1844. During that period, Scotland had no central bank. There were few regulations or restrictions on entry into the banking business. Private banks took deposits and issued their own private currencies backed by gold bullion. As Professor Lawrence White has documented, this system worked well. It was more stable, with less inflation than the more heavily regulated and politicized system of banking and money employed in England during the same period.[21] Michael Prowse of the *Financial Times* summarized Scotland's free-banking experience: "There was little fraud. There was no evidence of over-issue of notes. Banks did not typically hold either excessive or inadequate reserves. Bank runs were rare and not contagious. The free banks commanded the respect of citizens and provided a sound foundation for economic growth that outpaced that in England for most of the period."[22]

What worked well under the technological conditions of the eighteenth and nineteenth centuries will work even better with twenty-first-century technology. You will soon be able to deal in digital money from a private firm, issued much as American Express issues traveler's checks as receipts for cash. An institution of greater repute than any government, such as a leading mining company or the Swiss Bank Corporation, could create encrypted receipts for quantities of gold or even for unique bars, identified by molecular signatures and possibly even inscribed with holograms. These receipts will then trade as money, with almost no possibility that they can be counterfeited or inflated.

The new digital gold will overcome many of the practical problems that inhibited direct use of gold as money in the past. It will no longer be inconvenient, cumbersome, or dangerous to deal in large sums of gold. Digital receipts will not be too heavy to carry. Indeed, their only physical existence will be as elaborate patterns of computer code. Nor will it be difficult to divide digital receipts into units small enough to pay for even microvalue purchases. A wafer of physical gold tiny enough to pay for a chiclet would soon be lost or confused with one tiny enough to pay for two chiclets. But it will be as easy for the computer to distinguish these demoninations of digital money as if they were the size of a chipmunk and a rhinoceros.

The capacity of digital money to deliver micropayments will facilitate the emergence of new types of businesses that heretofore could not have existed, specializing in organizing the distribution of low-value information. The vendors of this information will now be compensated through direct-debit royalty schemes that overcome previously daunting transaction costs. When the cost of billing exceeds the value of a transaction, it probably will not take place. Use of cybermoney facilitates very-low-cost simultaneous billing, in which accounts are debited with use. We cited such an example above in imagining that you might pay a royalty equivalent to one-third of a penny to Bill Gates, or whoever owns the virtual-reality rights to tour the Louvre. Multiply this in a thousand ways. Virtual reality will create almost unlimited licensing opportunities that will nevertheless command only microroyalty payments. One day you will be able to replay the third game of the 1969 World Series, and pay microroyalties to the players whose images are used to make your virtual reality seem real.

ERADICATING INFLATION

Such possibilities notwithstanding, surely the most momentous consequence of the new digital money will be the end of inflation and the deleverage of the financial system. The economic implications are profound. The rise of inflation in the twentieth century, as we argued in *Blood in the Streets* and *The Great Reckoning,* was intimately connected with the balance of power in the world. Increasing returns to violence dictated sharply higher military expenditures, which in turn required ever more aggressive efforts to expropriate wealth. Governments found that they could effectively impose an annual wealth tax on all who held balances in their national currencies. This annual wealth tax on currency holders could also be seen as a transaction fee for allowing the users of currency to maintain their wealth in a convenient form provided by the issuers.*

Thinking of inflation as a transaction fee for the convenience of holding currency may be unusual, but consider it closely. During the Industrial Age we became so accustomed to thinking of the provision of currency as a service for which one does not pay directly, that it was easy to forget that the issuers of the dollars, pesos, pounds, and francs, namely governments, did require that we pay, and pay dearly—through inflation. The rate of this inflationary transaction fee on currency varied during the last half century from a low of 2.7 percent annually for the German mark, to rates perilously close to 100 percent. For example, between 1960 and 1991, when President Menem launched Argentina's currency-board reform, inflation struck seventeen zeros off successive versions of Argentine currency. If all the wealth of the world had been converted into Argentine pesos in 1960 and buried, it would not have been worth the effort to spade it up by 1991.

Argentina's example is a leading indicator for the next millennium. Currency will not be inflated because other nation-states will no longer be able to get away with it just as Argentina no longer can. The difference will be that private money dispersed over the Net will be even less susceptible to a reversal in policy than Argentina's automatic currency-board system, which

---

* Inflation had another lure during the industrial period when prices and wages were downwardly inflexible. Modest inflation increased output by reducing real wages and prices.

could be damaged by a credit contraction imported from other countries. Private money will not be inflatable because of competitive market pressures.

The death of inflation will take away the disguised profits that inflation previously conveyed to those who were the monopolistic issuers of currency. If all the disguised profits of issuing money were extinguished, a new method of payment would be needed to compensate the issuers of currency directly. Use of the new monetary system will therefore probably involve a more explicit transaction cost, perhaps a fee on the order of 1 percent per annum. This will be a small price to pay compared to the annual inflationary penalty of from 2.7 percent to 99 percent imposed by nation-states. All the more so, because there is a likelihood that overall prices will decline in the future as monopolies are eroded and competition intensifies worldwide.

Contracting Leverage

The emergence of digital money will not only defeat inflation once and for all; it will also contract leverage in the banking systems of the world. The ability of people everywhere to bypass regulatory authorities and shift their funds directly through the Internet is an entirely unprecedented consequence of the globalization of markets. It will be beyond the power of any government to regulate. When governments can no longer depreciate currency by printing money or defraud savers by expanding credit at will through captive banking systems, they will lose a major part of their indirect capacity to commandeer resources.

Higher Interest Rates

This will create an obvious dilemma for most Western governments. They will face sharp drops in revenue from taxation and the virtual elimination of leverage in the monetary system. At the same time, they will retain the unfunded liabilities and inflated expectations for social spending inherited from the industrial era. The result to be expected is an intense fiscal crisis with many unpleasant social side effects that we will consider in later chapters. The economic consequence of this transition crisis will probably include a one-time spike in real interest rates. Debtors will be squeezed as long-term liabilities contracted under the old system are liquidated, and concessionary credits dry up.

Altered by Competition

Governments facing serious competition to their currency monopolies will probably seek to underprice the for-fee cybercurrencies by tightening credits and offering savers higher real yields on cash balances in national currencies. Some governments may even seek to remonetize gold as another expedient to meet competition from private currencies. They may well reason that they could gain higher seigniorage profits from a loosely controlled nineteenth-century gold standard than would be the case if they allowed their national currency to be displaced entirely by commercial cybermoney. But not all governments will respond in the same way. Those in regions where computer usage and Net participation are low may opt for old-fashioned hyperinflation in the early stages of the cybereconomy. This will not enable these governments to capture the cash balances of the rich, but it will wring resources from those with little wealth or access to the cybereconomy. Governments using such tactics might nonetheless borrow internationally in cybermoney.

Still other governments may adapt to the opportunities created by the information economy, and facilitate local transactions in cybermoney. Those jurisdictions that first recognize the validity of digital signatures and provide local court enforcement of repossession for nonpayment of cyberdebts will stand to benefit from a disproportionate surge in long-term capital lending. Obviously, no cybermoney would be available for long-term credits in territories where local courts imposed penalties or permitted debtors to default without recourse.

Yield Gap

The combination of credit crises, competitive adjustments by national monetary authorities, and early transitional obstacles to lending cybercurrency will lead to a yield gap in the early stages of the information economy. Cybermoney will pay lower interest rates than national currencies and will probably also carry explicit transaction costs. Offsetting these apparent drawbacks to holding balances in digital money will be enhanced protection against losses due to predatory taxes and inflation. Because it will probably be gold-linked, cybermoney will also benefit from the appreciation of gold. The price of gold will probably rise significantly relative to other commodities, no matter which of the alternative government policies predominates.

Why?

The real price of gold almost always rises in deflation. A deflation, after all, reflects a shortage of liquidity. Gold is the ultimate form of liquidity.

The Deflation of the Industrial Age

Higher real rates all around will spur liquidation of high-cost, unproductive activities, and temporarily reduce consumption. We explored the logic of the credit cycle and its unwinding in *Blood in the Streets* and *The Great Reckoning*, so we will not rehearse those arguments here. Suffice it to say that the deflationary environment may drag on for some time, with more adverse consequences in the high-cost industrial economies of North America and Western Europe than in the low-cost economies in Asia and Latin America.

Lower Rates Long-Term

While the early consequences of the emergence of the cybereconomy are likely to include higher interest rates, the longer-term consequence will be just the opposite. The after-tax returns to savers will sharply increase as resources escape the grasp of governments. Dramatic improvements in the efficiency of resource use, and the liberation of capital to find the highest returns globally, should rapidly compensate for the output lost early in the transition crisis.

Investor Control over Capital

Conventional thinkers reviewing our argument at this point would conclude that the breakdown of income redistribution in the leading nation-states would doom the world to economic collapse. Do not believe it. We do not gainsay the fact that a transition crisis would be likely. But the view that the state improves the functioning of the economy by massive reallocation of resources is an anachronism, an article of faith roughly equivalent to the widespread superstitions at the close of the Middle Ages that fasting and flagellation were beneficial for a community. It should not be forgotten that governments waste resources on a large scale. Wasting resources makes you poor. A dramatic improvement in the efficiency of resource use will arise when revenues historically engrossed by governments come to be controlled instead by persons of genuine talent.

Tens of billions, then ultimately hundreds of billions of dollars will be controlled by hundreds of thousands, then millions of Sovereign Individuals. These new stewards of the world's wealth are likely to prove far abler than politicians in utilizing resources and deploying investment. For the first time in history, megapolitical conditions will allow the ablest investors and entrepreneurs rather than specialists in violence ultimate control over capital. It is not unreasonable to expect that the rates of return on this dispersed, market-driven investment could be double or triple the meager returns from the politically driven budget allocations of the nation-state era. It was not uncommon in the final decades of the twentieth century to find examples in any country of government investment that were substantially negative. We cited official Russian statistics in the revised version of *The Great Reckoning* from November 1992, suggesting that the whole of Russia's economy was "worth just $30 billion, less than a third of the value of its raw-material inputs. By implication, the output of Russia's economy would more than triple in value if the domestic manufacturing and service economy were shut down completely. Instead of contributing value, they subtract it." [23]

Admittedly, the example of Russia after the collapse of Communism is an extreme one, but there is ample evidence that reducing state control of resources tends to improve economic efficiency. Growth rates cited by the *Economist* suggest that economic liberty is strongly correlated with economic growth, with the most rapid rates of growth in the freest countries. The cybereconomy of the Information Age will be more free than any other commercial realm in history. It is therefore reasonable to expect that the cybereconomy will rapidly become the most important new economy of the new millennium. Its success will attract new participants from everywhere on the globe, in the same way that the wide use of fax machines made telecopying increasingly attractive for nonusers. But even more important, freedom from predatory violence will allow the cybereconomy to grow at far higher compound rates of growth than conventional economies dominated by nation-states.

That is perhaps the most important point to be made in anticipating the economic impact of the likely collapse of monopoly taxing and inflating capacities of government. Setting aside transition difficulties, which could last for decades, the long-term prospects for the global economy should be highly bullish. Whenever circumstances allow people to reduce protection costs and minimize tribute paid to those who control organized violence, the economy usually grows dramatically. As Lane said, "I would like to suggest that the most weighty single factor in most periods of growth, if any one factor has been most important, has been a reduction in the proportion of resources devoted to war and police." [24]

There could be great efficiency gains arising from a reduction of the resources devoted to predation and living off the spoils of predation. If the pricing of protection were placed on a competitive basis, with local monopolies competing for customers on a basis of price and quality, potentially huge gains to efficiency would be possible. The result to be expected would be much lower rates of taxation and less loss of resources and effort in political activity, which would no longer pay its previously huge dividends.

Would voters willingly forgo political windfalls to which they have become accustomed? That is an issue we take up at length elsewhere. But a simple answer is that we may have no choice. No one now demonstrates against rainy weather, or draught, however economically damaging or unpleasant it may be. No one, however criminally inclined, holds a pauper to ransom demanding a huge payment on pain of death. If it becomes impossible for politicians to obtain resources to redistribute, the public may respond in a rational way and forget about politics, just as well-intentioned people ceased organizing marches of penitents when the Middle Ages came to an end.

CHAPTER 8
THE END OF EGALITARIAN ECONOMICS

The Revolution in Earnings Capacity in a World Without Jobs

"God is not mocked: for whatsoever a man soweth, that shall he also reap."

—GALATIANS 6:7

Great changes in the dominant forms of production or defense change the structure of society, and the proportion of wealth and power of different groups. The Information Age means more than just a growing use of powerful computers. It means a revolution in lifestyles, institutions, and the distribution of resources. Because the role of covert violence in controlling resources will be sharply diminished, a new configuration of wealth will develop, without the coercive mediation by government that characterized the twentieth century. Because location will mean much less in the Information Society, there will be a diminished role in the future for all organizations that operate within rather than beyond geographic boundaries. Politicians, labor unions, regulated professions, lobbyists, and governments *per se* will be less important. Because favors and restraints of trade wrested from governments will be less valuable, fewer resources will be wasted either to promote or resist lobbying.

Those who have employed compulsion and local advantage to redistribute income are destined to lose much of their power. This will alter the command of resources. Privately generated wealth that heretofore has been commandeered by the nation-state will be retained instead by those who earn it. Increasing amounts of wealth will find their way into the hands of the ablest entrepreneurs and venture capitalists worldwide. Globalization, along with other characteristics of the information economy, will tend to increase the income earned by the most talented individuals in each field. Because the marginal value generated by superlative performance will be so huge, the distribution of earnings capacity throughout the entire global economy will take much the shape it does now in the performance professions like athletics and opera.

A MAGNITUDE BEYOND PARETO'S LAW

Pareto's law says that 80 percent of the benefit will depend on or go to 20 percent of those engaged. This may be approximately true, though, more strikingly, 1 percent of the population of the United States pays 28.7 percent of the income tax, suggesting that as societies advance into the Information Age they will experience an even more skewed distribution of incomes and abilities than Vilfredo Pareto observed at the end of the last century. People are quite accustomed to substantial inequalities of wealth. In 1828, 4 percent of New Yorkers were thought to have owned 62 percent of all the city's wealth. By 1845, the top 4 percent owned about 81 percent of all corporate and noncorporate wealth in New York City. More broadly, the top 10 percent of the population owned about 40 percent of the wealth across the whole United States in 1860. By 1890, records suggest that the richest 12 percent then owned about 86 percent of America's wealth.[1]

The 1890 numbers are close to what Pareto had in mind. They vary from his ratio of 80–20 percent mainly because a huge influx of penniless immigrants arrived in America at the end of the nineteenth century. The immigrants' share of total wealth was negligible; therefore, their arrival automatically made the total holdings of wealth more unequal. In fact, this is a striking illustration of the fact that any genuine upsurge in opportunity is almost inevitably bound to lead to at least a brief surge in inequality. By 1890, immigrants accounted for about 15 percent of the total U.S. population, but more than 40 percent in some of the northeastern states, where much of the income and wealth were generated.[2] Adjusting for the surge in immigration, late-nineteenth-century America fit Pareto's formula about as well as late-nineteenth-century Switzerland, where he lived.

The Information Age has already changed the distribution of wealth, particularly in the United States, and is one of the reasons for the bitterness of modern American politics, which we explore further in the next chapter. The Information Age requires a quite high standard of literacy and numeracy for economic success. A massive U.S. Education Department survey, "Adult Literacy in America," has shown that as many as 90 million Americans over the age of fifteen are woefully incompetent. Or in the more colorful characterization of American expatriate Bill Bryson, "They are as stupid as pig dribble." [3] Specifically, 90 million American adults were judged incapable of writing a letter, fathoming a bus schedule, or adding and subtracting, even with the help of a calculator. Those who cannot make sense of an ordinary bus timetable are unlikely to be able to make much of the Information Superhighway. From this third of Americans who have not prepared themselves to join the electronic information world, an angry underclass is being recruited. At the top of society is a small group, perhaps 5 percent, of highly educated information workers or capital owners who are the Information Age equivalent of the landed aristocracy of the feudal age—with the crucial difference that the elite of the Information Age are specialists in production, not specialists in violence.

The Megapolitics of Innovation

For no very good reason, most twentieth-century sociologists have assumed that technological progress would naturally tend to produce increasingly egalitarian societies. This was not true prior to about 1750. Beginning around that time, innovative new industrial technology began to open job opportunities for the unskilled and increase the scale of enterprise. The new technology of the factory not only raised the real earnings of the poor without any effort on their part; it also tended to increase the power of political systems, making them more able to redistribute income as well as more capable of withstanding unrest. Taking a longer view, there is no inherent reason to suppose that technology always tends to mask rather than accentuate the differences in human talents and motivation. Some technologies have been relatively egalitarian, requiring contributions of many independent workers of approximately equal utility; others have put power or wealth into the hands of a few masters while most people were little more than serfs. Both history and technology have shaped different nations in different ways. The Factory Age produced one shape, and the Information Age is producing another, less violent, and therefore more elitist and less egalitarian than the one it is replacing.

AMMON'S TURNIP

In the late nineteenth century a number of economists, of whom William Stanley Jevons was the most distinguished in England, started to develop mathematical economics. One of the first to apply probability theory to a major social question was the German economist Otto Ammon, whose work was first translated into English by Carlos C. Closson in an article in the *Journal of Political Economy* in 1899. The article was entitled "Some Social Applications of the Doctrine of Probability."[4] One might suppose that such an article was now of purely antiquarian interest. In fact, it deals with an economic problem that is again coming to the fore, and deals with it in what is still a stimulating way.

Otto Ammon was interested in the distribution of ability in society, and its relationship to the distribution of income and status. He took as his starting point the probable occurrence of total scores from four dice, each with six sides. Out of 1,296 possible throws, some totals will occur much more often than others.

The sum of 24 spots will appear once.

"	23	"	"	4	times.
"	22	"	"	10	"
"	21	"	"	20	"
"	20	"	"	35	"
"	19	"	"	56	"
"	18	"	"	80	"
"	17	"	"	104	"
"	16	"	"	125	"
"	15	"	"	140	"
"	14	"	"	146	"
"	13	"	"	140	"
"	12	"	"	125	"
"	11	"	"	104	"
"	10	"	"	80	"
"	9	"	"	56	"
"	8	"	"	35	"
"	7	"	"	20	"
"	6	"	"	10	"
"	5	"	"	4	"
"	4	"	"	once.	

It is immediately apparent that high and low scores are both comparatively rare. There are two possible totals, but the top four of these only occur thirty-five times out of the 1,296, and the bottom four only occur thirty-five times. The middle seven group of scores can be expected to occur 884 times;

the middle third of possible scores is the result in more than two-thirds of all throws. This produces the characteristic crowding toward the center of probability theory.

Otto Ammon argued that this random distribution of throws of the dice was matched by the distribution of human abilities. He was writing before the development of intelligence testing and IQs, and relied on the earlier work on intelligence of Francis Galton. Ammon did not consider that social utility, or success in life, depended simply on intelligence. He listed "three groups of mental traits which are largely decisive in the place which a man will occupy in life." These were:

1. *Intellectual traits;* among which I included all that belong to the rational side of man-power of quick comprehension, memory, power of judgement, power of invention, and whatever also belongs to this field.
2. *Moral traits;* namely, self control, will power, industry, perseverance, moderation, regard for family obligations, honesty and the like.
3. *Economic traits;* such as business ability, organizing talent, technical skill, caution, clever calculation, foresight, thrift and so on.

To these mental traits he added:

4. *Bodily traits;* power to work, endurance, power of undergoing exertions and of resisting excitements of every kind, vigour, good health, etc.

In Otto Ammon's view, the probable distribution of these qualities of intelligence, character, talent, and body were similar to those of scores on the dice. He went further and argued that there were, in fact, many more than four variables, and that they varied in more than six degrees. If instead of throwing four dice, one throws eight, then there are no less than 1,679,616 possible throws, yet the highest score, forty-eight, can still only be expected to occur once. The man or woman who scores very highly in all the factors that determine the place in life is much rarer than the probability of throwing four sixes would suggest; perhaps as rare as throwing eight sixes. Yet, Ammon notes, a mixture of high and low scores in these human qualities may produce "persons of unbalanced, inharmonious gifts, who, in spite of some brilliant qualities, cannot successfully meet the tests of life."

"Like a lonely mountain peak, or rather, like the spire of a cathedral, rise the men of high talent and of genius above the broad mass of mediocrity. . . . The number of the highly gifted is at all events so small that it is impossible that 'many' such can have been kept back in lower classes through the incompleteness of social institutions."

—OTTO AMMON

Traits and Incomes

Ammon then turns to the distribution of incomes. Of course, the statistics of the 1890s were much less adequate than they would be now, but German bureaucracy was already well developed, and Otto Ammon found in Saxony, Prussia, Baden, and other German states income curves that he thought were similar, both to his perceived distribution of human ability and to the probabilities of the dice. He found similar figures in Charles Booth's *Life and Labour of the People of London* (1892). Indeed, Booth's social distribution does look much as one might expect from Ammon's probability theory. Booth found in London 25 percent who were poor or worse, 51.5 percent who were comfortable, and 15 percent who were well-to-do, or better; if one takes the two lowest of Booth's categories they come to 9.5 percent. It was common before the welfare states of the twentieth century to speak of those who were least well off as the "submerged tenth." [5] The two highest of Booth's categories come to 7 percent.

From all this, Otto Ammon drew a number of interesting conclusions. He thought that people's abilities, broadly defined, determined their place in society and their income. He believed that high abilities naturally result in people rising in income and social position. "Like a lonely mountain peak, or rather, like the spire of a cathedral, rise the men of high talent and of genius above the broad mass of mediocrity. . . ." He also believed that the "true form of the so-called social pyramid is that of a somewhat flat onion or turnip." This turnip has a narrow stem above and a narrow root beneath. Such a social turnip is preferable as a metaphor to the social pyramid because, like modern industrial society, it has its mass in the middle while the pyramid has its mass at the bottom.

The Shape of the Turnip

Modern industrial societies are indeed all turnips, with a small wealthy and upper-professional class at the top, a larger middle class, and a minority poor class at the bottom. Relative to the middle, both the extremes are small. In modern London, if not in Washington, there are certainly more millionaires than homeless.

All of this is intriguing, but the immediate interest of Ammon's work lies in the major long-term shift we are experiencing in the relations, financial and political, between the top and the middle. The skills needed in the Factory Age, which is now passing, are undeniably different from those demanded by the Information Age. Most people could master the skills required for operating the machines of the mid-twentieth century, but those jobs have now been replaced by smart machines which, in effect, control themselves. A whole arena of low- and middle-skill employment has already disappeared. If we are correct, this is a prelude to the disappearance of most employment and the reconfiguration of work in the spot market.

"Yet it is a fact, acknowledged officially but quietly, that most of the unem-ployed youngsters have no qualifications whatsoever. . . ."[6]

—CLIVE JENKINS AND BARRIE SHERMAN

FEWER PEOPLE WILL DO MORE WORK

We can take the simple four-dice distribution of human ability and suppose that people could score in the Factory Age with a set of 4×2 or above. That would mean that over 95 percent of the population were above what Charles Booth called "the lowest limit of positive social usefulness." Indeed, 3 percent was set as the full-employment standard of the 1940s and 1950s. Suppose that in the Information Age the required score has risen to a 4×3, and the required minimum has gone up from 8 to 12. That would mean that nearly 24 percent would fall below this limit of "social usefulness."

Something similiar would happen at the top end of the scale. In the Factory Age, the required level of high ability was perhaps 4×4; suppose that in the Information Age it has risen to 4×5. In that case the proportion of people qualified for the top jobs, which are also the best paid, would fall from 34 percent to 5 percent.

These numbers are purely hypothetical. Obviously, we do not know what the shift in the skill requirements will be—or has already been—but there has certainly been a rise. Because of the shape of the turnip, a quite modest rise in the minimum skill requirement would put large numbers outside of a significant economic role. Equally, quite a small rise in the higher skill requirement would reduce the number of people qualified for the higher jobs very dramatically. Some shift is happening: we do not yet know how big it will be.

There is indeed no lack of social and political evidence that this shift is taking place in all advanced industrial societies, that its pace is accelerating, and that the movement is already a big one. The rewards for rare skills have increased and are increasing. This has been noted with displeasure by conventional thinkers. Consider, for example, *The Winner-Take-All Society*, by Robert H. Frank and Philip J. Cook.[7] It documents the growing tendency for the most talented competitors in many fields in the United States to earn very high incomes. Equally, the opportunities for middle skills are falling; a substantial number of low skills now fall outside the range that is rewarded with a comfortable living, though they may still find a place in small-scale services.

If the Information Age demands higher skills both at the top and bottom end, everyone except for the top 5 percent will be relatively at a disadvantage, but the top 5 percent will gain tremendously. They will both earn a higher share of income and keep a greater share of what they earn. At the same time, they will do a greater portion of the world's work than ever before. Many will emerge as Sovereign Individuals. In the Information Age, the turnip of income distribution will look more as it did in 1750 than in 1950.

Societies that have been indoctrinated to expect income equality and high levels of consumption for persons of low or modest skills will face demotivation and insecurity. As the economies of more countries more deeply assimilate information technology, they will see the emergence—so evident already in North America—of a more or less unemployable underclass. This is exactly what is happening. This will lead to a reaction with a nationalist, antitechnology bias, as we detail in the next chapter.

The Factory Age may prove to have been a unique period in which semistupid machines left a highly profitable niche for unskilled people. Now that the machines can look after themselves, the Information Age is pouring its gifts onto the top 5 percent of Otto Ammon's turnip. The Information Age was already looking far better for the top 10 percent, the so-called cognitive elite. Yet it will be the best of all for the top 10 percent of the top 10 percent, the cognitive double top. In the feudal age, it took one hundred semiskilled peasants to support one highly skilled warlord (or knight) on horseback. The Sovereign Individuals of the information economy will not be warlords but masters of specialized skills, including entrepreneurship and investment. Yet the feudal hundred-to-one ratio seems set to return. For better or worse, the societies of the twenty-first century are likely to be more unequal than those we have lived in during the twentieth.

MOST PEOPLE WILL GAIN FROM THE DEATH OF POLITICS

It is unlikely that the egalitarian economy and the nations it supports can disappear without a crisis. While a "crisis" by definition can last only for a short while, we nonetheless imagine that the trauma of the end of nations could reverberate for years. Without ignoring that trauma, whose dimensions we explore in greater detail later, it is important not to forget that in many areas of the globe the transition to the information economy will lead output to surge, with higher incomes all around. Indeed, in those areas that never shared fully in the benefits of industrialism but are now open to the free market, incomes are rising or will rise among all classes of people.

The deflation of compulsion as a feature of economic life will allow producers to retain assets that heretofore have been seized and redistributed. Redistribution usually meant that assets were dragooned into lower-value uses, thus reducing the productivity of capital. Wealth taken disproportionately from persons who were most adept at investing resources was reallocated by politicians to those who were less adept. In most cases, redistributed income was employed in lower-order economic activities. The effects of freeing resources from systematic compulsion will vary greatly among jurisdictions. This freezing of resources will bankrupt welfare states, and enhance diseconomies to scale that are undermining large governments and all institutions subsidized by large governments. On the other hand, the shift to the cybereconomy will reduce the economic drawbacks suffered by people operating under sovereignties in regions that have traditionally suffered from the inability to organize on a large scale.

"If the world operates as one big market, every employee will compete with every person anywhere in the world who is capable of doing the same job. There are lots of them and many of them are hungry." [8]

—ANDREW S. GROVE, PRESIDENT, INTEL CORP.

SHIFTING LOCATIONAL ADVANTAGES

Because there will no longer be rising returns to violence, there will be no advantage to living under a government that could capture them. Once-competent governments will no longer be the friends of wealth accumulation, but their enemies. High taxes, burdensome regulatory costs, and ambitious commitments to income redistribution will make territories under their control uninviting settings in which to do business.

Those who live in jurisdictions that remained poor or underdeveloped during the industrial period have the most to gain by the liberation of economies from the confines of geography. This is contrary to what you will hear. The main controversy surrounding the advent of the information economy and the rise of the Sovereign Individual will focus on the allegedly adverse effects on "fairness" arising from the death of politics. It is certainly true that the advent of the global information economy will deal a mortal blow to large-scale income redistribution. The main beneficiaries of income redistribution in the Industrial Age have been inhabitants of wealthy jurisdictions whose level of consumption is twenty times higher than the world average. Only within the OECD countries has income redistribution had noticeable effects in raising incomes of unskilled persons.

The greatest income inequalities have been observed *among* jurisdictions. Income redistribution has done little to alleviate them. In fact, we believe that foreign aid and international development programs have had the perverse effect of lowering the real incomes of poor people in poor countries by subsidizing incompetent governments. This is an issue we consider in more depth in analyzing the impact of the Information Revolution on morality.

A Century of Rising Income Inequality

During the industrial period, the factor that contributed most to determining the ordinary person's lifetime income was the political jurisdiction in which he happened to reside. Contrary to the common impression in rich economies today, income inequality rose rapidly during the industrial period. An estimate cited by the World Bank suggests that average per capita income in the richest countries ballooned from eleven times that in the poorest countries in 1870 to fifty-two times in 1985.[9] While inequality increased dramatically on a global basis, it often appeared otherwise to the fraction of the world inhabiting the wealthy industrial countries. Income inequality rose *among* jurisdictions rather than within them.

For reasons we have already explored, the character of industrial technology itself helped assure that income gaps would narrow within jurisdictions where halfway competent governments mastered the exercise of power on a large scale. When returns to violence were rising, as they were during the Industrial Age, governments that operated on a large scale tended to be controlled by their employees. This made it effectively impossible to impose controls on the claims these governments made over resources. Their unchecked control over resources conveyed an important military advantage so long as magnitude of power predominated over the efficiency with which it was used. A not-incidental corollary of government controlled by its employees was a sharp acceleration of income redistribution. Almost every society has some provision for income redistribution, at least on a temporary basis in extraordinary circumstances. However, a close reading of the history of the provision of aid to the poor shows that "welfare" benefits tend to be more generous when poverty is minimal. Income redistribution is more likely to be curtailed when incomes for large numbers weaken. Conditions in the wealthy industrial societies in the last half of the twentieth century were almost perfect for redistributing income. This led to much higher rewards for unskilled work within these favored jurisdictions. In due course, it even provided high levels of consumption for those who did not work at all.

The Paradox of Industrial Wealth

The irony is that it was also in these jurisdictions that more people became wealthy. This apparent paradox makes perfect sense once you understand the dynamics of megapolitics explored in previous chapters. Leading sectors of the industrial economy required the maintenance of order on a large scale to function optimally. This made them particularly vulnerable to extortion by unions and governments eager to maximize the number of persons under their sway. Yet widespread redistribution of income did not totally stifle the ablility of the industrial economy to function. Anyone lucky enough to be born in Western Europe, the former British settlement colonies, or Japan during the high-water period of industrialism was therefore likely to be far richer than a person of equivalent skills in South America, Eastern Europe, the late Soviet Union, Africa, and the landmass of Asia. The beneficial impact of information technology will include helping to overcome many of the obstacles to development that prevented the majority of the world's population from enjoying many of the benefits of free markets during much of the modern period.

> *"The indigenous characteristics of poor countries are strikingly inhospitable to effective large-scale organization, especially to large-scale organizations that have to operate (as governments do) over a large geographical area."* [10]
>
> —MANCUR OLSON

DISECONOMIES OF SCALE AND RETARDED GROWTH

As Mancur Olson has demonstrated, backwardness in the twentieth century was not due to lack of capital or specialized skills *per se.* In "Diseconomies of Scale and Development," an essay published in 1987, two years before the fall of the Berlin Wall, Olson wrote, "If capital had in fact been in scarce supply in the poor countries, its 'marginal productivity' and so the profitability of its use ought to be greater than in the prosperous countries. The low growth rates of many countries that received nonnegligible amounts of foreign aid and the low productivity of some modern factories that were built in poor countries have further lessened the credibility of the 'scarcity of capital' explanation of underdevelopment." [11] This must be right. Had capital or skill scarcity been the main deficiency, the returns earned by both in poor jurisdictions would have been higher than in developed countries. Both skilled personnel and capital would have flooded into these regions until the returns leveled out. In fact, the opposite was often the case. There was a substantial outmigration of educated people from backward jurisdictions. And the lucky few who did manage to accummulate capital in such places exported it as rapidly as possible to Switzerland and other advanced countries.

Better Government Could Not Be Imported

Olson argues, and we agree, that the true obstacle to development in backward countries has been the one factor of production that could not be easily borrowed or imported from abroad, namely government. This is a problem that worsened as the twentieth century unfolded. In 1900, Great Britain and France, along with some other European countries, were in the business of exporting competent government to regions where indigenous powers were incapable of functioning effectively on a large scale. But shifting megapolitical conditions in the twentieth century raised the costs and lowered the returns for this activity. Colonialism, or imperialism, as it was less fondly known, ceased to be a paying proposition. Shifts in technology raised the costs of projecting power from the center to the periphery and lowered the military costs of an effective resistance. Consequently, imperial powers withdrew, or stayed on only in tiny enclaves, like Bermuda or the Cayman Islands.

"If the postcolonial nation-state had become a shackle on progress, as more and more critics in Africa seemed to agree by the end of the 1980s, the prime reason could appear in little doubt. The state was not liberating and protective of its citizens, no matter what its propaganda claimed; on the contrary, its gross effect was constricting and exploitative, or else, it simply failed to operate in any social sense at all."[12]

—BASIL DAVIDSON

The indigenous governments that replaced colonial rule in the countries that were not settled by Europeans drew their leaders and administrators from populations who had little experience or skill at running any type of large-scale enterprise. In many cases, especially in Africa, infrastructure inherited from the departing colonial powers was rapidly looted, destroyed, or allowed to fall into disrepair. Telephone lines were torn down by scavengers and hammered into bracelets. Roads were no longer maintained. Rail lines became useless as roadbeds fell apart and locomotives broke down. In Zaire, the elaborate transportation infrastructure installed by the Belgians had almost totally disappeared by 1990. Only a few creaky riverboats continued to function, one of which was taken over as a kind of floating palace by the dictator.

Undependable communication and transport reflect the incompetence of backward nation-states at maintaining order. They have kept prices high and minimized opportunities for most of the world's population. As Olson emphasizes:

> First, poor transportation and communication tend to force a firm to rely mainly on local factors of production. When a firm's scale increases, it will have to go further afield to obtain factors of production, and the poorer the transportation and communications systems the faster these factor costs will rise with expanding output.
>
> The second and more important reason why poor transportation and communication systems work against effective large-scale enterprises is that they make it far more difficult to coordinate such enterprises effectively." [13]

Lightening the Burden of Bad Government

The ambitious poor of the world, more than anyone, stand to benefit as information technology disconnects the capacity to earn income from the locale in which one lives. New technologies, such as the digital cellular telephone, allow communications to function independently of the ability of the local police to defend every telephone pole in a jurisdiction from copper thieves. As wireless fax and Internet connections become available, it no longer matters so much whether desperately poor postal employees will pilfer mail just to steal the stamp.

In many cases, effective communications are even replacing the need for the physical transport of goods and services. Better communications and vastly increased computational power not only make coordination of complex activities cheaper and more effective; they also lower scale economies and dissolve large organizations. These changes all tend to reduce the penalty that persons in backward countries have suffered for living under incompetent governments. The Information Revolution will make it much less important whether governments are able to function capably. It will therefore be easier for persons living in traditionally poor countries to surmount the hurdles that their governments have heretofore placed in the path of economic growth.

Equal Opportunity in the Information Age

In the Information Age, familiar locational advantages will rapidly be transformed by technology. Earnings capacity for persons of similar skills will become much more equal, no matter in what jurisdiction they live. This has already begun to happen. Because institutions that have employed compulsion and local advantage to redistribute income are losing power, income inequality *within jurisdictions* will rise. Global competition will also tend to increase the income earned by the most talented individuals in each field, wherever they live, much as it does now in professional athletics. The marginal value generated by superior performance in a global market will be huge.

While public debate will focus on growing "inequality" in the OECD countries, individuals everywhere will enjoy far more nearly equal opportunity. They will no longer need to live in a jurisdiction that functions well on a large scale in order to succeed. Innate abilities and the willingness to develop them will be measured on a more equal playing field than ever before. Jurisdictional advantages that led to widening inequality between rich and poor economies during the industrial period will change dramatically.

Higher Returns in Poor Areas

The obstacles that governments in poorer regions place in the way of functioning free markets will be much diminished as the cybereconomy comes on line. As a consequence, capital and skills in short supply will in fact earn higher returns in many currently poor areas, much as the development theorists of the 1950s postulated they should. And both capital and skills will be far more readily importable. Emerging economies will no longer need to rely as much as during the Industrial Age upon local factors of production. Their enhanced ability to draw upon capital and expertise at a distance will lead to higher rates of growth. This will happen whether or not incompetent governments become more honest or better able to protect property rights. Lacking power over cyberspace, bad governments will simply be less able to stop people in their jurisdictions from benefiting from economic freedom.

Positive Reinforcement

In the new cybereconomy, the almost total portability of information technology will prohibit the hoarding of many of the jurisdictional advantages that arose in the Industrial Age. Enhanced competition between increasing numbers of jurisdictions will turn on new types of local advantage. Sovereignty will be commercialized rather than predatory. Governments will be obliged by the force of competition to set policies to appeal to those of their customers who make the greatest contributions to economic well-being, not to those who contribute little or whose economic contributions are negative.

This will represent a tremendous change from the common practice of the twentieth century. The ideology of the nation-state was that life can and should be regulated in a positive way by subsidizing undesirable outcomes and penalizing desirable ones. To be poor is undesirable; therefore, the poor were subsidized. To become rich is desirable; therefore, punitive taxes were laid on the rich to make life more "fair."

Because this whole policy approach was rooted in a megapolitical foundation that withstood all appeal, it mattered little what the perverse consequences of subsidizing dysfunction were. Nor was there much accounting for the skill, hard work, or ingenuity that went into earning the wealth that was redistributed. Outcomes were measured in terms of entitlements. The twentieth-century political view assumed that in order for outcomes to be "fair" they had to be equal.

The New Paradigm

The new megapolitical conditions of the twenty-first century will allow market tests to regulate outcomes in areas formerly dominated by politics. The market paradigm presupposes that results can be better regulated by rewarding desirable outcomes and penalizing undesirable ones. To be poor is undesirable, and to become rich is desirable. Therefore, incentives should reward wealth creation and encourage people to pay for the resources they consume. Life is more "fair" when people get to keep more of what they earn.

This is a view that will be heard more frequently in the new millennium than it was in the century now ending. Furthermore, it will be compelling as never before because it will be megapolitically founded. Capital in the Information Age is growing more mobile by the moment. The capacity to earn high income is no longer tied to residence in specific locations, as was the case when most wealth was created by manipulating natural resources. With every day that passes, it becomes easier for people using highly portable information technology to create assets that are far less subject to the leverage of violence than any form of wealth has ever been before.

Arbitrary political regulations that impose costs without creating offsetting market benefits will soon be nonviable. Powerful competitive forces are tending to equalize the prices of goods, services, labor, and capital across the globe. Governments will have less latitude to impose arbitrary policies than they are accustomed to enjoy. Any government that attempts to impose more burdensome regulations on an activity than other sovereignties will simply drive that activity away. In some cases, of course, driving away unwanted activities will please the market and make those jurisdictions all the more popular and prosperous. In this sense, certain regulations may be compared to the house rules imposed by the proprietors of a hotel chain. If they prohibit people from walking barefoot or smoking in the lobby, they will no doubt lose certain customers. But turning away those customers may not cost the jurisdiction customers overall, or even reduce its total revenues. Well-shod nonsmokers may pay more precisely because barefoot smokers are excluded. Equally, regulations that make it costly or impossible to operate a rendering plant in a certain jurisdiction may drive the rendering elsewhere without depriving the jurisdiction as a whole of income.

These examples demonstrate how regulations may in rare circumstances have a positive rather than a negative market value, especially in a world with a rapidly mulitiplying number of jurisdictions. Rules that preserve high standards of public health, clean air, and clean water will be highly valued in many locales. So will other, sometimes more exotic regulations and covenants of the kind that might be imposed by real estate developers or hotels catering to certain market segments.

No Customs House in Cyberspace

We expect the commercialization of sovereignty to rapidly lead to the devolution of many large territorial sovereignties. The very fact that information technology cannot be subjected to border controls of the kind that can still impede the trade of manufactures and farm goods has important implications. It means that protectionism will be less effective over time as trade in information displaces physical products in the generation of wealth. It also means that smaller regions will be ever less dependent upon the maintenance of extensive political jurisdictions in order to assure access to markets in which they can earn income.

Information technology exposes people working in formerly protected service sectors to foreign competition. If a firm in Toronto wished to hire a bookkeeper twenty years ago, that person had to be physically located in Toronto, or in a nearby community within commuting distance. In the Information Age, a bookkeeper in Budapest or Bangalore, India, could do the job, and download all the material needed in encrypted form over the Internet. Instant communication through satellite links makes any part of the world only a moment away by modem and fax. Someone in need of stock analysts could hire twenty-seven in India for the price of one on Wall Street. As information technology improves by a magnitude or more every eighteen months (Moore's Law), ever-greater numbers of service-sector workers will be exposed to price competition that is essentially beyond the capacity of politicians to impede. This competition will eventually apply as fully to the learned professions as to bookkeepers. Digital lawyers and cyberdoctors will proliferate in the Information Economy.

Death Watch for Nation-States

With the economic benefits formerly captured within the boundaries of nation-states falling away, the nation-states themselves will eventually collapse under their weighty liabilities. But the fact that all nation-states are on a death watch does not mean that they are all destined to expire at the same moment. Far from it. Devolutionary pressures will tend to be most intense in large political entities where incomes for most of the population are stagnant or falling. Jurisdictions in Latin America and Asia where per capita income is rising rapidly may endure for generations, or until lifetime income prospects there equate with those in the formerly rich industrial countries. At that point, there will no longer be easy cost-substituting gains to be had, and the politics of growth will become more challenging.

We also suspect that nation-states with a single major metropolis will remain coherent longer than those with several big cities, which imply multiple centers of interest with their various hinterlands.

Another spur to devolution will be high indebtedness of the central government. The three wealthy industrial countries with the highest relative indebtedness—Canada, Belgium, and Italy—are not coincidentally nations with advanced separatist movements. All three countries have suffered from chronic budget deficits and now have national debts that exceed 100 percent of GDP. As the national debt has mounted in each country, the appeal of separatist movements has grown as well. In Italy, the Northern League has emerged as a dynamic and popular regional political movement. Its platform is based upon a simple mathematical observation: northern Italy, or "Padonia," would be richer than Switzerland if large portions of its income were not siphoned off to subsidize Rome and the poorer south. The Northern League proposes an obvious solution: secede from Italy, and thus escape from some of the dire consequences of compound interest. Likewise, in Belgium, where the national debt exceeds 130 percent of GDP, the Flemings and Walloons are maneuvering like a hostile couple before a divorce. A growing minority among the Flemings argue that they are unfairly subsidizing the Walloons, and could improve their economic condition by splitting Belgium in two.

Canada's case differs in the detail that French Canada, the main region now agitating for separatism, has historically been subsidized by English Canada. But as the federal debt and deficit mount, the realization is dawning in Quebec that this form of income redistribution will decline. The Bloc Québecois is therefore flirting with an appeal that it lacked a decade ago—

the promise to raise after-tax income by abolishing the payment of Canadian federal tax. Separatist leaders also suggest that Quebec should leave Canada without shouldering a proportionate burden of the federal debt.

English Canadians resist this argument and tend to resent its implications because they are keenly aware of the large transfers made to Quebec over the years. Nonetheless, the appeal of the Parti Québecois is strong, and it seems only a matter of time until a secession referendum dissolves Canada. A similar fate awaits other nation-states when their financial circumstances deteriorate.

Another factor that bodes ill for Canada's long-term survival is the fact that it is a thinly populated country with a sprawling industrial-era infrastructure to maintain. The transition to the Information Age is inevitably depreciating physical infrastructure. As telecommuters replace factory employees and office workers, it will matter less whether freeways and other transportation thoroughfares are rebuilt and well-maintained. With fiscal crises pinching on all sides, more and more factions in Canadian life will retreat to the eighteenth-century exclusionary view of the financing of public goods advocated by Adam Smith. He wrote in *The Wealth of Nations:*

> Were the streets of London to be lighted and paved at the expense of the [national] treasury, is there any probability that they would be so well lighted and paved as they are at present, or even at so small an expense. The expense, besides, instead of being raised by a local tax upon the inhabitants of each particlar street, parish or district in London would, in this case, be defrayed out of the general revenue of the state, and would consequently be raised by a tax upon all the inhabitants of the kingdom, of whom the greater part derived no sort of benefit from the lighting and paving of the streets of London.[14]

For London, substitute Toronto, and you are inside an equation that will be running in the minds of many in Alberta and British Columbia. The logic of devolution will prove infectious.

When Canada breaks apart, this will lead to a marked increase in secessionist activity in the Pacific Northwest of the United States. Residents of Alaska, Washington, Oregon, Idaho, and Montana would find themselves at a distinct disadvantage in competition with Alberta and British Columbia as independent sovereignties.

AFTER THE NATION-STATE

In the place of nation-states you will see, at first, smaller jurisdictions at the provincial level, and ultimately, smaller sovereignties, enclaves of various kinds like medieval city-states surrounded by their hinterlands. As strange as it may seem to people inculcated with the importance of politics, policies of these new ministates will in many cases be informed more by entrepreneurial positioning than by political wrangling. These new, fragmented sovereignties will cater to different tastes, just as hotels and restaurants do, enforcing specific regulations within their public spaces that appeal to the market segments from which they draw their customers. This is not to say, of course, that there are not special problems arising from the organization of protection on a nomadic basis. We address these in the next chapter.

"Town air brings freedom."

—MEDIEVAL ADAGE

Noncitizens of the Pale

These difficulties notwithstanding, human ingenuity usually finds a way to create institutions to capture profitable opportunities, even where the demand arises from persons who can pay little. Where the potential customers are among the wealthiest persons on earth, that tendency should be all the more emphatic. Exit, or "voting with your feet," is always an option when dated products, organizations, or even governments lose their appeal and seem to offer little prospect of immediate improvement. Consider, for example, the growth of medieval towns that served as safe havens for serfs escaping feudal subjugation. Their role may prove analogous to the role of new jurisdictions in accommodating the coming exit from nation-states. The acceptance of aliens escaping from some lord as "citizens of the pale" defied the prevailing conventions of feudal law and episcopal authority. But nonetheless it was a generally successful alternative for those who employed it, contributing importantly to weakening the grip of feudalism. As medieval historian Fritz Rorig put it, the serf of a secular lord would be "a free burgher of the town after a year and a day."[15] It is reasonable to expect new institutional refuges to spring up, upon "new legal principles," to provide fiscal refuge to citizens of the state, much as the medieval town offered refuge to feudal subjects who lived within the shadows of its walls.

Economist Albert O. Hirschman, who explored the theoretical subtleties of "voting with your feet" in *Exit, Voice, and Loyalty,* first published in 1969, foresaw that technological advances would increase the likelihood of exit as a strategy for dealing with states in decline. He wrote, "Only as countries start to resemble each other because of the advances in communication and all-round modernization will the danger of premature and excessive exits arise. . . ."[16] That is precisely what is happening. Information technology is rapidly diminishing many of the differences among jurisdictions, making exit a much more attractive option. Of course, "premature and excessive exits" in Hirschman's vocabulary are understood from the point of view of what is optimal for the state being deserted. No doubt lords in medieval Europe believed that they suffered from "premature and excessive exits" of their serfs into towns where they achieved freedom.

To return to our earlier example, it is not as far-fetched as it might seem to suppose that there will be a number of ministates offering refuge to exiles fleeing the dying nation-states. These sovereignties will compete on terms and conditions of exile. Some, perhaps on the West Coast of North America, may well cater to people who do not smoke and are intolerant of secondhand smoke from those who do. Obviously, such regimes would not be popular with smokers. Rules banning their habit will seem an arbitrary imposition to many smokers.

In the industrial era of mass politics, such differences of opinion were fought out in political campaigns that ultimately forced one group or the other to abide by the wishes of the more powerful. But it is by no means essential that contentions about mutually exclusive choices be settled in a way that requires that the preferences of large numbers of people be suppressed.

Some individuals like to eat foie gras and others like hot dogs, and others still eat soya curd. They usually do not have to argue about their diet preferences because their culinary choices are not bound together. No one forces all to consume the same meal. Megapolitical conditions did, however, force common consumption of many kinds of collective and even private goods provided by governments in the industrial era. Why? Because there were great economic advantages to be captured by operating at a large scale. It was therefore impractical to divide sprawling jurisdictions into enclaves where everyone could have his own way, even on important items. The exclusionary approach to the provision of public goods argued by Adam Smith can be far more easily accommodated when the number of jurisdictions multiplies by ten or even a hundred times over. In the Information Age, growing numbers of sovereignties will be small enclaves rather than continental empires. Some may be North American Indian bands who will claim tax jurisdiction over their reservations and reserves much as they now claim the right to operate gambling casinos or to fish in defiance of limits.

Because information technology eliminates many of the drawbacks of devolving trading areas, it will be practical for the new sovereignties to operate more on the principles of clubs or affinity groups than those that governed territorial nation-states. Just as it is not crucial that every *potential* customer share the same taste in clothes, or watch the same television programs, it will be less important than it may seem that everyone agree with affinity points that define the governing style of fragmented sovereignties.

Widely dispersed tastes will result in widely divergent styles of fragmented sovereignty, much as there are increasingly wide choices in clothing style or television broadcasts. Some microstates may even be linked like hotel groups in franchises, or operate together to achieve advantages in police functions and other residual services of government. Those who like clean streets and resent finding gum under tabletops will find Singapore fetching. Fans of Beavis and Butthead won't. Those who like wild nightlife will prefer Macao or Panama, or some similar place. Customers uncomfortable with mores in one jurisdiction will be welcomed in others. While Salt Lake City may be smokeless, the new city-state in Havana, perhaps renamed Monte Cristo, will probably be shrouded in a cloud of cigar smoke.

"It means that all of the monopolies and hierarchies and pyramids and power grids of industrial society are going to dissolve before this constant pressure of distributing intelligence to the fringes of all networks. Above all, Moore's Law will overthrow the key concentration, the key physical conglomeration of power in America today: the big city—that big set of industrial cities that now lives on life-support systems—some $360 billion of direct subsidies from all the rest of us every year. Big cities are leftover baggage from the industrial era."[17]

—GEORGE GILDER

A peculiar irony of the re-emergence of micro-sovereignties or "city-states" is that it may coincide with the emptying out of many cities. The large city was largely an artifact of industrialism in the West. It arose with the factory system to capture scale economies in the manufacture of products with high natural resource content.

When the nineteenth century opened, cities of more than 100,000 were considered huge, and outside of Asia, where population statistics were doubtful, there were no cities of more than a million persons. The largest city in the United States in 1800 was Philadelphia, with a population of 69,403. New York had just 60,489. Baltimore was the third largest city in America with 26,114 inhabitants.[18] Most of what were to become the great metropolitan cities of Europe had populations that are tiny by twentieth-century standards. London, with a population of 864,845, was probably the biggest city in the world. Paris, with 547,756, was the only other city in Europe with more than half a million inhabitants in 1801.[19] Lisbon's population was 350,000.[20] Vienna had a population of 252,000.[21] Berlin had barely poked above 200,000 by 1819.[22] Madrid was home to 156,670.[23] The population of Brussels in 1802 was 66,297. Budapest had a population of just 61,000.[24]

There is an obvious temptation to think that the growth of big cities is a direct function of population growth. But this is not necessarily so. Every human on earth could be packed into Texas, with each family living in its own detached house with a yard, and still have some of Texas left over. As Adna Weber argued in the classic study *The Growth of Cities in the Nineteenth Century,* population growth alone does not explain why people live in urban settings rather than dispersed in the countryside. In 1890, Bengal had about the same population density as England. Yet Bengal's urban population was just 4.8 percent, while England's was 61.7 percent.[25]

Historically, cities were walled off from the countryside to keep marauders and the lower classes out. The growth of industrial employment in the nineteenth and twentieth centuries created big cities. Now the big city has become highly vulnerable to breakdown as industrialism has begun to fade. The perfect marker of this development is Detroit, the leading industrial city of the mid-twentieth century. At one time, a large fraction of the world's industrial output passed through Detroit. Now it is a hollowed-out shell, ridden by crime and disorder. In many blocks of downtown Detroit, one or more derelict buildings have been burned to the ground or torn down, leaving the impression that the city has survived a series of raids by World War II bombers.

Detroit stands as a reminder that many industrial cities are no longer viable. They will crumble away as information and ideas become more important factors imparting value than fabricating from natural resources. In many cases, the large city has already grown too large to support its own weight. To keep a metropolis functioning requires that a substantial number of support systems operate effectively at large scale. The very crowding together of millions of people implies a huge jump in vulnerability to crime, sabotage, and random violence. During the industrial era, the price of policing against these risks was repaid by the high-scale economies of production.

In the Information Age, only cities that repay their upkeep costs by offering a high quality of life will remain viable. Persons at a distance will no longer be obliged to subsidize them. A good marker for the viability of cities is whether those living at the core of the city are richer than those on its periphery. Buenos Aires, London, and Paris will remain inviting places to live and do business long after the last good restaurant closes in South Bend, Louisville, and Philadelphia.

Country States

Some city-states may prove to be merely enclaves with no cities attached. Perhaps they might be better thought of as village states or country states.

Natural resource endowments will be valued in different ways as well. When you can do business anywhere, you may well choose to do business in a beautiful place where you can breathe deeply without inhaling too much carcinogenic pollution. Communications technologies that minimize language difficulties will make it ever easier to abide almost anywhere that the environment is attractive. Thinly populated regions with temperate climates, and a large endowment of arable land per head, like New Zealand and Argentina, will also enjoy a comparative advantage because they enjoy high standards of public health and are low-cost producers of foods and renewable products. Such products will benefit from increased demand as the living standards of billions of people in East Asia and Latin America rise.

The Inequivalence Theorem

Many of the assumptions of economists about behavior are rooted in the tyranny of place. A distinct example is Ricardo's "Equivalence Theorem," which suggests that citizens in a country that runs huge deficits will adjust their expectations in anticipation of higher tax rates needed in the future to retire the debt. In this sense, there is an "equivalence" between financing spending by taxation and through debt. At least there was such an equivalence in the early nineteenth century when Ricardo wrote. In the Information Age, however, the rational person will not respond to the prospect of higher taxes to fund deficits by increasing his savings rate; he will transfer his domicile, or lodge his transactions elsewhere. For the same reason that producers sort among suppliers in search of the lowest costs, they will be even more strongly motivated to seek alternative suppliers of protection. The benefits of doing so will dwarf the margins to be realized by shifting to a new supplier of plastic tubes. The result to be expected is that Sovereign Individuals and other rational people will flee jurisdictions with large unfunded liabilities.

Cheap governments that have few liabilities and impose low costs on customers will be the domiciles of choice for wealth creation in the Information Age. This implies much more attractive prospects for doing business in areas where indebtedness is low and governments have already been restructured, such as New Zealand, Argentina, Chile, Peru, Singapore, and other parts of Asia and Latin America. These areas will also be superior platforms for doing business to unreformed, high-cost economies in North America and Western Europe.

The Erosion of Local Price Anomalies

Greatly reduced information costs will obviate most local pricing advantages. Not only will buyers be able to scan an immense number of outlets in search of the lowest prices on tradable goods; they will also be able to employ remote services to shop across jurisdictional boundaries. This will allow people to much more easily compare features of difficult-to-analyze products like insurance. And it will bypass restraints of trade imposed by local licensing procedures. Consequently, profit margins are likely to fall in any field where local price anomalies can be eroded by additional information and competition.

NEW ORGANIZATIONAL IMPERATIVES

The cybereconomy will significantly differ from the industrial economy in the way its participants interact. Information technology will dissipate many of the long-term organizational advantages of firms that arise from high transaction and information costs. The Information Age will be the age of the "virtual corporation."

Many analysts more knowledgable than we are about information technology have utterly failed to see that it is destined to transform the logic of economic organization. Not only does the new technology transcend borders and barriers; it also revolutionizes the "internal" costs of computation. Even the few businesses that will not be affected by exposure to greater cross-border competition because of improving information and communication technology will be exposed to new organizational imperatives. Rapidly falling information and transaction costs will decisively lower economies to scale, voiding many of the incentives that gave rise to long-lived firms and career employment during the industrial period.

Why Firms?

The classical economists like Adam Smith were almost silent on the question of firm size. They did not address what influences the optimal size of firms, why firms take the form they do, or even why firms exist at all. Why do entrepreneurs hire employees, rather than placing every task that needs doing out to bid among independent contractors in the auction market? Nobel Prize–winning economist Ronald Coase helped launch a new direction in economics by asking some of these important questions. The answers he helped to frame hint at the revolutionary consequences of information technology for the structure of business. Coase argued that firms were an efficient way to overcome information deficits and high transaction costs.[26]

Information and Transaction Costs

To see why, consider the obstacles you would have faced in trying to operate an industrial-era assembly line without a single firm to coordinate its activities. In principle, an automobile could have been produced without production being centralized under the oversight of a single firm. Economist Oliver Williamson, along with Coase, is another pioneer in developing the theory of the firm. Williamson defined six different methods of operation and control. Among them is the "entrepreneurial mode," "wherein each workstation is owned and operated by a specialist." [27] Another is what Williamson calls the "federated workstations" in which "an intermediate product is transferred across stages by each worker." [28] There is no physical reason why the thousands of employees could not have been replaced by a gaggle of independent contractors, each renting space on the factory floor, bidding for parts, and offering to assemble the axle or weld the fenders onto the chassis. Yet you would look in vain for an example of an industrial-era automobile factory organized and run by independent contractors.

Coordination Problems

Operating an industrial facility without the benefit of coordination through a single firm would have dissipated most of the economies to be realized by operating on a large scale. Massive transaction problems in coordinating a patchwork quilt of small firms would have effectively deautomated the assembly line. To work at all, such a system would have necessitated nonstop negotiation among the individual contractors. Instead of focusing on production, the multitude of contractors or entrepreneurs would have had to divert time and attention to fixing prices of components and working out the terms of their own constantly changing interactions. Simply monitoring production would have been a difficult problem.

The Authority to Act

With such a set of independent organizations struggling to assemble a car, creation and re-engineering of the models would have been a nightmare. You need only imagine the difficulty facing the designer in attempting to convince the hundreds of independent contractors on changes required to introduce a new model. In practice, almost unanimous consent would have been needed. Anyone holding out or objecting to any change in the specification of the product could either have effectively killed the model improvement or raised the cost of introducing it, thus further jeopardizing the gains from operating on a large scale.

Unnecessary Negotiation

An assembly line rented (or owned separately) by independent contractors would have been subject to numerous vulnerabilities avoided by operating within a single firm. The death, illness, or financial failure of individual contractors would have been an altogether too common occurrence in operations requiring the cooperation of thousands of people to build a single product under one roof. The auction market would certainly have been able to replace these contractors. But each succession would have required a negotiated settlement, such as a buyout of the previous operator by his replacement. It also would have required an agreement on assumption of the rental of the factory space, and perhaps a new lease on the welding machine or the press used for stamping out the taillight sockets. All of this would have been complicated.

Incentive Traps

Another crucial difficulty with an assembly line of independent contractors under the conditions of the Industrial Age was that capital requirements for the individual contractors would have differed dramatically. A plastic mold needed to produce a dashboard switch, for example, might have been relatively cheap, while the equipment needed to cast an engine block or stamp out the sheet metal on a fender could have cost millions. The high resource content and sequential nature of assembly-line production made problems arising from high capital costs inevitable, for reasons analyzed in the last chapter. Contractors with capital-intensive tasks would have essentially been dependent upon the cooperation of others to amortize their investments. The ability of the contractors with higher capital requirements to raise money and operate at a profit would have depended upon their securing the cooperation of many other participants in the process whose capital costs were far lower. In many cases, they would not have gotten it.

There would have been a substantial incentive for the small to exploit the great. Those who required less money to operate their particular function on the assembly line would have gained by failing to cooperate at crucial times. Like striking workers, they could have closed down the assembly line on one pretext or another, imposing little cost on themselves but much grief to those with larger capital investments. The production process would have been subject to constant gaming, with small-scale contractors exposing those with higher capital costs to ransom through their ability to thwart output. The maneuvering of smaller contractors to extract side payments from the large would have reduced the efficiency of the system.

The Firm Solution

In short, many of the economies to be achieved during the industrial era by operating an assembly line on a large scale would have been dissipated if the production had been divided among multitudes of individual contractors.

The single large firm was an efficient way of overcoming these drawbacks, notwithstanding its other limitations. Big business was bureaucratic. But to some extent bureaucracy and hierarchy were precisely what were required during the Industrial Age. Administrative and management teams monitored and coordinated production, with numerous middle managers passing orders down the hierarchy and other information back up the chain of command. The corporate bureaucracy also provided bookkeeping and accounting controls and minimized principal-agency problems, in which employees fail to act in the best interest of the firm that employs them. To achieve sophisticated accountancy under conditions of the Industrial Age required the work of many people. Having such an administrative bureaucracy in place was costly. It had to be paid whether production was active or slack. Because such administrators held crucial knowledge necessary to operate the business, they were usually paid a premium above what their skills would have commanded in the spot market.

"Organizational Slack"

The large numbers of professional managers and administrators also had the drawback of tending to "capture" the firm and operate it in their own interests rather than those of the shareholders. It was not uncommon in the industrial era, for example, to find firms spending lavishly on office furnishings, club memberships, and other perks that could be enjoyed by management but that might not have generated a direct return to investors. In a complicated business, it was impossible to easily monitor from the outside which overhead expenditures were essential and which were indulgences for the employees. It was also difficult to prevent a sometimes considerable fraction of corporate employees from shirking. The fact that it was technologically difficult to monitor performance made a large middle management necessary, and at the same time made it difficult to monitor the monitors.

These conditions all contributed to what became known as "organizational slack," a term coined in 1963 by Richard Cyert and James March in *A Behavioral Theory of the Firm.*[29] Careful examination suggested that numerous real firms were underperforming their potential substantially.

"Whether you produce results or not, the pay is the same.
"Whether you work hard or not, the pay is the same.
"Whether you care or not, the pay is the same."[30]

—CHRIS DRAY

"That's Not My Job"

As an entity aspiring to permanence, the large industrial firm had the draw-back we have already explored of being exposed to shakedowns by labor unions. It also shared some of the characteristics of bureaucracy seen in a more exaggerated form in government offices. Orders flowed from on high. Tasks were stereotyped and compartmentalized. These tasks were often rig-idly defined. Boundaries emerged among job categories, akin to those en-forced by the cartels regulating the learned professions. To have expected a bookkeeper to change a burned-out lightbulb in a lamp on his desk seemed as strange to many during the Industrial Age as calling on a lawyer to help cure your flu. Employees were neither expected, nor in many cases even permitted, to cross the compartmentalized boundaries between rigidly de-fined functions.

"That is not my job" was a widely heard slogan that underscored the "organizational slack" of the Industrial Age. Everyone's job was precisely defined in terms of stereotyped tasks that were not to be trespassed upon, however much that might improve productivity. Each employee in the corpo-rate bureaucracy was hired according to "qualifications" deemed likely to predict performance in his specific function. With few exceptions, everyone was paid based upon a job classification, with more or less uniform pay throughout the organization. Because specific performance in the adminis-trative hierarchies of Big Business often went unmeasured, as in state bu-reaucracies, work proceeded at a leisurely pace. So while the firm did capture the scale economies of mass production, it did so at the cost of other inefficiencies.

"In a market, you don't do something because somebody tells you to or because it is listed on page thirty of the strategic plan. A market has no job boundaries. . . . There are no orders, no translation of signals from on high, no one sorting out the work into parcels. In a market one has customers, and the relationship between a supplier and a customer is fundamentally nonorganizational, because it is between two independent entities."[31]

—WILLIAM BRIDGES

New Imperatives

The new megapolitical conditions of the Information Age will significantly alter the logic of business organization. Part of this is obvious. If information technology does nothing else, it dramatically lowers the cost of processing, computing, and analyzing information. One effect of such technology is to reduce the necessity of hiring large numbers of middle managers to monitor production processes. Indeed, automated machine tools made possible by advanced computational power are in many cases replacing hourly workers. And where the production process continues to be manned, the control and coordination process has largely been automated. Equipment fitted with microprocessors can monitor the progress of the assembly line much more effectively than managers ever could. Not only can the new equipment measure the speed and accuracy with which people work, it can also automatically compile accounts, and reorder components the moment they are taken out of inventory. The smallest operations can now afford financial control programs that account for their finances with greater speed and sophistication than even the largest corporations could have achieved through their production hierarchies a few decades ago.

The fact that information technology allows for dispersed, nonsequential output of products with reduced natural resource content dramatically reduces the vulnerability to gaming and extortion, as we have already explored. However, these are not the only characteristics of information technology that make it ever more attractive to contract out functions formerly done by employees. Capital costs are lower. Product cycles are shorter. The independent contractors themselves, including the one-person firms, have vastly more sophisticated information networks at their disposal. Soon they will be able to rely upon an array of digital servants to perform a wide variety of office functions, from answering the phone to secretarial services. Digital servants will be secretaries, advertising agents, travel agents, bank tellers, and bureaucrats.

The Disappearance of Good Jobs

To an increasing degree, individuals capable of creating significant economic value will be able to retain most of the value they create for themselves. Support staff that previously absorbed a large part of the revenue generated by the principal income creators in an enterprise will be replaced by low-cost automated agents and information systems. This implies that an organization will be better able to assure itself of the highest quality of service by contracting it out, rather than by keeping the function within the firm, where it will be relatively more difficult to reward individuals for performing a task well. A virtual corporation will eliminate most "organizational slack" by eliminating the organization.

"Good jobs" will be a thing of the past. A "good job," as Princeton economist Orly Ashenfelter put it, "is a job that pays more than you are worth." [32] In the Industrial Age, many "good jobs" existed because of high information and transaction costs. Firms grew bigger and internalized a wider range of functions because doing so allowed them to capture scale economies. Corporate bloat was also subsidized by tax laws. The high taxes that predominated in the late stages of the industrial era artificially magnified the advantages of forming a long-lived firm and hiring permanent employees. In most nations, tax laws and regulations substantially raised the costs of forming and dissolving firms on a project basis. They also have tended to force entrepreneurs to subsume independent contractors as employees. Legal interventions further temporarily inflated the supply of "good jobs" by making it costly and difficult to dismiss an employee, however little he might be contributing to the productivity of the firm.

Inevitably and logically, the character of business organization in the industrial era assured that the most highly skilled and talented people who created a disproportionate share of the value-added in an organization were paid proportionately less than their contribution was worth. This will change in the Information Age.

The microprocessing revolution is sharply increasing the availability of information and reducing transaction costs. This is devolving the firm. Instead of permanent bureaucracy, activities will be organized around projects, in much the way that movie companies already operate. Most of the formerly "internal" functions of the firm will be outsourced to independent contractors. The industrial-era employees who held "good jobs" but who contributed little and relied upon fellow workers to "cover" for them will soon find themselves bidding for contracts in the spot market. And so will many loyal, diligent employees. "Good jobs" will be an anachronism because jobs in general will be anachronistic.

In the extreme case of big Japanese corporations, employees expected to have a job for life. Even where they had no productive task to perform, they would be retained, sometimes merely showing up to sit at "a bare desk in the corner of a factory." Now even in Japan, the bloated white-collar workforce is being downsized. The headline of a story in the *International Herald-Tribune* told the tale: "Parting Is Such Sour Sorrow: Japan's Job-for-Life Culture Painfully Expires." [33]

In the postindustrial period, jobs will be tasks you do, not something you "have." Before the industrial era, permanent employment was almost unknown. As William Bridges put it, "Before 1800—and long after in many cases—*job* always referred to some particular task or undertaking, never to a role or position in an organization. . . . Between 1700 and 1890, the *Oxford English Dictionary* finds many uses of terms like *job-coachman, job-doctor,* and *job-gardener*—all referring to people hired on a one-time basis. *Job-work* (another frequent term) was occasional work, not regular employment." [34] In the Information Age, most tasks that were formerly captured within firms as an expedient to reduce information and transaction costs will migrate back to the spot market. "Just in time" inventory control and outsourcing are both practical because of information technology. They are steps toward the death of jobs. Already, major corporations such as AT&T have eliminated all permanent job categories. Positions in that large firm are now contingent. In Bridges's words, "Employment is becoming temporary and situational again, and categories are losing their boundaries."[35] In the new cybereconomy, "independent contractors" will telecommute across continents to nest together on the Information Age equivalent of the assembly line.

Hollywood Takes Over

The model business organization of the new information economy may be a movie production company. Such enterprises can be very sophisticated, with budgets of hundreds of millions of dollars. While they are often large operations, they are also temporary in nature. A movie company producing a film for $100 million may come together for a year and then dissolve. While the people who work on the production are talented, they have no expectation that finding work on the project is equivalent to having a "permanent job." When the project is over, the lighting technicians, cameramen, sound engineers, and wardrobe specialists will go their separate ways. They may be reunited in another project, or they may not.

As scale economies fall, and capital requirements for many types of information-intensive activities fall simultaneously, there will be a strong incentive for firms to dissolve. Business operations will be more ad hoc and temporary. Firms will tend to be more short-lived. Virtual corporations that assemble talents for specific purposes will be more efficient than long-standing companies. As encryption becomes widespread and the taxation of capital is forced down by competition, artificial scale economies that sustain the existence of "permanent" firms will fall away. This will happen whether taxes are reduced rapidly or slowly. If rapidly, the artificial costs of functioning on a project basis will disappear more quickly. If slowly, the main burden of paying the anachronistically high taxes will fall upon existing firms, while new enterprises will operate as virtual corporations, better enabling them to escape costly burdens imposed by the dying nation-state.

While special skills and talents will be more important than ever in the information economy, most of the artificial boundaries between professions will dissolve. Advanced information and retrieval storage technologies will make the trade secrets and specialized information of professions such as law, medicine, and accounting available to anyone. The economic value of memorization as a skill will fall, while the importance of synthesis and creative application of information will rise.

The full implications of this change will be retarded by antiquated regulation. But over the longer term, the power of governments to regulate the cybereconomy will wither to the vanishing point. Any artificial regulation of professional monopolies that raises costs without benefits that are valued in the market will ultimately be ignored.

There are other implications of the shift to an information economy:

- Local regulations that impose higher costs will be transformed to a market footing.
- There will be intensified competition among jurisdictions to domicile high value-added activities that in principle could be located anywhere. No stopping place is necessarily more compelling than the next.
- Business relations will gravitate toward reliance upon "circles of trust." Due to encryption, which gives individuals an ability to steal undetected, honesty will be a more highly valued ch.aracteristic of business associates.
- Patent and copyright regimes will change, due to ease of access to certain information.
- Protection will become increasingly technological rather than juridical. The lower classes will be walled out. The move to gated communities is all but inevitable. Walling out troublemakers is an effective as well as traditional way of minimizing criminal violence in times of weak central authority.
- Bulk goods will be heavily taxed and shipped locally, as in the Middle Ages, while luxury goods will be lightly taxed and shipped a great distance.[36]
- Police functions will increasingly be taken up by private guards linked to merchant associations.
- There may be a transitional advantage to private over publicly traded firms because private firms will enjoy greater leeway in escaping costs imposed by governments.
- Lifetime employment will disappear as "jobs" increasingly become tasks or "piece work" rather than positions within an organization.
- Control over economic resources will shift away from the state to persons of superior skills and intelligence, as it becomes increasingly easy to create wealth by adding knowledge to products.
- Many members of learned professions will be displaced by interactive information-retrieval systems.
- New survival strategies for persons of lower intelligence will evolve, involving greater concentration on development of leisure skills, sports abil-

ities, and crime, as well as service to the growing numbers of Sovereign Individuals as income inequality within jurisdictions rises..

Political systems that grew up at a time when there were rising returns to violence must undergo wrenching adjustments. Now that efficiency is growing in importance relative to the magnitude of power commanded by a system, small, efficient sovereignties, which produce more protection for their customers at lower cost, will be increasingly sustainable.

As in the medieval period, there are once again growing diseconomies of scale in the organization of violence. This is already reflected in the growing number of sovereign entities since the fall of Communism. We expect the number of sovereignties in the world to multiply rapidly as the logic of the Information Age is confirmed by experience.

Power will once again be exercised on a small scale. Enclaves and provinces may even find that they have substantial advantages over nations spanning continents in offering competitive terms to their "customers" for sovereignty services. This will be very different from the rapidly dying modern period, in which no entity could survive unless it could control military force sufficient to control a kingdom. In the past, when there were diseconomies of scale in exercising power, those who benefited most from the protection, like the wealthy merchants in the late medieval city-states, did control the government. In our view, you can look for something like this again. The lowering of predatory burdens and more efficient disposition of resources should result in rapid growth in areas where customers do exercise control over the local sovereignties.

As we explore next, whether these developments can or should proceed in the face of opposition from legions of losers will be among the more important controversies of the Information Age.

CHAPTER 9

NATIONALISM, REACTION, AND THE NEW LUDDITES

"Nationalism, of course, is intrinsically absurd. Why should the accident—fortune or misfortune—of birth as an American, Albanian, Scot, or Fiji Islander impose loyalties that dominate an individual life and structure a society so as to place it in formal conflict with others? In the past there were local loyalties to place and clan and tribe, obligations to lord or landlord, dynastic or territorial wars, but primary loyalties were to religion, God or god-king, possibly to emperor, to a civilization as such. There was no nation. There was attachment to patria, land of one's fathers, or patriotism, but to speak of nationalism before modern times is anachronistic."[1]

—WILLIAM PFAFF

http://www.ibm.com To say that the "world is getting smaller" is an informing figure of speech, reinforced by authorities as prestigious as IBM's advertising agency. Their "Solutions for a small planet" multicultural commercials for the Internet remind sports fans who may fail to realize it on their own that the terms of relations between individuals in widely dispersed jurisdictions have been changed by technology. We refer to the distinguished historian William McNeill for a useful footnote on the implications. He writes, "Continuing intensification of communications and transport, instead of favoring national consolidation, has begun to work in a contrary sense, inasmuch as its range transcends existing political and ethnic boundaries."[2] As the world "becomes smaller" and communications improve, the accidental and "intrinsically absurd" claims of nations and nationalism are bound to weaken.

THE GREAT TRANSFORMATION

The trouble with this reasonable expectation is that all previous history suggests that it cannot be accommodated in a reasonable way. The transition it implies will involve a crisis. It entails a radically new way of thinking, a new imagining of community that moves beyond nationalism and the nation-state. As Michael Billig has highlighted, "our beliefs about nation-hood, and about the naturalness of belonging to a nation," are "the products of a particular historical age."[3] That age, the Modern Age, may already be defunct. Its predominant institutions, nation-states, still endure, but they survive precariously upon an eroded foundation. As the other shoe drops, and nation-states collapse, we expect a nasty reaction, particularly in the wealthy countries where the "national economy" brought high income to unskilled work in the twentieth century.

We believe that when all is said and done, the change in megapolitical conditions occasioned by the advent of information technology will result in radical institutional change. The thesis of this book is that the massed power of the nation-state is destined to be privatized and commercialized. Like all truly radical institutional change, the privatization and commercialization of sovereignty will involve a revolution in the "common sense" of the way the world is comprehended. Such change seldom happens in a gradual, linear way. To the contrary. Indeed, for reasons we explored in *The Great Reckoning*, it is practically ruled out. We expect the Information Age to bring discontinuities—sharp breaks with the institutions and the consciousness of the past. Here is what to look for as the process unfolds:

1. Changes in economic organization of the kind described in previous chapters arising from the impact of microprocessing.
2. A more or less rapid falloff in importance of all organizations that operate within rather than beyond geographic boundaries. Governments, labor unions, licensed professions, and lobbyists will be less important in the Information Age than they became during the Industrial Age. Because favors and restraints of trade wrested from governments will be less useful, fewer resources will be wasted in lobbying.[4]
3. Wider recognition that the nation-state is obsolete, leading to wide-spread secession movements in many parts of the globe.

4. A decline in the status and power of traditional elites, as well as a decline in the respect accorded the symbols and beliefs that justify the nation-state.

5. An intense and even violent nationalist reaction centered among those who lose status, income, and power when what they consider to be their "ordinary life" is disrupted by political devolution and new market arrangements. Among the features of this reaction:

   a. suspicion of and opposition to globalization, free trade, "foreign" ownership and penetration of local economies;

   b. hostility to immigration, especially of groups that are visibly different from the former national group;

   c. popular hatred of the information elite, rich people, the well-educated, and complaints about capital flight and disappearing jobs;

   d. extreme measures by nationalists intent upon halting the secession of individuals and regions from faltering nation-states, including resort to wars and acts of "ethnic cleansing" that reinforce nationalist identification with the state and rationalize the state's claims on people and their resources.

6. Since it will be obvious that information technologies facilitate the escape of Sovereign Individuals from the power of the state, the reaction to the collapse of compulsion will also include a neo-Luddite attack on these new technologies and those who use them.

7. The nationalist-Luddite reaction will not be uniform across regions and population groups:

   a. The reaction will be less intense in rapidly growing economies where per capita income was low during the industrial era, and where the deepening of markets raises incomes among all skill groups.

   b. Reactionary sentiments will be most intensely felt within the currently rich countries, and especially in communities with high percentages of the value-poor and skill-poor who previously enjoyed high incomes.*

   c. The Unabomber notwithstanding, the neo-Luddites will attract most of their adherents among those in the bottom two-thirds of earnings capacity within the populations of leading nation-states.

   d. The nationalist and Luddite reaction will be strongest, however, not among the very poor but among persons of middling skills, under-achievers with credentials, who came of age during the industrial era and face downward mobility.

* The close relation between skills and values and, therefore, economic success is detailed by Lawrence E. Harrison in *Who Prospers? How Cultural Values Shape Economic and Political Success* (New York: Basic Books, 1992).

8. As new megapolitical conditions give rise to a new consciousness of identity, along with new, complementary ideologies and morality, the old imperatives of nationalism will lose their appeal.

9. The nationalist reaction will peak in the early decades of the new millennium, then fade as the efficiency of fragmented sovereignties proves superior to the massed power of the nation-state. We suspect that the congenital bullying by nation-states of alternative jurisdictions, exemplified by the Russian invasion of Chechnya, will tend to deprive nations and nationalist fanatics of the sympathy of the new generations that come to maturity under the megapolitical conditions of the Information Age.

10. The nation-state will ultimately collapse in fiscal crisis. Systemic crises typically arise when failing institutions suffer from rising expenses and falling income—a situation that is bound to beset the leading nation-states as retirement benefits and medical outlays balloon early in the twenty-first century. As we write, both the United Kingdom and the United States are burdened with multitrillion-dollar unfunded pension liabilities (comparable on a per capita basis) that neither is likely to tame. Other leading nation-states face similarly bankrupting burdens.

PARALLELS WITH THE RENAISSANCE

We previously outlined reasons for thinking that the collapse of the nanny state will have consequences closely parallelling those associated with the collapse of the institutional monopoly of the Holy Mother Church five centuries ago. Not unlike the nation-state today, the Church then had been in a position of unchallenged predominance for centuries. In some respects, the Church was even more firmly established than the state became five hundred years later. The Church had long claimed to act as "the universal authority at the head of Christian society."[5] That is the characterization of medieval intellectual historian John B. Morrall. Yet while few Europeans would have disputed the Church's claim to supremacy in Christendom before the technological revolution of the 1490s, the Church barely survived in its traditional role for another generation.

The Privatization of Conscience

By the early 1520s, millions of good Europeans had rejected the universal authority of the Catholic Church, a heresy punishable by torture and death just a few decades previously. Indeed, many medieval European cathedrals and churches were decorated with instructive carvings of heretics having their tongues torn out by demons.[6] The lesson these tortures conveyed must have impressed many illiterate parishioners who could have recognized the victims as heretics simply by their punishment. The iconography was unambiguous: heretics were those whose tongues were mutilated. Yet harsh as this punishment was, it was merely the warm-up for the ultimate punishment for heresy: death at the stake.

To the Church's dismay, however, the lesson was not sufficiently intimidating. The advent of the printing press inflated the supply of heretical arguments so dramatically that even the prospect of gruesome punishment ceased to deter would-be heretics. Indeed, not a few unlucky pioneers of religious freedom in early modern Europe did pay for their assertions of spiritual independence by having their tongues cut out. Others were burned at the stake. The agents of reaction in the Inquisition literally incinerated people for uttering what we would consider ordinary expressions of conscience.

All told, the Reformation and the reaction it inspired cost millions their lives. Battlefield deaths in the final half of the Thirty Years' War alone totaled 1,151,000.[7] Many more died from famine, disease, and at the hands of the Inquisition and other authorities. By no means all the violence was perpetrated by Catholic authorities. The bones of more than a thousand leading English Catholics thought to have been brutally murdered by King Henry VIII have been uncovered at the Tower of London. Some, including Sir Thomas More and Bishop St. John Fisher, were openly executed for refusing to abandon the old faith.[8] King Henry VIII's Catholic daughter, Queen Mary, on the other hand, insane with syphilis inherited from her father, incinerated three hundred Protestant heretics at the stake in the last two years of her reign. Such was the price paid as individuals of different persuasions asserted their religious convictions and the long-denied right to choose the church they supported.

Seen from our vantage at the end of the twentieth century, these expressions of personal belief were well within the range that should be protected by freedom of religion and freedom of speech. But there was neither freedom of religion nor freedom of speech in the early sixteenth century. The authorities of the day still drew their bearings from the waning medieval worldview. To their eyes gestures of individual autonomy in opposition to authority, especially the *plentitude potestatis* (fullness of power) of the pope were outrageous and decidedly subversive. As theological historian Euan Cameron said, religious reformers like Martin Luther adopted views that "meant a deliberate and decisive break with the institutional and spiritual continuity of the old Church."[9]

Heresy and Treason

In that spirit, we anticipate "a deliberate and decisive break" with the institutional and ideological continuity of the nation-state. By the end of the first quarter of the next century, millions of upright individuals will have committed the secular equivalent of sixteenth-century heresy—a kind of low treason. They will have withdrawn allegiance from the faltering nation-state to assert their own sovereignty, their right to choose not their bishops or their house of worship but their form of governance as customers. The privatization of sovereignty will parallel the privatization of conscience of five centuries earlier. Both are the mass defection of former supporters of · dominant institutions. As Albert O. Hirschman, an expert on "responses to decline in firms, organizations and states," has written, this type of exit is difficult because "exit has often been branded as *criminal,* for it has been labelled desertion, defection and treason." [10]

Sovereign Individuals will no longer merely accede to what is imposed upon them as human resources of the state. Millions will shed the obligations of citizenship to become customers for the useful services governments provide. Indeed, they will create and patronize parallel institutions that will place most of the services associated with citizenship on an entirely commercial basis. For most of the twentieth century, the productive have been treated as assets by the state, in much the way that the dairy farmer treats milk cows. They have been squeezed ever more vigorously. Now the cows will sprout wings.

Defection from Citizenship

Just as new megapolitical conditions undermined the monopoly of the Church in the sixteenth century, we expect the megapolitics of the Information Age to ultimately dictate the terms of governance in the twenty-first century, no matter how outrageous its new terms may seem to those who incorporate the values of modern politics as their own. The evolution from the status of "citizen" to that of "customer" entails a betrayal of the past as sharp as the transition from chivalry to citizenship in the early modern era. The defection of the information elite from citizenship will have a stimulus much like that which led millions of Europeans five hundred years earlier to renounce the infallibility of the pope.

If the parallel with the Reformation is not compelling, it may be partly because it is not immediately evident today that renunciation of loyalty to religious institutions was ever the big deal that treason became in the twentieth century. Outside of a few Islamic countries, heresy at the end of the twentieth century is a spiritual misdemeanor, no more shattering to an individual's reputation than a speeding ticket for driving forty-five in a thirty-mile zone.* Indeed, it is not uncommon in Europe and North America to find clergy and even bishops who do not believe in God or deny crucial tenets of the faith they espouse. Today, a heresy would almost need to be blatant devil worship to be noticeable. In most Western countries, religious doctrines are so ill-formed and sloppily held that few persons can identify the theological points that were the focus of controversy of heresies in the past.[11] This reflects the general shift of attention away from religion.

To some extent, religious leaders have actually helped to lead the late-twentieth-century defection from seriousness about spiritual issues by deflecting their energies away from spiritual preoccupations to become lobbyists and social agitators. Drawn like loose filings to the magnet of power, they devote much of their activities to pressuring political leaders to adopt redistributive policies crucial to the nationalist bargain. Witness the loud efforts of the Catholic Church in Argentina to pressure the government of President Carlos Menem to abandon economic reforms in favor of conventional inflationary monetary and Keynesian fiscal policies. Similar complaints have been lodged by religious leaders against efforts to restructure bloated budgets in New Zealand and many other countries. Catholic bishops lobbied vigorously against the reform of welfare in the United States.

A Fiscal Inquisition?

Simply put, contemporary religious leaders focus much of their declining moral authority on secular redemption and agitation to influence the state rather than on spiritual salvation. Given this record, they can be expected to participate as accomplices in the reaction against the coming secular reformation. As the nation-state is challenged and begins to wobble, it will no longer be able to fulfill the promises of material benefits that are central to popular support. The de facto bargain struck at the time of the French Revolution will lapse. The state will no longer be capable of guaranteeing its citizens low-cost or free schooling, much less medical care, unemployment insurance, and pensions in exchange for otherwise poorly paid military service. While the changing requirements of warfare will enable governments to defend themselves and territories under their dominion without fielding mass armies, this will hardly relieve governments of the criticism for breaking what has become an anachronistic bargain.

Indeed, as the new megapolitical logic takes hold, its consequences will prove wildly unpopular with the losers in the new information economy. It is therefore all but certain that many religious leaders, along with the primary

* For contemporary evidence of this, see Bruce Bawer, "Who's on Trial, the Heretic or the Church?" *New York Times Magazine*, April 7, 1996, p. 36f.

beneficiaries of government spending, will be at the forefront of a nostalgic reaction seeking to reassert the claims of nationalism. They will claim that no American, Frenchman, Canadian, or other nationality—fill in the blank—should be allowed to go to bed hungry. Even countries that have been at the forefront of reform and stand to benefit disproportionately from "market-friendly globalism," like New Zealand, will be tormented by reactionary losers. They will seek to thwart the movement of capital and people across borders. And they will not stop there. Demagogues, like Winston Peters, leader of the New Zealand First Party, are too lazy to think originally about how the new world will function. But, in due course, Winston and his crew will be tipped off to the logic of the information economy. They will seek to halt the diffusion of computers, robotics, telecommunications, encryption, and other Information Age technologies that are facilitating the displacement of workers in almost every sector of the global economy. Wherever you turn, there are politicians who will gladly thwart the prospects for long-term prosperity just to prevent individuals from declaring their independence of politics.

20/20 Vision

By 2020, or roughly five centuries after Martin Luther nailed his 95 subversive theses on the church door at Wittenberg, the perception of the cost-benefit ratios of citizenship will have undergone a similar subversive clarification. The vision of the nation-state among persons of ability and wealth, the Sovereign Individuals of the future, will have undergone the political equivalent of laser surgery. They will be seeing 20/20. In the twentieth century, as throughout the modern era, persistently high returns to violence made big government a paying proposition. The decisiveness of massed power mobilized the allegiance of the wealthy and ambitious to OECD nation-states, notwithstanding predatory taxes imposed on income and capital. Politicians were able to impose marginal tax rates approaching or exceeding 90 percent in every OECD country in the decade immediately following World War II.

As we have explored, the rich had little choice but to accede to such impositions. Circumstances obliged them to rely for protection upon governments that could master violence on a large scale. It rarely mattered, except perhaps to British policemen with the chance to take a posting to Hong Kong, that OECD governments imposed monopolistic taxes. Anyone with high earnings capacity who wished to enjoy leading-edge economic opportunity during the Industrial Age usually had little option but to reside in a high-tax economy. This meant shouldering a tax burden out of proportion to services rendered.

The Arithmetic of Politics

Nineteenth-century American Vice President John C. Calhoun shrewdly sketched the arithmetic of modern politics. Calhoun's formula divides the entire population of the nation-state into two classes: *taxpayers,* who contribute more to the cost of government services than they consume; and *tax consumers,* who receive benefits from government in excess of their contribution to the cost. With a few conspicuous exceptions, most OECD entrepreneurs were net taxpayers to an exaggerated extent as the twentieth century wound down. For example, in 1996, the top 1 percent of British taxpayers shouldered 17 percent of the total income tax burden. They paid 30 percent more than the bottom 50 percent of earners, who contributed just 13 percent of income tax payments. In the United States, the rich shouldered an even more exaggerated burden, with the top 1 percent paying 30.2 percent of the total income tax receipts in 1995.[12] Not only were the rich obliged to pay for service that, as Frederic C. Lane reminds us, "was of poor quality and outrageously overpriced," but their payments were often not proportionate to any service whatever.[13] The benefits for which the top taxpayers paid often went entirely to others. In most cases, the rich were glad to under-consume government services, which were typically of low quality. Government bureaus in almost every country were famously inefficient, largely because they tended to be controlled by employees who lacked an incentive to improve productivity. By practically any measure, the largest taxpayers during the industrial era paid many times more for government services than they would be worth in a competitive market.

This hardly went unnoted. Unhappily, however, the recognition that payments to government for protection were, in Lane's words, "wasteful by ideal standards" was seldom an actionable insight in the middle of the twentieth century. Rather it was simply a defect to be accepted, "one of various kinds of waste built into social organization."[14]

The alternative for the discontented was not to move from Britain to France, for example, or from the United States to Canada. Except in rare circumstances, that would have availed little. The leading nation-states all suffered from the same drawback. They all adopted more or less confiscatory tax regimes. To realize a significant increase in autonomy one had to escape the core countries of Europe and North America altogether and head for the periphery. Tax burdens were meaningfully lower in parts of Asia, South America, and on various remote islands. But there was usually a price to be paid for escaping predatory taxation—a loss of economic opportunity and, often, a decline in living standards. As we have explored, in the conditions of the Industrial Age, economic opportunity was constrained and living standards were subpar in most of the jurisdictions outside the core industrial nation-states that indulged in confiscatory taxation.

Consider the Communist systems as a paradigm. Along with many Third World regimes, they typically did not impose high income taxes—or even any at all.* Nonetheless, during the three-quarters of a century the Soviet Union existed, few, if any, entrepreneurs sought tax refuge there. While the Soviet income tax rates were not high, they afforded no advantage because the Soviets made a virtue of their refusal to recognize property rights. This imposed an even worse burden than taxation. The Communist systems made it all but impossible to organize a business and make any serious money. In effect, the Communist state confiscated pretax income.

Further, had anyone already possessing a secure income for some eccentric reason chosen to live in Moscow or Havana, he would have been hard-pressed to use money to purchase a decent standard of living. Outside of access to good cigars, caviar, excellent orchestras, and the ballet, life in the former Communist systems afforded few consumer pleasures. Most of the scarce good things of life were unavailable or were tightly rationed on the basis of political influence rather than open exchange. At the risk of validating the stereotype of critics of postmodern life who emphasize "the importance of consumption in the postmodern experience," the rising standard of goods and services available worldwide since the fall of Communism has surely made competition between jurisdictions more lively, thereby helping to weaken ties to nation and place.[15]

Under the old regime, consumer choices were so limited that even Castro himself would have been hard-pressed to secure a packet of decent dental floss had he wanted to clean cohiba fragments from his teeth. Until recently, not even the rich in many parts of the globe could enjoy the quality of life that was common among the middle classes in Western Europe or North America. Faced with this doleful situation, most persons of outstanding talent were moved to accept the nationalist bargain during the Industrial Age. They stayed put and paid outrageously high taxes for the doubtful protection offered by the particular nation-state that monopolized violence in the territory in which they were born.

"Paradise is now shut and locked, barred by angels, so now we must go forward, around the world and see if somehow, somewhere, there is a backway in."

—HEINRICH VON KLEIST

---

* Cuba only imposed an income tax in 1996 as an emergency measure in response to economic depression following the end of subsidies occasioned by the collapse of Communism in Europe.

The fall of Communism removed an "Iron Curtain" that had impaired travel and effectively blocked the globalization of commerce, thereby keeping the world artificially "large." The jet plane, in combination with the information technologies that undermined Communism, increased competition for high-end travel dollars. The parade of bankers trooping in and out of even the most remote provinces was a prodigious stimulus to the standard of accommodation and cuisine worldwide. By this, we are not referring to the spread of McDonald's hamburgers and Kentucky Fried Chicken franchises, in even such formerly forbidding venues as Moscow and Bucharest. Less noticed, but more important, has been the spread of leading hotel chains, and high-quality sit-down restaurants serving grand cru clarets rather than vodka and Coke. Thanks to this transformation, anyone who can afford it can now enjoy a high material standard of life almost anywhere on the planet. Indeed, it is now a rare country where there is not a first-class hotel and at least one restaurant that would interest a Michelin inspector.

As Hirschman anticipated a quarter of a century ago, technological advance has significantly increased the appeal of exit as a solution to unsatisfactory provision and pricing of services. He wrote: "Loyalty to one's country, on the other hand, is something we could do without. . . . Only as countries start to resemble each other because of the advances of communications and all-around modernization will the danger of premature and excessive exits arise, the 'brain drain' being a current example." [16] Note as we pointed out in chapter 8 that Hirschman's standard of "premature and excessive exits" is seen from the perspective of the nation-state being deserted, not from the perspective of the individual seeking a better life.

Nonetheless, his conclusion that similarities between countries will increase the attraction of defection and exit is unimpeachable. The fact that it is now easier to live well anywhere makes living where the cost is least onerous appealing. Yet more important than the fact that you can live well almost anywhere is the fact that you can now earn a high income anywhere. It is no longer necessary to reside in a high-cost jurisdiction in order to accumulate sufficient wealth to live, as Lord Keynes advised, "wisely, agreeably and well." For reasons we have already explored, microtechnology changes the underlying megapolitical foundation upon which the nation-state rests. In the Information Age, a new cybereconomy will emerge beyond the capacity of any government to monopolize. For the first time, technology will enable individuals to accumulate wealth in a realm that cannot be bent easily to the demands of systematic compulsion.

The new society, and therefore the new culture, will be defined at one end by what machines can do better than people, by automation that will do away with increasing numbers of low-skill tasks, and at the other by the power that information technology gives to people who actually have the talent to take advantage of it. Such a society will have greater tensions between a small class, who might be termed the information aristocracy, and a growing underclass, who might be termed the information poor. One of the differences between them will be that the information poor will either be tied by geography or will find little benefit from moving. The information aristocracy, as we discuss elsewhere, will be extremely mobile, since they will be able to earn money in any locale that is attractive to them, just as popular novelists have always been able to do. Robert Louis Stevenson could earn his living on an island in the Pacific a hundred years ago; now the information aristocracy can all do the same thing.

Market Competition Between Jurisdictions

Because information technology transcends the tyranny of place, it will automatically expose jurisdictions everywhere to *de facto* global competition on the basis of quality and price. In other words, governments exercising local territorial monopolies, like most other entities, finally will be subject to real market competition on the basis of how well they serve their customers. This will soon make it unavoidably obvious that the old logic that favored high-cost regimes in the industrial era has reversed. Leading nation-states, with their predatory, redistributive tax regimes and heavy-handed regulations, will no longer be jurisdictions of choice. Seen dispassionately, they offer poor-quality protection and diminished economic opportunity at monopoly prices. In the years to come, they may prove to be more socially unreceptive and violent than other regions such as Latin America where incomes have traditionally been more unequal. The leading welfare states will lose their most talented citizens through desertion.

The "Extranational" Age Ahead

As the era of the "Sovereign Individual" takes shape, many of the ablest people will cease to think of themselves as party to a nation, as "British" or "American" or "Canadian." A new "transnational" or "extranational" understanding of the world and a new way of identifying one's place in it await discovery in the new millennium. As indicated before, early evidence of this emerging mind-set was provided in the finding that almost half of teenaged viewers of MTV expect to leave the country of their birth in order to achieve the life they want for themselves. This new equation of identity, unlike nationality, will not be a product of the systematic compulsion that made nation-states and the state system universal in the twentieth century.

The mere fact that developments embracing the whole globe are commonly described as "international" shows how deeply the nationalist paradigm has penetrated into our way of conceiving the world. After two centuries of indoctrination in the mysteries of "international relations" and "international law," it is easy to overlook that "international" is not a long-standing Western concept. In fact, the word *international* was invented by Jeremy Bentham in 1789. It was first used in his book *An Introduction to the Principles of Morals and Legislation*. Bentham wrote, "The word *international*, it must be acknowledged, is a new one, though it is hoped sufficiently analogous and intelligible."[17] The word caught on, but not just in the narrow sense that Bentham intended. *"International"* came to be a sloppy synonym for anything that happens across the globe.

The International Age began in 1789, the same year as the French Revolution. It lasted for two centuries, until 1989, when the revolt against Communism in Europe began. We believe that that second revolution marked the end of the International Age, and not merely because the discredited Communist anthem was "The International." The command economy with state owner-ship was the most ambitious expression of the nation-state. The close rela-tionship between state power and nationalism was reflected in language. The most aggressive verb of the Modern Age was "to nationalize," meaning to bring under state ownership and control. It was a word that tripped easily off the tongues of demagogues in most parts of the globe during the Interna-tional Age. Now it is part of the vocabulary of the past. Nationalization has become anachronistic, precisely because state power has become anachro-nistic.

In the twilight of the modern era, the concentrated power of the state was undermined by the interaction between technological innovation and market forces. Now the next stage in the triumph of the market is about to unfold. Not only will individual nation-states begin to dissolve, but in our view even the club for nation-states, the United Nations, is destined to go bankrupt. We would not be surprised to see the UN liquidated sometime soon after the turn of the millennium.

If "international" were a stock, now would be the time to sell. The concept is likely to be supplanted in the new millennium, or at least narrowed to its original meaning for the compelling reason that the whole world will no longer be dominated by a system of interrelating sovereign nations. Relations will take on the novel "extranational" forms dictated by the grow-ing importance of microjurisdictions and Sovereign Individuals. A dispute between an enclave on the coast of Labrador and a Sovereign Individual will not rightly be described as an "international" dispute. It will be extra-national.

In the new age to come, communities and allegiances will not be territori-ally bounded. Identification will be more precisely targeted to genuine affin-ities, shared beliefs, shared interests, and shared genes, rather than the bogus affinities so prominent in the attention of nationalists. Protection will be organized in new ways that cannot be parsed by a sextant, a plumb line, or other early modern instruments in a surveyor's kit that demarcate territorial borders.

INVENTED COMMUNITIES AND TRADITIONS

The idea that humans must naturally place themselves in an "invented" community called a nation will come to be seen by the cosmopolitan elite as eccentric and unreasonable in the next century, as it would have been through most of human existence. The nation-state, as sociologist Anthony Giddens wrote, has "no precedent in history." [18] Michael Billig, an authority on nationalism, amplified that point:

At other times people did not hold the notions of language and dialect, let alone those of territory and sovereignty, which are so commonplace today and which seem so materially real to "us." So strongly are such notions embedded in contemporary common sense that it is easy to forget that they are invented permanencies. The mediaeval cobblers in the workshops of Montaillou or San Mateo might, with the distance of 700 years, now appear to us narrow, superstition-bound figures. But they would have found our ideas on language and nation strangely mystical; they would be puzzled why this mysticism could be a matter of life and death. [19]

We suspect that thinking people in the extranational future will be equally puzzled. As Benedict Anderson put it, nations are "imagined communities." [20] This is not to say that what is imagined is necessarily trivial. As Dr. Johnson observed, if not for imagination, a man would as gladly "lie with a chamber maid as a duchess." Still, for those who came of age during the twentieth century, "nations" may seem so inevitable a unit of organization that it is difficult to grasp that they are "imagined" rather than natural. In order to understand how different the future may be from the world with which we are familiar, it is necessary to see how nationalism has been imposed upon the "common sense" of the Industrial Age.

It is easy to overlook the degree to which the "national community" is formed by a continuing investment of imagination. There are no objective criteria to define accurately which group should be a "nation" and which should not. Nor, strictly speaking, are there "natural frontiers," as eminent historians Owen Lattimore and C. R. Whittaker have shown. "A major imperial boundary," Lattimore said, writing of imperial China, "is not merely a line dividing geographical regions and human societies. It also represents the *optimal limit of growth* of one particular society." [21] Or as Columbia University economist Ronald Findlay put it, "Insofar as they are considered at all in economics, the boundaries of a given economic system or 'country' are generally regarded as given, along with the population living within those boundaries. Yet it is obvious that, however sanctified these boundaries may have become in international law, they were all at one time or another contested between rival claimants and determined ultimately by the balance of economic and military power between the contending parties." [22]

Someone with all the data available on half the world's nation-states and a collection of fine satellite maps would not be able to predict where the boundaries of the other nation-states would fall. Nor is there any scientific way of distinguishing biologically or linguistically the members of one nationality from those of another. No autopsy procedure, however advanced, could distinguish genetically among the remains of Americans, Canadians, and Sudanese after a plane crash. The boundaries between states and nationalities are not natural, like the boundaries between species or the physical distinctions between breeds of animals. Rather, they are artifacts of past and ongoing efforts to project power.

"A language is a dialect with an army and a navy."

—MARIO PEI

LANGUAGES AS ARTIFACTS OF POWER

Surprisingly, much the same can be said of languages.

After centuries of nation-state dominance, the idea that "language" does not form an objective basis for distinguishing between peoples may seem ill-considered or even absurd. But look more closely. The history of modern languages clearly reveals the degree to which they were shaped to reinforce nationalist identification. Western "languages" as we now understand and speak them did not naturally evolve into their current forms. Nor are they objectively distinguishable from "dialects." In the modern world, no one wishes to speak a "dialect." Almost everyone prefers that his native tongue be considered the genuine article—a "language."

"Let no man say that the word is of little use in such moments. Word and Action are together one. The powerful energetic affirmation that reassures

hearts creates acts—that which is said is produced. Action here is the servant
of the word, it follows behind submissively, as on the first day of the world: He
said and the world was."

—MICHELET, August 1792

"Word and Action Are Together One"

Prior to the French Revolution, for example, the version of mongrelized
Latin spoken in southern France, *la langue d'oc* or Occitan, had more in
common with the vernacular spoken in Catalonia in northern Spain, than
with *la langue d'oïl*, the speech of Paris that became the basis of "French."
Indeed, when the "Declaration of the Rights of Man and the Citizen" was
published in the Parisian style, it was unintelligible to a majority living
within the current borders of France.[23] One of the challenges the French
revolutionaries faced was calculating how to translate their broadsides and
edicts into the patois of innumerable villages that were only vaguely intelligible to one another.

The people living within what became "France" had quite different ways
of speaking that were consciously conflated into one official language as a
matter of policy. Written French had been the official language of the courts
of justice since François I issued the Edict of Villers-Cotterêts in 1539.[24] But
this did not mean that it was widely intelligible, any more than "law French"
was widely intelligible in England after 1200, when it became the official
language of the courts of justice. Each was an "administrative vernacular,"
not a standardized language spoken and understood throughout the territory.

The French revolutionaries wanted to create something more comprehensive, a national language. Historian Janis Langins comments in *The Social
History of Language* that "an influential body of opinion among the revolu-
tionists believed that the triumph of the Revolution and the spread of enlight-
enment would be furthered by a conscious effort to impose a standard French
in the territory of the Republic."[25] This "conscious effort" included a good
deal of fussing over the use of individual words. Consider the telling example
of the adjective "revolutionary," first used by Mirabeau in 1789. After a
period of "somewhat wide and indiscriminant use," as Langins puts it,
"during the Terror there followed a period of suppression and oblivion for
several decades. . . . On June 12, 1795, the Convention decided to reform
the language as well as the institutions created by our former tyrants [i.e., the
vanquished Robespierrists] in replacing the word 'revolutionary' in official
designations."[26] This tradition of language engineering survives in the fin-
icky reception of the French authorities to words like "weekend" that have
made their way into French from English.

Two centuries ago, however, the national language engineers in France were not discriminating merely against words from across the English Channel; they faced a much bigger job eradicating local variants of speech within the territory of the republic. This exercise was not merely confined to suppressing *la langue d'oc*. The "French" spoken on the Riviera then was closer to the "Italian" spoken farther to the east than to Parisian French. Equally, the language of Alsace could arguably have been categorized as a form of German, which itself had numerous local varieties. Basque was spoken in the Pyrenees. Like Breton, spoken along the northwest coast of France, Basque had little in common with any of the vernacular "dialects" of Latin that were the basis of "French." There were also substantial numbers of Flemish speakers in the northeast. "The Parisian style of speech," as Michael Billig reminds us, was not spread through spontaneous market processes, but "imposed, legally and culturally, as 'French.' "[27]

What was true in France has been true elsewhere in the building of nation-states. Languages were often carried by armies and imposed by colonial powers. For example, the map of Africa after independence was defined according to the areas where the administrative languages of European powers predominated. Local dialects were seldom taught in schools. The distinctions between recognized "languages," which tended to define "nations," even nations with arbitrary colonial borders, and "dialects," which did not, were in large measure political.

In short, the imposition of a "national language" was part of a process used worldwide to enhance the power of the state. Encouraging or obliging everyone within the territory where the state monopolized violence to speak "the mother tongue" conveyed significant advantages in facilitating the exercise of power.

The Military Dimension of Language Uniformity

In a world where returns to violence were rising, the adoption of a national language conveyed military advantages. A national language was almost a precondition to consolidation of central power in nation-states. Central authorities that encouraged their citizens to speak the same tongue were better able to weaken the military power of local magnates. The standardization of language after the French Revolution made the cheapest and most effective form of modern military force—national conscript armies—feasible. A common language enabled troops from all regions of the "nation" to communicate fluently with one another. This was a prerequisite before massed conscript armies could displace independent battalions mustered and controlled not by the central authorities but by powerful local magnates.

Prior to the French Revolution, as we discussed in Chapter 5, troops were raised and commanded by local potentates who might or might not answer calls to battle issued from Paris or another capital. In either event, their stance was determined after careful negotiation. As Charles Tilly notes, the "ability to give or withhold support afforded . . . great bargaining power." [28] Furthermore, independent military units had the additional drawback, as far as the central authorities were concerned, of being capable of resisting government efforts to commandeer domestic resources. Clearly, central authorities, whether King or Revolutionary Convention, had a difficult challenge to collect taxes or otherwise strip resources from local potentates who commanded private armies capable of defending those assets.

"National armies" greatly enhanced the power of the national government to impose its will throughout a territory. Imposition of a national language played a decided role in facilitating the formation of national armies. Before national armies could form and function effectively it was obviously useful that their various members be able to communicate fluently.

It was therefore a military plus if everyone within a jurisdiction could comprehend orders and instructions, as well as convey certain intelligence back along the bureaucratic chain of command. The French revolutionaries demonstrated the value of this almost immediately. In addition to running the equivalent of a language school, they also set up special monthlong "crash courses" in which, as Langins writes, "hundreds of students from all over France would be trained in the techniques of gunpowder and cannon manufacture." [29]

The military advantage of the French approach was shown by their successes in the Napoleonic period, as well as by contrary examples of what happened to regimes that could not depend upon the mobilization benefits of a common tongue during war. One of many factors that contributed to the disastrous defeats and demoralization of the Russian forces in the early days of World War I was the fact that the czar's aristocratic officer corps tended to communicate in German (the other court language of the Romanovs was French), which the rank-and-file troops, not to mention the citizenry, did not understand.

This points to another important military advantage of a common language. It reduces the motivational hurdles to fighting a war. Propaganda is useless if incomprehensible. In this respect as well, the French revolutionaries were also well attuned to the possibilities. Their "dominant idea," according to Langins, was "the will of the people. . . . They therefore had to identify themselves with the popular will by *expressing* it in its own particular language." [30] Prior to 1789, mutual incomprehensibility among "citizens" was a drawback in expressing the "will of the people" and thus a check on the exercise of power at the national level. In more ways than one, multilingual states and empires faced higher obstacles in mobilizing for war during the industrial period.

At the margin, therefore, they tended to be supplanted by nation-states

276 THE SOVEREIGN INDIVIDUAL

that were better able to motivate their citizens to fight and mobilize resources for war. This is exemplified by nationalist consolidation, such as the invention of France and the French at the end of the eighteenth century. It is also illustrated by cases of nationalist devolution, such as the collapse of the Austro-Hungarian Empire after World War I. The new nation-states that emerged in the wake of the Hapsburg Empire—Austria, Hungary, Czechoslovakia, and Yugoslavia—were, as Keynes said, "incomplete and immature." Yet their claims to form independent nation-states grouped around national identities at least partly defined by language persuaded Woodrow Wilson and other Allied leaders drawing up the Treaty of Versailles.

The carving up of Central Europe after World War I illustrates what a double-edged sword language became in state-building. When returns to violence were rising, a common tongue facilitated the exercise of power and consolidated jurisdictions. However, when incentives to consolidate were weaker, factions formed by minorities around language disputes also tended to fracture multilingual states. The surge of separatist sentiment in the cities of the Austro-Hungarian Empire in the mid-nineteenth century followed epidemics that devastated the German-speaking populations. Prague was a German-speaking city when the nineteenth century opened. Like other cities, it grew rapidly as the century unfolded, mostly by migration, as vast numbers of landless Czech-speaking peasants were assimilated from the countryside. In the beginning, the newcomers found it necessary to learn German in order to get along, so they did. But when famine and disease carried away large numbers of German-speaking urban residents in midcentury, they were replaced by Czech-speaking peasants. Suddenly there were so many Czech speakers that it was no longer essential for the new residents to learn German. Prague became a Czech-speaking city and a hotbed of Czech nationalism.

Contemporary separatist movements now frequently form around language disputes in multilingual countries. This is evidently the case in Belgium and Canada, two nations that, as we noted earlier, will probably be among the first in the OECD to dissolve in the new millennium. Few governments can top the heavy-handed actions to enforce language uniformity imposed by the Parti Québecois in Quebec.[31] More surprisingly, language grievances also played a role in launching the early activities of the northern separatists in Italy, which also faces disintegration. In the early 1980s, the Lombard League, as it was then known, "declared Lombardian to be a separate language from Italian." Billig comments, "Had the League's programme been successful during the early 1980s, and had Lombardy seceded from Italy, establishing its own state boundaries, a prediction might be made: increasingly Lombardian would have come to be recognized as different from Italian."[32] This is not an arbitrary assertion. It reflects what has happened in similar cases. For example, after Norway became independent in 1905, Norwegian nationalists set about a concerted effort to identify and underline features of the "Norwegian language" that were distinct from Danish and Swedish. Similarly, activists favoring an independent Belarus changed road signs into "Belarusian," but apparently failed to make the point that Belarusian is a separate language rather than a dialect of Russian.

Now that the military imperatives favoring language uniformity have largely been outstripped, we expect the national languages to fade, but not without a fight. It is to be expected that the well-rehearsed adage that "war is the health of the state" will be tested as a recuperative. As the nation-state slides into irrelevancy, demagogues and reactionaries will foment wars and conflicts, along the lines of ethnic and tribal fighting that has racked the former Yugoslavia and numerous jurisdictions in Africa, from Burundi to Somalia. Conflicts will prove convenient for the pretexts they provide for those seeking to arrest the trend toward commercialization of sovereignty. Wars will facilitate efforts to sustain more exacting regimes of taxation and impose more severe penalties for escaping the duties and burdens of citizenship. Wars will help undergird the "them and us" dimension of nationalism. To the proponents of systematic coercion, commercialized sovereignty, which gives individuals a choice of sovereignty services based upon price and quality, will seem no less a sin than the assertion by individuals of the right to veto the judgments of the pope and choose their own path to salvation during the Reformation.

The parallel is underscored by the fact that both the new technology of printing at the end of the fifteenth century and the new information technology at the end of the twentieth place formerly occult knowledge at the disposal of individuals in a liberating way. The printing press brought the Scriptures and other holy texts directly within the reach of individuals who previously had to rely upon priests and the church hierarchy to interpret the Word of God. The new information technology brings within the reach of anyone with a computer hook-up information about commerce, investment, and current events that previously was available only to persons at the pinnacle of government and corporate hierarchies.

"[T]he development of printing and publishing made possible the new national consciousness and promoted the rise of modern nation states."[33]

—JACK WEATHERFORD

Rock and Roll in Cyberspace

Make no mistake, the advent of the Internet and the World Wide Web will be as destructive to nationalism as the advent of gunpowder and the printing press was conducive to nationalism. Global computer links will not bring back Latin as a universal language, but they will help shift commerce out of local dialects, like French in Quebec, into the new global language of the Internet and World Wide Web—the language that Otis Redding and Tina Turner taught the world, the language of rock and roll, English.

These new media will undercut nationalism by creating new affinities that supersede geographic boundaries. They will appeal to widely dispersed audiences that form wherever educated persons happen to find themselves. These new nonterritorial affinities will flourish, and in so doing help to create a new focus for "patriotism." Or rather, they will form new "in-groups" with whom individuals can identify without necessarily sacrificing their economic rationality. The history of the Jews during the past two thousand years shows that this is possible over the long term and in the face of hostile local conditions. As the comment from William Pfaff quoted at the head of this chapter suggests, it is ahistorical and wrong to think that loyalties to the land of one's fathers, the *patria,* necessarily entails loyalty to an institution resembling a nation-state. Geoffrey Parker and Lesley M. Smith make this even more clear in *The General Crisis of the Seventeenth Century,* showing that what appear to be examples of early modern nationalism are more often instances of patriots defending a much narrower *patria* —often against the encroachment of a state. They write, "All too often a supposed allegiance to a national community turns out, on inspection, to be nothing of the kind. The *patria* itself is at least as likely to be a home town or province as the whole nation." [34]

As Jack Weatherford lucidly explains in *Savages and Civilization,* the rise of the printing press, the first mass-production technology, had dramatic effects in contributing to the creation of politics, with its demands for allegiance to a broader nation-state. By the year 1500, there were printing presses operating in 236 places in Europe, "and they had printed a combined total of some 20 million books." [35] Gutenberg's first printed book was an edition of the Bible in Latin. He followed it with editions of other popular medieval books in Latin. As Weatherford explains, printing meandered in a direction that defeated early expectations that the ready availability of texts would spread the use of Latin and even Greek. To the contrary. There were two important reasons why the printing press did not reinforce the use of Latin. First, the printing press was a mass-production technology. As Benedict Anderson points out, "[I]f manuscript knowledge was scarce and arcane lore, print knowledge lived by reproducibility and dissemination." [36] Very few Europeans were multilingual in 1500. This meant that the audience for works in Latin was not a mass audience. The vast majority who were monoglot made up a much bigger market of potential readers. Furthermore, what was true of readers was even more true of writers. Publishers needed products to sell. Because there were few contemporary fifteenth- or sixteenth-century authors who could compose satifactory new works in Latin, publishers were driven by market necessity to publish works in the vernacular. Printing thus helped to differentiate Europe into linguistic subsets. This was encouraged not only by the publication of new works that established the identity of new languages, like Spanish and Italian, but also by the adoption of characteristic typefaces, such as Roman, Italic, and the heavy Gothic script that was common to German publishing until well into the twentieth century. The new vernacular publishing, what Anderson describes as "print capitalism," was very successful. Most notably, the printing press gave heresy the kind of decisive boost that we expect for the denationalization of the individual from the Internet. In particular, Luther became "the first best-selling author so known. Or to put it another way, the first writer who could 'sell' his new books on the basis of his name." [37] Astonishingly, Luther's works accounted for "no less than one third of *all* German-language books sold between 1518 and 1525." [38]

In many respects, the new technology of the Information Age will counter part of the megapolitical impact of fifteenth-century technology, the printing press, in stimulating and underpinning the rise of nation-states. The World Wide Web creates a commercial venue with a global language, English. It will eventually be reinforced with simultaneous-translation software, making almost everyone effectively multilingual, and helping to denationalize language and imagination. Just as the technology of the printing press undermined allegiance to the dominant institution of the Middle Ages, the Holy Mother Church, so we expect the new communications technology of the Information Age to undermine the authority of the nanny state. In due course, almost every area will become multilingual. Local dialects will rise in importance. Propaganda from the center will lose much of its coherence as immigrants and speakers of minority tongues are emboldened to resist assimilation into the nation.

MILITARY MYSTICISM

Far from being objective communities, in the same sense that, for example, "hunting-gathering bands" are objective, nations are imagined out of a mysticism inspired by a defunct military imperative. That was the imperative to link every person living within a territory through a sense of identity that can be made to seem more important than life itself. As Kantorowicz noted, it is not a coincidence that "at a certain moment in history the state in the abstract or the state as a corporation appeared as a corpus mysticism and that death for this new mystical body appeared equal in value to the death of a crusader for the cause of God!"[39] In this sense, the nation-state can be understood as a mystical construct. Yet as Billig notes, nationalism is "a banal mysticism, which is so banal that all the mysticism seems to have evaporated long ago." It "binds 'us' to the homeland—that special place which is more than just a place, more than a mere geophysical area. In all this, the homeland is made to look homely, beyond question and, should the occasion arise, worth the price of sacrifice. And men, in particular, are given their special, pleasure-saturated reminders of the possibilities of sacrifice."[40]

The imaginative link between the nation and home continues to be highlighted by nationalists at every opportunity. As Billig suggests, the nation is "imagined as homely space, cozy within its borders, secure against the dangerous outside world. And 'we' the nation within the homeland can so easily imagine 'ourselves' as some sort of family."[41] The clichés of nationalism, tirelessly and routinely repeated, include many commonplace metaphors of kinship and identity. They associate the nation with an individual's sense of "inclusive fitness," a powerful motive for altruism and sacrifice.

"That sacrificial altruism does exist in social insects, other nonhuman animals, and humans implies that maximization of self-interest cannot be solely defined in terms of an individual organism's wants and needs. Indeed, the presence of altruism, particularly toward kin, has required a whole rethinking of traditional notions of survival of the fittest in the biological sciences. This has resulted in a growing conviction that natural selection does not ultimately operate on the individual. . . ."[42]

—R. PAUL SHAW AND YUWA WONG

NATIONALISM AND INCLUSIVE FITNESS

Our main focus in this book is on objective "megapolitical" factors that alter the costs and rewards of human choices. The underlying premise upon which the predictive power of the analysis rests is that individuals will seek rewards and shun costs. This is an essential truth of what Charles Darwin called "the economy of nature." But it is not the whole truth. Simple reward optimization does not explain everything in life. However, it does illuminate two of the three main forms of human sociality, identified by Pierre Van Den

Berghe as "reciprocity and coercion."[43] By "reciprocity" Van Den Berghe means "cooperation for mutual benefit."[44] The most complex and far-reaching examples of reciprocity are market interactions: trading, buying, selling, producing, and other economic activities. "Coercion is the use of force for one-sided benefit, that is, for purposes of intra-specific parasitism or predation."[45] As we have explored in this volume and two previous books, we believe that coercion is a crucial element in human society, a larger one than is usually recognized. Coercion helps determine the security of property and limits the ability of individuals to enter into mutually beneficial cooperation. Coercion underlies all politics. The third element in Van Den Berghe's typology of human sociality is "kin selection," the cooperative behavior that animals undertake with their kin. Kin selection, which is described more fully below, is also a crucial feature of the "economy of nature."

As Jack Hirshleifer has written, "[T]he revival of Darwinian evolutionary selection theory as applied to problems of social behaviour, which has come to be known as sociobiology," has "a distinctly economic aspect." And:

> Looking over the whole realm of life, sociobiology is attempting to find the general laws determining the multifarious forms of association among organisms. For example, Why do we sometimes observe sex and families, sometimes sex without families, sometimes neither sex nor families? Why do some animals flock, others remain solitary? Within groups, why do we sometimes observe hierarchical dominance patterns, sometimes not? Why do organisms in some species partition territories, others not? What determines the selflessness of the social insects, and why is this pattern so rare in Nature? When do we see resources allocated peacefully, when by means of violence? These are questions both posed and answered in recognizably economic terms. Sociobiologists ask what are the net advantages of the observed association patterns to the organisms displaying them, and what are the mechanisms whereby these patterns persist in social equilibrium states. It is perhaps this assertion of *economic-behavioural continuity* between man and other life-forms (termed "genetic capitalism" by one detractor) that explains the hostility of some ideologues to sociobiology. . . .[46]

We introduce sociobiology into our analysis of nationalism because it provides perspective on aspects of human nature that help facilitate systematic coercion. We agree with natural scientist Colin Tudge, author of *The Time Before History,* that before we can understand the current world, much less gain a perspective on that to come, we need to understand the preface to history. That means we must "look at ourselves on the grand scale of time."[47] Tudge reminds us "that beneath the surface tremors of our lives there are much deeper and more powerful forces at work that in the end affect us all and all our fellow creatures. . . ."[48] We suspect that among "these deeper and more powerful forces" is a genetically influenced motivational component undergirding nationalism. As Hirshleifer points out, paraphrasing Adam Smith and R. H. Coase, *"human desires are ultimately adaptive responses* shaped by man's biological nature and situation on earth."[49] This comes to the fore with the obviously biological allusions in most discussions of nationalism. Even in the United States, a conspicuously multiethnic nation, the government is personified in familial terms as *"Uncle Sam."*

The Biological Inheritance

In short, human nature, the origin of species, and their development by natural selection are elements to be considered in understanding the continuing evolution of human society. In the present case we are considering the likely human response to new circumstances occasioned by information technology. Particularly, we are focusing on the reaction to the advent of the cybereconomy and its many consequences, including the emergence of economic inequality more pronounced than anything seen in the past. Keys to at least some of the expected response lie in our genetic inheritance.

When a new species is formed, it does not discard all the DNA that it carried in its previous form, but adds to it. The whole difference between a human being and a chimpanzee is contained in less than 2 percent of the DNA in each species; slightly over 98 percent of their DNA is common to both, and some of it can be traced back to very primitive early organisms, far down the historic chain of development.

GENETIC INERTIA

Human cultures similarly contain elements that are universal, some of which are indeed inherited from prehuman ancestors. How we seek food, how we mate, how we form families, how we relate to strange groups, how we defend ourselves are all complex mixtures of instinct and culture, with very primitive roots. They are also all capable of modern adaptations, such as those that have characterized the nation-state in the modern period. If we think of cultures in this way, we shall see them as parallel to genetic development. The three great differences are that cultures are transmitted by the information chain between human beings, not by the genetic chain between generations; they can to some extent—perhaps less than we think—be changed by conscious intelligent action; they change with the prevailing environment of costs and rewards, which mutates much faster than genetic change. Physically we are very similar to our ancestors of thirty thousand years ago; culturally we have moved quite far away from them.

Evolutionary Models

There are two biological models of the way in which species evolve. The scientific orthodoxy is neo-Darwinist. Random genetic changes produce different physical forms. Most of these forms have no advantage to survival, as for instance the albino blackbird, and these tend to die out. A small number of them are helpful to survival and spread through the species. There are still many difficulties in this theory, which may be sorted out by scientists in the next century, but randomness and the survival of favorable adaptations are the current scientific orthodoxy and have some explanatory power. The alternative is some variant of the theory of the early twentieth century French philosopher Henri Bergson, who believed that nature had some nonrandom creative purpose, an intelligent force seeking solutions. This concept has echoes in the work of such contemporary authorites as David Layzer and Stephen Jay Gould, who have stressed that genetic variation is not simply random but shows definite propensities.[50] This is not creationism in its strict biblical sense, but it avoids many of the problems of orthodox Darwinism.

"The great theoretical contribution of sociobiology has been to extend the concept of fitness to that of 'inclusive fitness.' Indeed, an animal can duplicate its genes directly through its own reproduction, or indirectly through the reproduction of relatives with which it shares specific proportions of genes. Animals, therefore, can be expected to behave cooperatively, and thereby enhance each other's fitness to the extent that they are genetically related. This is what is meant by kin selection. Animals, in short, are nepotistic, i.e., they prefer kin over non-kin, and close kin over distant kin. This may happen consciously, as in humans, or more commonly, unconsciously."[51]

—PIERRE VAN DEN BERGHE

GENETICALLY INFLUENCED MOTIVATIONAL FACTORS

The biological perspective on human behavior was enhanced by the introduction of the concept of "inclusive fitness" in 1963 by W. D. Hamilton in "The Evolution of Altruistic Behavior." Hamilton recognized that while humans are fundamentally given to self-oriented behavior, they also undertake occasional acts of altruism or self-sacrifice that offer no apparent benefits in terms of the life of the individual. Hamilton sought to reconcile these apparent contradictions by positing that the fundamental maximizing unit is not the individual organism but the gene. Individuals in any species will seek to maximize not simply their own personal well-being but what Hamilton called their "inclusive fitness." He argued that "inclusive fitness" involves not only personal survival in the Darwinian sense, but also the enhanced reproduction and survival of close relatives who share the same genes.[52] Hamilton's "inclusive fitness" thesis helps illuminate many otherwise curious features of human societies, including aspects of politics in nation-states.

Altruism: Misnomer or Fossil Kin Selection?

According to Van Den Berghe, "Altruism, then, is directed mostly at kin, especially at close kin, and is, in fact, a misnomer. It represents the ultimate genetic selfishness. It is but the blind expression of inclusive fitness maximization."[53] This is not to say, however, that there is no altruism absent the close genetic relationship referred to by Hamilton and Van Den Berghe. The uncertainties introduced by the fact that humans reproduce sexually rather than through asexual cloning all but guarantee that an inclination to "inclusive fitness maximization" would stimulate a good deal of "altruism" rebounding to the benefit of alleles other than the "selfish gene." In the first instance, there is always the possibility that some persons who undertake helping actions may do so in the mistaken assumption that they are helping close kin. The father who undertakes a sacrificial action for his offspring may not, in fact, be the progenitor but may merely think he is.* This is not merely a theme for soap operas; it is illustrative of a primordial puzzle—that survival of the "selfish genes" is probably facilitated if each apparent father behaves "as if" he actually is the father, despite the possibility that he is not.

Seen in their proper light, however, as Hirshleifer points out, many of the paradoxes of "altruism" are semantic muddles that frequently confuse or mislead people into losing sight of the context of competition in which "helping" could convey a survival advantage: " 'If an altruism choice of strategy is to be *viable* in competition with non-altruism, altruism must contribute to self-survival more than non-altruism does, and therefore it can't really be altruism.' All such muddles could be avoided if we drop the term 'altruism' and ask instead: What are the determinants of the entirely objective phenomenon that can be called *helping?*"[54]

This question is perhaps most interesting in the case of "kinship helping."

* The same logic, of course, applies to the son or daughter who sacrifices for those whom he takes to be his siblings but are not.

Hamilton's basic formulation of inclusive fitness involved a biological cost-benefit analysis in which an individual, or "the gene controlling helping behaviour," values the survival of an identical copy of itself equally to its own survival. Therefore, the willingness to undertake helping, let alone sacrifice, varies with the chance that another individual has an identical gene. "Specifically, a gene for kinship helping instructs a man (other things equal) to give his life if he can thereby save two siblings, four half-siblings, eight cousins, etc." [55]

PROBABILITY PROBLEMS OF INCLUSIVE FITNESS

While this biologic seems clear in principle, upon closer examination it disguises a number of difficulties. For example, the fact that one's siblings or children may have a 50 percent probability of sharing an identical gene does not, in strict logic, mean that it is actually expressed in them. Every individual carries two sets of each gene, one from the father and one from the mother. But this, of course, means that only half of the genes carried by an individual parent are necessarily present in offspring. Furthermore, there is always the risk of mutation in reproduction, which, unlikely though it may be, reduces the certainty of genetic cost-benefit analysis. So if the metaphor of "gene as optimizer" is taken seriously, the case of the pater who is not the progenitor is only the most clear-cut example of a broader problem. If it is indeed the survival of the "selfish gene" that is optimized by sacrificing for near-relatives, then any possibility that results in the substitution of another allele for the identical copy of the "selfish gene" may be considered one of those intricate tricks that Mother Nature plays on herself.

Uncertain Consequences

Altruism directed toward kin therefore involves problems. Not only is there the probability problem for the "selfish gene" that apparent relatives of its host may not, in fact, share its identical copies. There is also the difficulty of determining under conditions of uncertainty whether any given gesture of sacrifice will, in fact, primarily benefit relatives rather than others. (Sacrifice that primarily benefits others may actually harm the inclusive fitness of the selfish gene by reducing the prospects that it will be represented in succeeding populations.) Consider an awful example inspired by the news while we were writing. Suppose a parent in Dunblane, Scotland, learned on short notice that an armed lunatic was heading into a local school with the apparent intention of doing harm. By acting instantly, he or she could undertake the heroic but possibly doomed gesture of confronting the lunatic, and thereby possibly save his or her children at the school.

Or possibly not.

Even a ruthless lunatic intent on killing every child on the planet would be limited in the harm he could do before running short of ammunition or being subdued by others. Had the sacrificing parent decided not to intervene, more likely than not his children would have survived in any event, as most children at the school did. All the harm that a gallant act of sacrifice would have prevented probably would otherwise have fallen on the children of others. So by risking his or her life, primarily for the children of others, the father or mother in question might actually have reduced his "inclusive fitness." By depriving all his children of one of their parents, he would probably have left those children in a worsened position in the Darwinian struggle.

While this is admittedly a strained example, it is also realistic. It reflects the fact that there are countless circumstances in life in which large or small acts of helping have beneficial effects. In many cases, the direct beneficiaries of such actions cannot be easily isolated to closely related kin. And ironically, as we consider below, this may be part of the survival benefit that enabled those with less discriminate helping genes to endure all the millennia of unpleasantness until now.

Altruism and Genetic Inertia

If, as we believe, the "selfish gene" thesis is an accurate approximation of what motivates human action, it would be too simple to suppose that the helping or sacrificial behavior it engenders could operate narrowly and solely for the benefit of actual relatives. Imperfect knowledge makes distinguishing kin an uncertain art in some circumstances. And even assuming that kin were known, actual representation of any given "selfish gene" in the population of kin could not be ascertained as more than a matter of probabilities. Until recently, it would have been impossible to distinguish actual genetic markers among individuals. And we are still some distance from being able to practically distinguish which near-relatives actually express whatever "selfish gene" is optimizing its survival. Beyond that is the greater difficulty of confining benefits to kin rather than others.

Furthermore, it is also obvious from experience that humans sometimes divert their "nurturing instincts" for the benefit of nonkin if appropriate kin are unavailable. The most clear-cut example of this is the behavior of parents toward adopted children, or even the behavior of certain persons, usually childless, toward their household pets. It is not unheard of for such individuals to court serious injury and even death to rescue cats trapped in a tree. Certainly, in any given year, a not-insignificant number of persons perish in household accidents precipitated in some fashion by pets who find their way into jeopardy. What is true of pets is more true of adoptive children. It is certainly not a stretch to say that parents of adopted children often treat them "as if" they were kin, thus giving the concept of "kin selection" another meaning.

Such cases do not discredit the "selfish gene" theory as much as some critics would wish. To the contrary. We see examples of people behaving "as if" they were sacrificing for close relatives to advance their own inclusive fitness, as instances of "genetic inertia." In other words, they reflect the fact, noted by Howard Margolis in *Selfishness, Altruism and Rationality,* that "human society changed faster" than human genetic makeup. People, therefore, continue to act "substantially as if living in a small hunter-gatherer group."[56] A crucial characteristic of such groups was, as Van Den Berghe put it, that

> They were small in-bred populations of a few hundred individuals. . . . Members of the tribe, though subdivided into smaller kin groups, saw themselves as a single people, solidary against the outside world, and interlinked by a web of kinship and marriage making the tribe in fact a superfamily. A high rate of inbreeding assured that most spouses were also kinsmen."[57]

In short, for all of human existence prior to the advent of agriculture, ethnic groups were "inbreeding superfamilies." Given this past identity between the family and the in-group, there could well be a genetically influenced tendency to treat the in-group as kin. It is easy to imagine that such behavior could have had survival value in the past when every member of the "inbreeding superfamily" was kin. As Margolis suggests, it is easy to imagine that for "such small bands of hunter-gatherers, closely related, that inclusive selfishness (aside from any prospect of reciprocity or vengeance) would alone support a measure of commitment to group-interest. One can then argue that some tendency to group-interested motivation survives as a kind of fossil kin-altruism. . . ."[58] In other words, because we retain the genetic makeup of hunter-gatherers, our behavior toward in-groups reflects the kind of "altruism" that would be expected to optimize the survival success of in-groups comprised by "inbreeding superfamilies."

Presumably, as Margolis speculates, this tendency for group-interested behavior, arising from "fossil kin-altruism" or genetic inertia, contributed to the survival of *Homo sapiens* "while other humanoid species went extinct."[59]

Epigenesis

We see this "as if" behavior as a prime example of "epigenesis," or the tendency of genetically influenced motivational factors to innately bias humans to favor certain choices over others. In other words, the human mind is not a *tabula rasa*, or blank slate, but a hard drive with prewired circuits that make certain responses more readily learned and attractive than others. Thus the proposition that the mind is disposed to think in terms of an out-group that excites enmity or hostility and an in-group to which one feels great amity or loyalty usually reserved for kin.[60]

This epigenetic tendency to behave with an in-group as if it comprised close relatives creates a vulnerability to manipulation that has commonly been exploited by nationalists to engender sacrificial support for the state. In that sense, it is not a coincidence that nationalist propaganda everywhere is dressed up in the vocabulary of kinship.

"By the voice of her cannon alarming, fair France bids her children arise. Soldiers around us are arming. On, on, 'tis our mother who cries."[61]

—CHANT OF FRENCH SOLDIERS

Bogus Kinship

Consider the strong tendency of politicians everywhere to describe the state in terms borrowed from kinship. The nation is "our fatherland" or "our motherland." Its citizens are "we," "members of the family," our "brothers and sisters."[62] The fact that states as culturally different as France, China, and Egypt employ such similes is not a rhetorical coincidence, as we see it, but a prime example of "epigenesis" or the tendency of genetically influenced motivational factors to innately bias humans to favor certain choices.

How does this epigenesis work? The identification mechanism employed to harness emotional loyalty to the nation-state makes use of various devices that would have been markers of kinship in the primitive past "to link the individual's inclusive fitness concerns" with the interests of the state.[63] For example, Shaw and Wong focus on five identification devices used by modern nation-states to mobilize their populations against out-groups. These are:

1. a common language
2. a shared homeland
3. similar phenotypic characteristics
4. a shared religious heritage and
5. the belief of common descent[64]

Such characteristics, of course, would have distinguished the nucleus ethnic group in the primitive past. Much of the appeal of nationalism can be traced to the way that these identification devices have been adopted and dressed up in the language of kinship, as illustrated in the French soldiers' chant quoted above. Such mobilization devices, which refer to the state as the "fatherland" or the "motherland," are common worldwide because they work.

Genetic Accounting

The imaginary character of these kinship links as far as the state is concerned is evidenced by the fact that they possess none of the degrees of variability that characterize actual kinship. Even in extended families, where everyone is related, not everyone is related to the same degree. Parents and siblings are the closest relations, grandparents and cousins are less close, with distant, kissing cousins so remote that they are barely more likely than complete strangers to share any given gene in common. Husbands and wives generally are no longer closely related, as they tended to be in the Stone Age. In any event, all actual kinship is definable in mathematical terms as the "coefficient of relatedness," which Hamilton calculated as a measure of genetic overlap.[65]

By contrast, the national "family" is imagined to be totally and elastically coincident with the state's territorial dimensions. Nationality extends uniformly, like a liquid, into every crevice within the strictly defined boundaries. Benedict Anderson writes, "In the modern conception, state sovereignty is fully, flatly and evenly operative over each square centimeter of a legally demarcated territory."[66] And, of course, when it comes to sacrifice for the state, the coefficient of imaginary relatedness is always one.

This identification of inclusive fitness with the nation-state is interesting because it could help inform the disposition of humans to welcome or resist the changes of the new millennium. As we have explored earlier, prior to the Information Age all types of society were territorially based. They either formed around the home territory of the nucleus ethnic group, or, as with the nation-state, played upon the same motives of group solidarity to mobilize force for defense of a local territory against outsiders. In every case, it was the stranger outside of one's immediate territory who was feared as the enemy. Given the assumptions of kin selection in the primordial past, this made sense. When humanity emerged in its current genetic form, members of the tribe were close kin. They were members of a nucleus ethnic group, "the inbreeding superfamily."

Furthermore, there really was a practical economic reason, given the imperatives of kin selection, for the individual to identify the prosperity and survival of immediate kin with that of his tribe, or superfamily. A member of a hunter-gatherer tribe really did depend for his prosperity upon the success of the whole tribe. There was no independent property, nor any way that an individual or family could plausibly have hoped to survive and prosper if detached from the tribe. This strongly linked the individual's self-interest to that of the group. In Hirshleifer's words, "To the extent that members of a group share a common fate or outcome, helping one another becomes self-help." [67]

"Evidently primitive man—and the Lovedu can be regarded as representative of hundreds of similar peoples—considers as the norm a society in which, at any one moment of time, everyone's situation is precisely equal."

—HELMUT SCHOECK

New Circumstances, Old Genes

Now microtechnology is facilitating the creation of very different conditions from those to which we were genetically disposed by the conditions of the Stone Age. Information technology is creating economic inequality magnitudes outside the range of anything experienced by our ancestors in the pristinely egalitarian Stone Age. Information technology is also creating supraterritorial assets, which will help to subvert the embodiment of the in-group, the nation-state. Ironically, these new cyberassets will probably be of higher value precisely because they are established at a distance from home. All the more so if there is an invidious backlash of the kind we expect against the economic inequality arising from increasing penetration of information technology in the rich industrial countries. That very fact would tend to make assets held at long distance more valuable. They would not only be less exposed to envy, they would be more likely to be put beyond the reach of the most predatory group with which an individual must cope—his own nation-state.

Diseconomies of Nature and Nationalism

It is perhaps a mark of the importance of epigenesis in informing attitudes that so little notice has been taken of the ironies of in-group identification as it relates to the modern nation-state. The logic of violence in the modern period tended to confound the very impulse that gave rise to the tendency to identify fitness with the in-group in the first place. Why? Because rather than facilitating the survival and prosperity of near-relatives in a hostile world, the identification of the individual's "inclusive fitness" with a national in-group diluted the value of any act of sacrifice the individual might have made to the level of insignificance for his kin. The typical modern nation-state was simply too large to allow for a statistically significant "coefficient of relatedness" between the individual and other citizens of the nation that laid claim to him. Not only was the proportion of close relatives within the in-group sharply diminished from almost unity in the Stone Age to a bare chemical trace in the twentieth century; the "coefficient of relatedness" between the individual citizen and the rest of the nation would not, in most cases, have been significantly higher than with the whole human race. An "in-group" with tens of millions or even hundreds of millions (or in the case of the Chinese, more than a billion members) became so gigantic as to dilute the inclusive fitness effect of any sacrifice or benefit conveyed to the scale of a spit in the ocean. In strict logic, therefore, the modern nationalist, unlike the hunter-gatherer of the Stone Age, could not reasonably expect any gesture of sacrifice or helping for his "in-group" to enhance the survival prospects for his family in a meaningful way.

Notwithstanding the fact that national economies became the fundamental units of account in which well-being was measured in the modern era, the largest obstacle to the talented individual's success, and therefore to that of his kin, became the burdens imposed in the name of the nation, the in-group itself. This, at least, was true for those primarily engaged in reciprocal rather than coercive sociality—to revisit Van Den Berghe's categories of human behavior.[68]

The logic of the nation-state suggests that the ultimate price of citizenship is sacrifice and death. As Jane Bethke Elshtain observed, nation-states indoctrinate citizens more for sacrifice than aggression: "The young man goes to war not so much to kill as to die, to forfeit his particular body for that of the large body, the body politic."[69] The impulse to sacrifice is no less active where the taxpayer is concerned. Paying taxes, like bearing arms, is a duty, rather than an exchange in which one forgoes money to obtain some product or service of an equal or greater value. This much is acknowledged in common speech. People speak of a "tax burden" as they do not speak of the "food burden" of shopping for nutriments, or the "car burden" of purchasing an automobile, or a "vacation burden" for traveling, precisely because commercial purchases are generally fair exchanges. Otherwise, the buyers would not make them.

In this respect, nationalism shows how epigenesis can reverse the logic of the Darwinian "economy of nature." The nation-state facilitated systematic, territorially based predation. Unlike the situation faced by hunter-gatherers in the Stone Age, the main parasite and predator upon the individual at the end of the twentieth century was not likely to be the "outsider," the foreign enemy, but rather the presumed embodiment of the "in-group," the local nation-state itself. Thus the main advantage offered by the advent of assets that transcend territoriality in the Information Age is precisely the fact that such assets can be placed beyond the reach of the systematic coercion mobilized by the local nation-state in whose territory the would-be Sovereign Individual was resident.

If our view is correct, microtechnology will make it technically feasible for individuals to largely escape from the burdens of subordinate citizenship. They will be extranational sovereigns over themselves, not subjects, in the new "Virtual City," owing allegiance by contract or private treaty in a fashion more reminiscent of premodern Europe, where merchants secured commercial treaties and charters to protect themselves "from arbitrary seizures of property" and to obtain "exemption from seigneurial law." [70] In the cyberculture, successful persons will gain exemption from duties of citizenship arising from an accident of birth. They will no longer tend to think of themselves primarily as British or American. They will be extranational residents of the whole world who just happen to abide in one or more of its localities.

THE CYBERECONOMY AND OUR GENETIC INHERITANCE

The hitch, however, is that this technological miracle and the economic miracle it implies—escaping the tyranny of place—depend upon the willingness of individuals to entrust much of their wealth and futures to strangers. In strict genetic accounting, of course, those strangers would not necessarily be less genetically close than most of our "fellow citizens" upon whom in recent centuries we have been bound to depend.

The question is whether the perverse results of in-group amity in the case of the nation-state are negative or positive indicators for the cybereconomy. Will the "left-behinds" who stand to lose the benefits of coercive redistribution treat the death of the nation-state as as if it were an attack on kin? The first quarter century of the new millennium will tell. The emotional reactions could be complex. The fact that 115 million persons gave their lives fighting for nation-states in the twentieth century is stark evidence of the power of epigenesis.[71] It shows that many did consider the survival of their nations to be matters of life-and-death importance. The question is whether that attitude will carry over into a new age with different megapolitical imperatives.

The fact that genetically influenced sacrifice on behalf of the nation-state often militated against the evolutionary purpose of kin selection also tells you that humans are adaptable enough to adjust to many circumstances for which we were not genetically programmed in the conditions of the Stone Age. As Tudge elaborates in describing the "extreme generalness" of human beings: "We are the animal equivalent of the Turing machine: the universal device that can be turned to any task." [72] Which tendency will come to the surface in the coming transition crisis? Probably both.

The commercialization of sovereignty itself depends upon the willingness of hundreds of thousands of Sovereign Individuals and many millions of others to deploy their assets in the "First Bank of Nowhere" in order to secure immunity from direct compulsion. This type of trust has no obvious analogue in the primordial past. There were few assets in the Stone Age. Those that did exist were hoarded under the control of a tribe, an "in-breeding superfamily" that was paranoid about outsiders. Yet notwithstanding the evolutionary novelty of the cybereconomy, it gives humans the chance to express our most novel genetic inheritance—the intelligence that comes along with our outsized brains. Those among the information elite will certainly be smart enough to recognize a good thing when they see one.

Further, the creation of assets that are largely immune to predation should actually rebound in a practical way to increase the "inclusive fitness" of Sovereign Individuals. While the economic logic of participating in the cybereconomy turns the rationales of the nation-state upside down, it is compelling, especially for persons of high skills.

In order to optimize their advantage in shopping among jurisdictions, individuals must be willing to exit the nation-state and entrust their personal protection to police in another jurisdiction, or in some cases, to security personnel motivated mainly by market incentives in areas that may be distant from where they were born and reared. This implies a significant advantage in being multilingual and cosmopolitan in culture rather than jingoistic. And it further implies that anyone who is serious about realizing the liberating potential of the cybereconomy for himself and his family should begin to stake out a welcome for himself in several jurisdictions other than that in which he has resided during his main business career. For more details, see our discussion of strategies for achieving independence in the appendices.

Genuine Affinities

A new extranational understanding of the world and a new way of identifying one's place in it could change the habits of human culture, if not our inbred inclinations. The new extranational equation of identity that we expect to see take hold in the new millennium could make it easier to adopt to the new world than may seem likely. Unlike nationality, the new identities will not be a product of the systematic compulsion that made nation-states and the nation-state system universal in the twentieth century. In the new age to come, communities and allegiances will not be territorially bounded. Identification will be more precisely targeted to genuine affinities, shared interests, or actual kinship, rather than the bogus affinities of citizenship so tirelessly promoted in conventional politics. Protection will be organized in new ways that have no analogue in a surveyor's kit that demarcates territorial borders. Assets will increasingly be lodged in cyberspace rather than at any given place, a fact that will facilitate new competition to reduce the "protection costs" or taxes imposed in most territorial jurisdictions.

"Ambitious people understand, then, that a migratory way of life is the price of getting ahead."[73]

—CHRISTOPHER LASCH

ESCAPE FROM THE NATION-STATE

Notwithstanding the firm grip the nation-state as the "in-group" has had on the modern imagination, able people who do not already doubt the utility of affiliating with a grossly expensive "imagined community" soon will. Indeed, the partisans of the nation-state have already begun to complain of the growing detachment of the cognitive elites. The late Christopher Lasch, in his diatribe *The Revolt of the Elites and the Betrayal of Democracy,* assails those "whose livelihoods rest not so much on the ownership of property as on the manipulation of information."[74] Lasch laments the extranational character of the emerging information economy. He writes:

the markets in which the new elites operate is now international in scope. Their fortunes are tied to enterprises that operate across national boundaries. They are more concerned with the smooth functioning of the system as a whole than with any of its parts. Their loyalties—if the term is not itself anachronistic in this context—are international rather than regional, national or local. They have more in common with their counterparts in Brussels or Hong Kong than with the masses of Americans not yet plugged into the network of global communications.[75]

Although Lasch was far from a dispassionate observer, and he obviously meant his portrait of the information elite to be unflattering, his contempt for those who are liberated from the tyranny of place rests on a perception of some of the same developments that are the focus of this book. When we read Lasch's critiques or those of Mickey Kaus *(The End of Equality)*, Michael Walzer *(Spheres of Justice)*, or Robert Reich *(The Work of Nations)*, we see parts of our analysis confirmed, often unhappily, by authors who are deeply unsympathetic to many of the consequences of the deepening of markets, much less the denationalization of Sovereign Individuals. Lasch lambastes those with extranational ambitions "who covet membership in the new aristocracy of brains" for "cultivating ties with the international market in fast-moving money, glamour, fashion and popular culture." He continues:

> It is a question whether they think of themselves as Americans at all. Patriotism, certainly, does not rank very high in their hierarchy of virtues. "Multiculturalism," on the other hand, suits them to perfection, conjuring up the agreeable image of a global bazaar in which exotic cuisines, exotic styles of dress, exotic music, exotic tribal customs can be savored indiscriminately, with no questions asked and no commitments required. The new elites are at home only in transit, en route to a high-level conference, to the grand opening of a new franchise, to an international film festival or an undiscovered resort. Theirs is essentially a tourist's view of the world—not a perspective likely to encourage a passionate devotion to democracy.[76]

Economic Nationalism

Lurking behind criticisms of the "transients" who make up the virtual communities of the Information Age is a recognition that for many in the elite the benefits of transience already exceed their costs. Critics like Lasch and Walzer do not dispute that clearheaded cost-benefit analysis makes citizenship obsolete for persons of high skills. They do not propose that those among the information elite whose attitudes they despise have miscalculated where their best interests lie. Nor do they pretend that the compound-interest tables really show that continuing to pump one's money into a national social security program, much less income taxes, produces a better return than private investment. To the contrary, they understand arithmetic. They have seen the sums to their obvious conclusions. But rather than acknowledge the subversive logic of economic rationality, they recoil from it, counting it as "betrayal" for the information elite to transcend the tyranny of place and abandon "the unenlightened."[77]

Like Pat Buchanan, the social democrats are economic nationalists who resent the triumph of markets over politics. They denounce "the new aristocracy of brains" for being detached from place and not caring passionately about their view of where the best interests of the masses lie. While they do not explicitly recognize the denationalization of the individual as such, they rail against its early hints and manifestations, what Walzer describes as "the imperialism of the market," or the tendency of money to "seep across boundaries" in order to buy things which, as Lasch elaborates, "should not be for sale," such as exemption from military service.[78] Note the reactionary harking to the military demands of the nation-state as a sacred ground upon which money and markets should not trespass.

These criticisms of the information elite anticipate the terms of a popular reaction against the rise of Sovereign Individuals in the next millennium. As new, more market-driven forms of protection become available, it will become increasingly evident to the large numbers of able persons that most of the supposed benefits of nationality are imaginary. This will lead not only to better accounting of the opportunity costs of citizenship, it will also create new ways of framing allegedly "political" and even "economic" questions. For the first time, "an individual entrepreneur acting for and by himself" will be able to vary his own protection costs by moving between jurisdictions, without waiting for them to be effected by "group decision and group action," to quote Frederic C. Lane's formulation of an old dilemma.[79]

As the price paid for protection becomes subject "to the principle of substitution," this will lay bare the arithmetic of compulsion, intensifying conflict between the new cosmopolitan elite of the Information Age and "the information poor," the remainder of the population who are largely monoglot and do not excel in problem-solving or possess some globally marketable skill. These "losers" or "left-behinds," as Thomas L. Friedman describes them, will no doubt continue to identify their well-being with the political life of existing nation-states.[80]

MOST POLITICAL AGENDAS WILL BE REACTIONARY

Most of those who harbor an ardent political agenda, whether nationalist, environmentalist, or socialist, will rally to defend the wobbling nation-state as the twenty-first century opens. Over time, it will become ever more obvious that survival of the nation-state and the nationalist sensibility are preconditions for preserving a realm for political compulsion. As Billig points out, nationalism "is the condition for conventional (political) strategies, whatever the particular politics." [81] Therefore, the nationalist content in all political programs will swell like a glutton's paunch in the years ahead. Environmentalists, for example, will focus less on protecting "Mother Earth" and more on protecting the "motherland." For reasons we explore later, the nation and citizenship will be especially sacred to those who value equality highly. More than they may now understand, they will come to agree with Christopher Lasch, who followed Hannah Arendt in proclaiming, "It is citizenship that confers equality, not equality that creates a right to citizenship." [82]

The privatization of sovereignty will deflate the industrial-era premium on equality by severing ties of the creators of wealth to nation and place. Citizenship will no longer serve as a mechanism for enforcing income redistribution based upon the equality of the vote within a confined territory. The consequences will include another bruising for the progressive view of history. Contrary to the expectations of supposedly forward-thinking people when the twentieth century opened, the free market was not destroyed by the decades but left triumphant. The Marxists anticipated the eclipse of capitalism, which never happened, to lead to the transcendence of nation-states and the emergence of a universal class consciousness among workers. In fact, the state will be eclipsed, but in a very different way. Something more nearly the opposite to their expectation is happening. The triumph of capitalism will lead to the emergence of a new global, or extranational, consciousness among the capitalists, many of whom will become Sovereign Individuals. Far from depending upon the state to discipline the workers, as the Marxists imagined, the ablest, wealthiest persons were net losers from the actions of the nation-state. It is clearly they who have the most to gain by transcending nationalism as markets triumph over compulsion.

Perhaps not immediately, but soon, certainly within the span of a generation, almost everyone among the information elite will elect to domicile his income-earning activities in low-tax or no-tax jurisdictions. As the Information Age transforms the globe, it will impress an unmistakable object lesson in compound interest. Within years, let alone decades, it will be widely understood that almost anyone of talent could accumulate a much higher net worth and enjoy a better life by abandoning high-tax nation-states. We have already hinted at the staggering costs that the leading nation-states impose, but as this is the crux of an issue that is little understood, it is worth reemphasizing the opportunity costs of nationality.

Opportunity Costs

Far from suffering from the loss or curtailment of government services currently financed by high taxes, the information elite will flourish in an unparalleled fashion. Simply by escaping the excess tax burden they now pay, they will gain a tremendous margin for improving the material well-being of their families. As previously indicated, each $5,000 in tax paid annually reduces your lifetime net worth by $2.4 million if you can earn 10 percent annually from your investments. But if you could earn 20 percent, each $5,000 in annual tax payments would leave you $44 million poorer over a period of forty years. Cumulatively, paying $5,000 per year would therefore cost you more than a million dollars per year. At that rate, $250,000 per year in tax would soon translate to an annual loss of more than $50 million, or $2.2 billion in a lifetime. And, of course, sporadically higher earnings, for even a few years, especially early in life, imply a still more startling loss of wealth to predatory taxation.

Your authors have seen to our own satisfaction that higher than 20 percent returns are possible. Our colleagues at Lines Overseas Management in Bermuda earned triple-digit returns, averaging 226 percent per annum, during the years when we were writing this book. Their experience underscores what the spreadsheet suggests, that for many high-income earners and owners of capital, predatory taxation imposes a lifetime cost eqivalent to a large fortune. An individual with high earnings capacity paying taxes at Hong Kong rates could end up with a thousand times more wealth than someone with the same pretax performance paying taxes at North American or European rates. To subject your capital to recurring invasion by a high-tax jurisdiction is like running in a race and having someone shoot you every time you take a stride. If you could enter the same race with proper protection and run unhobbled, you would obviously go much farther, more quickly.

The Sovereign Individuals of the future will take advantage of the "transient" inclinations that so offend Christopher Lasch and other critics of the information elite, and they will shop for the most profitable jurisdictions in which to domicile. While this is contrary to the logic of nationalism, it accords with a compelling economic logic. A 10 percent, let alone a tenfold, bottom-line difference will frequently motivate profit-maximizing individuals to alter their lifestyles and production techniques, as well as their place of abode. The history of Western civilization is a record of restless change in which people and prosperity have repeatedly migrated to new areas of opportunity under the spur of meandering megapolitical conditions. A thousandfold difference in bottom-line returns would match the most potent stimulus that has ever put rational people in motion. Or put another way, most people, particularly those Thomas L. Friedman calls the "losers and left-behinds," if given a chance, would gladly leave any nation-state for $50 million, not to mention the still greater costs that nation-states impose in tax extracted from the top 1 percent of taxpayers. The rise of Sovereign Individuals shopping for jurisdictions is therefore one of the surest forecasts one can make.

THE COMMERCIALIZATION OF SOVEREIGNTY

Seen in cost-benefit terms, citizenship was already a dreadful bargain as the twentieth century drew to a close. This was highlighted by an unconsciously funny Parliamentary Research Note entitled "Is the Queen an Australian Citizen?" produced by Ian Ireland of the Australian Parliamentary Research Service in August 1995.[83] Ireland canvasses the Australian Citizenship Act of 1948, reviewing the four means by which one can obtain Australian citizenship. These are similar to the options for citizenship in other leading nation-states, namely:

> citizenship by birth
> citizenship by adoption
> citizenship by descent
> citizenship by grant

This is all unremarkable except that it focuses attention upon the distinction between sovereignty and citizenship. As Ireland says, "Under traditional legal and political concepts, the monarch is sovereign and the people are his/her subjects. Subjects are bound to the monarch by allegiance and subjection." Noting the obvious fact that Queen Elizabeth II is sovereign, he concludes that "there is an argument that the Queen is not an Australian citizen." [84]

Indeed, she is not. The Queen, long may she live, is fortunate to be beyond caring about being a citizen. She is sovereign, the Sovereign over her subjects. Like a handful of other monarchs in the world, the Queen is sovereign by birth, having inherited her status as a matter of custom that predates modern times. The idea of monarchy is ancient, going back to the earliest historic records of human life. Those countries that have retained their monarchy owe their constitution to their ancient history, but it still helps to decide the shape of their society, in terms of class prestige if not of political power. Postmodern individuals, without the Queen's head start, will be obliged to invent new legal rationales upon which to base the *de facto* sovereignty that information technology will hand them.

Sovereign Individuals will also have to cope with the corrosive consequences of envy—a difficulty that sometimes detains monarchs, but which will be more intensely felt by persons who are not traditionally venerated but invent their own sovereignty. As Helmut Schoeck wrote in his comprehensive survey, *Envy*, "Where there is only one king, one president of the United States—in other words, one member only of a particular status—he can live with relative impunity the kind of life which, even on a much smaller scale, would arouse indignation in the same society were it to be adopted by successful members of larger professional or social groups." [85] Monarchs, as embodiments of the nation, enjoy a certain immunity to envy that will not carry over to Sovereign Individuals.

The "losers and left-behinds" in the Information Society will surely envy and resent the success of winners, especially as the deepening of markets implies that this will be increasingly a "winners take all" world. Increasingly, rewards are already coming to be based upon relative performance, rather than absolute performance as was the case in industrial production. A factory worker was paid either on the basis of hours in attendence as measured by the time clock, or according to some criterion of output, such as pieces made, units assembled, or some similar measure.[86] Standardized pay was made possible by the fact that output was similar for everyone using the same tools. But the creation of conceptual wealth, like artistic performance, varies dramatically among persons using the same tools. In this respect, the whole of the economy is becoming increasingly like opera, where the highest rewards go to those with the best voices, and those who sing out of tune, however earnestly, do not normally attract large rewards. As many fields are opened to truly global competition, the return for ordinary performance is bound to fall. Middle talents will be in vast supply, some originating with persons who can rent their time for a fraction of the rates that prevail in the leading industrial countries. The losers will be the minor-league outfielders with "slider speed bats" whose reflexes are half a second shy of hitting a major league fastball. Instead of making a million dollars a year banging out home runs, they will make $25,000, with no supplementary income from celebrity endorsements. Others will strike out altogether.

> "Once a country opens itself up to the global market . . . , those of its citizens with the skills to take advantage of it become the winners, and those without become losers or left-behinds. . . . [U]sually one party . . . claims to be able to defy globalization or ease its pain. That is Pat Buchanan in America, the Communists in Russia and now the Islamic Welfare Party here in Turkey. . . . So what is happening in Turkey is much more complicated than just a fundamentalist takeover. It is what happens when widening globalization spins off more and more losers, when widening democratization gives them all a vote, while religious parties effectively exploit this coincidence to take power."[87]
>
> —THOMAS L. FRIEDMAN

Who will the losers be in the Information Age? In general terms, the tax consumers will be losers. It is usually they who could not increase their wealth by moving to another jurisdiction. Much of their income is lodged in the rules of a national political jurisdiction rather than conveyed by market valuations. Therefore, eliminating or sharply reducing the taxes that are negatively compounding against their net worths may not appear to make them much better off—the price of lower taxation is a diminished stream of transfer payments. They will lose income because they will no longer be able to depend upon political compulsion to pick the pockets of persons more productive than themselves. Those without savings who rely upon government to pay their retirement benefits and medical care will in all probability suffer a fall in living standards. This loss of income translates into a depreciation of what financial writer Scott Burns has dubbed "transcendental" or political capital.[88] This "transcendental" or imaginary capital is based not upon the economic ownership of assets but upon the *de facto* claim to the income stream established by political rules and regulations. For example, the expected income from government transfer programs could be converted into a bond capitalized at prevailing interest rates. This imaginary bond funded by the imagined community is *transcendental capital*. It will be suddenly depreciated by the "great transformation" that is destined to reduce the grip of political authorities upon the cash flow required to redeem their promises.

"On frontiers and on the high seas, where no one had an enduring monopoly in the use of violence, merchants avoided payment of exactions which were so high that protection could be obtained more cheaply by other means."[89]

—FREDERIC C. LANE

It does not take a giant stretch of the imagination to see that the information elite are likely to take advantage of the opportunities for liberation and personal sovereignty offered by the new cybereconomy. Equally, it is to be expected that the "left-behinds" will become increasingly jingoistic and unpleasant as the impact of information technology grows in the new millennium. It is difficult to guess at precisely what point the reaction will turn ugly. Our guess is that the recriminations will intensify when Western nations begin to unambiguously crack apart in the manner of the former Soviet Union.

Equally, every time a nation-state cracks up, it will facilitate further devolution and encourage the autonomy of Sovereign Individuals. We expect to see a significant multiplication of sovereign entities, as scores of enclaves and jurisdictions more akin to city-states emerge from the rubble of nations. These new entities will include many that will offer highly competitive pricing of protection services, imposing low taxes or none at all on income and capital. The new entities are almost bound to price their protection services more attractively than do the leading OECD nation-states. Seen simply as a matter of market segmentation, the area of the market that is most poorly served is the high-efficiency, low-cost end. Anyone who wishes to pay high taxes in exchange for a complicated array of state spending has ample opportunity to do so. Therefore, the most advantageous and profitable strategy for a new minisovereignty is almost bound to lie with a high-efficiency, low-price alternative. Such a minisovereignty could only with great difficulty expect to provide a more complete array of services than those on offer from the surviving nation-states. Since all nation-states will certainly not collapse at once, the statist alternative is likely to be well supplied, especially early in the transition. On the other hand, a no-frills regime of tolerable law and order can be provided relatively cheaply. If social unrest and crime spread in the old core industrial countries to the degree that we expect, tolerable law and order will be far more appealing in a jurisdiction than a national space program, a state-sponsored women's museum, or subsidized retraining schemes for displaced executives.

THE DENATIONALIZATION OF THE INDIVIDUAL

Citizenship will become less attractive and tenable as new institutions emerge to facilitate choice in the services governments now engross, begining with protection. This will make it practical for individuals to cease to identify themselves in national terms. Yet the demystification of citizenship will be a slow process. You are constantly exposed to a barrage of banal messages in the routines of daily life designed to reinforce your identification with your local nation-state. These messages make it highly unlikely for you to forget "your nationality." For many people, nationality is a crucial badge of identity. "We" are taught to see the world in terms of nationality. It is "our" country, "our" athletes compete in the Olympics. When they win, it is "our" flag that waves in the ceremony. "Our" anthem brings the judges and other competitors to attention in the awards ceremony. "We" are led to believe that it is "our" victory, although it is never quite clear how "we" participated, other than by being within the same territory as a citizen.

From First Person Plural to Singular

As information technology comes to the fore, it will help facilitate the global perspective already evident in the attitudes of MTV viewers, as well as create ways by which Sovereign Individuals can harness the latent possibilities of information technology to escape from the nationalist burden of taxation. Within the next few decades, for example, *narrow*-casting will replace *broad*casting as the method by which individuals obtain their news. This has significant implications. It amounts to a change in the imaginations of millions from first personal plural to singular. As individuals themselves begin to serve as their own news editors, selecting what topics and news stories are of interest, it is far less likely that they will choose to indoctrinate themselves in the urgencies of sacrifice for the nation-state. Indeed, their attitudes are more likely to be informed by the global culture to which they relate as consumers of entertainment than by the highly personal "news" narrow-casts to which they may subscribe. Much the same effect will arise from the privatization of education, again facilitated by technology. In the medieval period, education was firmly under the control of the Church. In the modern age, education has been under the control of the state. In the words of Eric Hobsbawm, "state education transformed people into citizens of a specific country: 'peasants into Frenchmen.' "[90] In the Information Age, education will be privatized and individualized. It will no longer be lumbered with the heavy political baggage that characterized education during the industrial period. Nationalism will not be constantly massaged into every corner of the mind's life.

The move to the Internet and the World Wide Web will also reduce the importance of location in commerce. It will create individual addresses that are not bounded territorially. Satellite-based digital telephone services will evolve beyond location-based land-line systems sharing a common international dialing code. The individual will have his own, unique global telephone address, like an Internet address, that will reach him wherever he happens to be. In due course, national postal monopolies will collapse, allowing privatized mail delivery by worldwide services with no particular ties to any existing nation-state.

These and other apparently small steps will help free the ordinary consumer, as well as the cognitive elite, from rote identification with the nation-state. The demystification of citizenship will be most dramatically accelerated by the emergence of practical alternatives to dealing within bounded territories monopolized by states. The building blocks of the cyber-economy—cybermoney, cyberbanking, and an unregulated global cybermarket in securities—are almost bound to come into existence on a large scale. As they do, the capacity of greedy governments to confiscate the wealth of "citizens" will shrivel.

While the leading states will no doubt attempt to enforce a cartel to preserve high taxes and fiat money by cooperating to limit encryption and prevent citizens from escaping their domains, the states will ultimately fail. The most productive people on the planet will find their way to economic freedom. It is unlikely that the state will even be effective at keeping people penned up where they can be physically held to ransom. The ineffectiveness of efforts to bar illegal immigrants convincingly shows that nation-states will be unable to seal their borders to prevent successful people from escaping. The rich will be at least as enterprising in getting out as would-be taxi drivers and waiters are at getting in.

For the first time since the medieval period of fragmented sovereignty, borders will not be clearly demarcated. As we explored earlier, there will be no distinct territory in which many future financial transactions will occur. Instead of accepting an inheritance of liabilities on the basis of an accident of birth, increasing numbers of Sovereign Individuals will take advantage of this ambiguity to desert their tax liabilities, moving beyond citizenship to become customers. They will negotiate private tax treaties as customers, along the lines now available in Switzerland, as analyzed in Chapter 8. A typical private tax treaty negotiated with the French-speaking Swiss cantons allows an individual or family to reside in exchange for a fixed annual tax payment of 50,000 Swiss francs (currently about $45,000). Note that this is not a flat-*rate* tax, but a flat amount of tax fixed without respect to income. If your annual income is 50,000 Swiss francs ($45,000), you should not enter into such a private tax treaty because your tax rate would be 100 percent. At an income of 500,000 Swiss francs, your rate is 10 percent. At SF5,000,000, the rate is just 1 percent. At SF50 million, your tax rate is just 1/10th of 1 percent. If this seems an incredibly good deal compared to a marginal rate of 58 percent in New York City, that is merely a measure of how predatory and monopolistic the pricing of government services generally became during the industrial period.

In fact, 50,000 Swiss francs is an ample annual payment for the necessary and useful services of government. The Swiss surely make a large profit from serving every millionaire who moves in and pays them 50,000 Swiss francs annually for the privilege. In many cases, the government's marginal cost to have another millionaire living in the jurisdiction is approximately zero. Therefore, its annual profit on the transaction will approach 50,000 Swiss francs. Any service that can be undercut and still allow the low-cost provider approximately a 100 percent profit is monopolized and overpriced to an extreme. What is remarkable is not that the rate of tax charged should fall as a percentage of income in this particular case, but that it should ever have seemed "fair" that different persons should pay wildly different amounts for the services of government during the twentieth century. This is particularly odd in that those who use government services the most pay the least, and those who use them least pay the most. All of them will provide an advantage as a domicile over the United States worth tens of millions over a lifetime to any high-income American. Unless U.S. taxes are reformed to become more competitive with those of other jurisdictions, and are no longer levied on the basis of nationality, thinking persons will renounce U.S. citizenship, notwithstanding the obstacles imposed by Clinton's exit tax, to take up passports that entail less onerous liabilities.

Governments in the industrial era priced their services on the basis of the success of the taxpayer, rather than in relation to the costs or value of any services provided. The movement to commercial pricing of government service will lead to more satisfactory protection at a far lower price than that imposed by conventional nation-states.

Citizenship Goes the Way of Chivalry

In short, citizenship is destined to go the way of chivalry. As the basis upon which protection is provided is reorganized once again, the rationalizations and motivating ideologies that complement the system will also inevitably change. Half a millennium ago, at the close of the Middle Ages, when the provision of protection in return for personal service generally ceased to be a paying proposition, people responded in the predictable way. They abandoned chivalry. Sworn oaths and personal fealty ceased to be taken as seriously as they had been for the previous five centuries. Now information technology promises to be equally subversive of citizenship. The nation-state and the claims of nationalism will be demystified just as the claims of the monopoly Church were demystified five centuries ago.

While reactionaries will respond by attempting to vilify innovators and revive nationalist sentiment, we doubt that the megapolitically defunct nation-state can exert a sufficiently strong tug of loyalties to withstand the competitive pressures unleashed by information technology. Most thinking individuals in a world of bankrupt governments will prefer to be well treated as customers of protection services, rather than be plundered as citizens of nation-states.

The wealthy OECD countries impose heavy tax and regulatory burdens upon individuals doing business within their borders. These costs may have been tolerable when the OECD nation-states were the only jurisdictions in which one could do business and reside at a reasonable level of comfort. That day has passed. The premium paid to be taxed and regulated as a resident of the richest nation-states no longer repays its cost. It will be ever less tolerable as competition between jurisdictions intensifies. Those with the earnings ability and capital to meet the competitive challenges of the Information Age will be able to locate anywhere and do business anywhere. With a choice of domiciles, only the most patriotic or stupid will continue to reside in high-tax countries.

For this reason, it is to be expected that one or more nation-states will undertake covert action to subvert the appeal of transience. Travel could be effectively discouraged by biological warfare, such as the outbreak of a deadly epidemic. This could not only discourage the desire to travel, it could also give jurisdictions throughout the globe an excuse to seal their borders and limit immigration.

The Drawback of Nationality Taxation

Unless there is an astonishing and almost miraculous change in policies, the successful investor or entrepreneur in the Information Age will pay a lifetime penalty of tens of millions, hundreds of millions, or even billions of dollars to reside in the countries with fiscal policies like those that have enjoyed the highest living standards during the twentieth century.

Absent a radical change, the penalty will be highest for Americans. The United States is one of just three jurisdictions on the planet that impose taxes based upon nationality rather than residence. The other two are the Philippines, a former U.S. colony, and Eritrea, one of whose exiled leaders fell under the spell of the IRS during its long rebellion against Ethiopian rule. Eritrea now imposes a nationality tax of 3 percent. While that is a pale imitation of the U.S. rates, even that burden makes Eritrean citizenship a liability in the Information Age. Current law makes U.S. citizenship even a larger liability. The IRS has become one of America's leading exports. More than any other country, the United States reaches to the corners of the earth to extract income from its nationals.

If a 747 jetliner filled with one investor from each jurisdiction on earth touched down in a newly independent country, and each investor risked $1,000 in a start-up venture in the new economy, the American would face a far higher tax than anyone else on any gains. Special, penal taxation of foreign investment, exemplified by the so-called PFIC taxation, plus the U.S. nationality tax, can result in tax liabilities of 200 percent or more on long-term assets held outside the United States. A successful American could reduce his total lifetime tax burden as a citizen of *any* of more than 280 other jurisdictions on the globe.

The United States has the globe's most predatory, soak-the-rich tax system. Americans living in the United States or abroad are treated more like assets and less like customers than citizens of any other country. The American tax regime is therefore more anachronistic and less compatible with success in the Information Age than those of even the notoriously high-tax welfare states of Scandinavia. Citizens of Denmark or Sweden face few legal obstacles in realizing their growing technological autonomy as individuals. Should they wish to negotiate their own tax rates, they are free to elect to pay taxes in Switzerland by private treaty, or move to Bermuda and pay no income taxes at all. A Swede or a Dane who wishes to pay high taxes because he believes the Scandinavian welfare state is worth what it costs is actually making a choice. He can elect to be taxed at any rate that prevails in any other jurisdiction in the civilized or uncivilized world. To change his tax rate, he need only move. Technology makes such a choice easier by the moment. Yet that option is denied to Americans.

Holding a U.S. passport is destined to become a major drawback to realizing the opportunities for individual autonomy made possible by the Information Revolution. Being born an American during the industrial period was a lucky accident. Even in the early stages of the Information Age, it has become a multimillion-dollar liability.

To see how great a liability, consider this comparison. Under reasonable assumptions, a New Zealander with the same pretax performance as the average of the top 1 percent of American taxpayers would pay so much less in taxes that the compounding of his tax savings alone would make him richer than the American would ever be. At the end of a lifetime, the New Zealander would have $73 million more to leave to his children or grandchildren. And New Zealand is not even a recognized tax haven. More than forty other jurisdictions impose lower income and capital taxation than New Zealand. If our argument is right, the number of low-tax jurisdictions is likely to rise rather than fall. All of them will provide an advantage as a domicile over the United States, worth tens of millions, if not hundreds of millions, over a lifetime. Unless U.S. taxes are reformed to become more competitive with those of other jurisdictions, and are no longer levied on the basis of nationality, thinking persons will renounce U.S. citizenship, notwithstanding the obstacles imposed by Clinton's exit tax.

The competitive conditions of the Information Age will render it possible to earn high incomes almost anywhere. In effect, the locational monopolies that nation-states exploited to impose extremely high taxes will be broken by technology. They are already breaking down. As they erode further, competitive pressures are almost bound to drive the most enterprising and able to flee countries that tax too much. As former *Economist* editor Norman Macrae put it, such countries "will be inhabited residually, mainly by dummies."

"[B]y the year 2012, projected outlays for entitlements and interest on the national debt will consume all tax revenues collected by the federal government. . . . There will not be one cent left over for education, children's programs, highways, national defense, or any other discretionary program."

—BIPARTISAN U.S. COMMISSION ON ENTITLEMENT AND TAX REFORM

The flight of the wealthy from advanced welfare states will happen at just the wrong time demographically. Early in the twenty-first century, large aging populations in Europe and North America will find themselves with insufficient savings to meet medical expenses and finance their lifestyles in retirement. For example, fully 65 percent of Americans have no savings for retirement at all. None. And those who do save save far too little. The average American will reach sixty-five facing expected medical bills of more than $200,000 before death and with a net worth of less than $75,000. Even the minority with private pensions are unlikely to be comfortable. The average pension will replace only 20 percent of preretirement income. Most of the assets of the typical retiree are not real wealth but "transcendental capital," the expected value of transfer payments. Most people have been conditioned to rely upon these transfer payments to make up the gap in their private resources. The catch is that they are unlikely to be forthcoming. Pay-as-you-go systems will lack the cash flow or resources to make good on them. A study conducted by Neil Howe showed that even if pretax incomes in the United States were to rise faster than they have over the past twenty years, average after-tax incomes in America would have to be pushed down by 59 percent by 2040 in order to finance Social Security and government medical programs at current levels.

This is not a problem that can be manipulated around the margins. The welfare state faces insolvency. Its financing predicament is even more acute in Europe than in North America. Italy is perhaps the worst case, followed closely by Sweden and the other Nordic welfare states that set the standard for generous terms in income-support programs. The *Financial Times* estimates that if "the present value of Italian state pensions is included, the country's public sector debt would rise to more than 200 percent of GDP." [91]

Indebtedness at such levels is all but mathematically hopeless. A comprehensive study of commercial indebtedness of Toronto Stock Exchange companies undertaken a few years ago showed that few survive debt ratios one-quarter as extreme as those facing the leading welfare states today. [92] Put simply, they are broke. As this reality is faced, grudgingly but inevitably, literally trillions in unfunded entitlement obligations will be written off.

Such is the logic of the cybereconomy. One possible hitch may be simple inertia, the nesting instinct that makes humans reluctant to pick up stakes and move. If there are other hitches, they may be hardwired into human nature. The economic logic of deploying assets in cyberspace could run counter to the biologic expressed in the ingrained suspicions of outsiders. Children in every culture show an aversion to strangers. Opponents of the commercialization of sovereignty will do their best to inflame doubts about the new global culture of the Information Age and the demise of the nation-state that it implies. Another possible hitch arising from epigenesis, or genetically influenced motivational factors, is the prospect that the "losers and left-behinds" will respond to developments that undermine the nation-state with the fury of hunter-gatherers protecting their families. In an environment where disoriented and alienated individuals will have increased power to disrupt and destroy, a backlash against the information economy could prove to be violent and unpleasant.

"Historically, collective violence has flowed regularly out of the central political processes of Western countries. People seeking to seize, hold, or realign the levers of power have continually engaged in collective violence as part of their struggles. The oppressed have struck in the name of justice, the privileged in the name of order, those between in the name of fear. Great shifts in the arrangements of power have ordinarily produced—and have often depended on—exceptional moments of collective violence."[93]

—CHARLES TILLY

VIOLENCE IN PERSPECTIVE

There are at least two contending theories about what precipitates violence in conditions of change. Historian Charles Tilly summarizes one theory: "[T]he stimulus to collective violence comes largely from the anxieties people experience when established institutions fall apart. If misery or danger compounds the anxiety, runs the theory, the reaction becomes all the more violent." In Tilly's view, however, violence is not so much a product of "anxiety" as it is a far more rational attempt to bully authorities into "meeting their responsibilities" motivated by a "sense of justice denied." According to Tilly's interpretation, "large structural changes" tend to stimulate collective violence of a "political" nature. "Instead of constituting a sharp break from 'normal' political life, furthermore, violent struggles tend to accompany, complement, and extend organized, peaceful attempts by the same people to accomplish their objectives. They belong to the same world as nonviolent contention." [94]

Whichever theory of violence is more correct, prospects for social peace during the Great Transformation would appear to be limited. The collapse of the nation-state surely counts as a conspicuous example of an "established institution falling apart." Therefore, anxieties are likely to be in full flower, as will the political inspiration for violence. This could be especially true in the leading welfare states, where populations are accustomed to relative income equality. Given that populations in the early stages of the information economy will have come of age during the industrial period, when political authorities did have the capacity to answer grievances with material benefits, it is reasonable to expect the "left-behinds" to continue to demand material benefits. It will probably take a slow, painful tutorial in the realities of the

cybereconomy before OECD populations are weaned away from expectations of being able to compel income redistribution on a large scale. In either
case, whether violence arises from "anxiety" or as a more calculating effort
to harness the benefits of systematic compulsion, conditions would appear
to make violence likely.

Constituencies of Losers

The collapse of coerced income redistribution is bound to upset those who
expect to be on the receiving end of the trillions in transfer programs. Mostly,
these will be "the losers or left-behinds," persons without the skills to
compete in global markets. Like the pensioners of the former Soviet Union
who formed the core of Zuganov's Communist support, the disappointed
pensioners of the dying welfare states will form a reactionary constituency
keen to prevent the sovereignty of the nation-states from being privatized,
thereby depriving the state of its license to steal. As they realize that governments they formerly controlled are losing their sovereignty over resources
and the ability to compel large-scale income transfers, they will become as
adamant as French civil servants in fighting arithmetic.

You may remember the violent reaction that greeted Prime Minister Alain
Juppe's quite modest proposals to scale back "demographically unsustainable" retirement benefits of state workers and economize the operations of
the nationalized railroad system. Symbolic of the absurdity of the *État-
Providence,* as the French call their social welfare system, is the rule that
allows "engineers on the computerized, high-speed TGV trains to retire at
age fifty, just like their predecessors who toiled on the coal-fired
locomotives. . . ."[95] A rowdy reaction to cutbacks of unsustainable benefits
is a distinct possibility in any OECD country. And even where populations
respond less angrily, you can expect the probable losers to do whatever is
within their power to forestall the erosion of state compulsion.

This will lead to some surprising twists. In the United States, for example,
nativist sentiment has historically been tinged with more than a slight tinc-
ture of racism. This is a tradition that began with the nineteenth-century
"White Caps" and Ku Klux Klan. Yet blacks, as a group, are major beneficiaries of income transfers, affirmative action, and other fruits of political
compulsion. They are also disproportionately represented in the U.S. military. Therefore, they are likely to emerge, along with blue-collar whites, as
among the most fervent partisans of American nationalism.

Politicians willing to cater to the insecurities of those whose relative
talents fall well down on Ammon's turnip will come noisily to the fore in
almost every country. From Slobodan Milosevic in Serbia to Pat Buchanan
in the United States to Winston Peters in New Zealand, to Necmettin Erba-

kan of Turkey's fundamentalist Islamic Welfare Party, demagogues will rail against the globalization of markets, immigration, and freedom of investment. Particular animus will be directed toward the rich and immigrants by those who imagine themselves to be the "global economy's casualties." In the words of Andrew Heal, they will "depise the entry of immigrants whose main entry criterion appears to be their wealth—or their lack of it, which, the specious logic goes, makes them welfare burdens." [96]

Fear of Freedom

The prospect of the dissappearance of the nation-state early in the new millennium seems timed to effect the maximum disruption in the lives of suggestible people. This will lead to widespread unpleasantness. More than a few observers have recognized a pattern of reaction that is common among those who feel left out by the prospect of a borderless world. As the larger, more inclusive national grouping begins to break down, with the more mobile "information elite" globalizing their affairs, the "losers and left-behinds" fall back upon membership in an ethnic subgroup, a tribe, a gang, a religious or linguistic minority. Partly, this is a practical and pragmatic reaction to the collapse of services, including law and order, formerly provided by the state. For persons with few marketable resources, it often proves difficult to purchase access to market alternatives to failed public services.

The transformation of what were formerly treated as public goods, such as education, provision of clean water, and neighborhood policing, into private goods is obviously easier to manage for those with sufficient resources to purchase high-quality private alternatives. For those wanting cash, however, the most practical alternative is often to depend upon kin, or join a mutual-aid group organized along ethnic lines, like the old ethnic Chinese "Hokkien" of Southeast Asia, or through a religious congregation. In those parts of the world where dynamic, proselytizing religions are active, part of the popularity of their programs depends on the fact that they tend to hark back to premodern mechanisms for providing social welfare and public goods. For example, Moslem-led vigilante groups have played a leading role in combating violent gangs in Cape Town, South Africa. [97] But as practical and pragmatic as such ethnic and religious organization of help can be, more is involved in the reactionary response to the withering of the state. There also seems to be a strong psychological component in the reaction against globalization.

The argument is not dissimilar to the psychological explanation for the appeal of fascism developed by Erich Fromm in his famous work *Escape from Freedom*, first published in 1941. [98] According to Fromm, social mobility introduced by capitalism had destroyed the fixed identities of traditional village life. The son of a farmer no longer knew that he would inevitably be a farmer, or even that he would be bound to live scrabbling to harvest a crop on the same poor ground that his father tilled. He now had a broad choice of occupation. He could become a schoolteacher, a merchant, a soldier; study medicine or take to the sea. Even as a farmer, he could emigrate to the United States, Canada, or Argentina and make a life far from the home of his forebears. This freedom that capitalism provided to people "to create their own identities" proved scary to those who were not prepared to make creative use of it. As Billig said, they yearned "for the security of a solid identity," and were "drawn towards the simplicities of nationalist and fascist propaganda." [99] Equally as Billig writes of the twilight of the industrial era, "There is a global psychology, which strikes the nation from above, withering loyalties with a free play of identities. And then, there is the hot psychology of caste or tribe, which hits at the soft underbelly of the state with a powerfully intolerant commitment and emotional ferocity." [100]

Andrew Heal views the same phenomenon from another perspective. He sees two great "global political and economic trends. . . . Trend one is the growth of the global economy. . . . The second is the rise of nationalist, ethnic and regionalist sentiment, whether it be Maori, Scottish, Welsh or from anti-immigrant factions, who even as their governments push them towards new, borderless horizons, pull themselves ever so hard the opposite way." [101] However you choose to look at them, whether as major "trends" or "psychological themes," it is clear that a strong reactionary sentiment in favor of nationalism and against the fall of borders and the deepening of markets is gathering its voice worldwide.

MULTICULTURALISM AND VICTIMIZATION

In its twilight, with a faltering capacity to redeem promises of something for nothing from an empty pocket, the welfare state found it expedient to foster new myths of discrimination. Many categories of officially "oppressed" people were designated, especially in North America. Individuals in groups with designated status as "victims" were informed that they were not responsible for shortcomings in their own lives. Rather, the fault was said to lie with "dead white males" of European descent, and the oppressive power structure allegedly rigged to the disadvantage of the excluded groups. To be black, female, homosexual, Latino, francophone, disabled, etc. was to be entitled to recompense for past repression and discrimination.

If Lasch's argument is to be believed, the purpose of heightening a sense of victimization was to undermine nations, making it easier for the new, footloose information elite to escape the commitments and duties of citizenship. We are not entirely convinced that the new elite, especially most of those in the mass media, are cunning enough to reason to such a posture. It would almost be reassuring to feel that they were. We see the growth of victimization as mainly an attempt to buy social peace by not only widening membership in the meritocracy as Lasch argues, but also by reconstituting the rationalizations for income redistribution. The new sport of victimology emerged in its most exaggerated form in North America because information technology penetrated more deeply there. We suspect, however, that new myths of discrimination will be common, to one degree or another, in all industrial societies in their senile state. The multiethnic welfare states in North America were simply more vulnerable to the temptation to foist the costs of income redistribution on the private sector. They were able to do this, while inflaming a sense of grievance and entitlement, by blaming the structure of society as a whole, and white men in general, for the economic shortcomings of various subcultures within society.

The Megapolitics of Innovation

Even before information technology began to threaten "creative destruction" of the industrial economy, it had clearly antiquated much of the cherished myth of Marxists and socialists. We examined the megapolitics of innovation in a previous chapter. The point we emphasized there is of importance in placing the social impact of the Information Revolution into perspective. The precedent of technology expanding employment opportunities in recent centuries seems like a dependable rule of economic life, but it need not be. It is possible for earnings to be concentrated in the hands of a prosperous minority.

REAL WAGES DROP BY 50 PERCENT

That is indeed what happened during the first two centuries or more of the modern period. From the time of the Gunpowder Revolution around 1500 until 1700, real incomes for the bottom 60–80 percent of the population in most of Western Europe fell by 50 percent or more.[102] In many places, real income continued to fall until 1750, and did not recover to 1500 levels until 1850.

Unlike the experience of the past 250 years, the income gains of the first half of the modern period, a time of dramatic expansion of Western European economies, were concentrated among a small minority. The current innovation of information technologies is quite different from the innovation of industrial technologies that the world experienced in recent centuries. The difference lies in the fact that most current technological innovations with labor-saving characteristics tend to create skilled tasks and reduce scale economies. This is the opposite of the experience since about 1750.

Industrial innovation tended to open job opportunities for the unskilled and increase the scale economies of enterprise. This not only raised the earnings of the poor without any effort on their part, it also tended to increase the power of political systems, making them more capable of withstanding unrest. Those who were displaced by mechanization and automation in the early phases of the Industrial Revolution tended to be skilled artisans, craftsmen and journeymen, rather than unskilled labor. This was certainly true in the textile industry, the first to employ mechanization and power equipment on a large scale, which led to a violent reaction by Luddites, who destroyed textile machinery and murdered factory owners during a rampage in the early nineteenth century. On the other hand, the followers of Captain Swing, the mythical leader of an 1830 rebellion in southeastern England, were day laborers. Their demands included imposing a levy on the local rich to provide them with money or beer, imposing a wage increase upon the local employers of day labor, and "destroying, or demanding the destruction of, new farm machinery, especially threshers" that reduced the call among farmers for rural day labor.[103]

Contrary to the romantic jabberings of Marxists and others who have transformed the violent opponents of labor-saving technology into heroes, they were an unpleasant and violent lot who opposed the introduction of technology that raised living standards worldwide for purely selfish reasons.

While the violent followers of Ned Ludd and Captain Swing jeopardized public order for many months in England, once suppressed by central authority their movements were bound to miscarry. The poor, unskilled majority were unlikely to be long attracted to a cause that promised to destroy machinery that offered them jobs and also raised their living standards by lowering the cost of items they needed, such as warm clothing and bread.

Higher Incomes for the Unskilled

Over time, industrial and agricultural automation was attractive to the have-nots because it created earnings opportunities for them and lowered their cost of living. New tools allowed those without skills to produce goods of quality equal to those made by persons of high skills. A genius and a moron on the assembly line would both produce the same product, and earn the same wage.

Over the past two centuries, industrial automation dramatically raised wages for unskilled work, especially in the small part of the world where conditions first allowed capitalism to flourish. The large scale of advanced industrial enterprise not only rewarded unskilled labor with unprecedented wages, it also facilitated income redistribution.

The welfare state arose as a logical consequence of the technology of industrialism. Because of their large scale and high capital costs, the leading industrial employers were the easiest targets to tax. And they could be relied upon to keep records and enforce the garnishment of wages that made the income tax technologically feasible as it had not been in previous centuries when economies were more decentralized. The net effect was that the growth of scale economies promoted by industrial innovation made governments richer, and presumably better able to maintain order.

The Process Is Reversed

In our judgment, the opposite is happening today. Information technology is raising earnings opportunities for the skilled and undermining institutions that operate at a large scale, including the nation-state.

This points to another irony of the Information Age—namely, the schizoid and fundamentally obstructionist attitude of critics of the free market toward the rise and fall of industrial jobs. In the early stages of industrialism, they were choked up about the supposed evil of industrial jobs, which lured landless peasants away from "the world we have lost." To hear the critics tell it, the advent of factory jobs was an unprecedented evil and "exploitation" of the working class. But now it appears that the only thing worse than the advent of factory jobs is their disappearance. The great-grandchildren of those who wailed about the introduction of factory jobs are now wailing about the shortage of factory jobs that offer high pay for low-skilled work.

The one coherent thread that runs through these complaints is a steadfast resistance to technological innovation and market change. In the early stages of the factory system, this resistance led to violence. It may again.

And not because capitalists are "exploiting the workers." The advent of the computer as a paradigm technology revealed the absurdity of that claim. It might have been half-credible for the inattentive to suppose that a barely literate auto worker had somehow been "exploited" in the production of an automobile by owners who conceived and financed the businesses that employed workers. The crucial role of conceptual capital in the production and marketing of tangible products was less obvious than it is in the output of the Information Age, which clearly involves mental work. Therefore, the plausibility of the assumption that entrepreneurs had somehow seized the value of information products actually created by workers was much diminished. Where the value was clearly created through mental work, as in the production of consumer software, it was little short of preposterous to suppose that it was actually the product of anyone other than the skilled persons who conceived it. In fact, far from assuming that the workers created all value, as Marxists and socialists did through most of the nineteenth and twentieth centuries, the obvious and growing trend away from unskilled employment gave rise to a spreading worry about quite the opposite problem—whether unskilled laborers still had any economic contribution to make.[104]

Hence the migration of the rationale for income redistribution away from "exploitation," which assumed a productive competence for those with low incomes, to "discrimination," which did not. "Discrimination," however, was alleged to account for the failure of those with low skills to develop more valuable ones.

This discrimination was also said to justify imposition of nonoptimal hiring criteria and other standards for opening "opportunity," or, more precisely, redistributing income to the lagging groups. In the United States, for example, race-based norming of achievement and aptitude tests allowed blacks to outscore white and Asian applicants while registering lower objective scores. Through this method and others, governments obliged employers to hire more blacks and other officially "victimized" groups at higher wages than might otherwise have been the case. Anyone who failed to comply faced costly court actions, including lawsuits involving large punitive damages.

The point of designating victims was not to incubate paranoid delusions of persecution and grievance among important subgroups of industrial society, or to subsidize the spread of counterproductive values. It was to relieve the bankrupt state of the fiscal pressures of redistributing income. Inculcating delusions of persecution was merely an unfortunate side effect. Ironically, the surge in concern about "discrimination" coincided with the early stages of a technological revolution that is bound to make actual arbitrary discrimination far less of a problem than it has ever been before. No one on the Internet knows or cares whether the author of a new software program is black, white, male, female, homosexual, or a vegetarian dwarf.

While the reality of discrimination is bound to be less oppressive in the future, that will not necessarily relieve the pressure for "reparations" to compensate various real or imagined wrongs. Every society, whatever its objective circumstances, gives rise to one or more rationalizations for income redistribution. They range from the subtle to the absurd, from the biblical injunction to love your neighbor as yourself, to the invocations of black magic. Sorcery, witchcraft, and the evil eye are the flip side of religious feeling, the spiritual equivalent of the Inland Revenue or the IRS. When people cannot be moved by love to subsidize the poor, the poor themselves will try to see that they are moved by fear. Sometimes this takes the form of an outright shakedown, a knife to the throat, a gun to the head. At other times, the threat is disguised or fanciful. It is no coincidence that most of the "witches" of the early modern period were widows or unmarried women with few resources. They terrorized their neighbors with curses that not infrequently moved those neighbors to pay up. It is by no means obvious that those who did so were only the superstitious. The malevolent intent of the evil eye was not a superstition but a fact. Even a poor woman could loose cattle or set someone's house ablaze. In that sense, the witchcraft trials of the early modern period were not altogether so preposterous as they seem. While the punishments were cruel and no doubt many innocents suffered from the hallucinations of neighbors under the influence of ergot poisoning, the prosecution of witches can be understood as an indirect way of prosecuting extortion.

We expect a return of extortion motivated by a desire to share in the rewards of achievement as the Information Age unfolds. Groups that feel aggrieved over past discrimination are unlikely to quickly relinquish their apparently valuable status as victims simply because their claims on society become less justified or harder to enforce. They will continue to press their claims until evidence in the local environment leaves no doubt that they will no longer be rewarded.

The growth of sociopathic behavior among Afro-Americans and Afro-Canadians tells you that. It says that there is little balance between black anger and a realistic appraisal of the extent to which black problems are self-inflicted consequences of antisocial behavior. Black anger has risen, even as black lifestyles have grown more dysfunctional. Out-of-wedlock births have soared. Educational attainment has fallen. Growing percentages of young blacks are implicated in criminal activities, to the point where there are now more black men in penitentiaries than in colleges.

These perverse results may have had the temporary effect of increasing the flow of resources to underclass communities during the twilight of industrialism by raising the shakedown threat against society as a whole. But the effect could be only temporary. By eliminating the beneficial impact of competition in challenging underachievers to conform to productive norms, the welfare state has helped to create legions of dysfunctional, paranoid, and poorly acculturated people, the social equivalent of a powder keg. The death of the nation-state and the disappearance of income redistribution on a large scale will no doubt lead some among the more pyschopathic of these unhappy souls to strike out against anyone who appears more prosperous than they. Therefore, it is reasonable to suppose that social peace will be in jeopardy as the Information Age unfolds, especially in North America and in multiethnic enclaves in Western Europe.

> *"We will never lay down Arms [till] The House of Commons passes an Act to put down all Machinery hurtful to Commonality, and repeal that to hang Frame Breakers. But We. We petition no more—that won't do—fighting must.*
> *"Signed by the General of the Army of Redressers*
> *Ned Ludd Clerk*
> *"Redressers for ever, Amen"*[105]

Neo-Luddites

Given past experience of antitechnological rebellion in the early nineteenth century and the long tradition of collective violence in both Europe and North America, no one should be surprised to see a neo-Luddite attack upon information technology and those who use it. The Luddites, referred to earlier, were cloth workers concentrated in West Yorkshire, England, who launched a terrorist campaign against automated cropping machines and the factory owners who adopted them in 1811–12.[106] With blackened faces, the Luddites raged through West Yorkshire, burning factories and murdering factory owners who dared to adopt the new technology. Most of the violence was the work of "croppers," highly skilled artisans whose labor in wielding gigantic scissors weighing up to fifty pounds was previously a crucial part of the production of woolen cloth. But the finishing work that the croppers performed, "raising the nap by teasels and cropping the cloth by shears," was, as Robert Reid, author of the best and most comprehensive discussion of the Luddite rising, *Land of Lost Content: The Luddite Revolt 1812,* observed, "too simple not to be mechanized."[107] The design of one such mechanized cropping machine had been sketched out by Leonardo da Vinci. Yet Leonardo's design for automatic cropping languished for centuries. Finally, by 1787, a device like Leonardo's was reinvented and brought into production in England. As Reid notes, "so long had all the constituent parts of the technology been known that the surprise is that it had not been introduced earlier. . . . The new equipment of the Industrial Revolution required so little strength and skill to use that many job openings were taken by women and young children, initially at low wages. One of these new machines, even operated by the relatively unskilled, could now crop in eighteen hours what a skilled cropper using hand shears took eighty-eight hours to do."[108]

Note that the workers who railed at mechanization were quite discriminating in their opposition to new technology. They only attacked and fought those technologies that displaced their own jobs or reduced the demand for skilled labor. When an entrepreneur named William Cooke introduced carpet-weaving machinery into the West Yorkshire district, this sparked no violence whatever. No attempts were made to burn Cooke's mill, or destroy his machinery, much less murder him. As Robert Reid explains in his history of the Luddite uprisings, Cooke's new technology excited no opposition because carpets were a product "in which no one in the valley had until then specialized." [109] Reid continues, "Because Cooke introduced a new product and created employment founded on no traditional practices whatever, his mill flourished. . . ." [110] This is an example with important application for the future. It suggests that thinking entrepreneurs in the next millennium will first introduce dramatic labor-saving automation in regions without a tradition of producing whatever product or service is in question.

If the past is a guide, the most violent of the terrorists of the early decades of the new millennium will not be homeless paupers but displaced workers who formerly enjoyed middle-class incomes and status. This was certainly the case in the Luddite uprising of 1812, in which the bulk of the Luddites were not an impoverished proletariat but skilled artisans who were accustomed to earning incomes five times or more greater than those of an average worker. The equivalent group today would probably be displaced factory workers. Unfortunately, scanning the demographics of most OECD countries, one finds more areas than not that could be highlighted as potential sites of violent reaction.

The world's nation-states will seek to counteract the cybereconomy and Sovereign Individuals who are able to take advantage of it to accumulate wealth. A furious nationalist reaction will sweep the world. Part and parcel of it will be an antitechonological reaction equivalent to the Luddite and other antitechnology rebellions in Britain during the Industrial Revolution. This should be considered closely, because it could be a key to the evolution of governance in the new millennium. One of the crucial challenges of the great transformation ahead will be maintaining order in the face of escalating violence, or alternatively escaping its brunt. Individuals and firms that are particularly associated with the advent of the Information Age, including those in Silicon Valley, and even the suppliers of electricity required to power the new technology, will have to maintain a special diligence against free-lance, neo-Luddite terrorism.

A lunatic like the Unabomber is unfortunately likely to stimulate brigades of imitators as frustration with falling incomes and resentment against achievement mount. We suspect much of the violence to come will involve bombings. As reported in the *New York Times,* domestic terrorism across the United States soared during the 1990s. "They increased by more than 50 percent in the last five years, and have nearly tripled over the last decade. The number of criminal explosions and attempts went from 1,103 in 1985 to 3,163 in 1994. . . . [I]n small towns and suburban neighborhoods, as well [as] among inner-city street gangs, there has been a proliferation of a sort of garden variety bomber." [111]

Defense Becomes a Private Good

Notwithstanding the penal taxes imposed by nation-states as a price of protection, they are unlikely to provide it effectively in the years to come. The falling scale of violence implied by the new information technology makes the provision of a massive military establishment far less useful. This implies not only a declining decisiveness in warfare, meaning that states will be less able to actually protect citizens, it also implies that the apparent extraterritorial hegemony of the United States as the world's superpower will be less effective in the next century than the hegemony of Great Britain was in the nineteenth century. Until the onset of World War I, power could be effectively and decisively projected from the core to the periphery at relatively low cost. In the twenty-first century, the threats that major powers pose to the safety of life and property will necessarily diminish with the return to violence. Falling returns to violence suggest that nation-states or empires capable of exercising military power on a large scale are unlikely to survive or come into being in the Information Age.

As the fiscal requirement for provision of an adequate defense falls, it will become ever more credible to treat protection services as if they were private goods. After all, security threats on a diminished scale will be increasingly defensible by security forces of the kind that can be engaged commercially, such as by employing walls, fences, and security perimeters to screen out troublemakers. Further, a wealthy individual or firm may be able to afford to hire protection against most threats that would be likely to arise in the Information Age. At the margin, the diminished scale of military threats will increase the danger of anarchy, or competitive violence within a single territory. But it will also intensify competition among jurisdictions in the provision of protection on competitive terms. This will mean intensified shopping among jurisdictions for protection services, passport and consular services, and the provision of justice.

In the long run, of course, Sovereign Individuals will probably be able to travel on nongovernmental documents, issued like letters of credit by private agencies and affinity groups. It is not farfetched to suppose that a group will emerge as a kind of merchant republic of cyberspace, organized like the medieval Hanseatic League, to facilitate negotiation of private treaties and contracts among jurisdictions as well as to provide protection for its members. Imagine a special passport issued by the League of Sovereign Individuals, identifying the holder as a person under the protection of the league.

Such a document, if it comes into existence, will be only a temporary artifact of the transition away from the nation-state and the bureaucratic age it fostered. Before the modern period, passports were generally unnecessary to pass frontiers, which were loosely defined in most cases. While letters of safe conduct were sometimes employed in medieval frontier societies, they were normally issued by the authorities whose realm was to be visited, rather than the jurisdiction from which the traveler originated. More important than a passport were letters of introduction and credit, which allowed a traveler to find lodging and negotiate business. That day will come again. Ultimately, persons of substance will be able to travel without documents at all. They will be able to identify themselves on a foolproof biometric basis through voice-recognition systems or retinal scanning that recognizes them uniquely.

In short, we expect that sometime in the first half of the next century the world will experience the genuine privatization of sovereignty. This will accompany conditions that could be expected to shrivel the realm of compulsion to its logical minimum. Yet to the secular inquisitors and reactionaries of the next millennium, the placing of the once "sacred" attributes of nationality onto a market footing to be bought and sold as a matter of cost-benefit calculation will be both infuriating and threatening.

We argue in this book that it will no longer take a nation-state to fight an Information War. Such wars could be undertaken by computer programmers deploying large numbers of "bots" or digital servants. Bill Gates already possesses a greater capacity to detonate logic bombs in vulnerable systems globally than most of the world's nation-states. In the age of the Information War, any software company, or even the Church of Scientology, would be a more formidable antagonist than the accumulated threat posed by the majority of the states with seats in the United Nations.

This loss of power by nation-states is a logical consequence of the advent of low-cost, advanced computational capacity. Microprocessing both reduces returns to violence and creates for the first time a competitive market for the protection services for which governments charged monopoly prices in the industrial period.

In the new world of commercialized sovereignty, people will choose their jurisdictions, much as many now choose their insurance carriers or their religions.* Jurisdictions that fail to provide a suitable mix of services, whatever those may be, will face bankruptcy and liquidation, just as incompetent commercial enterprises or failed religious congregations do. Competition will therefore mobilize the efforts of local jurisdictions to improve their capacity to provide services economically and effectively. In this respect, competition between jurisdictions in providing public goods will have a similar impact to that observed in other sectors of life. Competition usually improves customer satisfaction.

---

* See Stephen J. Dubner, "Choosing My Religion," *New York Times Magazine*, March 31, 1996, p. 36f.

COMPETITION AND ANARCHY

It is important to bear in mind that the competition between jurisdictions that we anticipate is not mainly competition among organizations employing violence in the same territory. As indicated earlier, competitive organizations using violence tend to increase the penetration of violence in life, reducing economic opportunity. As Lane put it,

> In the use of violence there were obviously great advantages of scale when competing with rival violence-using enterprises or establishing a territorial monopoly. This fact is basic for the economic analysis of one aspect of government: the violence-using, violence-controlling industry was a natural monopoly, at least on land. Within territorial limits the service it rendered could be produced much more cheaply by a monopoly. To be sure, there have been times when violence-using enterprises competed in demanding payments for protection in almost the same territory, for example, during the Thirty Years' War in Germany. But such a situation was even more uneconomic than would be competition in the same territories between rival telephone systems.[112]

Lane's comment is informative in two respects. Firstly, we agree with his general conclusion that sovereignties will tend to exercise territorial monopolies because doing so will allow them to offer cheaper and more effective protection services. The second interesting aspect of Lane's comment is his dated comparison with monopoly telephone service. Obviously, we now know that telephone systems need not be monopolies. This introduces a caution into the analysis. Changes in technological conditions may to some extent obviate the general conclusion that anarchy within territorial limits is nonviable. For example, if cyberassets grow to large scale in a realm that puts them outside the reach of compulsion, the pricing of protection services may be much less a matter of "demand" and more a matter of market negotiation.

Nonetheless, what we refer to here is something different from generalized anarchy—namely, competition among jurisdictions, each enjoying a monopoly of violence in its own territory. We see such jurisdictions competing to offer the greatest value possible in the cost-effective provision of protection services that appeal to their "customers." Admittedly, there will no doubt be greater ambiguities in the provision of protection services in the Information Age, with more complete private provision of policing and defense services than we have been accustomed to seeing before. Yet the competition we envision is different from a clash of multiple protection agencies battling on a large scale to provide service to different customers in the same territory, which is *anarchy*.

Be that as it may, the multiplication of sovereignties, with individuals assuming more of the role of sovereigns in cases when they accumulate sufficient resources, inevitably implies that there will be an increase in the scope for anarchy in the world. The relations between sovereignties are always anarchic. There is not and never has been a world government regulating the behavior of individual sovereignties, whether ministates, nation-states, or empires. As Jack Hirshleifer writes, "[W]hile associations ranging from primitive tribes to modern nation-states are all governed internally by some form of law, their external relations with one another remain mainly anarchic."[113] When there are more sovereign entities in the world, inevitably more relations transpire in more than one jurisdiction and are therefore anarchic.

It is important to note that anarchy, or the lack of an overwhelming power to arbitrate disputes, is not synonymous with total chaos or the absence of form or organization. Hirshleifer notes that anarchy can be analyzed: "intertribal or international systems also have their regularities and systematic analyzable patterns."[114] In other words, just as "chaos" in mathematics can entail an intricate and highly ordered form of organization, so "anarchy" is not entirely formless or disordered.

Hirshleifer analyzes a number of anarchic settings. These include, in addition to relations among sovereignties, gang warfare in Prohibition-era Chicago and "miners versus claim jumpers in the California gold rush." Note that even though California was part of the United States by the onset of the gold rush in 1849, conditions in the goldfields were properly described as anarchy. As Hirshleifer notes, "[T]he official organs of law were impotent."[115] He argues that topographical conditions in the mountainous camps, plus effective vigilante organization by miners to combat claim jumpers, made it difficult for gangs of outsiders to seize gold mines, in spite of the lack of effective law enforcement. In other words, under certain conditions, valuable property can be effectively protected even under anarchy.

The question is whether Hirshleifer's theoretical analysis of the dynamics of the spontaneous order of the Darwinian "natural economy" is of any relevance to the economy of the Information Age. We suspect it is. While we do not anticipate generalized anarchy, or goldfield conditions everywhere, we do anticipate an increase in the number of anarchic relations in the world system. In light of this expectation, Hirshleifer's argument about conditions under which "two or more anarchic contestants" can "retain viable shares of the socially available resources in equilibrium" is suggestive.[116] In particular, he explores when anarchy is prone to "break down" into *tyranny* or dominance hierarchies, which happens when the anarchic parties can be subdued by an overwhelming authority.

These issues may be more important to understand in the Information Age than they were in the Industrial Age. Part of the reason that the finer distinctions about the dynamics of anarchy were less crucial in recent centuries than they may be in the new millennium is precisely because the returns to violence were rising through the modern period. This meant that massing larger and larger military forces, as nation-states did in recent centuries, tended to make for decisive warfare. Decisive warfare, almost by definition, subdues anarchy by placing contestants for the control of resources under the domination of a more powerful authority. On the other hand, declining decisiveness in battle, which corresponds to the superiority of the defense in military technology, contributes to the dynamic stability of anarchy. Therefore, the apparent impact of information technology in reducing the decisiveness of military action should make the anarchy between minisovereignties more stable and less prone to be replaced through conquest by a large government. Less decisiveness in battle also implies less fighting, which is an encouraging deduction for the world in the Information Age.

Viability

Another important condition for anarchy to be sustained is viability or income adequacy. Individuals who lack a sufficient income to sustain life are likely either to (1) devote a great deal of effort to fighting in order to seize enough resources to survive, or (2) capitulate to another contestant in exchange for food and sustenance. Something similar to this occured with the rise of feudalism during the transformation of the year 1000. We expect increasing numbers of low-income persons in Western countries who previously would have depended upon transfer payments from the state to affiliate with wealthy households as retainers. Nonetheless, the mere fact of inviability by some contenders in a Hobbesian melee (or war of all against all) is inconclusive. As Hirshleifer says, "[T]he mere fact of low income under anarchy, . . . of itself provides no clear indication as to what is likely to happen next." [117]

The Character of Assets

Still another interesting condition for the sustainability of anarchy is that resources be "predictable and defendable." In Hirshleifer's analysis, "[A]narchy is a social arrangement in which contenders struggle to conquer and defend durable resources." [118] He defines "durable resources" to include "land territories or movable capital goods." [119] In the Information Age, digital resources may prove to be predictable, but they will not be "durable resources" of the kind that Hirshleifer identifies with territoriality and anarchy. Indeed, if digital money can be transferred anywhere on the planet at the speed of light, conquest of the territory in which a cyberbank is incorporated may be a waste of time. Nation-states wishing to suppress Sovereign

Individuals would have to seize simultaneously both the world's banking havens and its data havens. Even then, if encrypted systems are designed properly, nation-states would merely be able to sabotage or destroy certain sums of digital money, not seize it.

The conclusion is that the most predictable and vulnerable assets of the rich in the coming Information Age may be their physical persons—in other words, their lives. Which is why we fear Luddite-style terrorism in the coming decades, some of it perhaps covertly encouraged by agents provocateurs in the employ of nation-states.

Over the long term, however, we doubt that the leading nation-states will succeed in suppressing Sovereign Individuals. For one thing, existing states, especially in capital-poor regions, will find that they have more to gain by harboring Sovereign Individuals than by maintaining solidarity with the North Atlantic nation-states and upholding the sanctity of the "international" system. The fact that bankrupt, high-tax welfare states want to keep "their citizens" and "their capital" in "their country" will not be a compelling motive to be observed by hundreds of fragmenting sovereignties elsewhere.

We say this, notwithstanding the fact that there are thousands of multinational organizations designed to condition the behavior of the world's various sovereignties. There can be little doubt that some of these organizations, like the European Union and the World Bank, are influential. But remember that the jurisdictions that make Sovereign Individuals welcome stand to benefit significantly from their presence. Even a pigheaded power like the United States, which is bound by current trends to work vigorously to prevent the emergence of a cybereconomy outside the control of the U.S. government, will ultimately not wish to exclude those residents of the globe with positive bank balances who do not wish to be Americans. This is especially likely inasmuch as shopping is now a major fascination of travelers. Ultimately, although well after others, the United States, or fragments thereof, will join in the commercialization of sovereignty because of competitive pressures.

Demand Creates Supply

Those pressures will be felt more vigorously early on in nation-states with the weakest balance sheets. Among the new "offshore" centers will be fragments and enclaves of current nation-states, like Canada and Italy, which will almost surely disintegrate well before the end of the first quarter of the twenty-first century. The birth of a global market for high-quality, cost-efficient jurisdictions will help bring such jurisdictions into being. As in ordinary commerce, small-scale competitors will be more nimble and better able to compete. The thinly populated jurisdiction can more easily structure itself to operate efficiently.

The information elite will seek high-quality protection on contract for a reasonable fee. While this fee will fall well short of what would be required to redistribute a noticeable benefit to the whole populations of nation-states as they are now structured, with tens of millions to hundreds of millions of citizens, it would not be trivial in a jurisdiction with a population in the tens of thousands or hundreds of thousands. The tax payments and other economic advantages accruing from the presence of a small number of exceedingly rich individuals imply a far higher per capita benefit to a jurisdiction with a small rather than a huge population.

Since it will be practically immaterial where one domiciles his businesses, except in the purely negative sense that some addresses will imply higher liabilities than others, small jurisdictions will find it easier to set commercially successful terms for protection. Therefore, jurisdictions with small populations will enjoy a decided advantage in formulating a fiscal policy attractive to Sovereign Individuals.

We believe that the age of the nation-state is over, but this is not to say that the attraction of nationalism as a tug on human emotions will be immediately quieted. As an ideology, nationalism is well placed to draw upon universal emotional needs. We have all had the experience of awe, such as one might feel on first seeing a giant waterfall, or first standing at the entrance to a great cathedral. We have all had the experience of belonging, such as we might feel at a family Christmas party, or as a member of a successful team in some sport. Human culture calls for a response to both of these powerful emotions. We are illuminated by the historic culture of our own country, which is itself part of the larger culture of humanity. We are comforted by the knowledge that we belong to a cultural group, which gives us both a sense of participation and of identity.

The impact of these cultural symbols can have the strongest emotional effect. The American associations of the Flag, the National Anthem, or the family feast at Thanksgiving Day, the English associations of the monarchy or cricket—all have a real hold on the imaginations of American and English people, respectively, a hold that is reinforced by repetition and goes deep into the subconscious mind. Such symbols help to tell us what sort of people we are, and remind us of a national culture. When anti–Vietnam War demonstrators wanted to shock the rest of the United States, they burned the flag. Alienated English attack the monarchy, and have even been known to dig holes in cricket pitches.

These trigger points are superficial, but not unimportant. They are the associations we were taught to bleed for. Whatever the change in megapolitical conditions or resulting change in institutions, they will probably remain important in the imaginations of persons who came of age, as we did, in the twentieth century.

CHAPTER 10
THE TWILIGHT OF DEMOCRACY

"Democratic theory is the moral Esperanto of the present nation-state system, the language in which all Nations are truly United, the public cant of the modern world, a dubious currency indeed—and one which only a complete imbecile would be likely to take quite at its face value, quite literally." [1]

—JOHN DUNN

It is no secret that democracy has been relatively rare and fleeting in the history of governments. In those times, ancient and modern, where democracy has prevailed, it has depended for its success upon megapolitical conditions that reinforced the military power and importance of the masses. Historian Carroll Quigley explored these characteristics in *Weapons Systems and Political Stability*.[2] They have included:

1. **Cheap and widely dispersed weaponry.** Democracy tends to flourish when the cost to purchase useful weapons is low.

2. **Weapons that can be used effectively by amateurs.** Democracy is more likely when anyone can use effective weapons without extended training.

3. **A military advantage for a large number of participants on foot in battle.** As Quigley points out, "[P]eriods of infantry dominance have been periods in which political power has been more widely dispersed within the community and democracy has had a better chance to prevail." [3]

This is hardly a comprehensive catalogue of the conditions under which democracy can exist. If it were, democracy would not have become a triumphant system at the end of the twentieth century. Weapons were arguably more expensive in the twilight of the industrial era than ever. And many of the most effective weapons definitely required specialists to be used effectively. Furthermore, the Gulf War between the United States, its allies, and Iraq proved how vulnerable large contingents of infantry are, even when nestled in trenches and dug-in fortifications. So why has democracy appeared to flourish under these conditions as the twentieth century winds down?

DEMOCRACY, THE FRATERNAL TWIN OF COMMUNISM?

We offered a paradoxical explanation in Chapter 5, namely that democracy flourished as a fraternal twin of Communism precisely because it facilitated unimpeded control of resources by the state. This conclusion may seem silly to the Manchichaean "common sense" of the industrial era. We do not deny that within the terms of industrial society, democratic systems and Communism were stark opposites. But seen from a megapolitical perspective, as they may more likely be seen from the vantage of the Information Age, the two systems had more in common than you would have been led to suspect.

In a setting where weaponry was grotesquely expensive, democracy became the decision mechanism that maximized control of resources by the state. Like state socialism, democratic systems made available huge sums to fund a massive military establishment. The difference was that the democratic welfare state placed even greater resources in the hands of the state than could the state socialist systems. That is saying something, because the state socialist or Communist systems laid claim to practically every asset worth having.

Seen dispassionately, democracy was superior to state socialism as a recipe for enriching the state. As we explained earlier, democracy made substantially more money available to the military because democracy was compatible with private ownership and capitalist productivity.

The state socialist system was predicated upon the doctrine that the state owned everything. The democratic welfare state, by contrast, made more limited initial claims. It pretended to allow private ownership, although of a contingent kind, and thereby harnessed superior incentives to mobilize output. Instead of mismanaging everything from the start, democratic governments in the West allowed individuals to own property and accumulate wealth. Only after the wealth had been created did the democratic nation-states step in to tax a large fraction of it away.

The word "Large" should be capitalized. For example, in 1996 the lifetime federal tax rate at the highest brackets in the United States stood at seventy-three cents on the dollar. For owners of corporations, who received their income through dividends, the rate was eighty-three cents on the dollar. And for anyone who sought to leave or give wealth to grandchildren, the federal tax rate was ninety-three cents on the dollar. When state and local taxes are considered as well, democratic government at all levels confiscates the lion's share of each dollar earned in the United States. Predatory tax rates made the democratic state a *de facto* partner with a three-quarters to nine-tenths share in earnings. This was not the same thing as state socialism, to be sure. But it was a close relation.

The democratic state survived longer because it was more flexible and collected more prodigious quantities of resources compared to those available in Moscow or East Berlin.

"Inefficiency, Where It Counted"

We have described the megapolitical advantages of democracy as a decision rule for a powerful government as "inefficiency, where it counted." Compared to Communism, the welfare state was indeed a far more efficient system. But compared to a genuine laissez-faire enclave like colonial Hong Kong, the welfare state was inefficient. Growth rates in Hong Kong were fabulous, but their superiority lay precisely in the fact that the resident of Hong Kong, not the government, was able to pocket 85 percent of the benefits of faster growth.

Hong Kong, of course, was never a democracy. Indeed, it is a mental model of the kind of jurisdiction that we expect to see flourish in the Information Age. In the Industrial Age, Hong Kong had no need to be a democracy, as it was spared the unpleasant necessity of gathering resources to support a formidable military establishment. Hong Kong was defended from the outside, so it could afford to maintain a really free economy.

It was precisely the capacity to rake in resources that made democracy supreme during the megapolitical conditions of the Industrial Age. Mass democracy went hand in hand with industrialism. As Alvin Toffler has said, mass democracy "is the political expression of mass production, mass distribution, mass consumption, mass education, mass media, mass entertainment, and all the rest."[4]

Now that information technology is displacing mass production, it is logical to expect the twilight of mass democracy. The crucial megapolitical imperative that made mass democracy triumph during the Industrial Age has disappeared. It is therefore only a matter of time until mass democracy goes the way of its fraternal twin, Communism.

Mass Democracy Incompatible with the Information Age

A moment's reflection shows that the technology of the Information Age is not inherently a mass technology. In military terms, as we have indicated, it opens the potential for "smart weapons" and "Information War," in which "logic bombs" could sabotage centralized command and control systems. Not only does information technology clearly point toward the perfection of weapons operated by specialists; it also reduces the decisiveness of warfare, improving the relative position of the defense. Microtechnology makes possible dramatic gains in the military power of individuals, while reducing the importance of massed infantry formations. As the Rand Corporation reported to the secretary of defense: "Interconnected networks may be subject to attack and disruption not just by states but also by nonstate actors, including dispersed groups and even individuals."[5] What is more, this implies that cyberwar will realize the potential diseconomies to scale inherent in mass, centralized systems.

In the words of the Rand experts, "Information-based techniques render geographical distance irrelevant; targets in the continental United States are just as vulnerable as in-theatre targets."[6] Whereas there used to be safety implied in residence within the boundaries of large, superpower nation-states like the United States, in the Information Age the logic of aggregating power could be reversed. Peoria may be far from any potential military front, but it will no longer be safe from cyberattack by almost any potential antagonist. Residing within the borders of a superpower will mean putting yourself within the bull's-eye. Instead of federating, locales may make themselves more secure by disaggregating. The advent of cyberwar will increase the vulnerability of centralized command-and-control systems, while increasing the competitive viability of dispersed systems.

The feedback mechanisms this will stimulate could accelerate the devolutionary process. As the Rand experts suggest, in order to lessen the vulnerability to cyberattack of the command-and-control systems that have evolved during the late stages of the nation-state, governments will be obliged to increase "the exploitation of new software encryption techniques." This will make these mainly private-sector systems far less vulnerable to sabotage, while accelerating the commercial dispersion of hard encryption, which will help free them from state domination. This, too, will give impetus to devolution. As we argued earlier, it will further propel the dispersion of resources into cyberspace, where they will be beyond the reach of politics.

Ultimately, this means the end of mass democracy, especially in its predominant form, representative misgovernment, either of the congressional or parliamentary type.

THE MEGAPOLITICS OF MISREPRESENTATION

When megapolitical conditions change in a big way, as they are changing now, the organization of government inevitably changes as well. In fact, the form of representative government has traditionally been an artifact of the distribution of raw power. This is shown by the very fact that representatives are chosen on a geographic basis, rather than in some other way.

Think about it. In principle, a legislature would be just as representative if its members were chosen according to any arbitrary division of the population. Parliamentary ridings or congressional districts could be based on birthdays, or even alphabetical constituencies. Everyone born on January 1 could vote from one list of candidates. Those born on January 2 from another. Or every person whose name began with "Aa" to "Af" could choose among one list of candidates. Those whose names began with "Ag" would chose among another. And so on.

No such system exists now for several reasons. A first and sufficient reason is that it was technologically impractical in the eighteenth century. But even more important is the fact that birthday or alphabetical constituencies would not have reflected or even approximated the distribution of raw power that the vote had to manifest at that time. Persons who shared no more than birthdays or the first few letters of their names in common would have been and still would be extremely hard to organize into any coherent power base.

Why Do Geographic Cross Sections Count More?

The vote really did begin as a proxy for a military contest. And so it remains, if only in a veiled way. Such contests can be organized along geographic lines, and more rarely, along kinship or religious lines. They cannot be organized on the basis of birthdays or first initials. Nor can they be organized effectively according to occupations, except where occupations are confined within hereditary guilds, like the castes in India, or cluster locally the way farmers do in Iowa.

The whole point of current formulas of representation is that they mobilize interests that are vested geographically, rather than along some other dimension. Historically, the key to military success was to control territory. All military threats have formed locally. Representative systems are geared to provide a different venue for the expression of that power. The fact that they inevitably tend to promote local vested interests is an artifact of the formula of representation. Geographic constituencies induce representatives to target favors for special groups at the expense of the common interests that all residents of a country share.

New Possibilities Ahead

As analysis by Public Choice economists has shown, apparently minor shifts in the way an election is structured, or the way the vote is calculated, have large and predictable consequences in altering the outcome.[7] This is why serious students of politics today have to be serious students of constitutions. And it is one of the considerations that led us to look beyond constitutions to the ultimate metaconstitution as determined by the prevailing megapolitical factors of a given environment.

Technological change has already swept away some of the foundations for confining the vote to geographic constituencies. When modern representative systems emerged in the eighteenth and nineteenth centuries, almost all communications were local. Most people lived and died within a few miles of where they were born, and the whole of their commerce and communication was conducted locally. Today there is instantaneous communication worldwide. You can do business with someone five thousand miles away almost as easily as with a neighbor. To an increasing extent, the economy is transcending geographic limitations. Society is far more mobile.

And so is wealth in the Information Age. Unlike a steel mill, a computer program cannot easily be held hostage to the local political process. A steel mill can scarcely be moved when legislators determine to tax it or regulate its owners. A computer program can be transmitted by modem at the speed of light anywhere in the world. The owner can pack his 486 laptop computer and fly away. This, too, undermines the megapolitical foundations of geographic constituencies.

A major difficulty that all representative democratic systems share in light of our analysis is that their geographic constituencies are bound to overrepresent the vested interests of industrial-era enterprises. The "losers" or "left-behinds" are perfect constituents, geographically concentrated and politically needy. The history of industrial democracy confirms this. "Winners" from new industries were chronically underrepresented in legislative deliberations even in the high tide of the Industrial Age in the 1930s.[8] The tendency of politicians to represent the existing, established competitors, not the new enterprises that might come into being or the potential customers of new enterprises, is probably an inherent feature of representative government. As Mancur Olson argued in *The Rise and Decline of Nations*, long-lived industries tend to develop more effective "distributional coalitions" to lobby and struggle over political booty.[9]

This problem is magnified immeasurably when it comes to the economy of the Information Age. The more creative participants in the new economy are geographically distributed. Therefore, they are unlikely to form a sufficient concentration to gain the attention of legislators, the way that salmon fishers in Scotland or wheat farmers in Saskatchewan do. Indeed, many of the dynamic personalities of the new economy are unlikely to be citizens of even the most encompassing jurisdiction. Thus they will have little "voice" in the legislative deliberations of representative democracies. As a telling example, consider the disreputable efforts of American math Ph.D.s to block foreign mathematicians from taking jobs in the United States.[10] Their xenophobic representations to Congress to block employers from hiring on the basis of merit are all too likely to be heeded. The antiquated geographic representation left over from the Industrial Age takes no heed of the foreign mathematicians, or any other crucial contributors to prosperity who are not voters.

"Why do people believe in the legitimacy of democratic institutions? Answering that question is almost as difficult as explaining why people believe in particular religious dogmas, for as is the case with religious beliefs, the degree of understanding, of skepticism and faith, varies widely across the society and over time."[11]

—JUAN J. LINZ

Few have begun to think in a concerted way about the consequences of technological change in undermining industrialism and altering income distributions. Obviously, democracy is not likely to be much more than a recipe for legalized parasitism if incomes diverge as widely as they may in the information economy. Fewer still have noticed the implied incompatibility between some of the institutions of industrial government and the megapolitics of postindustrial society. Whether these contradictions are explicitly acknowledged or not, however, their consequences will become increasingly obvious as examples of political failure compound around the world. Institutions of government that emerged in the modern period reflect the megapolitical conditions of one or more centuries ago. They survived the transition from agrarian society to urban industrialism. But the Information Age may require new mechanisms of representation to avoid chronic dysfunction and even Soviet-style collapse.

You can expect to see crises of misgovernment in many countries as political promises are deflated and governments run out of credit and institutional support. Ultimately, new institutional forms will have to emerge that are capable of preserving freedom in the new technological conditions, while at the same time giving expression and life to the common interests that individuals share.

All this points to the end of mass democracy as we have known it in the twentieth century. The question is, What will take its place? If the only alternative to mass democracy were dictatorship in which the individual has no say in his destiny, then one might be tempted to join the neo-Luddites' "revolt against the future."

New Institutions

Happily, however, dictatorship is not the sole alternative to mass democracy. Information technology facilitates choice. Instead of collective choice within the constrained setting of "mass production, mass consumption, mass education, mass media, mass entertainment, and all the rest," information technology will facilitate genuine, consumer choice of customized sovereignty services. This will be possible because operating at a mass scale will no longer be imperative. We believe that the technology of the Information Age will give rise to new forms of governance—just as the Agricultural Revolution and, later, the industrial era brought forth their own distinctive forms of social organization.

What might such new institutions be? To understand, forget anything you read in misnamed "political science" texts. The new institutions of governance for the Information Age will trespass the boundaries of conventional thinking. The progress toward such institutions of the new age has already begun. They are little-recognized improvisations for restructuring underutilized assets, the benefits of sovereignty. The world's nation-states, anxiously looking over their shoulders at secession movements and the powerful forces of devolution, have clubbed together to form the strongest border-fixing cartel that they can possibly enforce. While the number of new states in the world has increased in the 1990s, this happened mainly in two clusters, thanks to the collapse of multiethnic Communist dictatorships in the former Soviet Union and Yugoslavia. It is notable that other leading nation-states, including the United States, maneuvered to preserve the Soviet Union for as long as possible. And few governments welcomed the breakup of Yugoslavia. The independence of the former Yugoslav republics was recognized only after secessionists had wrested control that they could enforce through their own military efforts. The leading powers were content to see unarmed or poorly armed separatists slaughtered by their Serb tormentors. Even faraway China, a powerful nation-state with no direct interest in preserving the rump of Yugoslavia, vigorously opposed efforts to achieve self-determination for oppressed ethnic Albanians in Kosovo. Ironically, this border-fixing fetish is more likely to dictate the path of devolution to fragmented sovereignty than to actually forestall devolution. The fierce resistance of vulnerable nation-states across the globe to overt secession and political disaggregation makes recognized sovereignty a valuable form of transcendental capital that can be voluntarily fragmented and sublet by the states possessing it.

An example of how sovereignty can be voluntarily fragmented to create essentially private, tax-free jurisdiction is the Agulhas Bay Concession Free Zone, comprising fifty square kilometers of the island of Principe off the coast of West Africa. Although the territory remains within the borders of the Democratic Republic of São Tomé and Principe, the administration of the zone is privatized. Governance there is determined according to contract administered by WADCO, the West African Development Corporation Ltd., a private company chartered in South Africa. The language of record in the zone is not the official Tomean tongue, Portuguese, but English. The currency of record is not the Tomean local Monopoly money, the dobra, but the globe's money, the U.S. dollar. Security is provided not by police forces of the Democratic Republic of São Tomé and Principe, but by private police employed by WADCO. São Tomean commercial law is inapplicable to commercial dealings within the zone, and São Tomean courts have no jurisdiction. All disputes must be settled by transnational arbitration, under the Paris ICC rules. With a few tightly regulated and trivial exceptions, São Tomean taxes do not apply within the zone, nor do official monopolies. Telecommunications, for example, are automatically deregulated within the zone. Subject to the payment of rent and adherence to other terms of the concession, WADCO is entitled to automatically and repetitively renew its lease on private, fragmented sovereignty for terms of fifty years, from the first renewal date, 2047.

What WADCO has achieved in São Tomé and Principe can and will be matched by others in many different jurisdictions. One of the true pioneers of twenty-first-century development, Joaquin Aguirre has created a similar zone of private sovereignty in the Central Aguirre Portuaria, in eastern Bolivia. Aguirre, a multimillionaire, novelist, and inventor, a cofounder of the United Nations, and a former Senator of the Bolivian Republic, is a pioneer many times over. Half a century after he helped to found the United Nations, Aguirre is now a prototype for the Sovereign Individual of the twenty-first century. His Zona Franca, which is free of most Bolivian taxes, duties, and regulatory impositions, points the way toward the new form of privatized city-state which will increasingly be achieved by successful individuals in the Information Age. It also demonstrates conclusively that the lives of the masses, so often eulogized by the apologists of big government, can be dramatically improved by the economic development catalyzed by free trade zones such as that launched by Señor Aguirre. As time passes, the number of de facto city states in the world will multiply significantly. Indeed, if you achieve sufficient financial independence as an individual, you will be able to achieve ultimate independence, like Joaquin Aguirre. In the event that no one else's piece of fragmented, commercialized sovereignty offers you a comfortable home base, you can launch your own proprietary ministate, as independent as any dukedom of the Middle Ages. Instead of playing tug-of-war with demagogues and political hacks to keep your assets from being wrested away and divided among the many clamoring hands of mass democracy, you will be able to establish your own private realm of governance.

The dramatic phase change from mass democracy to the ultimate form of self-government, individual sovereignty, need not involve a radical shift in public opinion, nor a miraculous vote by disenchanted electors opting to scrap mass democracy. Such a revolution can begin, indeed, already has begun, invisibly, with the leasing of sovereign territory for use as tax-free zones, "Zona Francas," and free ports. In due course, sovereignty will fragment repeatedly until it is so completely fissured that dividing it further would not yield a value sufficient to offset the transaction costs of devolution. Given Moore's Law and Gilder's Corollary, that bandwidth triples each year, there is no basis at present to foresee any early end to the devolutionary trend. To the contrary, we anticipate that the apparently solid power of nation-states currently devoted to mass democracy will splinter in tens of thousands of fragments into a system more reminiscent of the medieval period than the modern industrial age.

In due course, even nation-states that retain rump institutions of mass democracy will experience a significant shift in policies to accommodate the new metaconstitutional realities. As William Keech, a faithful advocate of democracy, argues in *Economic Politics: The Costs of Democracy:* "People learn to want what they see they can get, but they can also change their minds if they see that they do not like what they wanted and what they got." [12] In other words, the fact that mass democracy with conventional institutions of representative government is hailed everywhere as the twentieth century draws to an end could be a "sell signal." It by no means assures that such decision rules will stand the test of time, even in their own terms. Remember, when you look outside politics, there is scarcely any evidence of executives, administrators, coaches, or other professional leaders being selected democratically. To the contrary, the most successful leaders are routinely hired by proprietors through selection processes in which those with the greatest interests at stake have an unequal and disproportionately greater say in determining the outcome. If democratic selection were truly a superior method to identify competent leaders, you would expect to see it as a universal decision rule. Instead, it is confined almost solely to the political realm. In short, it is more reasonable on current evidence to assume that the provision of sovereignty services is hobbled by the dominance of democratic decision-making than it is to assume the opposite, namely, that corporate and business organizations suffer because they are run by executives installed by proprietors rather than according to a show of hands.

By the middle of the twenty-first century it is likely that the proliferation of proprietary jurisdictions of fragmented sovereignty will have conclusively demonstrated the advantages of proprietary administration. Voters will see that they suffer for being saddled with mass democracy. Therefore, as Professor Keech suggests, they will come to see that the benefits derived from employee control of government are outweighed by its costs. They will migrate toward reform. Even electorates in Europe and North America that now seem so strongly committed against reform could eventually vote to make their regions more accommodating to proprietary governance. Majorities may willingly, even gladly abandon the farce of politics in favor of proprietary management of government which actually aims toward achieving the optimum setting for concluding and enforcing contracts.

To the extent that government with its familiar accoutrements survives at all, it may be informed in entirely new ways. Somewhere, in some jurisdiction, sometime before the crack of doom, someone will realize the potential that computer technology offers to make possible truly representative government. The supposed problem of excessive campaign expenditures and the undoubted annoyance of chronic political campaigning could be resolved in an instant. Rather than being elected, representatives could be selected by sortition entirely at random, with a high statistical probability that their talents and views would match those of the population at large.

This would be merely a modern version of the ancient Greek system of selection by lot. As E. S. Staveley details in his authoritative history, *Greek and Roman Voting and Elections,* numerous positions in Athens, from the magistrates to the archons, were selected by sortition as a substitute for elections. This was cleverly accomplished, in spite of mechanical limitations on the randomization of chances, through use of an allotment machine, "or, as it was called by the Athenians, the *cleroterion.*"[13]

A series of black and white beans were used as random counters to determine who would be selected to fill various offices, as well as "to determine the order in which the tribal sections in the Council were to take their turns as *prytaneis.*"[14] The classic provenance of this idea may give it an extra measure of credibility. But its main appeal is precisely that it would avoid the drawbacks of self-selection in politics. It would statistically assure that fewer lawyers and egomaniacs engrossed the public's business.

Legislatures could be composed of true representatives. Since they would not be brought together by the pursuit of power, and would have a negligible chance of being selected again by sortition in any event, they would be free to conduct the affairs of government and formulate policy on the basis of a rational analysis of the issues.

Straight Commission

Today, politicians bent on optimizing votes have little incentive to analyze problems coherently. It is hardly surprising, therefore, that their records in actually solving problems are so pathetic as compared to entrepreneurs, business executives, and coaches of sports teams, who are rewarded according to performance. Performance-based compensation for legislators would not make everyone chosen at random as effective as Lee Kuan Yew. But paying leaders on the basis of their performance is just a logical extension of Lee's successful "Flexiwage" program in Singapore, which pays government employees on the basis of the real growth of the Singapore economy. There is every reason to believe that performance would be greatly enhanced if the pay of legislators and executives were keyed to some objective measure of performance, such as the growth of after-tax per capita income. Pay them on the basis of performance, and the chance that they would perform would increase a thousandfold.

The gain to society from policies that improve real income net of taxes could be huge. Why not pay prime ministers and presidents even a tiny share of the gain that their policies promote? The funding for such payments could be collected by a small, unobtrusive tax. Such an arrangement would free society from the threat it now faces from ambitious men with specialized political talent like Richard Nixon and Bill Clinton.

"They brought him gold, silver and clothing; but the 'Christ' distributed all these things to the poor. When gifts were offered he and his female companion would prostrate themselves and offer up prayers; but then rising to his feet, he would order the assembly to worship him. Later, he organized an armed band, which he led through the countryside, waylaying and robbing travellers they met on the way. But here too his ambition was not to become rich but to be worshipped. He distributed all the booty to those who had nothing—including, one may assume, his own followers."[15]

—NORMAN COHN

Messianic Personalities

Too little attention has been paid to the fact that electoral politics lures disordered, messianic personalities into positions of power. Such persons existed, and often posed serious threats to social order even in agrarian societies before the emergence of democratic political systems. Reviewing the careers of Eudo de Stell, the Breton Christ, Adelbert in the eighth century, Eon in the eleventh, Tanchelm of Antwerp, Melchior Hoffman, and Bernt Rothmann and their ilk, several points stand out. The more immediately obvious their political talents seem to be, the greater the damage they appear to have inflicted. Because the state was not yet engaged in organizing widespread systematic coercion, these early protopoliticians frequently took it upon themselves to rob and loot in order to obtain cash to distribute to their followers among the poor.

Protopoliticians in action

The stories of their antics give one the impression of talents out of time, like reading about seven-foot men running up and down a court before the invention of basketball. Today, thanks to the NBA, freakishly tall men are making millions dribbling and dunking. If basketball disappeared, they would recede again into the crevices of society, probably appearing mostly as circus attractions and in sideshows.

Demagogues before politics was invented were drawn to the nearest approximation of politics the agrarian world had to offer: itinerant preaching. They harangued crowds and, like politicians, eloquently promised a better life to those who would follow them. Then as now, the poor were the chief targets of demagogues. Norman Cohn's great history of millenarian movements, *The Pursuit of the Millennium,* recounts the careers of numerous messianic leaders before polling. It is easy to recognize in his descriptions the strong similarities in personality type with the charismatic politician of the modern period.

[T]he leader has—like pharaoh and many another "divine king"—all the attributes of an ideal father: he is perfectly wise, he is perfectly just, he protects the weak. But on the other hand, he is also the son whose task is to transform the world, the Messiah who is to establish a new heaven and a new earth and who can say of himself: "Behold, I make all things new!" And both as father and as son this figure is colossal, superhuman, omnipotent. He is credited with such abundance of supernatural powers that it is imagined as streaming forth as light. . . . Moreover being thus filled with this divine spirit the eschatological leader possesses unique miracle-working powers. His armies will be invariably and triumphantly victorious, his presence will make the earth yield prodigious crops, his reign will be an age of such perfect harmony as the old, corrupt world has never known.

This image was of course a purely phantasic one, in the sense that it bore no relation to the real nature and capacity of any human being who ever existed or ever could exist. It was nevertheless an image which could be projected on to a living man; and there were always men about who were more than willing to accept such a projection, who in fact passionately desired to be seen as infallible, wonder-working saviours. . . . And the secret of the ascendancy which they exercised never lay in their birth nor to any great extent in their education, but always in their personalities. Contemporary accounts of these messiahs of the poor commonly stress their eloquence, their commanding bearing and their personal magnetism. Above all one gets the impression that even if some of these men may perhaps have been conscious impostors, most of them really saw themselves as incarnate gods. . . . And this total conviction would communicate itself easily enough to the multitudes whose deepest desire was precisely for an eschatological saviour.[16]

While this passage is marvelously concise in describing the would-be millenarian saviors who frequently unsettled medieval society, it cannot give the full flavor of Cohn's magisterial survey. One cannot read the whole work without recognizing in the antics of these *prophetae* the familiar characteristics of the modern demagogue: the eloquence, "the personal magneticism," the "messianic pretensions," and the recurring desire to be worshiped as tribune of the poor.

The main difference that one discerns between the reception of medieval society to these impostors and that afforded by democracy at the end of the twentieth century is that in the Middle Ages such persons were normally executed, whereas, at the end of the twentieth century, modern democratic politics provides them with an open channel by which to legitimately seize power in the nation-state.

A system that routinely submits control over the largest, most deadly enterprises on earth to the winner of popularity contests between charismatic demagogues is bound to suffer for it in the long run.

Pay Leaders to Do a Good Job

As suggested above, it would be easy to stipulate a superior method for securing talented leadership for an organization: hiring it. This is the method most widely and successfully used in competitive economies. A rational selection process, combined with a constructive incentive structure to reward positive leadership, would bring able people to the helm of government. It would also mobilize new types of talent who otherwise would not normally take an interest in the problems of governance.

The most talented executives in the world could be attracted to run faltering governments if they could be paid on the basis of results they actually achieve for society. A leader who could significantly boost real income in any leading Western nation could justly be paid far more than Michael Eisner. In a better world, every successful head of government would be a multimillionaire.

Electronic Plebiscites

Another obvious alternative to representative misgovernment would be electronic plebiscites whereby citizens, perhaps a representative fraction selected by tamper-proof sortition, could cast their ballots directly on legislative proposals. Computer technology allows decisions to be determined, with electronic plebiscites. Plebiscites could be easily combined with allotment to narrow the numbers voting on specific issues. In any event, in principle, it is far less challenging for would-be voters to understand political issues than to attempt to fathom politicians and evaluate these politicians' evaluations of the same issues, much less know what those politicians would actually do upon assuming office. This is particularly difficult in that politicians and their handlers are becoming increasingly proficient at packaging and manipulating the images they present to the public.

COMMERCIALIZED SOVEREIGNTY

We expect to see something new emerge to replace politics. While any of the possibilities we canvass above might be tried with some advantage, our expectation is not that politics will be reformed or improved, but that it will be antiquated and, in most respects, abandoned. By this we do not mean to say that we expect to see dictatorship, but rather entrepreneurial government —the commercialization of sovereignty.

Unlike dictatorship, or even democracy, commercialized sovereignty will not foreclose choice. It will afford every individual greater scope for expressing his views. And for those with the talent to take advantage of it, commercialized sovereignty will permit more practical scope for decision-making and self-determination than any form of social organization that has heretofore existed.

Customized Government

Lest this sound millenarian, consider that microtechnology miniaturizes and disaggregates. It facilitates customization rather than mass production. You can now go into a store and purchase blue jeans that will be cut from a pattern customized to your measurements and sewn up half a world away. When new institutions at last evolve to fit the new megapolitical realities of the Information Age, you will be able to obtain governance at least as well customized to meet your personal needs and tastes as blue jeans.

Alvin Toffler, of all people, has criticized the idea that information technology could make citizens into customers. Toffler says, wrongly we believe, "That is far too narrow of a model. Whether we like it or not, there is a world of religion and feeling out there that cannot be simply reduced to contractual relationships." [17] For reasons we explored earlier, we would agree that it will be difficult to "reduce the world of nationalist feeling" to "contractual relationships." But to say that is not to argue that it is impossible, much less that it would be a bad arrangement. A little less irrational gusto in nationalism could save millions of lives.

"Entry, Exit" and "Voice"

Of course, the commercialization of sovereignty is an unfamiliar concept, apparently even to Alvin Toffler. But its central idea—the *economic* mode of expression—is commonplace in the lives of people living at the end of the twentieth century. In any marginally free economy, consumers can act to express their desires directly by purchasing services and products. Or by withdrawing their custom. When you become dissatisfied with one version of a product or a provider of a service, you can directly express your dissatisfaction by means of "exit." In other words, you can shift your business elsewhere.

In the previous chapters, we analyzed how the advance of information technology will soon make it feasible for you to create assets in cyberspace that will be all but immune from predatory invasion by nation-states. This will create a *de facto* metaconstitutional requirement that governments actually provide you with satisfactory service before you pay their bills. Why? Because income taxation will become almost as voluntary in fact as it is supposed to be in theory.

Avoiding "Cumbrous Political Channels"

In effect, if information technology evolves as it may, it will assure that governments are actually controlled by their customers. As a customer, you will first have hundreds, then thousands of options to reduce your protection costs directly by contracting a private tax treaty with a nation-state or by defecting from nation-states altogether to emerging minisovereignties. These contract "entry" and defection or "exit" options are economic expressions of your desires as a customer. Voting with your feet and your money has the great advantage that it leads to results that you desire.

How do your "entry" and "exit" options as a customer compare with the *political* mode of expression in democracy? Persons who become dissatisfied with some product or service, especially one provided by or heavily regulated by the government, can give "voice" to their views by writing letters to the president in the United States, or seeking a meeting with their member of Parliament or another appropriate elected official elsewhere. Sometimes, such love letters work. But not always. Not usually. Failing success, at first, persons seeking to employ their "voice" for change can then organize a demonstration, take out a full-page advertisement in a newspaper, or even seek elective office themselves.

The political mode of expression does provide a channel for articulate statements and oratory. But it entails the drawback that you can seldom obtain satisfaction or improve your position by your own action. When faced with a substandard product or service of government, you are obliged to continue paying for it until you can persuade the whole political process to accede to your request for a change.

In Western countries, and now in practically the entire earth, this has come to mean the necessity of securing majority support of a democratic political system. The requirement to involve a majority imposes massive transaction costs between you and achieving what in all likelihood is a relatively straightforward and rational goal.

Milton Friedman discussed the merits of the economic, as opposed to the political, mode of expression in advancing his proposal for school vouchers in *Capitalism and Freedom:*

> Parents could express their views about schools directly, by withdrawing their children from one school and sending them to another, to a much greater extent than is now possible. In general they can now take this step only by changing their place of residence. For the rest, they can express their views only though cumbrous political channels.[18]

Albert O. Hirschman, speaking as a partisan of politics, took exception to Friedman's preference for "exit as the 'direct' way of expressing one's unfavorable views of an organization. A person less well trained in economics might naively suggest that the direct way of expressing one's views is to express them!"[19]

Whether it is more direct or effective to express your opinions through market mechanisms, such as providing or withdrawing your support as a customer, or through "cumbrous political channels" is a complex and contentious question. Different persons will answer it in different ways. For those whose primary engagement with political expression is to demand benefits at the expense of others, shifting to the economic mode of expression may indeed seem a dismal substitute to writing to a politician and demanding more.

Economic Expression and "Reciprocal Sociality"

For those who intend to engage their fellows in "reciprocal" rather than "coercive" or parasitic sociality, the economic mode of expression opens the prospect of achieving far greater satisfaction at a lower cost in time and trouble. Professor Hirschfield notwithstanding, this is easily demonstrated.

Any set of economic expressions, comprising entry, on-going contracts, and exits, could be converted into an expression of political "voice" simply by involving multitudes of people in the decision-making. Try it as an experiment. All you would require to test it are a few hundred people who feel there is not enough politics in their lives. Instead of spending their disposable income in thousands of discrete purchases over a year's time, they would convert this multitude of economic decisions into a handful of political ones.

To start, all would agree to pool their disposable income and thereafter forgo purchases on an individual basis. Instead of thousands of dollars to spend individually in thousands of ways, everyone would get one vote or perhaps a few votes depending upon the number of offices to be filled. Rather than spending money directly to obtain what you want at any time you wished, you would spend your vote or votes on the handful of occasions when elections were held to select representatives who would then decide how the now gigantic collective purse would be spent.

You, along with the others, would then share in the consumption of those items, and only those items that the ruling committee approved in the name of the majority.

Does that seem like a "cumbrous political channel" for expression yet? Just wait. This model holds all the potential for oratory and persuasion that one finds in politics at the national level. And most of the potential for frustration.

For example, if you like fresh broccoli, and the group has an ordinary distribution of tastes in food, you are in trouble. Chances are that some or most of the others in your group would prefer to spend more of the common food allowance on red meat than on fresh vegetables. To prevent the canteen committee from going to a warehouse store and squandering the whole annual vegetable budget on canned peas and corn, you might have to step forward and give "voice" to your views. You could draw the group's attention to the relative merits of ingesting more vitamins and phytonutrients like sulforaphane in broccoli, as compared to more saturated fats and cholesterol from red meat.

Just exactly how you make this or any point understood, of course, would be as much of a puzzle in this constructed political model as it is to advocates of any political cause or candidacy. You could give a speech, but that, of course, requires that a good fraction of the group whom you need to persuade is already assembled somewhere and prepared to listen. You could print up flyers, provided that such a "campaign expenditure" were permitted by the house rules of your political game. You could write letters. But both of these options depend upon the other participants being literate enough to read.

"It paints a picture of a society in which the vast majority of Americans do not know that they do not have the skill they need to earn a living in our increasingly technological society and international marketplace."

—RICHARD RILEY,
U.S. SECRETARY OF EDUCATION, IN "ADULT LITERACY IN AMERICA"

Ninety Million Alzheimer's Patients?

If your group in this model political exercise happened to be Americans, you would be hard-pressed to get any persuasive message to sink in, particularly if the members of the group were similar to the U.S. electorate as a whole. The perception that disproportionally large numbers of citizens of the world's most powerful nation-state are underachievers has been bleakly confirmed by the most thorough survey ever undertaken of the competence of American adults. The study, "Adult Literacy in America," shows that finding a literate audience for any political argument is by no means easy. A large fraction, perhaps a majority of Americans over the age of fifteen, lack basic skills essential to evaluating ideas and formulating judgments. According to the U.S. Education Department, 90 million Americans cannot write a letter, fathom a bus schedule, or even do addition and subtraction on a calculator. This is about what you would expect if 90 million Americans were progressing through various stages of Alzheimer's Disease. Thirty million were judged so incompetent that they could not even respond to questions.

So if your health message did not turn the tide, which is otherwise finding its own level, then you could call for help from animal rights activists. Perhaps you could get them to picket your opponents in the canteen committee or make a fuss about the evil of killing cows at the homes of influential members.

This example could be extended indefinitely, which is probably far longer than the patience of rational people would permit. It clearly demonstrates that (1) any economic expression of entry or exit can be converted into a political expression of voice by making it a collective decision; and (2) that collective decisions, in spite of the invitation they offer to eloquence, are, indeed, cumbrous and often intractable.

This is exactly what experience has shown. It is far from easy to mobilize the effort required to change the course of a democracy. To reiterate, that may well be the reason that democratic welfare states survived centuries of competition with alternative methods of government to predominate at the end of the industrial era. Democracy succeeded as a political system precisely because its operation made it difficult for customers to control the government or limit the state's claims on resources.

However, since an unlimited partnership by the state in your affairs will no longer convey a military advantage in the Information Age, ingenious people will find superior ways to obtain the few valuable services that governments actually provide. As spelled out earlier, it is likely that actual power will be contracted out from collective mechanisms that no longer pay their way. We expect to see efficiency predominate over massed power. As Neil Munro succinctly put it, "[I]t is computerized information, not manpower or mass production that increasingly drives the U.S. economy and that will win wars in a world wired for 500 TV channels. The computerized information exists in cyberspace—the new dimension created by endless reproduction of computer networks, satellites, modems, databases and the public Internet." [20]

Massed armies will mean little in such a world. Efficiency will mean more than ever before. Because microtechnology creates a new dimension in protection, as we explored in Chapter 6 and elsewhere, individuals for the first time in human existence will be able to create and protect assets that lie entirely outside the realm of any individual government's territorial monopoly on violence. These assets, therefore, will be highly susceptible to individual control. It will be perfectly reasonable for you and significant numbers of other future Sovereign Individuals to "vote with your feet" in opting out of leading nation-states to contract for protection of your assets and your person with an outlying nation-state or a new minisovereignty that will only charge a commercially tolerable amount, rather than the greater part of your net worth. In short, you would probably accept $50 million to move to Bermuda.

Exit First, Contract Later

The early stimulus to commercialization of sovereignty will have to come from persons expressing themselves economically by exit. This option will be most difficult in the United States, where it will also be most valuable. The "Berlin Wall" for capitalists imposed by President Bill Clinton and the Republican Congress contradicts the Declaration of Independence, which proclaims the right of individuals to renounce the dominion of predatory governments. It also undoes the slogan so confidently expressed by American nationalists in the 1960s, "Love it or leave it." By imposing penal taxes on those who leave, the exit tax is meant to compel loyalty. Yet this vindictive legislation, reminiscent of the penalties imposed on fleeing property owners in the last days of the Roman Empire, may inadvertently set the framework for a more rational policy later in the Information Age.

At some point, when enough able persons have left and compounded sufficiently large fortunes offshore, it will become appealing to U.S. authorities, and those of other high-tax countries to allow citizens or green card holders to buy their way out of future tax liabilities by paying an exit tax but not requiring that they actually exit. After all, it is economically in the interest of any sovereignty that economically productive persons remain within its territory and create value rather than departing to a more welcoming jurisdiction. In other words, the exit tax could become the model for a lump-sum buyout. The government imposing an exit tax would realize far higher benefits by allowing those exiting to resume residence under terms of a private treaty like those currently available in Switzerland and elsewhere.

Such moves on the part of the United States or other governments would be rational income-optimizing gestures. Eventually, competition in protection services will force down tax rates and adjust the terms of taxation to more civilized standards. Rather than depending upon legislatures to enact acceptable tax regimes, Sovereign Individuals in the future will be able to negotiate acceptable, customized policy packages by private treaty.

OFFENDING THE TRUE BELIEVERS

Of course, we do not contend for a moment that much of this will be popular any time soon. The denationalization of the individual and the commercialization of sovereignty it implies will offend remaining true believers in the clichés of twentieth-century politics. Like the late Christopher Lasch, they see the atrophy of politics as a threat to the well-being of a majority of the population. In their view, a revival of industrial-era politics, with its commitment to redistribute income, could be a solution to the distresses so many feel with the competitive pressures brought to bear by information technology.

E. J. Dionne, Jr., is a political reporter for the *Washington Post*. Like Lasch, he harks back, nostalgically, to politics. He also speaks for a social democratic leveling impulse that is bound to find louder voice in the decades to come as the new megapolitical realities of the Information Age more decisively undermine institutions left over from the modern world. Dionne sees the material improvements in living standards that were widely shared within rich jurisdictions in the twentieth century as owing mainly to democratic politics rather than to technological or economic development. His message is that hope for the future requires extending the dominion of politics over the technologies of the Information Age:

> The overriding need in the United States and throughout the democratic world is for a new engagement with democratic reform, the political engine that made the industrial era as successful as it was. The technologies of the information age will not on their own construct a successful society, any more than industrialism left to itself would have made the world better. . . . Even the most extraordinary breakthroughs in technology and the most ingenious applications of the Internet will not save us from social breakdown, crime or injustice. Only politics, which is the art of how we organize ourselves, can even begin to take on such tasks."[21]

Dionne and others like him fail to understand that the conditions that made twentieth-century life particularly conducive to systematic compulsion were not chosen by any human agency. The "art of how we organize ourselves" is a statement that would not have been intelligible prior to the modern period. Societies are too complex to be rightly considered the fruit of any willful effort of conscious self-organization. The nation-states of the modern period emerged spontaneously as a coincidental by-product of industrial technology that raised returns to violence. Now information technology is reducing the returns to violence. This makes politics anachronistic and irretrievable, no matter how earnestly people might wish to preserve it into the next millennium.

"Not of to-day nor yesterday, the same
Throughout all time they live; and whence they came
None knoweth."

—SOPHOCLES, *Antigone*

"THEY DON'T MAKE THEM LIKE THEY USED TO"

The fervent desire to "make laws," which seems so much a part of the "common sense" of twentieth-century politics, is by no means universal to all cultures. Its disappearance in the future could be seen as part of a cycle that has waxed and waned with the centuries. For example, early Greeks, among others, believed that laws could not be made. In the words of philosopher Ernst Cassirer, the Greeks believed "the 'unwritten laws,' the laws of justice, have no beginning in time."[22] Like other prepolitical peoples, they felt that no one could improve upon the natural, "geometrical" laws of justice that had not been created by any human power.

They did not believe in a "lawgiver." As Cassirer put it, "It is by rational thought that we are to find the standards of moral conduct, and it is reason, and reason alone, that can give them their authority." In this sense, any attempt to impose laws upon society through legislation would be like trying to alter geometry by legislation.

Legislation as Sacrilege

For very different reasons, a similar resistance to "lawmaking" prevailed through much of the medieval period. As John B. Morrall writes, "[F]or the Germans, law was something which had existed from time immemorial." It was "a guarantee of the rights" of individual members of the tribe.[23] Kings and councils

> had as yet no intention of creating new law. Such an intention would have been, from the point of view of these early medieval times, not only superfluous . . . but even semi-blasphemous, for law, like kingship, possessed its own sacrosanct aura. Instead, king and councillors thought of themselves as merely explaining or clarifying the true meaning of the already existing and complete body of law.
>
> Germanic custom handed on to the medieval mind an idea which it was never able to forget, even when in practice it behaved otherwise. This idea was that good laws were rediscovered or restated but never remade.[24]

After the excesses of twentieth-century legislation, there is something quaint about that ancient attitude. The desire to put the coercive power of the state to work for private ends, particularly the redistribution of income, became almost second nature.

Regrets

Little wonder, then, that there are sad songs for politics in its last days. They are entirely predictable. And not only because they reflect the blindness of most thinkers to the imperatives of megapolitics. Few political reporters, like Dionne, are prepared to accept the apparent atrophy and demise of politics, when doing so might put them back on the crime beat. At the end of the Middle Ages, voices were raised in support of reviving chivalry. Consider *Il Libro del Cortegiano,* or *The Book of the Courtier,* written by Count Baldassare Castiglione in 1514, and published at Venice in 1528 by Aldus.

Castiglione's longing for a return to virtues of chivalry was deeply felt, but longing for a defunct way of life could not bring it back in the sixteenth century. Nor will it in the twenty-first century.

As we have attempted to convey in explaining our theory of megapolitics, technological imperatives, not popular opinion, are the most important sources of change in today's world. If our theory of megapolitics is valid, the reason the modern age, with its concept of citizenship and politics organized around the state, supplanted the feudal system and chivalry organized around personal oaths and relationships was not a matter of ideas, but shifts in costs and benefits arising from new technology. Chivalry did not die because Castiglione or others failed to convince a disinterested populace who had any control over the matter that there was no need for honor or morality in the affairs of state. To the contrary, Castiglione's *Courtier* is critical of princes and the kind of behavior his contemporary, Niccolo Machiavelli, commended in his *Il Principe*, or *The Prince*. But so what? Machiavelli ultimately reached a larger audience with his book, not because his argument in *The Prince* was more eloquent but because his advice better suited the megapolitical conditions of the modern age.

As the distinguished twentieth-century philosopher Ernst Cassirer said in discussing "The Moral Problem in Machiavelli,"

> The book describes, with complete indifference, the ways and means by which political power is to be acquired and maintained. About the right use of this power it does not say a word. . . . No one had ever doubted that political *life*, as matters stand, is full of crimes, treacheries and felonies. But no thinker before Machiavelli had undertaken to teach the *art* of these crimes. These things were done, but they were not taught. That Machiavelli promised to become a teacher in the art of craft, perfidy, and cruelty was a thing unheard of.[25]

In short, *The Prince* was a radical work that spelled out a modern recipe whereby an aspiring ruler could succeed in advancing his career at any cost to others. Machiavelli endorsed conduct that proved well suited to the nature of politics in an age of power. But the art of the double-cross, which was a shrewd policy for politicians in the modern era, was outrageous and subversive in terms of the culture of chivalry that had grown up in previous centuries.

As we explored earlier, the virtues of chivalry included an emphasis on extreme fidelity to oaths. This was a necessity in a society where protection was organized in exchange for personal services. The bargains upon which feudal society rested were not such that they would have reemerged spontaneously among people free to determine where their best interests lay under conditions of duress. Therefore, feudal commitments that were the basis of chivalry had to be shorn up with a strong sense of honor. In that context, little could have been more subversive than Machiavelli's suggestion that the Prince should not hesitate to lie, cheat, and steal when so doing served his interests.

As the twentieth century drew to a close, Machiavelli's arguments were still being examined for their importance in understanding modern politics and various twentieth-century crimes and tyrannies. Castiglione's work, by contrast, is all but forgotten. In a year's time, *Il Libro del Cortegiano* may be read from cover to cover by a handful of literature students at the graduate level and a few connoisseurs of the history of manners.

Sometime within the next few decades, the new megapolitics of the Information Age will antiquate *The Prince*. The Sovereign Individual will require a new recipe for success, one which will highly emphasize honor and rectitude in deploying resources outside the grip of the state. We can predict that such advice will not be read with pleasure by E. J. Dionne, Jr., and the other living social democrats.

Policy Set by Customers

This will be especially true early in the transition, when most jurisdictions will still be lumbered with the necessity of formulating policies whose advocates can attract popular assent from a majority of the population. Later, as democracy fades away and the market for sovereignty services deepens, the market conditions that constrain "policy" will become more broadly understood.

What we now think of as "political" leadership, which is always conceived in terms of a nation-state, will become increasingly entrepreneurial rather than political in nature. In these conditions, the viable range of choice in putting together a "policy" regime for a jurisdiction will be effectively narrowed in the same way that the range of options open to entrepreneurs in designing a first-class resort hotel or any similar product or service is defined by what people will pay for. A resort hotel, for example, would seldom attempt to operate on terms that required guests to perform hard labor to repair and extend its facilities. Even a resort hotel owned or controlled by its employees, like the typical modern democracy, would try in vain to force customers to comply with such demands, especially after better accommodations became available. If the customers would rather play golf than do heavy labor in the hot sun, then on that question, at least, the market offers little scope for imposing arbitrary alternatives. In such conditions, presently "political" issues will recede into entrepreneurial judgments, as fragmented jurisdictions seek to discover which policy bundles will attract a viable cross-section of customers.

The Atrophy of Politics

As this becomes understood, there will be a sea change in attitudes. Populations in devolving jurisdictions will no longer expect to select from the same range of wish-fulfilling policy options that engrossed political debate in the twentieth century. With income-earning capacity more highly skewed than in the industrial era, jurisdictions will tend to cater to the needs of those customers whose business is most valuable and who have the greatest choice of where to bestow it.

Under such conditions, it may matter much less than we are accustomed to assume whether or not policies that are commercially optimal for a jurisdiction would appeal to the "median voter" in a focus group.

In short, the commercialization of sovereignty will facilitate the control of governments by their customers. This will tend to make the opinions of noncustomers irrelevant, or less relevant, just as the opinions of Big Mac eaters about foie gras are irrelevant to the success of three-star French restaurants, like L'Arpège in Paris.

"THE BETRAYAL OF DEMOCRACY"

Like the late Christopher Lasch, objectors will not only complain that information technology destroys jobs; they will also complain that it negates democracy because it allows individuals to place their resources outside the reach of political compulsion. For this reason, the reactionaries of the new millennium will find the financial privacy facilitated by information technology especially threatening. They will recoil from the prospect that income and capital taxation would truly depend upon "voluntary compliance." They will support novel and even drastic means of squeezing resources out of anyone who appears to be prosperous, such as "presumptive taxation" and holding of wealthy persons to outright ransom.

Community Property

Hints of what is to come are near the surface as we write. Early evidence that the capacity of governments to control international markets is slipping away offends those who believe that individuals are, by right, assets of nation-states. They want to enforce their ability to treat the citizens of a country as assets, not as customers. The reactionaries believe that all income should be considered revenues of the community, meaning that it should be at the disposal of the state.[26]

We have already discussed arguments advanced by Lasch in *Revolt of the*

Elites and the Betrayal of Democracy. But his is not the only diatribe in support of the nation-state. Harvard University political theorist Michael Sandel argues in *Democracy's Discontent* that "Democracy today is not possible without a politics that can control global economic forces, because without such control it won't matter who people vote for, the corporations will rule."[27] In other words, the state must retain its parasitic power over individuals, in order to assure that political outcomes can diverge from market outcomes. Otherwise collective decisions to compel diseconomic outcomes would be meaningless.

In our view, Sandel's lament, like that of Lasch, is no more than half right. We concede that democracy will lose much of its importance if governments lack the power to compel individuals to behave as politicians insist. This is obvious. Indeed, democracy as it has been known in the nineteenth and twentieth centuries is destined to disappear. But Sandel misses the real importance of the triumph of markets over compulsion. His invocation of "corporate rule" as a danger attendant upon the collapse of the nation-state is strikingly anachronistic.

Corporations will hardly be in a position to rule the markets of the new global economy. Indeed, as we have suggested, it is far from obvious that corporations will even continue to exist in their familiar modern form. Far from it. Firms are almost bound to be transformed in the megapolitical revolution that comes with the introduction of the Information Age. As we have previously discussed, microprocessing will alter the "information costs" that help determine the "nexus of contracts" that define firms. As economists Michael C. Jensen and William H. Meckling suggest, corporations are merely one legal form that provides "a nexus for a set of contracting relationships among individuals."[28]

Whether the corporation can even survive, much less "rule" as "a domain of bureaucratic direction that is shielded from market forces," is itself likely to be determined, in the words of economists Louis Putterman and Randall S. Kroszner, by "the completeness of market forces and the ability of market forces to penetrate intrafirm relationships."[29]

As we argued earlier, it is doubtful that firms will be able to survive the increasing penetration of market forces into what have heretofore been "intrafirm relationships." As a result, firms will tend to dissolve as information technology makes it more rewarding to rely upon the price mechanism and the auction market to undertake tasks that need doing rather than having them internalized within a formal organization. As information technology increasingly automates the production process, it will take away part of the *raison d'être* of the firm, the need to employ and motivate managers to monitor individual workers.

"Why Are There Firms?"

Remember, the question "Why are there firms?" is not as trivial as it may seem on casual observation. Microeconomics generally assumes that the price mechanism is the most effective means of coordinating resources for their most valued uses. As Putterman and Kroszner observe, this tends to imply that organizations like firms have no inherent "economic *raison d'être*." [30] In this sense, firms are mainly artifacts of information and transaction costs, which information technologies tend to reduce drastically.

Therefore, the Information Age will tend to be the age of independent contractors without "jobs" with long-lasting "firms." Equally, when economic success depends upon talented individuals, they may receive outsized pay and extravagant bonuses to provide their services, much as professional athletes and movie stars command huge rewards for their talents. In any event, as technology lowers transaction costs, the very process that will enable individuals to escape from domination by politicians will also prevent "rule by corporations." Corporations will compete with "virtual corporations" from across the globe to a degree that will disturb and threaten all but a few. Most corporations as institutions will be lucky to survive intensified competition as markets become more complete.

The consequence to be expected is not that individuals will be at the mercy of corporations. To the contrary. Corporations, per se, will have no more power to rig markets than politicians. It is rather that individuals will finally be free to determine their own destinies in a truly free market, ruled neither by big governments nor corporate hierarchies.

This erosion of transaction costs will also put the lie to recently fashionable notions of "stakeholder capitalism." Such notions, dear to Tony Blair of Britain's Labour Party as well as some within Bill Clinton's entourage, are predicated upon the ability of the state to manipulate the corporation. Socialism having collapsed, interventionists now dream of achieving the ends of socialism through more market-efficient means by heavily regulating the firm. This new redistributive theory holds that the management, shareholders, employees, and "community" are all "stakeholders" of firms. The argument is that they all derive benefits from long-lasting firms, and even depend upon these benefits. Therefore, regulation ought to protect the stakes that managers, employees, and local taxing authorities have in the continuation of their historic relations with the firms.

"Stakeholder capitalism" is a doctrine that ultimately presupposes not only an ability of the state to manipulate the decision-making of corporations, but even more basically presupposes the existence of corporations as long-standing organizations capable of functioning independently of price signals in the auction market.

We suspect that the deepening of markets will not only diminish the taxing capacity of the nation-state, it will also erode the capacity of politicians to impose their will arbitrarily upon the owners of resources by regulation. In a world where jurisdictional advantages will be subject to market tests, and many local markets will be opened to competition from anywhere, it is hardly to be expected that local "communities" will have many effective ways of isolating favored firms from global competitive pressures. Therefore, they will have few ways of assuring that corporations lumbered with higher costs (for example, to retain unnecessary employees and management personnel, and keep unneeded facilities open to accommodate local political pressures) will be able to offset those costs and stay in business. In the Industrial Age, politicians could close markets and restrict entry to a few favored firms to meet employment and other objectives. In the future, when information will be freely tradable anywhere on the globe, the power of governments to insulate local businesses from global competitive pressures will be minimal.

Neither is it likely that calls for a "new social contract" focused on a so-called independent or volunteer sector to absorb the time of otherwise unemployed or marginalized workers "in the community" will prove viable.[31] Jeremy Rifkin imagines "a new partnership between the government and the third sector to rebuild the social economy. . . . Feeding the poor, providing basic health care services, educating the nation's youth, building affordable housing and preserving the environment. . . ."[32]

The Eclipse of Public Goods

Of course, the apologists for coercion will argue that the waning of state power will lead to an inability to procure or enjoy public goods. This is unlikely, both for competitive and other reasons. For one thing, with locational advantages mostly dissipated by technology, jurisdictions that fail to provide essential public goods, such as maintenance of law and order, will rapidly lose customers. In the most extreme failures, such as those already evidenced in Somalia, Liberia, Rwanda, and the former Yugoslavia, hordes of penniless refugees are likely to spill over borders seeking more satisfactory provision of law and order. But these extreme examples of desertion, or voting with one's feet, will differ only by their urgency from straightforward jurisdictional shopping. In any event, corporations will force local jurisdictions to meet the needs of their customers.

"Competitive Territorial Clubs"

This is more than merely a theory, as articulated first by economist Charles Tiebout in 1956.[33] As economist Fred Foldvary has documented in *Public Goods and Private Communities: The Market Provision of Social Services,* there is no essential reason that social services and many public goods must be provided by political means. Foldvary's examples, among others, also confirm the controversial theorem of Nobel Prize–winning economist Ronald Coase that "government intervention is not needed to resolve externality issues," such as problems of pollution.[34] Entrepreneurs can provide collective goods by market means. Many already do so now in real world communities. Foldvary's case studies show how the privatization of communities can result in new mechanisms for providing and financing public goods and services.[35]

The Road to Prosperity

Microtechnology itself will facilitate new means of financing and regulating the provision of goods heretofore treated as public goods. In retrospect, some of these goods will prove to have been private goods in disguise. Highways represent a key example. So long as congestion was a minor problem, roads and highways could be treated as if they were public goods, albeit subject to the criticisms leveled by Adam Smith that they disproportionally benefit those living nearby at the expense of those in remote regions who are dragooned into paying for them while enjoying few of the benefits.

In the Information Age, it will be technologically feasible to impose tolls, including congestion fees, that accurately price access to highways, runways, and other infrastructure without interrupting traffic flow. Thus the provision transportation infrastructure could be discretely privatized and financed directly by those who use the service. Economist Paul Krugman estimates that market pricing of U.S. transportation infrastructure would add from $60 billion to $100 billion annually to GDP in the United States, while improving the efficiency of resource use and reducing pollution.[36]

Furthermore, it is not to be forgotten that the most costly part of what modern nation-states do—redistributing income—is not the provision of a public good at all, but the provision of private goods at public expense. "Public expense" here is a euphemism for "at the expense of those who pay the taxes."

What of a genuine public good, like the provision of a military force capable of deterring attack by a great power? Such a force has traditionally been expensive. Obviously, as we have already explored, a government that lacks an unchecked ability to confiscate the incomes and property of its citizens would be unable to finance participation in another great power conflict like World War II.

Yet this fiscal limit poses less of a threat than the reactionaries will pretend, for the simple reason that there will be no more conflicts like World War II. The very technology that is liberating individuals will see to that.

Up from Politics

Instead of leaving the quality and character of such services to the mercy of politics, "governments" can be run entrepreneurially and converted into what Foldvary describes as "competitive territorial clubs." [37] We suspect that ultimately, the decision-making process by which such "competitive territorial clubs" are organized will mean much less than their success in meeting market tests of performance. Today, few consumers care when they buy a product or service whether the firm that sells it is a sole proprietorship, a limited liability company, or a corporation controlled by outside directors dominated by pension plans. Equally, we doubt that the rational consumer of sovereignty services in the Information Age will care whether Singapore is a mass democracy or a proprietorship of Lee Kwan Yew.

CHAPTER 11
MORALITY AND CRIME IN THE "NATURAL ECONOMY" OF THE INFORMATION AGE

"Corruption . . . is far more widespread and universal than previously thought. Evidence of it is everywhere, in developing countries and, with growing frequency, in industrial countries. . . . Prominent political figures, including presidents of countries and ministers, have been accused of corruption. . . . In a way this represents a privatization of the state in which its power is not shifted to the market, as privatization normally implies, but to government officials and bureaucrats."[1]

—VITO TANZI

We believe that as the modern nation-state decomposes, latter-day barbarians will increasingly come to exercise real power behind the scenes. Groups like the Russian mafiyas that pick the bones of the former Soviet Union, other ethnic criminal gangs, nomenklaturas, drug lords, and renegade covert agencies will increasingly be laws unto themselves. They already are. Far more than is widely understood, the modern barbarians have already infiltrated the forms of the nation-state without greatly changing its appearances. They are microparasites feeding on a dying system. As violent and unscrupulous as a state at war, these groups employ the techniques of the state on a smaller scale. Their growing influence and power is part of the downsizing of politics. Microprocessing reduces the size that groups must attain in order to be effective in the use and control of violence. As this technological revolution unfolds, predatory violence will be organized more and more outside of central control. Efforts to contain violence will also devolve in ways that depend more upon efficiency than magnitude of power.

The surge of covert criminal activity and corruption within nation-states will form an important subplot as the world changes. What you will see could be a covert and sinister version of a bad movie, *Invasion of the Body Snatchers*. Before most nation-states visibly collapse they will be dominated by latter-day barbarians. As often as not, as in the famous B-movie from the 1950s, they will be barbarians in disguise. The Pod People of the future, however, will not be aliens from space but criminals of various affiliations who fill official positions while owing at least partial allegiance outside the constitutional order.

The end of an era is usually a period of intense corruption. As the bonds of the old system dissolve, the social ethos dissolves with it, creating an environment in which people in high places may combine public purposes with private criminal activity.

Unfortunately, you will not be able to depend upon normal information channels to give you an accurate and timely understanding of the decay of the nation-state. "Persistent make-believe" of the kind that disguised the fall of the Roman Empire is probably a typical feature of the decomposition of large political entities. It now disguises and masks the collapse of the nation-state. For a variety of reasons, the news media cannot always be depended upon to tell you the truth. Many are conservative in the sense that they represent the party of the past. Some are blinded by anachronistic ideological commitments to socialism and the nation-state. Some will be afraid for more tangible reasons to reveal the corruption that is likely to loom ever larger in a decaying system. Some will lack physical courage that might be required for such a task. Others will fear for their jobs or be shy of other retribution for speaking up. And, of course, there is no reason to suspect that reporters and editors are any less prone to corrupt consideration than building inspectors or Italian paving contractors. To a larger extent than you might expect, important organs of information that appear to be keen to report anything and everything may prove to be less dependable information sources than is commonly supposed. Many will have other motivations, including shoring up support for a faltering system, that they will place ahead of honestly informing you. They will see little and explain less.

BEYOND REALITY

As artificial reality and computer game technologies continue to improve, you'll even be able to order a nightly news report that simulates the news you would like to hear. Want to watch a report showing yourself as the winner of the decathlon at the Olympics? No problem. It could be tomorrow's lead story. You'll see any story you wish, true or false, unfold on your television/computer with greater verisimilitude than anything that NBC or the BBC can now muster.

We are rapidly moving to a world where information will be as completely liberated from the bounds of reality as human ingenuity can make it. Certainly, this will have tremendous implications for the quality and character of the information you receive. In a world of artificial reality and instantaneous transmission of everything everywhere, integrity of judgment and the ability to distinquish the true from the false will be even more important.

But this will be less of a change from our current circumstances than many people would imagine. The distinctions between true and false are commonly blurred for reasons that have been amplified by technology. We say this recognizing that many of the consequences of the Information Revolution have been liberating.

Technology has already begun to transcend geographic proximity and political domination. Governments can erect barriers to hinder the trade in goods, but they can do much less to halt the transmission of information. Almost every diner at any restaurant in Hong Kong is connected by cellular phone to the whole globe. The hard-line coup plotters in Moscow in August 1991 could not shut down Yeltsin's communications because he had cellular phones.

More Information, Less Understanding

As the barriers to transmission of information have fallen, there has been more of it, which is good. But there has also been more confusion about what it means. The modern technology that helps liberate information from political controls and impediments of time and place also tends to raise the value of old-fashioned judgment. The kind of insight that helps discern what is important and true from the mountain of facts and fantasies is growing in value almost daily. This is true for at least three reasons:

1. The very glut of information now available puts a premium on brevity. Brevity leads to abbreviation. Abbreviation leaves out what is unfamiliar. When you have many facts to digest and lots of phone calls to return, the natural desire is to make each information-processing event as concise

as possible. Unfortunately, abbreviated information often provides a poor foundation for understanding. The deeper and richer textures of history are precisely the parts that tend to be edited out in the twenty-five-second sound-bites and misconstrued on CNN. It is much easier to convey a message that is a variation on an already understood theme than it is to explore a new paradigm of understanding. You can report a baseball or a cricket score much more easily than you can explain how baseball or cricket is played and what it means.

2. Rapidly changing technology is undermining the megapolitical basis of social and economic organization. As a consequence, broad paradigmatic understanding, or unspoken theories about the way the world works, are being antiquated more quickly than in the past. This increases the importance of the broad overview and diminishes the value of individual "facts" of the kind that are readily available to almost anyone with an information retrieval system.

3. The growing tribalization and marginalization of life have had a stunting effect on discourse, and even on thinking. Many people have consequently gotten into the habit of shying away from conclusions that are obviously implied by the facts at their disposal. A recent psychological study disguised as a public opinion poll showed that members of individual occupational groups were almost uniformly unwilling to accept any conclusion that implied a loss of income for them, no matter how airtight the logic supporting it. Given increased specialization, most of the interpretive information about most specialized occupational groups is designed to cater to the interests of the groups themselves. They have little interest in views that might be impolite, unprofitable, or politically incorrect. There is no better example of this general tendency than the broad drumbeat of views implying bright prospects for investing in the stock market. Most of that information is generated by brokerage firms, few of which will tell you that stocks are overvalued. Their income is derived from transaction business that depends on the majority of customers being ready to buy. Independent, contrary voices are seldom heard.

For these and other reasons, the Age of Information has not yet become the Age of Understanding. To the contrary, there has been a sharp drop-off in the rigor of public discourse. The world now could know more than at any time in the past. But there is almost no public voice left to assess the meaning of events and say what is true. This is why we have been fascinated to see the tepid interest, particularly in the U.S. media, in reporting hints of sensational corruption at high levels of the U.S. government.

A central theme we have wrestled with in this book is how changing technology and other "megapolitical" factors alter the "natural economy." The "natural economy" is the Darwinian "state of nature" where outcomes

are determined, sometimes unfairly, by physical force. In the "natural economy," an important strand of behavior is what biologists call "interference
competition."

Interference Competition

"Interference competitors," as Jack Hirshleifer put it, "gain and maintain
control over resources by directly fighting off or hampering their rivals. . . ."[2]
However much we may wish that human behavior were always subject to the
rule of law and "other socially enforced rules of the game" ("political
economy"), there is ample evidence that many people "play by the rules"
only when it suits them. Hirshleifer, an authority on conflict, put it this way:
"[T]he persistence of crime, war and politics teaches us that actual human
affairs still remain largely subject to the underlying pressures of natural
economy."[3]

In other words, economic outcomes are determined only partly by the
peaceful and law-abiding behavior of the *Homo economicus* described in
textbooks, who honor property rights "and will not simply take what does
not belong to them."[4] Actual outcomes are also shaped by conflict, including
overt violence. As economist Hirshleifer points out, "Even under law and
government, the rational, self-interested individual will strike a balance between lawful and unlawful means of acquiring resources—between production and exchange on the one hand and theft, fraud and extortion on the
other."[5]

MUGGING IN THE INFORMATION AGE

Michelle R. Garfinkel and Stergios Skaperdas explore this in a useful book
on violence, crime, and politics, *The Political Economy of Conflict and
Appropriation:* "Individuals and groups can either produce and thus create
wealth or seize the wealth created by others."[6] They quote a tale of modern
interference competition originally reported by the *Economist:* "An American businessman, recently arrived in Moscow to open an office, was met at
his hotel by five men with gold watches, pistols and a print-out of his firm's
net worth. They demanded 7% of future earnings. He took the first flight to
New York, where muggers are less sophisticated."[7]

This tale of mugging in the Information Age owes more to new technology than the simple fact that thugs in Russia now have access to financial
profiles and credit reports on their victims through the Internet.

Falling Decisiveness of Military Power

For good and for ill, by making large-scale military power less decisive, information technology has radically reduced the capacity of the nation-state to impose its authority in an unruly world. If once, as Voltaire said, God was "on the side of bigger battalions," there appears to be less divine support with every day that passes for generating large returns to violence. Instead, we see the opposite—more evidence of diminishing returns to violence—which strongly implies that large conglomerations like the nation-state will no longer justify their huge overhead costs.

The most obvious evidence of the declining decisiveness of centralized power is the rise of terrorism. High-profile bombings in the United States in the mid-nineties show that even the world's military superpower is not immune from attack.

Another important manifestation of falling returns to violence is the worldwide growth of gangsterism and organized crime, along with its corollary, political cronyism and corruption. They reflect a generally amoral atmosphere in which the state can coerce but not protect. As its monopoly of violence frays, new competitors edge into the scene, like the bully-boys who tried to impose their own private taxes on the American businessman in Moscow.

Small groups, tribes, triads, gangs, gangsters, mafias, militias, and even solitary individuals have gained increasing military effectiveness. They will exercise far more real power in the "natural economy" of the next millennium than they did in the twentieth century. Weapons that employ microchips have tended to shift the balance of power toward the defense, making decisive aggression less profitable and therefore less likely. Smart weapons, like Stinger missiles, for example, effectively neutralize much of the advantage that large, wealthy states formerly enjoyed in deploying expensive air power to attack poorer, smaller groups.

Information War Ahead

Looming ahead is the widely discussed but little-understood possibility of "Information War." It also points to diminishing returns to violence. "Logic bombs" could disable or sabotage air-traffic control systems, rail-switching mechanisms, power generators and distribution networks, water and sewage systems, telephone relays, even the military's own communications. As societies become more dependent upon computerized controls, "logic bombs" could do almost as much damage as physical explosions.

Unlike conventional bombs, "logic bombs" could be detonated remotely, not just by hostile governments but by groups of free-lance computer programmers, and even talented individual hackers. Note that an Argentine teenager was arrested in 1996 for repeatedly hacking into Pentagon computers. While to date hackers have not tended to tamper with computer-controlled systems in destructive ways, this is not because there are truly effective ways of stopping them.

When the age of Information War finally arrives, it is unlikely that its antagonists will only be governments. A company like Microsoft certainly has a greater ability to conduct Information War than 90 percent of the world's nation-states.

The Age of the Sovereign Individual

This is part of the reason why we have entitled this book *The Sovereign Individual*. As the scale of warfare falls, defense and protection will be mounted at a smaller scale. Therefore, they will increasingly be private rather than public goods, provided on a for-profit basis by private contractors. This is already evident in the privatization of policing in North America. One of the more rapidly growing occupations in the United States is the "security guard." Projections indicate that the number of private security guards will increase 24 percent to 40 percent above 1990 levels by the year 2005.[8]

The privatization of policing is already a well-defined trend. Yet as Anglo-Irish guru Hamish McRae points out, this is hardly the result of any deliberate decision of government. He writes in *The World in 2020*:

No government has made a specific decision to move out of some policing tasks, nor indeed, have any moved out; the private sector has moved in. Partly as a result of the perceived failures of the police, partly as a result of other changes in society, private security firms have gradually been taking over much of the job of protecting ordinary civilians in their offices or shopping centres. As the gated communities of Los Angeles show, people are even moving some way back towards the medieval concept of a city, where the citizens live behind town walls patrolled by guards, and where access is possible only at controlled gates.[9]

We believe that this is only a foretaste of more comprehensive privatization of almost every function undertaken by governments in the twentieth century. Because information technology has undermined the capacity of centralized authority to project power and provide physical security for systems that operate at a large scale, the optimal size of almost every enterprise in the "natural economy" is falling.

To respond to this technological change will entail a massive investment requirement (read opportunity) to redesign vulnerable systems with distributed rather than concentrated capabilities. If vulnerabilities of large scale are not removed, the systems that retain them will be subject to catastrophic failure.

Sooner or later, by default if not by design, services and products provided by large bureaucratic agencies and corporations will devolve into highly competitive markets, managed not from a "headquarters" but through a distributed, decentralized network.

The corporation with a headquarters that can be surrounded by pickets or sabotaged by terrorists will be vulnerable until it ultimately becomes a "virtual corporation" without a location, "dwelling in many places concurrently," as Kevin Kelly, executive editor of *Wired* magazine writes in *Out Of Control*.[10] Kelly understands that technology has changed the imperative to bring production processes under centralized control. "For most of the industrial revolution, serious wealth was made by bringing processes under one roof. Bigger was more efficient." Now it isn't.

Kelly foresees the possibility that an automobile of the future, the Upstart Car, could be designed and brought to production by as few as a dozen people collaborating in a virtual corporation.

In the future, excessive scale could be not only counterproductive but dangerous. Larger enterprises make more tempting targets. As practitioners of the underground economy demonstrate, one of the secrets of avoiding taxation is to avoid detection. This will be much easier for small-scale, "virtual corporations" than old-line corporations operating out of a skyscraper headquarters with their names in lights. They are bound to be more vulnerable to the attentions of "men with gold watches, pistols and a print-out of the firm's net worth," the gangsters who will impose their own private brand of taxation in other parts of the globe as they do in Russia. Enterprises on all scales will be vulnerable to criminal shakedowns and impositions from organized criminal gangs.

"[C]onsider the definition of a racketeer as someone who creates a threat and then charges for its reduction. Governments' provision of protection, by this standard, often qualifies as racketeering."[11]

—CHARLES TILLY

Nature Hates Monopolies

As the monopoly on violence enjoyed by the "bigger battalions" breaks down, one of the first results to be expected is increasing prosperity for organized crime. Organized crime, after all, provides the main competition to nation-states in employing violence for predatory purposes. Although it is impolite to say so, it should not be forgotten, as political scientist Charles Tilly reminds us, that governments themselves—"quintessential protection rackets with the advantage of legitimacy—qualify as our largest examples of organized crime." [12]

If you knew nothing else about the world other than the fact that an important monopoly was breaking down, one of the simplest and surest predictions you could make is that its nearest competitors would stand to benefit most. It is therefore not a coincidence that drug cartels, gangs, mafias, and triads of various sorts are proliferating around the world.

Sistema del Potere

From Russia to Japan to the United States, organized crime is a far more important factor in the operation of economies than economic textbooks would prepare you to believe. What the Sicilians call the *"sistema del potere,"* the "system of power," of organized crime has an increasingly important role to play in determining how economies function.

European police officials report that international crime syndicates, including Russian and Italian mafias, played "a dominant role" in financing the genocidal wars that have racked the Balkans in recent years.

Drug traffickers have also played a key role in financing recent civil wars and insurgencies in other parts of the globe. Julio Fernandez, chief of the Spanish national police drug squad in Catalonia, says, "From 1986 to 1988, 80 percent of the heroin in Spain was carried here by Tamil Tiger guerrillas working with Pakistani residents in Barcelona or Madrid. As soon as we destroyed that network with arrests, it was replaced with Kurds from Turkey, who completely dominated it for the next two years." [13] Chances are, whenever a new civil war or insurgency gets under way, the desperately poor combatants will finance their military effort by delivering drugs and laundering drug money.

Drug-Financed Discounting

Organized criminal syndicate activities have placed downward pressures on prices of commodities other than drugs. At the micro level, crime syndicates subsidize apparently legitimate businesses from the spoils of criminal enterprise. They can launder drug profits and other illicit funds by selling ordinary goods below cost, thus undercutting the prices of their clean competitors and putting many out of business.

Yakuza Deflation

In Japan, the powerful Yakuza gangs played a key role in Japan's hyperactive real estate bubble of the late 1980s. In spite of the fact that ninety thousand Yakuza make somewhere between $10.19 billion (official estimate) and $71.35 billion (estimate of Professor Takatsugu Nato) annually, a high proportion of the uncollectible loans that have threatened the solvency of Japan's banks were made to Yakuza-backed deals.[14] The deflation pressures—"price destruction," as the Japanese call it—that have characterized Japan's economy are a consequence.

A Blind Eye

Russia's mafiyas, as Yeltsin himself has admitted, have merged with "commercial structures, administrative agencies, interior ministry bodies, city authorities . . ."[15] Because of the immunity the mafiyas have achieved by merging with police, they are able to enforce collection of their private taxes through blatant violence. Authoritative sources indicate that four of five Russian businesses now pay protection money. "According to some reports, local small businesses in Russia have to pay 30 to 50 percent of their profits to racketeers, not just the meager 7 percent demanded from the American businessman."[16]

In 1993 there were 355,500 crimes in Russia officially designated as examples of "racketeering," including almost "30,000 premeditated murders," mostly gangland assassinations of businessmen. According to a former interior minister, General Viktor Yerin, "The bulk were contract killings, because of conflicts in the sphere of commercial and financial activity." In most cases, authorities turned "a blind eye."

Criminal organizations "through their control over coercion and corruption," as economists Gianluca Fiorentini and Sam Peltzman write in *The Economics of Organized Crime,* play a key role in the economy.[17] In theory, this influence can sometimes be beneficial because it constrains regulation and may encourage governments to improve their delivery of public goods. The presence of a powerful mafia "constrains the monopolistic role of government authorities."[18] Governments in territories with powerful organized crime groups can only with great difficulty entertain policies that the mafias oppose.

Collusion

In fact, it is notable how infrequently most governments are willing to directly confront the mafias that are their main competitors in the use of organized coercion. In strictly economic terms, this is not surprising. The most profitable arrangement that "the elected members of the public administration" can strike is a "collusive agreement" with organized crime. Fiorentini and Peltzman note that "there has been evidence of large-scale agreements where organized crime ensures political support for groups of candidates, while the latter repay the favour through a favourable management of public procurements and the provision of public services or subsidies." [19]

Contrary to the impression conveyed by Hollywood, penetrating and defrauding governments now appears to be one of the main focuses of criminal organizations like the Sicilian mafia. "Most scholars think that by now the greatest business of the Sicilian mafia is precisely that of appropriating the different sources of public expenditures and of organizing frauds against the local, national and European Community schemes of subsidization." [20]

Narco Republics

As we warned in *The Great Reckoning*, many governments in the world are thoroughly corrupted by drug lords. Mexico is an indisputable example. Former Mexican federal deputy attorney general Eduardo Valle Espinosa put the Mexican system in perspective in his resignation statement: "Nobody can outline a political project in which the heads of drug trafficking and their financiers are not included. Because if you do, you die." Valle indicated that bribes make serving as a Mexican police chief so lucrative that candidates pay up to $2 million just to get hired. In a strict profit-and-loss accounting, buying a local police office can be a lucrative investment. Drug cartels are willing to pay fortunes to even low-ranking Mexican officials because the money buys them immunity from prosecution for their crimes.

Colombia is another country where the top rungs of government are dominated by drug lords. The U.S. authorities have recently revoked the U.S. visa of Colombian president Ernesto Samper on grounds that he knowingly received political contributions from drug dealers in exchange for favors.

Pot Calls the Kettle Black

Anyone who has followed the reports in our newsletter, *Strategic Investment,* during the 1990s will immediately recognize the irony in the Clinton administration's posturing about Samper. There is credible evidence that U.S. President Bill Clinton has done everything Samper is accused of, and worse. Even if you would not take our word for it, Clinton's background is highlighted in gaudy detail in two well-researched books by authors on opposite sides of the political divide.

Roger Morris, who takes a generally left-wing perspective, was a national security official in the Nixon administration, as well as a senior aide to Dean Acheson, President Lyndon Johnson, and Walter Mondale. Morris has a doctorate from Harvard University. His book, *Partners in Power,* details a sordid past for Clinton that makes Samper seem like a Boy Scout.

Morris recounts Clinton's fatherless childhood in Hot Springs, Arkansas, a center of gambling, prostitution, and organized crime to which most of his family had some connection. Clinton's step-uncle, Raymond Clinton, to whom Bill Clinton referred as a "father figure," was reputedly a leading "Godfather" figure in the Dixie mafia.

Morris alleges that Bill Clinton became a CIA recruit and spent his student days at Oxford monitoring anti–Vietnam War activists. As Morris sees things, Clinton remained a CIA asset through his period as governor, facilitating a CIA drug- and gun-running operation centered in Mena, Arkansas. Morris seems to indict the CIA as a whole for drug trafficking, rather than entertaining the possibility that Clinton threw in with a corrupt faction of the agency, which seems more probable to us. Either interpretation, however, still suggests that the main covert intelligence agency of the U.S. government either directly or indirectly participates in organized drug running on a large scale. If the CIA is not an adjunct of organized crime, it is tripping dangerously close to being so.[21]

One Chance in 250,000,000

Nonetheless, *Partners in Power* contains details that would interest any student of the corruption of modern American politics. And by no means, however, are all of Morris's fingers pointed at Bill Clinton. His wife comes in for some critical attention as well. For example, consider this exerpt from Morris's account of Hillary Clinton's miraculous commodity trading: "In 1995 economists at Auburn and North Florida Universities ran a sophisticated computer statistical model of the First Lady's trades for publication in the *Journal of Economics and Statistics,* using all the available records as well as market data from the *Wall Street Journal.* The probability of Hillary Rodham's having made her trades legitimately, they calculated, was less than one in 250,000,000."[22]

Morris musters many incriminating details about the drug-running and money-laundering operation that prospered in Arkansas under Clinton. "By the sheer magnitude of the drugs and money its flights generated, tiny Mena, Arkansas, became in the 1980s one of the world centers of the narcotics trade. . . ."[23] Morris quotes an intimate as testifying about Clinton that "He knew."

Clinton not only knew of the cocaine smuggling but told state trooper

L. D. Brown, a former bodyguard whom Clinton helped to land a position with the CIA, that the drug running was not a CIA operation. " 'Oh, no,' Clinton said, 'That's Lasater's deal.' "[24]

Dan Lasater, convicted cocaine distributor, was one of Clinton's major financial supporters, a man who made millions from Arkansas state business and once reportedly gave $300,000 in cash in a brown paper bag to then Kentucky Governor John Y. Brown. According to Morris, Lasater "was never merely another big donor to be paid special deference, but an extraordinary intimate whom Clinton visited regularly at his brokerage and who came to the mansion whenever he pleased."[25] Morris recounts that Lasater's driver, who frequently brought him to the mansion, was "a convicted murderer who carried a gun and was widely known to deal drugs on the side."[26] According to Morris's account, the President of the United States appears to have been on warmer terms with a drug dealer than the relationship alleged between Colombian president Ernesto Samper and the Cali cartel.

"Whew! Bob says things about Bill Clinton that even Hillary wouldn't say."

—P. J. O'ROURKE

R. Emmett Tyrell, Jr., editor-in-chief of *The American Spectator,* is not a left liberal like Morris. But his account *Boy Clinton* contains many of the same details cited by Morris in painting a portrait of Clinton as a corrupt politician, intimately linked to drug dealing and other crimes. Indeed, the Prologue to *Boy Clinton* quotes L. D. Brown, Clinton's former bodyguard, making the sensational allegation that Clinton was complicit in death-squad activity designed to eliminate witnesses who were knowledgeable about drug dealing at Mena.

Specifically, Brown testifies that he was personally dispatched to Puerto Vallarta, Mexico, on June 18, 1986, with a Belgian-made F.A.L. light automatic rifle. Traveling under the alias Michael Johnson, Brown was to have shot and killed Terry Reed.

Reed, as you may remember, came to public attention in 1994 as the coauthor of *Compromised: Clinton, Bush and the CIA.* The thesis of *Compromised* is that the CIA has "co-opted the presidency," and that its "black operations, like a cancer have metastasized the organs of government." More specifically, Reed and his coauthor claim that both Clinton and Bush were deeply compromised by involvement in illegal activities in Arkansas, including drug trafficking.

Brown did not kill Reed, as instructed. He and Reed managed to survive to tell at least part of their tales, which makes them luckier than others who were involved with Clinton, then and later. Consider the late Jerry Parks, who provided security for the Clinton-Gore headquarters in 1992 and was shot dead, in a gangland-style assassination, in September 1993. In another bizarre twist to a twisted tale, London's *Sunday Telegraph* has revealed, on the basis of exclusive information provided by Parks's widow, that Parks was hired to spy on Bill Clinton by the late Vincent Foster.

Why Foster wanted to compile a dossier of compromising information on Clinton is anyone's guess. (He said he was doing it for Hillary.) But in any event it belies the official depiction of Foster as a naïve country boy, so shocked by the ruthless ways of Washington that he killed himself in despair. That never-plausible story becomes less plausible with each new revelation.[27]

The Mob's President

While the world as a whole draws back from the disturbing conclusion that the President of the United States is tainted by close association with organized crime and criminals, that is what the evidence suggests. Morris quotes a former U.S. Attorney who tracked organized crime figures and their interests. He claims that Clinton's election as governor in 1984 "was the election when the mob really came into Arkansas politics, the dog-track and racetrack boys, the payoff people who saw a good thing. . . . it went beyond our old Dixie Mafia, which was penny-ante by comparison. This was eastern and West Coast crime money that noticed the possibilities just like the legitimate corporations did."[28]

Apparently, others of like mind have continued to notice the possibilities with Clinton. *New York* magazine, following an earlier piece in *Reader's Digest,* reports that "the president's key allies in the trade-union movement are also men affiliated with what to all appearances are some of the dirtiest, most mobbed-up unions in America."[29] Of particular interest is Clinton's close relationship with Arthur Coia. Coia, who is one of Clinton's "prime fund raisers," is president of the Laborers International Union of North America, "one of the most flamboyantly corrupt unions in labor history."[30]

Apparently, the Justice Department under Mr. Clinton struck what *New York* describes as a "weirdly generous deal" with Coia "to keep his job in the face of compelling charges from that very same Justice Department that he is a long-time associate of organized-crime figures."[31]

Whether or not Terry Reed's thesis is correct that "the CIA has co-opted the presidency," there is obviously a strong temptation for individuals within a covert organization authorized to undertake "black operations" to indulge in Professor Hirshleifer's rational choice of employing "unlawful means of acquiring resources."

Given the technological change that is reducing the decisiveness of massed military power in the world, one should perhaps expect to see increasing corruption, if not outright takeover of governments by organized criminal enterprises.

Hirshleifer argues, and we agree, that "the institutions of political economy can never be so perfect as to entirely displace . . . the underlying realities of natural economy." [32] Power is devolving in the "natural economy." This implies far-reaching shifts in the internal margins of power in society.

Political corruption, as Vito Tanzi shrewdly notes, "represents a privatization of the state in which its power is not shifted to the market, as privatization normally implies, but to government officials and bureaucrats." [33] In effect, this has happened to the FBI and other police agencies under Clinton. The "rule of law" is becoming whatever Clinton and his cronies want it to be.

As of now, there seems little evidence that details of these corrupt connections will carry any weight with voters, even if they were taken up and discussed in the mass media. To the contrary. There seems to be little concern about hints that the President of the United States is complicit in drug running, money laundering, and worse.

This brings to mind the late Walter Lippmann's fear that voters lacked the perception to see through what he called fictitious personalities. He thought that voters "are ill-served by flattery and adulation. And they are betrayed by the servile hypocrisy which tells them that what is true and what is false, what is right and what is wrong, can be determined by their votes." [34]

Lippmann perceived a "breakdown in the constitutional order" that could be "the cause of the precipitate and catastrophic decline of Western society. . . . We have fallen far in a short span of time. . . . What we have seen is not only decay—though much of the old structure is dissolving—but something which can be called an historic catastrophe." [35]

The problem is that political judgments seem less a response to the real world than to a pseudoreality that the general public has constructed about phenomena beyond their direct knowledge. [36] But it is a mistake for you to be governed by the limits of what others see. Even if you do not give a twig whether Vincent Foster was murdered, and his murder covered up by the top police agencies and responsible officials of the U.S. government, including even the current special prosecutor, Kenneth Starr, you might want to consider evidence of the broader pattern of ties between organized criminal enterprise and the White House.

In the long run, political corruption at the highest levels makes nonsense of conventional celebration of the possibilities of democracy for the deliberate mastery of public problems. In the Information Age it will be much less important that government be large and powerful than that it be honest. Most of the services that governments historically provided are destined to devolve into the private market in the next millennium. But it is doubtful on the evidence from around the world whether you can long depend upon a corrupted system with corrupt leaders for the security of your family and investments.

As Morris says, "[T]he Clintons are not merely symptomatic, but emblematic of the larger bipartisan system at its end-of-century dead end." [37]

Vito Tanzi, in his essay on corruption, shows that "the only way to deter corruption is to reduce significantly the scale of public intervention." [38] The Information Revolution will significantly reduce "the scale of public intervention" and on that basis holds out hope for a rebirth of morality and honesty. The other obvious implication of the Information Revolution for morality is an increased vulnerability that comes with the possibility of cybercommerce and virtual corporations communicating with unbreakable encryption. Internal thieves within an organization, even a virtual organization, will be more difficult to detect and it will be all but impossible to recover money that is stolen or received covertly for selling trade secrets, patents, or other valuable economic assets.

Crime pays, and many find it attractive to supplement lawful, productive pursuits with unlawful, predatory ones. Unlike the usual situation that prevailed in Western societies through most of the past two centuries, criminals are not merely misfits, without social standing. When crime pays, you tend to get a better class of criminal because little social odium attaches to crime. The Sicilian Mafia, for example, along with many drug dealers who employ local labor at inflated rates, command respect and popular support on their home turf.

THE MORAL ORDER AND ITS ENEMIES

All strong societies have a strong moral basis. Any study of the history of economic development shows the close relationship between moral and economic factors. Countries and groups that achieve successful development do so partly because they have an ethic that encourages the economic virtues of self-reliance, hard work, family and social responsibility, high savings, and honesty. This is also true of social subgroups. The business success of Jews, particularly of religious Jews, of the Puritans in New England, of the Quakers in British business in the eighteenth and nineteenth centuries, or of the Mormons in modern America, all show the economic benefits that result from cultures with a strong moral framework.

One can take the Quakers as an example. The Quakers became successful businesswise, and were particularly successful as bankers, for a number of reasons. They set themselves the highest possible standard of trustworthiness. They would not swear oaths, but regarded every business commitment as being as binding as an oath. "My word is my bond" was for them an absolute principle. They believed in a quiet style of living, decent but frugal. As a religious duty, they avoided spending money on the vanities of this world. They avoided quarrels, and thought war was always sinful. They thought that the businessman had a moral obligation to give fair value, and as merchants they developed a reputation for maintaining high quality with moderate prices. "Caveat emptor"—let the buyer beware—was not good enough for them. In an age when most merchants followed a high-price, high-margin theory of trade, the Quaker morality led them naturally to a low-margin, high-turnover policy. As Henry Ford later showed, this can be potentially far more profitable. They followed this business policy because they thought it their duty not to cheat their customer, but it turned out to be the best way to expand their businesses. The Quakers proved good people to do business with, so their customers came back; there were profits on both sides. As a high-saving community, which honored its obligations, the Quakers had an advantage as bankers, and membership in the Quakers was itself a business asset which inspired confidence.

Unfortunately such business advantages can be eroded by the very success they produce. Countries go through a cycle, which formed the basis of Adam Ferguson's sociological theory in the eighteenth century, from poverty and hard work, to riches, to luxury, to decadence, and on to decline. The ancient Romans themselves looked back to the virtues of the Republican period, when the Empire was being built, and deplored the luxury and laziness that they regarded as the cause of their decline. This erosion of the industrious virtues by prosperity can happen surprisingly quickly. The Germans are still a capable and efficient people, but they are not working anything like as hard as they did when they were rebuilding their country after the ruin of defeat in 1945. In two generations, they have gone from working long hours, almost with their bare hands, in conditions of acute poverty, to working short hours for the highest pay and the most expensive welfare on earth.

In October 1995, the Petersburg Declaration was signed by sixteen German associations of employers. It is a catalogue of well-justified complaints, which reflect the decline in Germany's industrial morale.

> Germany's tax burden reached record highs in 1995, particularly due to the solidarity surcharge and payments for nursing care insurance. With total corporate taxation amounting to more than 60 per cent, Germany is far above the comparative international level of 35 to 40 per cent. Public sector habits such as regulated promotions, jobs for life and higher pension payments have to be replaced by the free market rules of meritocratic promotion and compensation. ... Due to the fact that Germany has the highest labour costs in the world,

wage policies have to contribute to the reduction of unemployment by alleviating the costs for enterprises. . . . Wage increases should be measured according to competitiveness and productivity. . . . The behaviour of the unions has to change. The yearly ritual of campaigns, demands, workers' mobilization, threats, and warning strikes is damaging.

This anxiety that the Germans, particularly the young and the heirs of prosperity, have lost the habit of work is shared by Chancellor Kohl.

The existing Volkswagen labor contract gives the highest pay for any car workers on earth, to which welfare taxes have to be added, in return for a 28-hour week—four days of seven hours each. Postwar Germany is now a massive exporter of jobs. The British were regarded in the middle of the nineteenth century as the most efficient industrial nation, a reputation they had certainly lost a hundred years later. The cycle of prosperity undoubtedly undermines virtues of hard work and modest expectations, which exist at the early stages of successful industrial development. Nations are not able to retain their early virtues, just as individuals can become greedy and lazy with too easy a success.

Global investment undoubtedly rewards these industrious virtues and penalizes those who become greedy and lazy, as it should. Indeed, one could say that sound investment has to be based on a moral as well as a purely financial assessment. The Englishman in the eighteenth century who subscribed to the capital of a Quaker bank was likely to do very well. In the nineteenth century, the Quakers invested in chocolate businesses, since they thought that cocoa was healthier than alcohol. It probably is. Yet an investment in Fry's or Cadbury's was certainly a good investment. Investors should be concerned to avoid the periods of decadence. Even if Germany retains a strong position in the European market, and high industrial skills, high labor costs and short working hours have already reduced Germany's future potential.

Social morality and economic success are insolubly linked. But what factors help to maintain, or tend to undermine, the social morality? Arnold Toynbee, the great philosophic historian of the first half of the twentieth century, formulated the theory of the challenge and response. Societies are invigorated by challenges, and develop virtue they did not even know they possessed.

There has always been a human recognition that hard times may develop, and normally do develop, healthier responses than those of periods of prosperity. In our individual lives, we all try to make ourselves comfortable, we hope to live in a house that we enjoy, have a job that we like, have enough money in the bank, and so on. The struggle to achieve these objectives is a rewarding one. We study at school, we train ourselves, we work hard at our business or profession, with these objectives in mind.

In far too many people the achievement of these objectives creates something of a trap. The struggle is better than the achievement. The great Swiss psychologist Carl Jung had an American businessman as his patient early in this century. The businessman had these very ambitions as a young man. He had worked to establish his own business, and to make enough money to retire by the age of forty. He married a young and attractive woman, he bought a beautiful home, he had a young family, his business was highly successful, and by the age of forty he had indeed been able to sell out and retire, a rich and independent man with nothing apparently to worry about. At first he enjoyed his freedom, was able to do things he had long promised himself. He took his family to Europe. They visited art galleries and so on. Gradually these interests, and his sense of freedom itself, began to pale. He started to look back at the time when he was not free, when he was working all hours at his business and had all the usual business worries, as the happy period of his life. He fell into a depression, which led his wife to bring him to Jung as a patient. Jung diagnosed him, in effect, as having no outlet for his creative energy, which had turned in on him, and was destroying him. The diagnosis may well have been correct, but it did not lead to a cure. The businessman never recovered from his nervous breakdown.

For human beings it is the struggle rather than the achievement that matters; we are made for action, and the achievement can prove to be a great disappointment. The ambition, whatever it may be, sets the struggle in motion, but the struggle is more enjoyable than its own result, even when the objective is fully achieved. And, of course, for most people, the objectives can be achieved only partially. Most of us do not have as much money as we would like, and do not live in our dream house. We have to settle for something less.

This sense that virtue is dynamic, that it consists in the effort rather than the result, developed strongly in the nineteenth century, and in different ways. There is a well-known poem by Arthur Hugh Clough that brought comfort to many people in the life-and-death struggle of the Second World War. It is worth noting that suicide rates in the warring countries fell in the Second World War; even the struggle of war can be better than the depression of inactivity.

Say not, the struggle nought availeth,
The labour and the wounds are vain,
The enemy faints not, nor faileth,
And as things have been they remain.

If hopes were dupes, fears may be liars;
It may be, in yon smoke concealed,
Your comrades chase e'en now the fliers,
And, but for you, possess the field.

For while the tired waves, vainly breaking,
Seem here no painful inch to gain,
Far back, through creeks and inlets making,
Comes silent, flooding in, the main.

And not by eastern windows only,
When daylight comes, comes in the light,
In front, the sun climbs slow, how slowly,
But westward, look, the land is bright.

This active competition still appeals to the modern sensibility. Indeed, it is how many modern men and women lead their lives, in a continuous struggle to seize the opportunities of a potentially hostile environment. We all live in a competitive world, and most of us do not wish to contract out of it. There is, of course, the contemplative spiritual temperament, but it is quite rare.

A similar nineteenth-century perception of this dynamic morality was developed by William James, the greatest of American philosophers, in an address to the Yale Philosophical Club in 1891:

> The deepest difference, practically, in the moral life of man is the difference between the easy-going and the strenuous mood. When in the easy-going mood the shrinking from present ill is our ruling consideration. The strenuous mood, on the contrary, makes us quite indifferent to present ill, if only the greater ideal be attained. The capacity for the strenuous mood probably lies slumbering in every man but it has more difficulty in some than others in waking up. It needs the wilder passions to arouse it, the big fears, loves and indignation; or else the deeply penetrating appeal of some one of the higher fidelities, like justice, truth, and freedom. Strong relief is a necessity of its vision; and a world where all the mountains are brought down and all the valleys are exalted is no congenial place for its habitation. This is why in a solitary thinker this mood might slumber on forever without waking. His various ideals, known to him to be mere preferences of his own, are too nearly of the same denominational value: he can play fast or loose with them at will. This too is why, in a merely human world without a God, the appeal to our moral energy falls short of its maximal stimulating power. Life, to be sure, is even in such a world a genuine ethical symphony; but it is played in the compass of a couple of poor octaves, and the infinite scale of values fails to open up.

William James believed that the dynamic morality, which consists in doing rather than being, in acting rather than refraining from action, can be extended into the religious sphere. There is also a powerful development of the morality of competition and survival in the work of Adam Smith (1776), Thomas Malthus (1798), and Charles Darwin (1859). As this is the dominant moral doctrine of the present world economic order, its central theme needs careful consideration.

The dominant idea of Darwinism is that species survive through adaptation to their environment, and that this process of natural selection shapes the characteristics of the species. In animals the process is the result of random mutations, which are now known to belong to a genetic process Darwin himself could only guess at. The survival of human societies depends, however, on cultural choices that are based on human intelligence. Culture changes human society as genes change other species. Change can therefore take place much faster in our societies. It does not have to work through many generations as it does when it depends on random genetic mutations. In place of the natural selection in animals, human beings have developed cultural selection, with some cultures, at some stage of human history, developing new technologies that gave them a decisive advantage in wealth creation or mustering power. The cultural edge of new technologies, such as Iron Age man had over Bronze Age man, or electronic man has over mechanical man, are decisive. Adam Smith may not have been the first writer on economic matters to reduce the welfare of nations to the action of individuals, but he put it most succinctly and with the greatest authority:

> Every individual is continually exerting himself to find out the most advantageous employment for whatever capital he can command. It is his own advantage, indeed, and not that of the society, which he has in view. But the study of his own advantage naturally, or rather necessarily, leads him to prefer that employment which is most advantageous to the society.

Thomas Malthus, the founder of population studies, saw that the Adam Smith argument could be applied not only to the development of the economy of nations but also to the survival of human populations. He is well known for his proposition that "Population, when unchecked, increases in a geometrical ratio. Subsistence increases only in an arithmetical ratio. A slight acquaintance with numbers will show the immensity of the first power in comparison of the second."

Malthus even saw, long before Darwin, that the same principle applied throughout nature:

> Through the animal and vegetable kingdoms, nature has scattered the seeds of life abroad with the most profuse and liberal hand. She has been comparatively sparing in the room, and the nourishment necessary to rear them. The germs of existence contained in this spot of earth, with ample food, and ample room to expand in, would fill millions of worlds in the course of a few thousand

years. Necessity, that imperious all-pervading law of nature, restrains them within the prescribed bounds.

The way the world develops, even at this stage of Adam Smith and Malthus, had already come to be understood by the end of the eighteenth century as dynamic, which it had always been in fact. The human species, itself one among many, is forced to compete by the mismatch between its unlimited capacity for generation and its limited ability to grow food. The survival of human societies, as of animal species, depends on successful adaptation to the environment. A dynamic morality is therefore concerned with overcoming the problems of adaptation. This is best achieved by individuals who adapt their own actions to the opportunities of the environment, and therefore employ resources available in the society to the greatest advantage.

Malthus already saw that Adam Smith's ideas had changed the world, and he wrote that his new argument about population was not new: "The principles on which it depends have been explained in part by Hume and in part by Dr. Adam Smith." He also saw that this constant competition for survival was a moral, not merely a practical, matter. The last paragraph of the 1798 "Essay" reads:

> Evil exists in the world, not to create despair, but activities. We are not patiently to submit to it, but to exert ourselves to avoid it. It is not only the interest, but the duty of every individual, to use his utmost efforts to remove evil from himself, and from as large a circle as he can influence; and the more he exercises himself in this duty, the more wisely he directs his efforts, and the more successful these efforts are; the more he will probably improve and exalt his own mind, and the more completely does he appear to fulfil the will of his Creator.

Perhaps one can illustrate Darwin's sense of the importance of this argument from his summary of the contents of Chapter 3 of his epoch-making book, *On the Origin of Species,* first published in 1859. He called this crucial chapter "Struggle for Existence." The subject readlines are: "Bears on Natural Selection—The term used in a wide sense—Geometrical powers of increase—Rapid increase of naturalized animals and plants—Nature of the checks to increase—Competition universal—Effects of climate—Protection from the number of individuals—Complex relations of all animals and plants throughout nature—Struggle for life most severe between individuals and varieties of the same species; often severe between species of the same genus—The relation of organism to organism the most important of all relations."

Since 1776, it has been evident that the best way to optimize the wealth of nations is to allow individuals to optimize their own return on capital in conditions of free competition. Since 1798, it has been evident that the relative survival of populations depended on societies having sufficient economic and political success to be able to feed themselves, protect themselves from infectious diseases, and protect their populations in war. Since 1859, it has been evident that the whole drama of life, in the human, the animal, or the vegetable kingdom, consists of a continuous struggle for survival, in which those species or cultures that are nearest to each other may be the greatest rivals. This struggle requires a dynamic morality, which actively wards off evil and does not merely respond to it when it happens.

These ideas have been so powerful that it has been impossible for anyone to think about the nature of humanity, or the problems of morality, since the time in which they were developed, without responding to them. Karl Marx believed in the struggle for survival just as much as Charles Darwin, but he believed it was a war between social classes, themselves formed by economic forces. Adolf Hitler believed in the struggle for survival, and saw his own political career almost exclusively in those terms. But he believed that the struggle was one between different races. Marx, Lenin, Stalin, Mao, and Hitler can all be called social Darwinists, in that they saw the struggle for survival, "Mein Kampf" as Hitler called it, as the central political issue. The Marxists saw social classes as though they were separate species; the Nazis saw races in the same light.

This, however, makes not a dynamic morality, such as Malthus envisaged, but a dynamic immorality. Both Marxism and Nazism wished to solve the same problem, the problem of the struggle for survival, but by destroying competition. They invaded foreign territories, they promoted conflict between different classes who competed for social power, or different races who were seen either as economic exploiters (the normal charge made against Jews by anti-Semites) or as a dangerous underclass (the fear held of blacks by their white enemies). The Second World War was an attempt by Adolf Hitler, which failed, to secure an advantage in survival terms of the German people, by destroying potential competition, particularly Slavs and Jews. By an interesting paradox, defeat in war proved more advantageous to Germany than the victory of the Nazis could ever have been.

The alternative to destructive "interference" competition is collaborative competition, and collaborative competition is the central idea of Adam Smith, and also of Malthus and of William James. The archetype of destructive competition is the conqueror. He destroys his competitors in order to seize their assets, which may include taking over their countries and may involve the enslavement of their peoples. The archetype of collaborative competition is the merchant. It is in the interest of the merchant that the customer should be satisfied with the transaction, because only a satisfied customer comes back for more trade. It is also in the interest of the merchant that the customer should be prosperous, because a prosperous customer has the money to go on buying. Conquest implies the destruction of the other party; commerce implies the satisfaction of the other party. As modern technology has made conquest an extraordinarily dangerous policy, commerce has become the only rational approach to the problems of survival.

This interdependence is strengthened by another central idea of Adam Smith—not new with him—which is the specialization of function. The *Wealth of Nations* starts with a celebrated passage in which Adam Smith observes that "the greatest improvement in the productive powers of labour, and the greater part of the skill, dexterity and judgement with which it is any where directed, or applied, seem to have been the effects of the division of labour." He points out that "the important business of making a pin is, in this manner, divided into about eighteen distinct operations, which, in some manufactories, are all performed by distinct hands." The more complete the specialization of function, the more efficient the manufacture is likely to be, but obviously such an economy is highly interdependent. If it is to be successful, it has to be collaborative.

A successful social morality must therefore have certain characteristics. It must be strong—a weak morality will be vulnerable and ineffective. It must contribute to the struggle for survival, but in ways that are collaborative rather than murderous. Hitler had a strong morality of survival, but its destructive quality nearly destroyed his own society. It must be dynamic, to match the dynamic changes of modern technology, and indeed of all modern social systems. It must be economically efficient. The mixture of egalitarian and authoritarian ideas in the Leninist system simply did not work. Yet these are not all the characteristics that such a social morality might be expected to possess. It has a broader purpose of making the society a good one to live in, and of binding people together. Also, moralities have to adapt and survive; a brittle morality may be acceptable in our generation only to be rejected in the next. A traditional social morality may be too inflexible to adapt to successive changes in social structure. On the other hand a purely relativist system is not a morality at all; it gives no clear signals on how to behave.

We can first of all put all social morality inside a context. A strong community, even a virtual community, depends upon the morality being widely accepted. The most successful periods in the history of societies tend to be those in which the collective morality is fully shared. Such a morality not only performs specific functions such as reducing crime, and helping to support family and social structures, but gives citizens a sense of purpose and direction. Such a consensus on morality historically seems to depend on there being a dominant religion, whether that is a state religion of the early Roman Empire; the religion of the Jews, which has been the thread of survival for a dispersed people; the Islamic religion with its social rules; the Catholicism of the Middle Ages; or the Protestantism of early New England. The three ideas of a people, a morality, and a religion depend upon one another, and each tends to reinforce the others.

In such a moral society, the individual citizen is able to work toward personal objectives inside a framework of social support. Admittedly the moral laws may be somewhat arbitrary, or at least may appear arbitrary to outsiders. The Orthodox Jew loses the freedom to eat pork or shellfish, or to work on the Sabbath. The loyal Catholic may lose the freedom to use artificial contraceptives, let alone to have an abortion. The Moslem may lose the freedom to drink alcohol. The pious Confucian may have the inconveniently long period of mourning for his reverend father—even Confucius himself warned that mourning rituals could be exaggerated. Yet the adherent to each of these systems of belief regards these observations as a small price to pay for a shared and coherent sense of world order, in which the individual has a settled place. An Orthodox Jew could well argue that the observance of the Sabbath is a small price to pay for the benefits of the Law or the strength of the Jewish family. A shared morality in a tolerant society was the ideal of John Locke and of early philosophers of liberty. They did not at all believe that a society, of any kind, can be maintained without rules, but they thought that the rules ought to be subject to the best of reason, and that people should be coerced to accept only the essential rules. They did recognize that coercion was inevitable in social morality, particularly in the protection of life or of property, because they considered that no society can survive if there is no security. They applied an almost absolute tolerance to variations in personal choices that did not affect the welfare of others. The Confucian, mourning his father for forty days, could live next door to the Jew, honoring the Sabbath, without either disturbing the other, or wanting to coerce him into following his own religious practices.

From this combined doctrine of social morality in essential matters and tolerance in personal decisions, one actually gets a core moral standard that has to be imposed on all citizens and a voluntary ethic that citizens accept as individuals or as members of subgroups in society. When a Benedictine monk takes vows of poverty, chastity, and obedience, he does so as a member of such a subgroup. He does not call on all Catholics, let alone on all his fellow citizens, to take the same vows, or to observe the same rules. He will be obedient to the orders of his abbot, but he does not expect anyone outside his abbey to pay any attention to them. The adherence to these optional parts of social morality does not need to be universal, but the core morality does have to be shared, and people who will not accept the core morality damage society as well as themselves. In the extreme example, a society overrun with robbers who do not hesitate to murder, as large parts of Europe were after the fall of the Roman Empire, offers nobody a satisfactory life, not even the robbers themselves; they are always particularly threatened by other murderers. This is equally true of some inner-city areas of the United States today. Anarchy is not the ideal society, because without the enforcement of law there is no human security.

When one looks at the forces that are hostile to the morality of society, one needs to consider this core morality, which is broadly similar in most modern religious belief systems. Two, at least, of the Ten Commandments of the Old Testament, for Christians, or the Torah, for Jews, can be regarded as universal for anything one could recognize as a religion: "Thou shalt not kill" and "Thou shalt not steal." One can even go beyond that. Almost all serious agnostics would regard both murder and theft—the ultimate threat to life and the ultimate threat to property—as forbidden, and would accept that society has the right to punish people who kill or rob. They might disagree about the appropriate punishment for a particular crime, but not about the right of society to punish as such.

The original phrase of John Locke has it precisely. Everyone has a right to "life, liberty and estate." In 1776 Thomas Jefferson added another of John Locke's phrases, "the pursuit of happiness." That makes a very fine phrase, and a very fine aspiration, but "life, liberty and estate" is more down to earth than "life, liberty, and the pursuit of happiness." Society depends absolutely on the right to life and the right to property. In practice history shows that these rights can be protected only when there is liberty. If the state is all-powerful, then the state becomes the great enemy of life, as in wars of aggression, and of individual property, by taking an inordinate share of the national wealth for its own often undesirable and always wasteful purposes.

The core morality is, however, under attack in the most advanced nations, partly by the very forces of modernity that give these nations their technical edge. The United States is the world's leading technological power. Many people, including most Americans, would have regarded the United States as a moral example to the rest of the world at any time up to the early 1960s. Now that view is seldom expressed, even by Americans who are proud of their country. One could not listen, as the world did, to the O.J. Simpson trial and regard the United States as the simple virtuous Republic it began by being.

If one looks back at the labels of the old America, they reflected the needs of a frontier society, which colored the attitudes of its citizens even in the big cities. Frontiers are democratic places. People feel themselves to be equal, and the early Americans threw off the class hierarchies of Europe. Even indentured laborers, sent over from England as prisoners, established themselves as independent tradesmen, farmers, or free laborers once their indenture period was over. Wages were higher than in Europe, and the cost of essentials was low, though imported manufactures were expensive. On the frontier itself people depended very much on one another, but the living, if hard, was a good one by European standards. Immigrants might start as low wage earners in the slums of Boston and New York, but they usually escaped from the slums quite soon, and generation after generation found prosperity. After the Civil War, the blacks saw themselves as though they were another immigrant group, and many of them shared these American values and objectives. From these the black middle class developed.

This aspiration, strengthened by the actual experience of the frontier, and by the influence of the churches, both Protestant and Catholic, framed the patriotism of Americans. They believed that they lived in God's own country, a notion uniquely guided by democratic ideals and Christian faith, the first and most successful of the world's democracies. The picture is familiar enough; it is personified in the image we all, or almost all, have of Abraham Lincoln, though one can still find some Americans in the South who see Lincoln as the man who unleashed the horrors of the first modern war to prevent free states from leaving a Union they no longer trusted.

Nevertheless, the image of Lincoln, craggy, simple, honest, and eloquent, is still the supreme American image, and it is essentially a moral one. Many Americans still feel the vivid original contrast between the democratic energy of the new country and the tired hierarchies of Europe. This ideal of an essentially dynamic meritocracy is hard for the foreigner to recognize in present-day Los Angeles, New York, Houston, or Washington, even though its traces, and something more than traces, can still be found in the great suburban belts or in the rural areas. The American Puritan ethic, with all its historic importance, survives best north of the snowline, but the entrepreneurial dynamism is more widespread.

Americans would point to the decay of the big cities, which have become breeding grounds for crime, especially the narco-business, as the worst symptom of the decline of a communal sense of morality. Most Americans also recognize that there is a clash of several different moral cultures, all competing in their claims and their authority. The "politically correct" culture rejects many, but not all, of the moral principles that upheld the old culture. It aggressively emphasizes the role and the rights of groups who are seen as having been historically exploited by a dominant white male culture, and rejects that culture, despite its being the founding culture of the United States.

The dominant male culture of the first half of the twentieth century centered on the survival of the nuclear family. This historically gave the husband-father at least a nominal dominance in the home, though in practice the home was often run by the wife-mother with the often meek acceptance of the nominal master. It gave the male boss a real dominance in the workplace, a dominance that the feminist movement has so far challenged but not reversed. The interest of the family, and historic Christian teaching, outlawed abortion. The old morality thought abortion was unlawful killing, was never allowable, and the adherents of the traditional morality still think that. Adherents of the new morality think the opposite. In *Roe* v. *Wade* the Supreme Court based the constitutional right to abortion, which had hitherto been regarded as a question for the individual states, on the doctrine of a right to privacy, itself remote from any language actually to be found in the Constitution or its amendments.

A woman's privacy was held to include the right to have or not to have children, whatever the consequences to the embryo might be. The Supreme Court did not regard the embryo as enjoying any constitutional rights—embryos being the same extraconstitutional entities in the late twentieth century that slaves had been in the first half of the nineteenth. "Life, liberty, and the pursuit of happiness" did not apply to slaves, and the language of the Declaration of Independence was not applied to embryos by the justices in *Roe* v. *Wade.*

The abortion debate is the extreme example of the conflict between the old and new morality, though there are equally remarkable conflicts in other areas where the old social organization with its morality has been challenged by the new. Traditional Christian morality, in Protestant and Catholic churches alike, laid great emphasis on sexual roles: No heterosexual intercourse outside or before marriage. No genital homosexual relationships. Lesbianism was less emphasized, because society hardly recognized its existence. When Queen Victoria was first told of it, she stoutly refused to believe that such things happened between women. Political correctness is the morality of supposedly oppressed groups. The homosexuals claimed an equal validity for their lifestyle, and challenged the traditional opposition to their sexual conduct. "Homophobia" was regarded as being itself an outrageous form of prejudice, like racial discrimination. To be critical of gays is regarded by the new morality as being as unacceptable as being critical of blacks, Jews, or women.

At the same time other sexual taboos were being eroded or abolished. In the 1960s there was a new wave of free love, partly based on the apparent security of the female contraceptive pill, but also promoted by moodchanging drugs and pop music. It led to an increasing amount of nonmarital cohabitation. By the 1990s it was thought absolutely normal in Britain, a rather more old-fashioned society than most of the United States, for Prince Edward to sleep with his girlfriend at Buckingham Palace, in the same stable but unmarried intimacy that students were sleeping with each other in their 1960s lodgings. Few people thought it odd that Queen Elizabeth II, the head of the Church of England, condoned her youngest son's conduct, her three elder children's marriages having already broken down. Those few who complained were regarded as hopelessly out of date and priggish. Yet there were still many people who regarded the old morality as preferable, even if they did not practice it themselves, or seriously expect their children to do so, beyond a fairly early age.

The politically correct movement has had its own puritanical side. Because it sprang from the perceived interests of women, seen as the largest of the oppressed groups, it had a certain hostility to male sexuality, both in aggressive and in what would previously have been regarded as harmless forms. Some women took the view that all men were by nature rapists, and the natural horror at rape was exaggerated into a general denunciation of the male gender. Others concentrated on sexual harassment, a real grievance—many men have very crude sexual manners—which became ludicrous in some trivial cases. Sexual harassment was even alleged in mere looks, without any word being uttered, let alone physical contact. As a result the new morality could be very censorious. White people could be accused of racial prejudices, not because they were prejudiced but because they were white. Men could be accused of sexual harassment because their expressions showed that they found a woman attractive, something that in an earlier generation had been regarded as a compliment rather than an insult.

The politically correct and the fundamentalist Christian groups are bitterly critical of each other, yet in the modern world they look rather alike. They both assume the authority of a particular moral doctrine as though it were universal, even though their moral doctrines are different. Both indeed can be criticized for the same defect, for an exaggerated and overconfident moralism, lacking in depth, in historic sense, or in tolerance. Both are attacked for their supposed resemblance to seventeenth-century Puritanism, to the self-confident moralists like Oliver Cromwell in England—he nearly emigrated to New England—or the Salem witch hunters. Neither the women's movement, in its more dogmatic form, nor the conservative preachers of the Bible belt can be accused of any lack of morality, but of its overdevelopment and rigidity. The heart of these moralities sometimes seems to have turned to stone. This sort of hardening of the moral arteries is as damaging to the consensual morality of society as the "anything goes" anarchy against which it protests.

It is a distortion of moral forces, a coarsening into self-righteousness. Pharisaism, the conviction that one is uniquely virtuous, is as old as humankind, and was particularly offensive to Jesus Christ. The erosion of morality, the belief that ethical choices are purely a matter of private preference, as much a matter for the individual as the choice of clothes, is a more recent phenomenon. This belief reflects the absence of any shared morality at all. It takes to a quite new stage the classical doctrine of liberty, and turns "the pursuit of happiness" from what John Locke originally meant by the phrase, and Jefferson understood by it in 1776, into a hedonism that is reckless of consequences.

The phrase "the pursuit of happiness" is taken from John Locke's *Essay on Human Understanding* (1691): "the highest perfection of intellectual nature lies in a careful pursuit of true and solid happiness, so the care of ourselves that we mistake not imaginary for real happiness, is the necessary foundation of our liberty." He does go on to say that "everyone does not place his happiness in the same thing. . . . the mind has a different relish as well as the palate. . . . Men may choose different things, yet all choose right, supposing them only like a company of poor insects, whereof some are bees, delighted with flowers and their sweetness, others beetles delighted with other kinds of viands." Yet he goes on to argue that to prefer vice to virtue is "manifestly a wrong judgement." He puts particular weight on the religious argument, but considers also that "wicked men have the worse part here." He believes that "morality, established upon its true foundations, cannot but determine the choice in anyone who will consider."

The Lockean doctrine of liberty undoubtedly gives a wider range to human preferences than more authoritarian moral systems that seek to treat all people alike, and impose uniformity of conduct. Yet soon the classic doctrine of liberty recognizes the need for collective moral imperatives, including respect for other people in society, particularly their lives and the peaceful ownership of their possessions under the law. A general erosion of the collective morality threatens liberty, both directly, in that it introduces an element of anarchy, and indirectly, by encouraging the most authoritarian forces of society. We can see the history of public morality as a cycle between disorder and authoritarianism; the modern authoritarian moralities, both feminism and fundamentalism, have emerged as a cyclical response to the hedonism of the 1960s.

We have already described some of the attributes of the new world of the next century. It will be shaped by two main forces, the shift of technology that is opening up the economies of Asia and the new global electronic communications that are making the citizen progressively less dependent on his or her local government. The new technology will replace, or has already replaced, many of the middle human skills—the production line worker, the office clerk, now increasingly the middle manager. But it has rewarded the rarer skills, creating an international cognitive elite of highly skilled people for whom the new communications open up the widest possible market for their skills. Like most elites, the cognitive elite tend to be a bit above themselves, are rather arrogant, and think they can set their own standards. They are alienated from society as a result.

During the first half of the next century there will be a massive transfer of wealth from the Old West to the New East. Political failures—and China is still a politically backward country—may delay this transfer of wealth and strategic power, but are most unlikely to prevent it. They cannot reverse it.

This process of the shift in wealth would in any case put the greatest possible pressure on the white-dominated countries of the Northern Hemisphere, on Europe and North America. At present about 750 million people belong to the advanced countries of this area; until very recently Japan was the only Asian, nonwhite country to have reached the Euro-American standard of living, though there were ethnically European populations in New Zealand, in Australia, and in the white population of southern Africa. Even in 1990, the total population of the advanced industrial countries was only about 15 percent of the world population of 5 billion. The shape of the distribution of the world's wealth was 15 percent rich, 85 percent poor, very like the income distribution in advanced industrial societies a hundred years ago. By 2050, in an accelerating process, the expectation is that the advanced economies will include about 3 billion people out of a world population that may have risen to 7 billion, or a wealth distribution of 40 percent rich, 60 percent poor. By the end of the century these figures could well be reversed, and the distribution could be 60 percent rich and 40 percent poor, with poverty particularly concentrated in Africa. The shift between nations will be toward a greater equality of wealth, but inside nations it will probably be toward greater inequality. The efficient users of talent and capital will have a decisive advantage over those with moderate skills or little capital. This wealth will be highly mobile. The poor in the advanced world will not be able to tax the rich on the twentieth-century scale; those countries that try to do so will fall back in an intensely competitive race.

Of course, the total productivity of the world economy will continue to rise, perhaps by an average of 3 percent over the whole world, if there are no world wars. If that proves correct, the total world product will double every twenty-five years, making it more than four times as large as it is now by 2050, and sixteen to twenty times as large by 2100. Even if the world population has increased to 8 billion by 2100, that will give the world GDP per head by the end of the century ten times its present level. Such an increase in wealth can take care of the rise in the new industrial societies, and the multimillion-dollar incomes of the cognitive elite, and still provides a decent and rising standard of living for the rest of the advanced workforce. But the differentials will be very different from those of the twentieth century. In world terms the poor nations will see their incomes grow much faster than those of the rich nations; in national terms, the incomes of the rich, as in the America of the 1990s, will grow much faster than middle or low incomes. In the next century we shall witness the creation of a world superclass, perhaps of 500 million very rich people, with 100 million being rich enough to emerge as Sovereign Individuals.

This process will have an inevitable consequence. Societies will become much less homogeneous; the nation-state will become weaker, or crumble altogether; the cognitive elite will see itself as cosmopolitan. Already people who work in the same global functions are developing a culture that is much closer to that of their fellow workers in other parts of the world than to their fellow citizens in the old nation-states. A London investment banker will probably feel more at home in Seoul than he will in Glasgow; a Washington civil servant may feel more at home in Bonn than in black areas of Washington itself. We can already see the splintering effect that this process has on moral values. The morality of the individual is partly framed by education, by what the individual has been taught as a child; it is also partly framed by experience of life. Both the education and the experiences of the cognitive elite will be cosmopolitan, and will tend to divorce people from their local communities.

As we move toward the next century, a high proportion of people in the growing cognitive elite have been given little religious or moral education in the family. The commonest religion of the elite is an agnostic humanism. Many such families are themselves split by divorce, remarriage, and subsequent third marriages. The marriage pattern in Hollywood is not universal in the United States, but the cognitive elite in Euro-America has a high divorce rate, probably averaging a third or more. The children of these divorced parents seldom have a basic religious education, and are aware of the variations of moral attitude between parents, stepparents, and stepsiblings. If one compares the initial moral education of this group with that of an Irish or Polish village, the peasant education obviously provides much the stronger religious training of the two. A godless, rootless, and rich elite is unlikely to be happy, or to be loved.

This inadequacy in the initial moral education of what will be the dominant economic group of the next century is likely to be reinforced by their life experience. These people will have the discipline of an advanced technical education, of one sort or another, to fit themselves for their new role as the leaders of the new electronic universe. But they will learn from that only some of the moral lessons that have historically been the framework for human social conduct. By the standards of Confucius, Buddha, or Plato (500 B.C.), St. Paul (A.D. 50), or Mahomet (A.D. 600), they may be moral illiterates. They will have been taught the lessons of economic efficiency, the use of resources, the pursuit of money, but not the virtues of humility or self-sacrifice, let alone chastity. Essentially most of them will have been brought up as pagans with a set of values closer to those of the late Roman Republic than to Christianity. Even these values will be highly individualistic, rather than shared. Societies, as we have argued, can only be strong if real moral values are widely shared. The advanced nations are already moving into the situation where many people will hold weak or limited moral values, others will compensate with fierce adherence to irrational values, and few values will be held in common across the whole of society. No doubt, some of the "competitive territorial clubs" that we described earlier will impose exacting moral standards for residence.

Differences in wealth have not in themselves historically produced fundamental differences in religious values. In dense and stable societies with strong traditions, a steep hierarchical structure, "the rich man in his castle, the poor man at his gate," may conceal values that run through the hierarchy, but this depends upon the strength of the communal feeling of the rich and the poor, and the strength of the social traditions. Neither of these conditions exists now, and both community feeling and tradition are being weakened by the economic and technological revolution that is taking place. The lives of the many and the few are becoming more and more distant from each other. The technological revolution has been achieved by breaking away from the old ways of doing things. In every field it has been the radical who has won, and the conventional thinker who has fallen behind, who has literally fallen out of the race. Our politics may be led by conventional thinkers—Bill Clinton, Helmut Kohl, John Major—but our most successful businesses are led by radicals with a keen understanding of the new technological world; the archetype is Bill Gates. Conventional thinking has been discredited by its inability to deal with the rapidity and the sheer force of change.

Yet morality is not like that. If we take the science of Moses, formed about 1000 B.C., it has very little to tell us. The account of the creation in the Book of Genesis may well contain a theological truth—God made the universe and humankind—but it does not give a scientific account of the actual development of physical structures. Yet if we take the morality of Moses—the Ten Commandments—that has a great deal to tell us.

Respect for parents and faithfulness in marriage are the best ways to preserve family life; family life is the best way to bring up morally healthy children. Stealing damages the thief and the people from whom things are stolen, and is a disincentive to work and saving. Social order depends on the truth of witnesses. It is wrong to murder, and so on.

In science, three thousand years completely changed what human knowledge is; in morality, we may actually have fallen back. The average psychotherapist probably gives the patient less good moral advice on how to lead his life than the average Jew would have received from his teacher in the period of Moses. Of course, Christianity itself is still available, but it is for most of the world a pale ghost of its former self. Few people have the faith of the earlier ages, or even of the less sophisticated communities; one does not look for saints on Park Avenue.

The destruction of tradition has been a necessary condition of scientific progress. If we all still believed that the sun revolved around the earth, then we could not have developed satellite communications. Indeed what we believe to be science itself is only a series of hypotheses, imperfect explanations due to be replaced by other explanations, stronger but still imperfect. Yet the destruction of tradition has been a disaster to the moral order of the world.

Confucius taught that we should always behave with moderation (he called the Golden Mean *chum yum*, at least as it was translated by seventeenth-century scholars). He also taught that we should respect authority and treat others as we would wish to be treated ourselves. That teaching is twenty-five hundred years old. As a tradition it influenced China for all recorded history, but Confucianism seems an outmoded tradition to many modern Chinese, who do not value moderation, who respect force rather than authority, and certainly do not treat others as they would wish to be treated themselves. With the loss of tradition, societies can lose the whole vocabulary of their moral consensus. China, with all its advancing power, is now a morally backward country compared to Tibet, impoverished and oppressed as the Tibetans are.

A good social morality has certain characteristics. It should contribute to the survival of society and of individuals, in a dynamic rather than static way. It should include tolerance and avoid self-righteousness. It should be religious, rather than merely agnostic. It should not pretend to decide questions of scientific fact. It should be neither anarchic nor authoritarian. It should be widely shared and deeply held. Such a social morality is particularly important to the family and to the raising of children as independent and responsible adults. It provides the focus of a good society.

We find that any such morality is supported by the logic of interdependence that comes from commerce and fellow-feeling, but is threatened by the attacks of a facile scientism, by the alienation of a superclass and a subclass, by the loss of the rootedness of the old geographical economies. Perhaps there will be a reaction against these trends. They must be recognized as extremely dangerous to the societies of the next century.

As what Isaiah Berlin called "the most terrible century in Western history" winds down, the age of giantism in social structure also draws to a close. The final days of the twentieth century are destined to be a time of downsizing, devolution, and reorganization. It will be the time of the social dinosaurs trapped in the tar pit. And a time of scavengers. Birds will pick the bones of dinosaurs. Governments, corporations, and unions will be obliged to adjust against their inclinations to new metaconstitutional conditions established by the penetration of microtechnology. It has profoundly shifted the boundaries within which violence is exercised. Today's world has already changed more than we commonly understand, more than CNN and the newspapers tell us. And it has changed in precisely the directions indicated by a study of megapolitical conditions. As we argued first in *Blood in the Streets* and then in *The Great Reckoning,* when change occurs in technology or the other factors that set the boundaries where violence is exercised, the character of society inevitably changes with them. Everything that is attached to the way humans interact, including morality and the common sense of the way we see the world, will change as well. After a period of slack morality, which is indicative of the end of an era, we will see the awakening of a sterner morality, with more exacting demands to meet the more exacting requirements of a world of competitive sovereignty.

Several features of the new morality can be foreseen. For one thing, it will emphasize the importance of productivity and the correctness of earnings being retained by those who generate them. Another corollary point will be the importance of efficiency in investment. The morality of the Information Age applauds efficiency, and recognizes the advantage of resources being dedicated to their highest-value uses. In other words, the morality of the Information Age will be the morality of the market. As James Bennett has argued, the morality of the Information Age will also be a morality of trust. The cybereconomy will be a high-trust community. In a setting where unbreakable encryption will allow an embezzler or thief to securely place the proceeds of his crimes outside the range of recovery, there will be a very strong incentive to avoid losses by not doing business with thieves and embezzlers in the first place. Just as in the example of the Quakers cited earlier, a reputation for honesty will be an important asset in the cyber-economy. In the anonymity of cyberspace, this reputation may not always apply to a known person, but it will be reliably verifiable through identification of cryptographic keys. The possibility for radiating difficulties if encryption or certification of encrypted identities becomes corrupted by gangsters or others is daunting enough that it should strongly militate against the hiring of any person whose behavior could be indicative of a lack of trustworthiness. Bennett envisions "A Gentleman's Club of Cyberspace," protected areas that would require heightened security measures for participation, "possibly using biometric validation such as voice-print identification. The proprietors would assume the responsibility of vouching for the identity of the participants and to some extent their trustworthiness, achieving a 'gentleman's club in cyberspace' (although ladies would be welcome these days). In these areas, people could carry on transactions with greater security and confidence than in the general realm of cyberspace. Thus the twenty-first century may see a return to a Victorian-like emphasis on trustworthiness and character in an environment no Victorian could have envisioned."

The protected areas of cyberspace may also offer guarantees to reduce risk similar to the extraterritorial guarantees of protection offered by the Counts of Champagne to protect merchants traveling to and from Champagne fairs. Other jurisdictions actually "indemnified traveling merchants against any losses they might incur while passing through the territory under the jurisdiction of the given noble."

"Guards of the Fair," officials originally appointed by the counts, provided security and a "tribunal of justice" for merchants at the fair. They ultimately volved into more independent entities, with a separate seal, notarizing contracts and enforcing performance, with the power to "bar from future fairs any trader found guilty of not paying his debts or fulfilling his contracted promises. This was evidently so severe a penalty that few willingly risked this denial of opportunities for future profit. Short of that, however, the guards could seize the goods of a defaulting debtor and sell them for the benefit of his creditors." [39]

Ostracism as means of enforcement of contracts declined in importance when the number of alternative markets rose. With the new information technology now available, however, ostracism of cheats and those defaulting on contracts could again be a potent enforcement mechanism with the fragmented sovereignties of the next stage of society. Computer linkages can police cyberspace with unforgeable information about credit and fraud. As the world will be in this sense particularly a small community, cheats and frauds will be discouraged.

In addition to emphasizing the morality of earnings and efficiency and placing a renewed stress on character and trustworthiness, the new morality is also likely to stress the evil of violence, particularly kidnapping and extortion, which will grow in importance as means of "shaking down" individuals whose resources will not otherwise be easy prey to crime.

Still another likely spur to sterner morality will be the end of entitlements and income redistribution. When the hope of aid for those falling behind is based primarily upon appeals to private individuals and charitable bodies, it will be more important than it has been in the twentieth century that the recipients of charity appear to be morally deserving to those voluntarily dispensing the charity.

"Subsidies, windfalls, and the prospect of economic opportunity remove the immediacy of needing to conserve. The mantras of democracy, redistribution, and economic development raise expectations and fertility rates, fostering population growth and thereby steepening a downward environmental and economic spiral." [40]

—VIRGINIA ABERNETHY

In some ways the new information world will be better positioned to encourage seriousness over moral issues. The promises of income redistribution that enflamed expectations among the unlucky and unsuccessful in the United States, Canada, and Western Europe have also had a perverse effect internationally. There is strong evidence suggesting that foreign aid and promises of intervention to forestall famine and increase living standards have been major factors stimulating population growth that exceeds the carrying capacities of backward economies. The startling growth of world population since World War II, with its often destructive impact on forests, soils, and water resources, can be traced to intervention on a global scale. This intervention short-circuited the negative feedback consequences that had long kept local populations in balance with the resources needed to support them.

Of course, many who lived in local environments with few resources and little or no growth were only too pleased to be assured that constraining limitations of their village life could be put aside. They eagerly adopted the optimistic message carried by international aid workers, Peace Corps volunteers, local revolutionaries, and the competing ideologues of the Cold War, who told one and all that a better day lay ahead. This was precisely the wrong message.

An important consequence of redistribution among cultures has been to make those who lived in nonindustrial civilizations and adhered to nonindustrial values artificially competitive. International aid, rescue missions to counter famine and disease, and technical intervention fooled many into believing that their life prospects had sharply improved—without the necessity on their part of updating their values or significantly altering their behavior.

International income redistribution not only encouraged an unsustainable surge in the world's population, it contributed in important ways to cultural relativism and widespread confusion over the crucial role of culture in fitting people to prosper in their local environment. Today most people believe that cultures are more matters of taste than sources of guidance for behavior that can mislead as well as inform. We are too keen to believe that all cultures are created equal, too slow to recognize the drawbacks of counterproductive cultures. This is especially true of the hybrid cultures that have begun to emerge in the hothouse of subsidy and intervention in many parts of the world in this century. Like the criminal subculture of America's inner cities, they retain incoherent bits and pieces of cultures appropriate to earlier stages of economic development, and combine them with values for informing behavior in the Information Age.

The Information Revolution, therefore, will not merely release the spirit of genius, it will also unleash the spirit of nemesis. Both will contest as never before in the millennium to come.

The shift from an Industrial to an Information Society is bound to be breathtaking. The transition from one stage of economic life to another has always involved a revolution. We think that the Information Revolution is likely to be the most far-reaching of all. It will reorganize life more thoroughly than either the Agricultural Revolution or the Industrial Revolution. And its impact will be felt in a fraction of the time. Fasten your seat belts.

AFTERWORD
DEVOLUTION AND THE LAW OF DIMINISHING MARGINAL RETURNS

"What is bloated beyond its proportions inevitably collapses. . . . What is concentrated, coherent, and connected to its past has power. What is dissipated, divided, and distended rots and falls to the ground. The bigger it bloats, the harder it falls."

—ROBERT GREENE AND JOOST ELFFERS, *The 48 Laws of Power* [1]

Heretofore, the history of human societies is that they have tended to evolve in the direction of greater "complexity" or sociopolitical control. Small hunting and gathering bands evolved into agriculture states, which gave way to larger-scale industrial nation-states. As archaeologist and historian Joseph A. Tainter writes in *The Collapse of Complex Societies,* "Human history as a whole has been characterized by a seemingly inexorable trend toward higher levels of complexity, specialization, and sociopolitical control. . . . " [2] Now, however, the emergence of the next stage of economic development, the Information Society, promises to reverse the apparently "inexorable trend" toward greater levels of centralization.

Tainter's work raises many interesting questions pertinent to the themes of this book. For example, if Tainter is correct in supposing that devolution of centralized control and less redistribution of resources imply collapse, then it is unlikely that the industrial nation-state in its current form could long coexist with devolved microstates hosting Sovereign Individuals. The nation-states may be incapable of surviving on a diet of stable, much less diminished, resources. As Tainter details, when hypertrophied systems have exhausted their potential, as we believe nation-states have today, "the Law of Diminishing Marginal Returns" frequently sets in. In "many crucial spheres" the returns for increased investments in centralized sociopolitical control decline, or even become negative. Hence, the phenomenon of "Parkinson's Law," in which the number of employees and expense of operating the British Admiralty skyrocketed over the twentieth century, while the number of ships in the British Navy shrank dramatically.

Similar manifestations of the "Law of Diminishing Returns" are certainly in evidence in the United States and other leading economies as the twentieth century draws to a close. As Roger Lane, Professor of Social Sciences at Haverford College, wrote in "On the Social Meaning of Homicide Trends in America," "the old institutions of social control—law, schools, police, prisons—have lost their effectiveness, despite frequent infusions of manpower and money."[3] There is unambiguous evidence of increasing costs for the overall burdens of government. For example, total taxes rose from 27.8 percent of U.S. median income in 1957 to 37.6 percent in 1997.[4] This is a strong hint, if not absolute proof, of diminishing marginal returns on the whole range of government activity in the United States.

In the past, sharply diminishing marginal returns have been a prelude to collapse. The argument of this book is that the increased capacity of individuals to protect their transactions and their assets from predatory taxation implies a decline in the redistribution of resources, along with less centralized social control, less regulation and regimentation, and, ultimately, devolution of territory. All these developments have historically been manifested in "collapse." In Tainter's terms, "collapse" is what happens when a centralized control system is no longer worth what it costs.

> "Whenever we have a threshold phenomenon, whether in physical, biological or social systems, the configuration of the system at the moment when the threshold is reached becomes unstable and the slightest, even infinitesimal displacement in the configuration in the proper direction leads eventually to a finite change in the configuration of the system. Therefore a change in the behavior of a single individual, no matter how small, may precipitate in an unstable social configurational process that leads to a finite and sometimes radical change."
> —Nicholas Rashevsky, *Looking at History Through Mathematics*[5]

While most individual adaptations to change are admittedly marginal and evolutionary in character, there can be revolutionary "paradigm shifts." Sometimes, even great empires tumble as a consequence. The marginal returns from further investment in centralized control can become so overwhelmingly negative that it is no longer economically rational for most individuals to continue to support the old system. Tainter explains the fall of the Roman Empire in these terms. In his words, "If accounts are to be believed, at least a portion of the overtaxed peasantry openly welcomed the relief they thought the barbarians would bring from the burdens of Roman rule. And a much larger portion were evidently apathetic to the impending collapse. . . . The costs of empire had risen dramatically, while in the face of barbarians' successes the protection that the State could offer to many of its citizens proved increasingly ineffectual. To many, there were simply no remaining benefits to the Empire, as both barbarians and tax collectors crossed and ravaged their land. As Gunderson notes, '. . . the net value of local autonomy exceeded that of membership in the Empire.' Complexity was no longer yielding benefits superior to disintegration, and yet it cost so much more."[6]

Tainter quotes other authorities in support of his thesis that collapse can bring "with it a corresponding rise in the marginal return on social investment:"

> "Zosimus, a writer of the second half of the fifth century A.D., wrote of Thessaly and Macedonia that, '. . . as a result of this exaction of taxes city and countryside were full of laments and complaints and all invoked the barbarians and sought the help of the barbarians.' . . . '[B]y the fifth century,' concludes R. M. Adams, 'men were ready to abandon civilization itself in order to escape the fearful load of taxes.' "[7]

Rashevsky's analysis of the "role of determinism versus indeterminism" in history emphasizes the vulnerability of systems to radical change that can be precipitated even by a single individual when the system becomes unstable and reaches a "threshold" condition. When conditions are ripe for change (such as when diminishing marginal returns for supporting a centralized system no longer yield "benefits superior to disintegration"), then the opportunity for a radical change is so robust that practically anyone can precipitate it. Rashevsky writes, "The individual who precipitates a finite change does not have to be an *exceptional* individual. He may be *any* individual. The situation is analogous to that in a physical system, where at a point of instability an accidental displacement of any one of the trillions of *identical* molecules precipitates a finite transition to a stable state."[8]

We cannot specify who will precipitate the collapse of the overgrown nation-state system, or when it will happen. But extrapolating from Tainter's and Rashevsky's analyses of the dynamics of social change, we can foresee collapse coming. The most developed and heretofore successful nation-states are all characterized by dwindling populations and massive, unfunded old-age pension liabilities. Absent unprecedented immigration from underdeveloped countries, or an unexpected influx of angels willing to work overtime and pay confiscatory tax rates, leading states in Europe, North America, and Australasia will fall far short of the revenues needed to maintain the social benefits currently delivered. Actuaries forecast rising taxes and lower benefits, i.e., diminishing marginal returns, especially for entrepreneurs who shoulder a disproportionate share of the tax burden.

IRS figures show that one-tenth of one percent of Americans paid a majority of income taxes in the United States as of 1997. These are precisely the persons to whom efficient minisovereignties can offer new opportunities for domicile at a negligible cost in taxes. The difference between the protection costs of a commercialized sovereignty and the predatory taxes imposed by the old nation-states could amount to the equivalent of many millions or even billions of dollars in lifetime income.

Conventional microeconomics is based upon the proposition that individuals who spot a $100 bill in the street will pick it up. Opportunities to save millions or billions would be tens of thousands or millions of times more compelling. People will act in the indicated way when faced with choice between confirming their costly allegiance to institutions beset by declining marginal returns, or shifting to new arrangements that demand less and promise more.

"Of all 36 ways to get out of trouble, the best way is—leave."

—CHINESE PROVERB

The argument of this book clearly informs the decision to redeploy your capital, if you have any. Citizenship is obsolete. To optimize your lifetime earnings and become a Sovereign Individual you will need to become a customer of a government or protection service rather than a citizen. Instead of paying whatever tax burden is imposed upon you by grasping politicians, you will be better positioned to prosper in the Information Age by freeing yourself to negotiate a private tax treaty that obliges you to pay no more for services of government than they are actually worth to you.

Based upon the history of other dominant systems facing collapse, those who opt for the *ultimum refugium* and get out early will be better off for having done so. This is already evident in the rash of laws passed during the 1990s to penalize Americans renouncing citizenship. The dangers of a nationalist reaction to the crisis of the nation-state make it important not to underestimate the scope for tyranny and mischief. Not withstanding the fact that the right to expatriate is enshrined in the U.S. Declaration of Indepenlence, the U.S. is likely to be one of the more tyrannical jurisdictions blocking the emergence of commercialized sovereignty. You should aim never to leave your money in any jurisdiction that claims the right to conscript you, your children, or your grandchildren.

Whatever your current residence or nationality, to optimize your wealth you should aim to primarily reside in a country other than that from which you hold your first passport, while keeping the bulk of your money in yet a third jurisdiction, preferably a tax haven.

To better acquaint yourself with the alternatives, we recommend that you travel widely to visit attractive locales where you might wish to secure the right to reside in an emergency.

If you are truly ambitious, you may even wish to carve out a minisovereignty of your own. We provide contacts in the appendices who can help you negotiate your own tax-free zone, or zona franca, from a recognized government that is prepared to sublet its sovereignty under the right circumstances.

Suppose you are just starting out . . .

But suppose you agree with the premises of this book and are excited by the prospect of the Information Age, but lack the ready capital to deploy in order to take advantage of opportunities to benefit from commercialized sovereignty? What do you do?

Any recipe for easy success is bound to disappoint. Opportunities to succeed abound as a consequence of the Information Revolution. Which one is right for you to capture is beyond our scope to say. If you are intent in accumulating capital in order to realize your full potential as a Sovereign Individual, you should make it one of your priorities to study and evaluate the works of the various gurus who attempt to teach useful hints about how to succeed.

Any good business bookstore or one of the on-line booksellers, like Amazon.com, can offer you a wide selection of manuals on success. Read as many as you can, not with the idea that any one set of rules will automatically make you financially independent, but with the understanding that success is a choice. If you are to succeed, you must arm yourself with the perspective and habits that characterize successful persons.

If you are still at the stage of selecting a career, resist the temptation of jumping to an easy conclusion that the best route to success in the Information Age is to become a computer programmer. Yes, it is true that programmers have been in great demand as the Information Revolution unfolded in the last quarter of the twentieth century. But as computational power has increased, artificial intelligence has developed apace. A company called Authorgenics has already demonstrated the capacity to create object-oriented software without programmers. You won't be highly paid by studying to do something that can be done with Aladdin's Lamp. The problem with specializing in software or any other rapidly evolving field at the center of the Information Revolution is that your area of expertise could soon be outdated.

This underscores the wisdom of the traditional liberal education, which aimed to encourage students to develop their critical faculties and thinking skills. Success in business, as in most areas of life, depends upon being able to solve problems. If you can teach yourself how to solve problems, you have a bright career ahead of yourself. No matter where you live, you will find problems galore in need of solving. In most cases, those who would benefit from solutions of their problems will pay you handsomely to effect them.

APPENDIX
RESOURCES FOR ACHIEVING INDEPENDENCE

"It takes a great deal of boldness and a great deal of caution to make a great fortune . . . it requires ten times as much wit to keep it."

—EMERSON, *The Conduct of Life*

STRATEGIC INVESTMENT AND OTHER INFORMATION SERVICES FROM JAMES DALE DAVIDSON AND LORD REES-MOGG

If you enjoyed this book, you may enjoy reading *Strategic Investment,* the private financial advisory service edited by James Dale Davidson and Lord Rees-Mogg.

Strategic Investment offers readers continuing insights into the emergence of the Information economy, along with advice about ways to profit from geopolitical developments.

Time after time, *Strategic Investment* has scooped the world in forecasting headlines before they happened. In its very first issue in 1984, *Strategic Investment* pinpointed a little-known member of the Soviet Politburo—Mikhail Gorbachev. Before Gorbachev had even assumed power, *Strategic Investment* obtained an interview with him and forecast that he and his wife would become international celebrities, pull back Soviet troops from around the globe, and seek cooperation rather than confrontation with the West.

Strategic Investment analyzed the pending fall of the Berlin Wall in February 1989, ten months before the bulldozers actually broke through the Wall. Years before the banking crisis, the S&L bankruptcies, and the real estate bust became news, *Strategic Investment* told readers what to expect. Among other *Strategic Investment* bull's-eyes: the 1987 stock market plunge, the collapse of oil prices in 1986, the ditching of apartheid in South Africa, the 1990 crash of the Japanese stock market, the rout of Iraq in the 1991 Gulf War, and the collapse of the Soviet Union.

A six-month trial subscription in the United States is available for just $60 (in Canada and elsewhere—US$75). Send your order to Strategic Investment, 108 N. Alfred Street, Suite 200, Alexandria, VA 22314; phone: (703) 836-8250.

James Dale Davidson also offers an investment club for accredited investors, *Strategic Opportunities.* A one-year trial subscription is $995 within the United States, $1025 elsewhere.

Also be sure to check *Strategic On-line* at http://www.strategicinvestment. com.

James Dale Davidson and Lord Rees-Mogg offer private consultation to individuals and corporations. For more details, contact Davidson and Rees-Mogg at 108 N. Alfred Street, Alexandria, Virginia, Suite 200 22314. Phone (703) 548-836-8250 or 888-281-8250. Or contact them by E-mail at http://www.sovereignindividual.com.

TO CREATE YOUR WEALTH OFFSHORE

For investment of sums in excess of $100,000, contact Lines Overseas Management. Headquartered in Bermuda, with offices in multiple offshore jurisdictions, Lines Overseas Management provides a full range of brokerage and investment banking services. For information, contact LOM's head office at 73 Front Street, Hamilton, HM 12 Bermuda; phone: 441-295-5808. Or visit the LOM page on the World Wide Web at http://www.oceanis.com.

Offshore Trust and Corporate Services

From its inception as the oldest independent trust company in Bermuda, St. George's Trust Company has provided the highest quality of personal service to an exclusive clientele. Through a network of legal and accounting advisers in the United Kingdom, the United States, Canada, Hong Kong, and the leading offshore jurisdictions, St. George's offers services that are innovative, customized, and multijurisdictional.

Whether your objectives are wealth building and estate planning, asset protection, overcoming political obstacles or instability, avoiding exchange controls or forced heirship, securing corporate voting control, or financing commercial ventures, St. George's Trust Company can develop a trust or corporate structure tailored to meet your individual requirements. For personal service and attention to detail, St. George's Trust, Waterstreet Administration, and associated companies provide the best that Bermuda and the Cayman Islands have to offer, with over a quarter century of trust, investment, and private banking experience.

Contact St. George's Trust, P.O. Box HM 3051, Hamilton, HM NX Bermuda; phone: 441-295-1820; fax: 441-295-5491, or look up St. George's on the World Wide Web at http://www.oceanis.com.

Secure Your Own Tax-Free Zone

If you would like to carve out your minisovereignty, contact The Services Group at 2300 Clarendon Boulevard, Arlington, Virginia 22201. Phone: 703-528-7444. Fax: 703-522-2329. E-mail: TSG@TSGINC.com. The Services Group was involved in negotiating the tax-free zone from the Democratic Republic of São Tomé and Principe, and is also a shareholder of WADCO, the South African company that obtained the concession discussed earlier. They have an up-to-date understanding of terms and conditions under which tax-free zones are being established, and they know which countries are inclined to entertain concessions.

The Sovereign Society

The Sovereign Society is a recently formed group of would-be Sovereign Individuals, inspired by the first edition of this book, who have clubbed together to help one another achieve independence. The group develops and circulates information about alternative passports and reports on efforts by governments to curtail choice of sovereignty services. Regular Membership is $295 per year. For more information, contact The Sovereign Society, 105 W. Monument Street, Baltimore, Maryland 21202. Or visit their Web site: http://www.*sovereignsociety.com.*

Global Alternative Residence and Lifestyle Tours

To participate in upcoming alternative residence and lifestyle trips with James Dale Davidson and Lord Rees-Mogg to areas of emerging opportunity, contact Lisa Eden at 888-281-8250.

NOTES

Chapter 1. The Transition of the Year 2000:
The Fourth Stage of Human Society

1. Danny Hillis, "The Millennium Clock," *Wired,* Special Edition, Fall 1995, p. 48.
2. Ericka Cheetham, *The Final Prophecies of Nostradamus* (New York: Putnam, 1989), p. 424.
3. Dr. Edward Yardeni, *Year 2000 Recession: "Prepare for the worst. Hope for the best,"* Version 5.0, May 13, 1998, B1.2.
4. Michael Grasso, *The Millennium Myth: Love and Death at the End of Time.* Wheaton, Illinois: Quest Books, 1995.
5. Johan Huizinga, *The Waning of the Middle Ages,* trans. F. Hopman (London: Penguin Books, 1990), p. 172.
6. Marshall McLuhan, *Understanding Media.* New York: Signet, 1964, p. 19.
7. James George Frazer, *The Golden Bough: A Study in Magic and Religion* (New York: Macmillan, 1951), p. 105.
8. For more detail about fragmented sovereignties as a precursor and alternative to the nation-state, see Charles Tilly, *Coercion, Capital and European States AD 990–1992* (Oxford: Blackwell, 1993).
9. The German GPI index stood at 33.20 on December 31, 1948, and 112.90 on June 30, 1995, which represents a compound annual depreciation of 2.7 percent. The U.S. CPI stood at 24 on December 31, 1948, and 152.50 on June 30, 1995. The cumulative U.S. inflation was 635 percent for the period.
10. Janet L. Abu-Lughod, *Before European Hegemony: The World System A.D. 1250–1350* (Oxford: Oxford University Press, 1991), p. 62.
11. Jack Cohen and Ian Stewart, *The Collapse of Chaos* (New York: Viking, 1994).
12. See James Dale Davidson and Lord William Rees-Mogg, *The Great Reckoning,* 2nd ed. (New York: Simon & Schuster, 1993), p. 53.
13. Frederic C. Lane, "Economic Consequences of Organized Violence," *The Journal of Economic History,* vol. 18, no. 4 (December 1958), p. 402.
14. Nicholas Colchester, "Goodbye Nation-State, Hello . . . What?," *New York Times,* July 17, 1994, p. E17.

15. Norman Macrae, "Governments in Decline," *Cato Policy Report,* July/August 1992, p. 10.

16. Arthur C. Clarke, *Profiles of the Future: An Enquiry into the Limits of the Possible* (London: Victor Gollancz Ltd., 1962), p. 13.

17. Ibid.

18. A. T. Mann, *Millennium Prophecies: Predictions for the Year 2000* (Shaftesbury, England: Element Books, 1992), pp. 88, 112, 117.

19. Yardeni, *op. cit.,* p. 45.

20. Cited in Frooso, *op. cit.,* p. 40.

21. Ibid.

22. William Playfair, *An Inquiry into the Permanent Causes of the Decline and Fall of Powerful and Wealthy Nations: Designed to Show How the Prosperity of the British Empire May be Prolonged* (London: Greenland and Norris, 1805), p. 79.

23. Guy Bois, *The Transformation of the Year One Thousand: The Village of Lournard from Antiquity to Feudalism* (Manchester, England: Manchester University Press, 1992).

24. *Ibid.,* p. 150.

25. Quoted in S. B. Saul, *The Myth of the Great Depression* (London: Macmillan, 1985), p. 10.

26. Oswald Spengler, *The Decline of the West,* trans. Charles Francis Atkinson, quoted in I. F. Clark, *The Pattern of Expectation, 1644–2001* (London: Jonathan Cape, 1979), p. 220.

Chapter 2. Megapolitical Transformations in Historic Perspective

1. Huizinga, *op. cit.,* p. 7.

2. *The Compact Edition of the Oxford English Dictionary,* vol. 1 (Oxford: Oxford University Press, 1971), p. 1828.

3. Michael Hicks, *Bastard Feudalism* (London: Longmans, 1995), p. 1.

4. *Ibid.,* p. 102.

5. See S. A. Cook et al., eds., *The Cambridge Ancient History,* vol. 12 (Cambridge: Cambridge University Press, 1971), pp. 208–22.

6. *Ibid.,* pp. 209–20.

7. Will Durant, *The Story of Civilization,* vol. 4, *The Age of Faith* (New York: Simon & Schuster, 1950), p. 43.

8. C. W. Previte-Orton, *The Shorter Cambridge Medieval History,* vol. 1 (Cambridge: Cambridge University Press, 1971), p. 102.

9. *Ibid.,* p. 131.

10. *Ibid.,* p. 137.

11. *Ibid.*

12. Durant, *op. cit.,* p. 43.

13. Ramsay MacMullen, *Corruption and the Decline of Rome* (New Haven: Yale University Press, 1988), p. 192.

14. Quoted in *ibid.,* p. 193.

15. Quoted in David Kline and Daniel Burstein, "Is Government Obsolete?" *Wired,* January 1996, p. 105.
16. Lane, "Economic Consequences of Organized Violence," *op. cit.*
17. *Ibid.*
18. Susan Alling Gregg, *Foragers and Farmers: Population Interaction and Agricultural Expansion in Prehistoric Europe* (Chicago: University of Chicago Press, 1988), p. 9.
19. Stephen Boyden, *Western Civilization in Biological Perspective* (Oxford: Clarendon Press, 1987), p. 89. See also Marvin Harris, *Cannibals and Kings* (New York: Vintage, 1978), pp. 29–32.
20. Geoffrey Parker and Lesley M. Smith, eds., *The General Crisis of the Seventeenth Century* (London: Routledge & Kegan Paul, 1985), p. 8.
21. See Charles Woolsey Cole, *French Mercantilism: 1683–1700* (New York: Octagon Books, 1971), p. 6.
22. Chris Scarre, ed., *Past Worlds: The Times Atlas of Archaeology* (New York: Random House, 1995), p. 58.

Chapter 3. East of Eden: The Agricultural Revolution and the Sophistication of Violence

1. Boyden, *op. cit.*, p. 4.
2. Gregg, *op. cit.*, xv.
3. Boyden, *op. cit.*, p. 62.
4. *Ibid.*, p. 67.
5. *Ibid.*
6. Quoted in E. J. P. Veale, *Advance to Barbarism: The Development of Total Warfare* (New York: Devin-Adair, 1968), p. 37.
7. R. Paul Shaw and Yuwa Wong, *Genetic Seeds of Warfare: Evolution, Nationalism and Patriotism* (Boston: Unwin Hyman, 1989), p. 4.
8. See Carleton S. Coon, *The Hunting Peoples* (New York: Nick Lyons Books, 1971), p. 275.
9. Gregg, *op. cit.*, p. 23.
10. Boyden, *op. cit.*, p. 69.
11. Shaw and Wong, *op. cit.*, p. 69.
12. For more details about the Kafirs, see Schuyler Jones, *Men of Influence in Nuristan* (London: Seminar Press, 1974).
13. See Samuel L. Popkin, *The Rational Peasant* (Berkeley: University of California Press, 1979), p. 13.
14. See Bois, *op. cit.*
15. See Frances and Joseph Gies, *Cathedral, Forge, and Waterwheel: Technology and Invention in the Middle Ages* (New York: HarperCollins, 1994), p. 40.
16. Quoted in *ibid.*, p. 42.
17. Bois, *op. cit.*, p. 78.
18. *Ibid.*, p. 118.
19. Gies, *op. cit.*, p. 45.

20. Bois, *op. cit.*, p. 116.
21. *Ibid.*, p. 26.
22. *Ibid.*, p. 64.
23. Gies, *op. cit.*, p. 47.
24. Bois, *op. cit.*, p. 52.
25. *Ibid.*, p. 150
26. Gies, *op. cit.*, p. 2.
27. *Ibid.*, p. 46.
28. *Ibid.*, pp. 56–57.
29. *Ibid.*, p. 58.
30. Bois, *op. cit.*, p. 87.
31. *Ibid.* While the precise sequence of events during the feudal revolution is difficult to reconstruct because of the paucity of records, the broad outline of the thesis suggested by Guy Bois strikes us as likely to be correct. It is not only plausible in itself, but it makes sense of otherwise anomalous facts and fits with our theories as well.
32. *Ibid.*, p. 136.
33. *Ibid.*, pp. 57 and *passim*.
34. A. R. Radcliffe-Brown, "Religion and Society," in *Structure and Function in Primitive Society* (London: Cohen & West, 1952), pp. 153–77.
35. Bois, *op. cit.*, p. 36.
36. Gies, *op. cit.*, p. 112.
37. *Ibid.*, p. 114.
38. *Ibid.*, p. 117.
39. The details about bridges and infrastructure are mainly from *ibid.*, pp. 148–54.
40. Bois, *op. cit.*, p. 136.
41. See Norman Cohn, *Cosmos, Chaos, and the World to Come: The Ancient Roots of the Apocalyptic Faith* (New Haven: Yale University Press, 1993), chaps. 1–3, especially p. 60.
42. Bruce M. Metzger and Michael D. Coogan, eds., *The Oxford Companion to the Bible* (Oxford: Oxford University Press, 1993), p. 178.
43. Boyden, *op. cit.*, p. 118.

Chapter 4. The Last Days of Politics: Parallels Between the Senile Decline of the Holy Mother Church and the Nanny State

1. Clarke, *op. cit.*, p. 9.
2. Martin van Creveld, *The Transformation of War* (New York: The Free Press, 1991), p. 52.
3. *The Compact Edition of The Oxford English Dictionary, op. cit.*, p. 1074.
4. See T. C. Onions, ed., *The Oxford Dictionary of English Etymology* (Oxford: Oxford University Press, 1966), p. 693.
5. John Urquhart, "Former Premier Sues Canada for Libel in Probe of Alleged Airbus Kickbacks," *Wall Street Journal,* November 21, 1995, p. A11.
6. Huizinga, *op. cit.*, p. 172.

7. *Ibid.*, p. 150.
8. *Ibid.*, p. 56.
9. *Ibid.*, p. 65.
10. *Ibid.*, p. 22.
11. van Creveld, *op. cit.*, p. 52.
12. Huizinga, *op. cit.*, p. 21.
13. *Ibid.*, p. 83.
14. *Ibid.*, pp. 88–89.
15. *Ibid.*, p. 95.
16. *Ibid.*, p. 90.
17. *Ibid.*, p. 87.
18. Norman Cohn, *The Pursuit of the Millennium: Revolutionary Millenarians and Mystical Anarchists of the Middle Ages,* revised and expanded edition (Oxford: Oxford University Press, 1970), p. 127.
19. *Ibid.*
20. *Ibid.*, p. 128.
21. C. Northcote Parkinson, *Parkinson's Law and Other Studies in Administration* (Boston: Houghton Mifflin, 1957), p. 60, quoted in Tilly, p. 4.
22. van Creveld, *op. cit.*, p. 50.
23. Playfair, *op. cit.*, p. 72.
24. Huizinga, *op. cit.*, p. 26.
25. *Ibid.*, p. 57.
26. *Ibid.*
27. Frederic C. Lane, *Venice: A Maritime Republic* (Baltimore: Johns Hopkins University Press, 1973), p. 275.
28. Adam Smith, *An Inquiry into the Nature and Causes of the Wealth of Nations* (Chicago: University of Chicago Press, 1976), pp. 8–9.
29. See H. J. Habakkuk and M. Postan, eds., *The Cambridge Economic History of Europe*, vol. 6, *The Industrial Revolution and After: Incomes, Population and Technological Change* (Cambridge: Cambridge University Press, 1966).
30. Euan Cameron, *The European Reformation* (Oxford: The Clarendon Press, 1992), p. 68.
31. *Ibid.*
32. Huizinga, *op. cit.*, p. 198.
33. Cameron, *op. cit.*, pp. 26–27.
34. Huizinga, *op cit.*, p. 149.
35. E. J. Burford, *The Bishop's Brothels* (London: Robert Hale, 1993), p. 103.
36. *Ibid.*, p. 102.
37. *Ibid.*
38. *Ibid.*, p. 103.
39. Huizinga, *op. cit.*, p. 151.
40. Cameron, *op. cit.*, p. 31.
41. *Ibid.*, p. 24.
42. *Ibid.*, p. 15.
43. Huizinga, *op. cit.*, p. 27.

44. Burford, *op. cit.*, p. 103.
45. Huizinga, *op. cit.*, p. 173.
46. *Ibid.*
47. William Manchester, *A World Lit Only by Fire: The Medieval Mind and the Renaissance* (Boston: Little, Brown, 1992), pp. 75–76.
48. *Ibid.*, p. 79.
49. *Ibid.*, pp. 82–84.
50. Huizinga, *op. cit.*, p. 154.
51. *Ibid.*
52. *Ibid.*, p. 155.
53. *Ibid.*
54. *Ibid.*, p. 9.
55. These examples of religious ritual are from Cameron, *op. cit.*, pp. 10–11.
56. Keith Thomas, *Religion and the Decline of Magic* (London: Penguin, 1971), p. 800, quoted in Cameron, *op. cit.*, p. 10.
57. Huizinga, *op. cit.*, p. 161.
58. Cameron, *op. cit.*, p. 19.
59. Huizinga, *op. cit.*, p. 148.
60. For more details on sharp differences between fifteenth-century and sixteenth-century perspectives on poverty, see Robert Jutte, *Poverty and Deviance in Early Modern Europe* (Cambridge: Cambridge University Press, 1994), pp. 15–17.
61. Cameron, *op. cit.*, p. 127.
62. *Ibid.*, p. 14.
63. *Ibid.*, p. 11.
64. *Ibid.*, p. 5.
65. Huizinga, *op. cit.*
66. *Ibid.*, p. 199.
67. *Ibid.*, p. 203.
68. *Ibid.*, p. 27.
69. *Ibid.*, p. 22.

Chapter 5. The Life and Death of the Nation-State: Democracy and Nationalism as Resource Strategies in the Age of Violence

1. Quoted in Tilly, *op. cit.*, p. 84.
2. See John Keegan, *A History of Warfare* (London: Hutchinson, 1993), p. 321.
3. Jim Taylor and Watts Wacker, *The 500-Year Delta: What Happens After What Comes Next.* New York: HarperCollins, 1997, pp. 38–39.
4. Ibid., p. 39.
5. *The Cambridge Ancient History, op. cit.*, pp. 263–64.
6. Cook et al., *op. cit.*, p. 268.
7. For more on the logic of hydraulic societies, see Karl A. Wittfogel, *Oriental Despotism: A Comparative Study of Total Power* (New Haven: Yale University Press, 1957).

8. Tilly, *op. cit.*, p. 28.
9. Lane, "Consequences of Organized Violence," *op. cit.*, p. 406.
10. *Ibid.*
11. *Ibid.*, p. 412.
12. Tilly, *op. cit.*, pp. 96–126.
13. *Ibid.*, p. 130.
14. *Ibid.*, p. 110.
15. This example in *ibid.*, p. 139.
16. *Ibid.*, p. 115.
17. See Mancur Olson, *The Logic of Collective Action* (Cambridge: Harvard University Press, 1965).
18. Josep R. Llobera, *The God of Modernity: The Development of Nationalism in Western Europe* (Oxford: Berg Publishers, 1994), pp. ix–x.
19. *Ibid.*, p. xiii.
20. See William McNeill, *Polyethnicity and National Unity in World History* (Toronto: University of Toronto Press, 1986).
21. *Ibid.*, p. 7.
22. Hernando de Soto, *The Other Path* (New York: Harper & Row, 1989).
23. *Ibid.*
24. *Ibid.*, p. 6.

Chapter 6. The Megapolitics of the Information Age: The Triumph of Efficiency over Power

1. Neil Munro, "The Pentagon's New Nightmare: An Electronic Pearl Harbor," *Washington Post*, July 16, 1995, p. C3.
2. Thomas Hobbes, *Leviathan*, chap. 13 of "The Natural Condition of Man as Concerning Their Felicity and Misery."
3. Thomas Schelling, *Arms and Influence* (New Haven: Yale University Press, 1966).
4. Kevin Kelly, *Out of Control: The New Biology of Machines, Social Systems, and the Economic World* (Reading, Mass.: Addison-Wesley, 1995), pp. 45–46.
5. *Ibid.*, pp. 2–4.
6. *Ibid.*, p. 4.
7. Heinz Pagels, *The Dreams of Reason* (New York: Bantam Books, 1989), quoted in Roger Lewin, *Complexity: Life at the Edge of Chaos* (New York: Macmillan, 1992), p. 10.
8. Lane, "Economic Consequences of Organized Violence," *op. cit.*, p. 402.
9. Frederic C. Lane, "The Economic Meaning of War and Protection," in *Venice and History: The Collected Papers of Frederic C. Lane* (Baltimore: The Johns Hopkins Press, 1966), pp. 383–84.
10. Shi Mai'an and Lao Guanzhong, *Outlaws of the Marsh*, trans. Sidney Shapiro (Bloomington: Indiana University Press, 1981), p. 12.
11. George F. Will, "Farewell to Welfare States," *Washington Post*, December 17, 1995, p. C7.

12. Robert S. McElvaine, *The Great Depression: America, 1929–1941* (New York: Times Books, 1984), p. 292.

13. *Ibid.,* p. 293.

14. Smith, *op. cit.,* p. 75.

15. *Ibid.,* p. 76.

16. *Ibid.*

17. Among the first Argentine unions to organize was the railroad union in 1887. See Carmelo Mesa-Lago, *Social Security in Latin America: Pressure Groups, Stratification, and Inequality* (Pittsburgh: University of Pittsburgh Press, 1978), p. 161.

18. For details of the planning and construction of the C&O Canal, see Robert J. Brugger, *Maryland: A Middle Temperament 1634–1980* (Baltimore: The Johns Hopkins Press, 1990), pp. 202–3f.

19. Irving J. Sloan, *Our Violent Past: An American Chronicle* (New York: Random House, 1970), p. 177.

20. For details about violence in the rail strikes of 1877, see *ibid.,* and Brugger, *op. cit.,* pp. 341–44.

21. Sloan, *op. cit.,* p. 202. See also S. S. Boynton, "Miners' Vengeance," *Overland Monthly,* vol. 22 (1893), pp. 303–7.

22. Benjamin Schwartz, "American Inequality: Its History and Scary Future," *New York Times,* December 19, 1995, p. A25.

23. McElvaine, *op. cit.,* p. 293.

24. *Ibid.*

25. *Ibid.*

26. Henry C. Simons, "Some Reflections on Syndicalism," *Journal of Political Economy,* March 1944, p. 22.

27. Kelly, *op. cit.,* pp. 191–92.

28. Gayle M. Hanson, "A Riveting Account of 'Life' in Postmodernist Cyberspace," *Washington Times,* December 24, 1995, p. B7.

29. A concise introduction to the academic investigation of anarchy can be found in Gordon Tullock, ed., *Explorations in the Theory of Anarchy* (Blacksburg, Va.: Virginia Polytechnic Institute and State University, 1972). See also Murray N. Rothbard, *Power and Market: Government and the Economy* (Menlo Park, Calif., 1970); and Robert Nozick, *Anarchy, State and Utopia* (New York: Basic Books, 1974).

30. See Pierre Clastres, *Society Against the State: The Leader as Servant and the Humane Uses of Power Among the Indians of the Americas* (New York: Urizen Books, 1977); and Jones, *op. cit.*

31. Lane, "Economic Consequences of Organized Violence," *op. cit.,* p. 403.

32. Charles Tilly, "War Making and State Making as Organized Crime," in Peter B. Evans, Dietrich Rueschemeyer, and Theda Skocpol, *Bringing the State Back In* (Cambridge: Cambridge University Press, 1985), p. 169.

33. *Ibid.*

34. Lane, "Economic Consequences of Organized Violence," *op. cit.,* p. 402.

35. David J. Elkins, *Beyond Sovereignty: Territory and Political Economy in the Twenty-first Century.* Toronto: University of Toronto Press, 1995, pp. 13–14.

36. *Ibid.,* p. 29.
37. Jim Taylor and Watts Wacker, *The 500-Year Delta: What Happens After What Comes Next.* New York: HarperCollins, 1997, p. 40.
38. *Ibid.,* p. 67.
39. *Ibid.,* pp. 41–42.
40. George Gilder, "Fiber Keeps Its Promise: Get Ready. Bandwidth Will Triple Each Year for the Next 25, Creating Trillions in New Wealth." *Forbes ASAP,* April 7, 1997.
41. See Neal Stephenson, *Snow Crash.* New York: Bantam Books, 1993.
42. Keith B. Richburg, "Two Years After U.S. Landing in Somalia, It's Back to Chaos," *Washington Post,* December 4, 1994, p. A1.
43. Cited in Tilly, *Coercion, Capital and European States, op. cit.,* p. 85.
44. Lane, "Economic Consequences of Organized Violence," *op. cit.,* p. 411.
45. *Ibid.*
46. *Ibid.*
47. *Ibid.,* p. 412.
48. *Ibid.,* p. 403.
49. *Ibid.,* p. 404.
50. Esther Dyson, *Release 2.1: A Design for Living in the Digital Age.* New York: Broadway Books, 1998, p. 131.
51. Rees Davies, "Frontier Arrangements in Fragmented Societies: Ireland and Wales," in Robert Bartlett and Angus MacKay, eds., *Medieval Frontier Societies* (Oxford: Oxford University Press, 1992), p. 80.
52. See Thomas W. Lippman, "Seychelles Offers Investors Safe Haven for $10 Million," *Washington Post,* December 31, 1995, p. A27.
53. See "ROM of Ages," *Wired,* January 1996, p. 52.
54. Quoted in James Adams, "Dawn of the Cyber Soldiers," *The Sunday Times* (London), October 15, 1995, pp. 3–5.
55. Kelly, *op. cit.,* p. 19.
56. George Melloan, "Welfare State Reform Is Mostly Mythological," *The Wall Street Journal,* October 14, 1996, p. A19.

Chapter 7. Transcending Locality: The Emergence of the Cybereconomy

1. John Perry Barlow, "Thinking Locally, Acting Globally," *Time,* January 15, 1996, p. 57.
2. *Ibid.*
3. M. C. Seymour, ed., *Mandeville's Travels* (Oxford: Oxford University Press, 1968), p. 122.
4. R. C. Johnson, "The Transportation of Vagrant Children from London to Virginia, 1618–1622," in H. S. Reinmuth, ed., *Early Stuart Studies* (Minneapolis: University of Minnesota Press, 1970), pp. 143–44, quoted in Jutte, *op. cit.,* p. 168.
5. John Dos Passos, *The Big Money* (New York: Harcourt, Brace & Co., 1936).
6. Clarke, *op. cit.,* p. 29.
7. Quoted in Kline and Burstein, *op. cit.,* p. 105.

8. Clarke, *op. cit.*, p. 20.
9. *Ibid.*
10. *Ibid.*, p. 21.
11. Lane, "Economic Consequences of Organized Violence," *op. cit.*, p. 404.
12. James Bennet, "The Information Revolution and the Demise of the Income Tax," *Strategic Investment*, November 1994, pp. 11–12.
13. Lane, "Economic Consequences of Organized Violence," *op. cit.*, p. 404.
14. Abu-Lughod, *op cit.*, p. 177.
15. Quoted in Henry Mark Holzer, *Government's Money Monopoly* (New York: Books in Focus, 1981), p. 4.
16. Abu-Lughod, *op. cit.*, p. 332.
17. Friedrich A. von Hayek, *The Denationalization of Money* (London: Institute of Economic Affairs, 1976), p. 47.
18. See Chapter 1, note 6.
19. Hayek, *op. cit.*, p. 40.
20. *Ibid.*
21. See Lawrence White, *Free Banking in Britain* (London: Institute of Economic Affairs, 1995).
22. Michael Prowse, "Bring Back Gold," *Financial Times*, February 5, 1996, p. 12.
23. Davidson and Rees-Mogg, *op. cit.*, p. 203.
24. Lane, "Economic Consequences of Organized Violence," *op. cit.*, p. 413.

Chapter 8. The End of Egalitarian Economics:
The Revolution in Earnings Capacity in a World Without Jobs

1. Benjamin Schwarz, "American Inequality: Its History and Scary Future," *New York Times*, December 19, 1995, p. A25.
2. Adna Ferrin Weber, *The Growth of Cities in the Nineteenth Century* (New York: Macmillan, 1899; reprinted by Cornell University Press, 1963), p. 249.
3. Bill Bryson, *The Lost Continent* (New York: Harper Perennial, 1989), p. 72.
4. This article is reprinted in vol. 4 of Adrian Darnell's collection, *Early Mathematical Economists*, 6 vols. (London: Pickering & Chatto, 1991).
5. For example, see Weber, *op. cit.*, p. 2.
6. Clive Jenkins and Barrie Sherman, *The Collapse of Work* (London: Methuen, 1979), p. 103.
7. Robert H. Frank and Philip J. Cook, *The Winner-Take-All Society* (New York: The Free Press, 1995).
8. Clay Chandler, "Buchanan's Success Frightens Business," *Washington Post*, February 22, 1996, p. D12.
9. Stephanie Flanders and Martin Wolfe, "Haunted by the Trade Spectre," *Financial Times*, July 24, 1995, p. 11. They quote from the World Bank's most recent world development report, on workers in an integrating world economy.
10. See Mancur Olson, "Diseconomies of Scale and Development," *Cato Journal*, vol. 7, no. 1 (Spring/Summer 1987).
11. *Ibid.*

12. Basil Davidson, *The Black Man's Burden: Africa and the Curse of the Nation State* (New York: Times Books, 1992), p. 290.

13. Olson, *op. cit.*

14. Adam Smith, *The Wealth of Nations*, p. 724. This point was suggested by an argument by Edwin G. West in his *Adam Smith and Modern Economics* (Aldershot, England: Edward Elgar Publishing, 1990), pp. 88–89.

15. Fritz Rorig, *The Medieval Town* (Berkeley: University of California Press, 1967), p. 28.

16. Albert O. Hirschman, *Exit, Voice, and Loyalty* (Cambridge: Harvard University Press, 1969), p. 81.

17. Tom Peters and George Gilder, "City vs. Country: Tom Peters & George Gilder Debate the Impact of Technology on Location," *Forbes,* February 1995.

18. Weber, *op. cit.*, p. 21.

19. *Ibid.*, p. 46 for London, p. 73 for Paris.

20. *Ibid.*, p. 120.

21. *Ibid.*, p. 95.

22. *Ibid.*, p. 84.

23. *Ibid.*, p. 119.

24. *Ibid.*, p. 101.

25. *Ibid.*, p. 5.

26. See Ronald Coase, "The Nature of the Firm," reprinted in Louis Putterman and Randall S. Kroszner, eds., *The Economic Nature of the Firm: A Reader,* 2nd ed. (Cambridge: Cambridge University Press, 1996), pp. 89–104.

27. Quoted by West, *op. cit.*, p. 58; see also Oliver E. Williamson, "The Organization of Work: A Comparative Insititutional Assessment," *Journal of Economic Behaviour and Organisation,* vol. 1, no. 1.

28. Quoted by West, *op. cit.*, p. 59; see also Williamson, *op. cit.*

29. Richard Cyert and James March, *A Behavioral Theory of the Firm* (Englewood Cliffs, N.J.: Prentice-Hall, 1983).

30. Chris Dray, "Civil Servants Lead Lives of Quiet Collusion," *Globe and Mail,* February 2, 1996, p. A14.

31. William Bridges, *Jobshift: How to Prosper in a Workplace Without Jobs* (Reading, Mass.: Addison-Wesley, 1994), pp. 62, 64.

32. See Al Ehrbar, " 'Re-Engineering' Gives Firms New Efficiency, Workers the Pink Slip," *Wall Street Journal,* July 22, 1992, p. A14, quoted by Bridges, *op. cit.*, p. 39.

33. Sheryl WuDunn, "Parting Is Such Sour Sorrow: Japan's Job-for-Life Culture Painfully Expires," *International Herald Tribune,* June 13, 1996, p. 13.

34. Bridges, *op. cit.*, pp. 31–32.

35. *Ibid.*, p. 58.

36. Abu-Lughod, *op. cit.*, p. 186.

Chapter 9. Nationalism, Reaction, and the New Luddites

1. William Pfaff, *The Wrath of Nations: Civilization and the Furies of Nationalism* (New York: Simon & Schuster, 1993), p. 17.

2. William H. McNeill, "Reasserting the Polyethnic Norm," in John Hutchinson and Anthony D. Smith, eds., *Nationalism* (Oxford: Oxford University Press, 1994), p. 300.

3. Michael Billig, *Banal Nationalism* (London: Sage Publications, 1995), p. 16.

4. See Gordon Tullock, *Rent-Seeking* (Aldershot Harts, England: E. Elgar, 1993).

5. John B. Morrall, *Political Thought in Medieval Times* (New York: Harper, 1958), p. 48.

6. For example, see the façade of the cathedral at Angoulême, France.

7. See Karen A. Rasler and William R. Thompson, *War and State Making: The Shaping of the Global Powers*. Studies in International Conflict, vol. 2 (Boston: Unwin Hyman, 1989), p. 13.

8. Julian Large, "Bishop Died for Standing Firm Against Henry VIII," *Daily Telegraph*, June 16, 1996, p. 2.

9. Cameron, *op. cit.*, p. 97.

10. Hirschman, *op. cit.*, p. 17.

11. For an informative survey of heresy through the Reformation, see Malcolm Lambert, *Medieval Heresy*, 2nd ed. (Oxford: Blackwell, 1992).

12. See David Smith, "What Clarke Could Learn from Reagan," *The Sunday Times* (London), June 16, 1996, p. 6.

13. Lane, "Economic Consequences of Organized Violence," p. 404.

14. *Ibid.*

15. See M. Featherstone, *Consumer Culture and Postmodernism* (London: Sage, 1991), and J. F. Sherry, "Postmodern Alternative: The Interpretative Turn in Consumer Research," in T. Robertson and H. Kassarjian, eds., *Handbook of Consumer Research* (Englewood Cliffs, N.J.: Prentice-Hall, 1991), discussed in Billig, *op. cit.*

16. Hirschman, *op. cit.*, p. 81.

17. Jeremy Bentham, *An Introduction to the Principles of Morals and Legislation*, J. H. Burns and H. L. A. Hart, eds. (London: Methuen, 1982), p. 296, cited by Billig, *op. cit.*, p. 84.

18. Anthony Giddens, *Social Theory and Modern Sociology* (Cambridge: Polity Press, 1987), p. 166, quoted in Billig, *op. cit.*

19. Billig, *op. cit.*, p. 36.

20. Benedict Anderson, *Imagined Communities* (London: Verso, 1983), quoted by Billig, *op. cit.*, p.10.

21. Owen Lattimore, *Inner Asian Frontiers of China* (New York: Beacon Press, 1960), p. 60. Cited by Ronald Findlay, "Towards a Model of Territorial Expansion and the Limits of Empire," in Michelle R. Garfinkel and Stergios Skaperdas, eds., *The Political Economy of Conflict and Appropriation* (Cambridge: Cambridge University Press, 1996), p. 54.

22. Findlay, *op. cit.*, p. 41.

23. Billig, *op. cit.*, p. 25.

24. See Anderson, *op. cit.*, p. 93.

25. Janis Langins, "Words and Institutions During the French Revolution: The Case of 'Revolutionary' Scientific and Technical Education," in Peter Burke and Roy

Porter, *The Social History of Language* (Cambridge: Cambridge University Press, 1987), p. 137.

26. *Ibid.*, pp. 140, 142.
27. Billig, *op. cit.*, p. 27.
28. Tilly, *Coercion, Capital, and European States*, p. 22.
29. Langins, *op. cit.*, p. 143.
30. *Ibid.*, p. 139.
31. See Rheal Seguin, "PQ Ready to Harden Laws on Language: English Signs Face Ban in Quebec," *Globe and Mail*, August 29, 1996, p. A1.
32. Billig, *op. cit.*, p. 35.
33. Jack Weatherford, *Savages and Civilization: Who Will Survive?* (New York: Fawcett Columbine, 1994), p. 143.
34. Geoffrey Parker and Lesley M. Smith, *The General Crisis of the Seventeenth Century* (London: Routledge & Kegan Paul, 1985), p. 122.
35. Weatherford, *op. cit.*, p. 144.
36. Anderson, *op. cit.*, p. 90.
37. *Ibid.*, p. 91.
38. *Ibid.*
39. F. H. Kantorowicz, quoted by Llobera, *op. cit.*, p. 83.
40. Billig, *op. cit.*, p. 175.
41. *Ibid.*, p. 109.
42. Shaw and Wong, *op. cit.*, pp. 26–27.
43. Pierre Van Den Berghe, "A Socio-Biological Perspective," in Hutchinson and Smith, eds., *Nationalism*, p. 97.
44. *Ibid.*
45. *Ibid.*
46. Jack Hirshleifer, *Economic Behaviour in Adversity* (Chicago: University of Chicago Press, 1987), p. 170.
47. Colin Tudge, *The Time Before History: 5 Million Years of Human Impact* (New York: Scribners, 1996), p. 17.
48. *Ibid.*, pp. 17–18.
49. Hirshleifer, *op. cit.*, p. 172.
50. See Stephen Jay Gould, "Evolutionary Biology of Constraints," *Daedalus*, Spring 1980, and David Layzer, "Altruism and Natural Selection," *Journal of Social and Biological Structures* (1978), cited by Howard Margolis, *Selfishness, Altruism and Rationality* (Chicago: University of Chicago Press, 1984).
51. Van Den Berghe, *op. cit.*, p. 96.
52. See W. D. Hamilton, "The Evolution of Altruistic Behavior," *American Naturalist*, 1963, pp. 346–54.
53. Van Den Berghe, *op. cit.*, p. 96.
54. Hirshleifer, *op. cit.*, p. 179.
55. *Ibid.*
56. Margolis, *op. cit.*, p. 32.
57. Van Den Berghe, *op. cit.*, p. 98.
58. Margolis, *op. cit.*, p. 32.

59. *Ibid.*
60. Shaw and Wong, *op. cit.*, pp. 68–74.
61. Quoted by Shaw and Wong, *op. cit.*, p. 91.
62. See Billig, *op. cit.*, p. 71.
63. Shaw and Wong, *op. cit.*, p. 106.
64. *Ibid.*
65. See Hamilton, *op. cit.*, and W. D. Hamilton, "The Genetical Evolution of Social Behavior, I and II," *Theoretical Biology*, vol. 7, pp. 1–16, 17–52.
66. Anderson, *op. cit.*
67. Hirshleifer, *op. cit.*, p. 188.
68. Van Den Berghe, *op. cit.*, p. 97.
69. J. B. Elshtain, "Sovereignty, Identity, Sacrifice," in M. Ringrove and A. J. Lerner, eds., *Reimaging the Nation* (Buckingham, England: Open University Press, 1993), pointed out by Billig, *op. cit.*
70. See Abu-Lughod, *op. cit.*, p. 90.
71. Charles Tilly, "Collective Violence in European Perspective," in T. R. Gurr, ed., *Violence in America*, vol. 2, *Protest, Rebellion, Reform* (Newbury Park, Calif.: Sage Publications, 1989), p. 93.
72. Tudge, *op. cit.*, p. 168.
73. Christopher Lasch, *The Revolt of the Elites and the Betrayal of Democracy* (New York: W. W. Norton & Company, 1995), p. 5.
74. *Ibid.*, p. 34.
75. *Ibid.*, pp. 34–35.
76. *Ibid.*, p. 6.
77. *Ibid.*, p. 21.
78. *Ibid.*, p. 21.
79. Lane, "The Economic Meaning of War," in *Venice and History: The Collected Papers of Frederic C. Lane*, p. 385.
80. See Thomas L. Friedman, "Don't Leave Globalization's Losers Out of Mind," *International Herald Tribune*, July 18, 1996, p. 8.
81. Billig, *op. cit.*, p. 99.
82. Lasch, *op. cit.*, p. 88.
83. Ian Ireland, "Is the Queen an Australian Citizen?" Parliamentary Research Service, Australia, no. 6, August 28, 1995.
84. *Ibid.*, p. 2.
85. Schoeck, *op. cit.*, p. 265.
86. For a critical view of compensation according to relative performance, see Robert H. Frank and Philip J. Cook, *The Winner-Take-All Society*, pp. 24f.
87. Friedman, *op. cit.*
88. For more on transcendental capital, see James Dale Davidson, *The Squeeze* (New York: Summit Books, 1980), pp. 38–55.
89. Lane, "Economic Consequences of Organized Violence," p. 404.
90. Eric Hobsbawm, "The Nation as Invented Tradition," in Hutchinson and Smith, *Nationalism*, p. 77.
91. John Plender, "Retirement Isn't Working," *Financial Times*, June 17–18, 1995.

92. See V. H. Atrill, *How All Economies Work* (Calgary, Canada: Dimensionless Science Publications, 1979), p. 27f.

93. Tilly, "Collective Violence in European Perspective," p. 62.

94. *Ibid.*, p. 68.

95. See Dick Howard, "French Toast: Can Politicians Anywhere Tangle with Entitlements Without Getting Burned?" *The New Democrat*, July/August 1996, p. 39f.

96. Andrew Heal, "New Zealand's First," *Metro*, July 1996, p. 86.

97. See Roger Matthews, "South Africa Calls Up Troops for War on Crime," *Financial Times*, August 31/September 1, 1996, p. 1.

98. Erich Fromm, *Escape from Freedom* (London: Routledge & Kegan Paul, 1941).

99. Billig, *op. cit.*, p. 137.

100. *Ibid.*, p. 135.

101. Andrew Heal, "New Zealand's First," p. 85.

102. Robert Jutte, *Poverty and Deviance in Early Modern Europe* (Cambridge: Cambridge University Press, 1994), pp. 29, 74.

103. Tilly, "Collective Violence," p. 77.

104. For a well-documented look at the impact of disappearing factory jobs on persons with low skills, see William Julius Wilson, *When Work Disappears: The World of the New Urban Poor* (New York: Alfred A. Knopf, 1996).

105. Tilly, "Collective Violence," p. 78.

106. Robert Reid, *Land of Lost Content: The Luddite Revolt 1812* (London: Penguin, 1986).

107. *Ibid.*, p. 44.

108. *Ibid.*, p. 45.

109. *Ibid.*, p. 26.

110. *Ibid.*

111. Timothy Egan, "Terrorism Now Going Homespun as Bombings in the U.S. Spread," *New York Times*, August 25, 1996, p. 1.

112. Lane, "Economic Consequences of Organized Violence," p. 402.

113. Jack Hirshleifer, "Anarchy and Its Breakdown," in Michelle R. Garfinkel and Stergios Skaperdas, eds., *The Political Economy of Conflict and Appropriation* (Cambridge: Cambridge University Press, 1996), p. 15.

114. *Ibid.*, p. 15.

115. *Ibid.*, p. 34.

116. *Ibid.*, p. 17.

117. *Ibid.*, p. 37.

118. *Ibid.*, p. 16.

119. *Ibid.*

Chapter 10. The Twilight of Democracy

1. John Dunn, *Western Political Theory in the Face of the Future*. Cambridge, Eng.: Cambridge University Press. 1979, p. 2.

2. Carroll Quigley, *Weapons Systems and Political Stability* (Washington, D.C.: University Press of America, 1983).

3. *Ibid.*, p. 56.
4. Quoted in Kelly, *op. cit.*, p. 46.
5. Molander, et al. Strategic Information Warfare, *op. cit.*, p. xv.
6. *Ibid.*, p. xiv.
7. See Dennis C. Mueller, *Public Choice*, vol. 2 (Cambridge: Cambridge University Press, 1989), pp. 43–226.
8. See Michael A. Bernstein, *The Great Depression: Delayed Recovery and Economic Change in America, 1929–1939* (Cambridge: Cambridge University Press, 1987).
9. Mancur Olson, *The Rise and Decline of Nations: Economic Growth, Stagflation, and Social Rigidities* (New Haven: Yale University Press, 1982).
10. Michael M. Phillips, "Math Ph.D.s Add to Anti-Foreigner Wave: Scholars Facing High Jobless Rate Seek Immigration Curbs," *Wall Street Journal*, September 4, 1996, p. A2.
11. Juan J. Linz and Alfred Stepan, eds., *The Breakdown of Democratic Regimes* (Baltimore, Md.: The Johns Hopkins University Press, 1978), p. 18.
12. William Keech, *Economic Politics: The Costs of Democracy*. Cambridge: Cambridge University Press, 1995, p. 221.
13. E. S. Staveley, *Greek and Roman Voting and Elections* (Ithaca, N.Y.: Cornell University Press, 1972), p. 62.
14. *Ibid.*, p. 65.
15. Norman Cohn, *The Pursuit of the Millennium* (Oxford: Oxford University Press, 1970), p. 41.
16. *Ibid.*, pp. 84–85.
17. Quoted in Kelly, *op. cit.*, p. 46.
18. Milton Friedman, *Capitalism and Freedom* (Chicago: University of Chicago Press, 1962), p. 91. Discussed by Hirschman, *op. cit.*, pp. 16–17.
19. Hirschman, *op. cit.*, p. 17.
20. Neil Munro, "The Pentagon's New Nightmare: An Electronic Pearl Harbor," *Washington Post*, July 16, 1995, p. C3.
21. E. J. Dionne, "Why the Right Is Wrong," *Utne Reader*, June 1996, p. 32.
22. Ernst Cassirer, *The Myth of the State* (New Haven: Yale University Press, 1946), p. 81.
23. John B. Morrall, *Political Thought in Medieval Times* (New York: Harper Torchbooks, 1962), p. 15.
24. *Ibid.*, p. 16.
25. Cassirer, *op. cit.*, pp. 142, 150.
26. For example, see Robert J. Shapiro, "Flat Wrong: New Tax Schemes Can't Top Old Progressive Truths," *Washington Post*, March 24, 1996, p. C3, and Thomas L. Friedman, "Politics in the Age of NAFTA," *New York Times*, April 7, p. E11.
27. Quoted by Friedman, *op. cit.*
28. See Louis Putterman and Randall S. Kroszner, "The Economic Nature of the Firm: A New Introduction," in Louis Putterman and Randall S. Kroszner, eds., *The Economic Nature of the Firm: A Reader* (Cambridge: Cambridge University Press, 1996), p. 17.

29. *Ibid.*
30. *Ibid.*, p. 9.
31. See Jeremy Rifkin, *The End of Work: The Decline of the Global Labor Force and the Dawn of the Post-Market Era* (New York: G.P. Putnam), 1995.
32. *Ibid.*, p. 250.
33. See Charles M. Tiebout, "A Pure Theory of Local Expenditure," *Journal of Political Economy* 64 (1956), pp. 416–24.
34. Mueller, *op. cit.*, pp. 28–29.
35. Fred Foldvary, *Public Goods and Private Communities: The Market Provision of Social Services* (Aldershot, Hants, England: Edward Elgar Publishing, Ltd., 1994).
36. Paul R. Krugman, "The Tax-Reform Obsession," *New York Times Magazine*, April 7, 1996, p. 37.
37. Foldvary, *op. cit.*, pp. 66f.

Chapter 11. Morality and Crime in the "Natural Economy" of the Information Age

1. Vito Tanzi, "Corruption: Arm's-length Relationships and Markets," in Gianluca Fiorentini and Sam Peltzman, eds., *The Economics of Organized Crime* (Cambridge: Cambridge University Press, 1995), pp. 167, 170.
2. Hirshleifer, *op. cit.*, p. 176.
3. *Ibid.*, p. 169.
4. Michelle R. Garfinkel and Stergios Skaperdas, eds., *The Political Economy of Conflict and Appropriation* (Cambridge: Cambridge University Press, 1996), p. 1.
5. Hirshleifer, *op. cit.*, p. 173.
6. Garfinkel and Skaperdas, *op. cit.*, p. 1.
7. *Ibid.*
8. Hamish McRae, *The World in 2020* (London: Harper Collins, 1995), p. 188.
9. *Ibid.*, pp. 188–89.
10. Kevin Kelly, *Out of Control* (Reading, Mass.: Addison-Wesley, 1994), p. 189.
11. Tilly, "War Making and State Making as Organized Crime," in Evans, Rueschemeyer, and Skocpol, *op. cit.*, p. 171.
12. *Ibid.*, p. 169.
13. Frank Viaino, "The New Mafia Order," *Mother Jones*, May/June 1995, p. 55.
14. See Velisarios Kattoulas, "Japan's Yakuza Claim Place Among Criminal Elite," *Washington Times*, November 25, 1994, p. A22.
15. Viaino, *op. cit.*, p. 49.
16. Garfinkel and Skaperdas, *op. cit.*, p. 2.
17. Fiorentini and Peltzman, *op. cit.*, p. 15.
18. *Ibid.*
19. *Ibid.*, p. 16.
20. *Ibid.*

21. For additional explicit evidence of CIA complicity in drug running, see Michael Levine, *The Big White Lie: The Deep Cover Operation That Exposed the CIA Sabotage of the Drug War* (New York: Thunder's Mouth Press, 1994).

22. Roger Morris, *Partners in Power* (New York: Henry Holt, 1996), p. 233.

23. *Ibid.*, p. 393.

24. *Ibid.*, p. 411.

25. *Ibid.*, p. 418.

26. *Ibid.*

27. For a thorough review of the Foster story, see Christopher Ruddy, *Vincent Foster: The Ruddy Investigation*, available for $19.95 from 1-800-711-1968.

28. Morris, *op. cit.*, p. 331.

29. See Jeffrey Goldberg, "Some of the President's New Union Pals Seem to Have Some Suspicious Pals of Their Own," *New York*, July 9, 1996, p. 17.

30. *Ibid.*, p. 19.

31. *Ibid.*

32. Hirshleifer, *op. cit.*, p. 173.

33. Tanzi, *op. cit.*, pp. 167, 170.

34. Walter Lippmann, *The Public Philosophy* (New Brunswick, N.J.: Transaction Publishers, 1989), p. 14.

35. *Ibid.*, p. 15.

36. Paul Roazen, "Introduction," in Lippmann, *op. cit.*, p. xv.

37. Morris, *op. cit.*, p. 469.

38. Fiorentini and Peltzman, *op. cit.*, p. 16.

39. James Bennett, "Cyberspace and the Return of Trust," *Strategic Investment*, October 1996.

40. Virginia Abernethy, "Optimism and Overpopulation," *Atlantic Monthly*, December 1994, p. 88.

Afterword and Appendix

1. Quoted in *Wired*, March 1999, p. 33.

2. Joseph A. Tainter, *The Collapse of Complex Societies* (Cambridge, Mass.: Cambridge University Press, 1988), p. 3.

3. Roger Lane, "On the Social Meaning of Homicide Trends in America," in *Violence in America*, Vol. 1, ed. Ted Robert Gurr (Newbury Park: Sage Publications, 1989), p. 57.

4. See Robert Higgs, "A Carnival of Taxation," *The Independent Review*, Volume III, Number 3, Winter 1999, p. 437.

5. Nicholas Rashevsky, *Looking at History Through Mathematics* (Cambridge, Massachusetts: MIT Press, 1968), p. 119.

6. Tainter, *op. cit.*, pp. 150–51.

7. Tainter, *op. cit.*, p. 147.

8. Rashevsky, *op. cit.*, pp. 119–20.

INDEX

CPSIA information can be obtained
at www.ICGtesting.com
Printed in the USA
LVHW090032260422
716518LV00003B/3

9 780684 832722